SCHAUM'S OUTLINE OF

GERMAN GRAMMAR

Second Edition

•

by

ELKE F. GSCHOSSMANN-HENDERSHOT

Former Instructor, Rutgers University

SCHAUM'S OUTLINE SERIES
McGRAW-HILL PUBLISHING COMPANY

New York St. Louis San Francisco Auckland Bogotá Caracas Hamburg Lisbon London Madrid Mexico Milan Montreal New Delhi Oklahoma City Paris San Juan São Paulo Singapore Sydney Tokyo Toronto

Elke Gschossmann-Hendershot, a native of Germany, received her formal schooling in Regensburg, Germany, and completed her postgraduate work at Rutgers University, New Jersey. She has teaching experience at various levels, from elementary school through college. She designed programs for the Army Language School and served as supervisor for Deutsche Sprachschule. Her most recent teaching assignment was at Rutgers University, New Jersey.

Schaum's Outline of
GERMAN GRAMMAR

7 8 9 10 11 12 13 14 15 16 17 18 19 20SH SH 89

ISBN 0-07-025097-9

Sponsoring Editor, Paul Farrell
Editing Supervisor, Marthe Grice
Production Manager, Nick Monti

Library of Congress Cataloging in Publication Data

Gschossmann-Hendershot, Elke.
Schaum's outline of German grammar.

(Schaum's outline series)
1. German language–Grammar–Outlines, syllabi, etc.
I. Title. II. Series.
PF 3118.G8 1983 438.2'421 81-23684
ISBN 0-07-025097-9

Preface

Like the first edition, the second edition of this review book has been designed and developed in order to make the study of German grammar easier. The book is divided into nine chapters. Each chapter concentrates on the basic problem areas of the language: nouns and articles; prepositions; adjectives and adverbs; numbers, dates, and time; verbs; interrogatives; negatives; pronouns; and word order and conjunctions.

Each grammatical or structural point is introduced by a simple explanation in English. The explanation is further clarified by many concrete examples. It is recommended that you first read the explanation and then study the illustrative examples. Once you have done this, go on to the exercises that follow. You should write out the answers to these exercises and then compare your answers to those that appear at the end of the book. It is recommended that you correct yourself immediately before proceeding to the next exercise.

One of the most difficult and tedious tasks in acquiring a second language is learning the many forms that exist in the language, whether they are noun, adjective, or verb forms. In Schaum's Outline of German Grammar all forms have been logically grouped in order to make their acquisition as simple as possible and also to minimize what at first appears to be irregularities. By grouping verbs with vowel changes in the different tenses, the mastering of the different forms is greatly facilitated.

Schaum's Outline of German Grammar can be used as a review text or as a companion to any text. In order to reinforce each point you are learning in your basic text, you may wish to get additional practice by doing the clear, logically organized exercises provided throughout this book.

I would like to express my gratitude to Conrad J. Schmitt for his help in developing my manuscript and for his many valuable suggestions.

ELKE F. GSCHOSSMANN-HENDERSHOT

CONTENTS

CONTENTS

Chapter 1

Nouns and Articles

CAPITALIZATION

All German nouns and words used as nouns are capitalized: **der Herr, das Haus, die Alte, der Reisende, das Lesen.**

GENDER

All German nouns have a grammatical gender. A noun is either masculine, feminine or neuter. The definite article **der** (*the*) accompanies a masculine noun, **die** accompanies a feminine noun and **das** a neuter noun.

Nouns that refer specifically to male beings, such as father, uncle, etc., are usually masculine. Those that refer to female beings, such as mother, daughter, etc., are usually feminine. However, nouns referring to things are not always neuter but can have a masculine or feminine gender. For this reason the gender of each noun should be memorized.

Although no definite rules for gender can be given, the following generalizations may be helpful in memorizing the gender of frequently used nouns.

GENDER IDENTIFICATION BY NOUN GROUPS

Nouns Referring to People

Nouns referring to male beings (people and animals) are usually masculine. Nouns referring to female beings are usually feminine.

Masculine		*Feminine*	
der Vater	*father*	**die Mutter**	*mother*
der Mann	*man*	**die Frau**	*Mrs., woman*
der Sohn	*son*	**die Tochter**	*daughter*
der Bruder	*brother*	**die Schwester**	*sister*
der Herr	*Mr., gentleman*	**die Dame**	*lady*
der Onkel	*uncle*	**die Tante**	*aunt*

der Lehrer	*teacher*		**die Lehrerin**	*teacher*
der Kater	*cat*		**die Katze**	*cat*
der Hahn	*rooster*		**die Henne**	*chicken*
der Junge	*boy*	BUT:	**das Mädchen**	*girl*

Nouns referring to young people and animals are usually neuter. All diminutives ending in **-chen** or **-lein** are neuter.

Neuter

das Mädchen	*girl*	**das Kind**	*child*
das Fräulein	*Miss, young woman*	**das Kalb**	*calf*
das Kätzchen	*kitten*	**das Küken**	*chick*
das Schwesterlein	*little sister*		

1. Supply the appropriate definite article.

1. ______ Lehrer kommt.
2. ______ Kalb ist klein.
3. ______ Dame ist freundlich.
4. ______ Mann ist alt.
5. ______ Kaninchen ist weiss.
6. ______ Tante bringt es.
7. ______ Büchlein liegt hier.
8. ______ Katze schläft.
9. ______ Sohn schreibt.
10. ______ Tochter ist hübsch.
11. ______ Junge ist gross.
12. ______ Küken ist gelb.
13. ______ Lehrerin ist intelligent.
14. ______ Mutter kocht.
15. ______ Kind weint.
16. ______ Kater ist schwarz.
17. ______ Lehrer sitzt dort.
18. ______ Mädchen ist klein.
19. ______ Henne ist braun.
20. ______ Fräulein sieht uns.

Masculine Nouns

Names of all calendar days

der Montag	*Monday*	**der Freitag**	*Friday*
der Dienstag	*Tuesday*	**der Samstag**	*Saturday*
der Mittwoch	*Wednesday*	**der Sonntag**	*Sunday*
der Donnerstag	*Thursday*		

Names of all calendar months

der Januar	*January*	**der Mai**	*May*	**der September**	*September*
der Februar	*February*	**der Juni**	*June*	**der Oktober**	*October*
der März	*March*	**der Juli**	*July*	**der November**	*November*
der April	*April*	**der August**	*August*	**der Dezember**	*December*

Names of all seasons

der Frühling	*spring*	**der Herbst**	*fall*
der Sommer	*summer*	**der Winter**	*winter*

Names of all cardinal directions

der Süden	*south*	**der Westen**	*west*
der Norden	*north*	**der Osten**	*east*

2. Supply the appropriate definite article.

1. _______ Sommer ist eine warme Jahreszeit.
2. _______ Süden Deutschlands ist malerisch.
3. _______ August und _______ Juli sind Sommermonate.
4. _______ Frühling kommt bald.
5. _______ Sonntag ist ein Ruhetag.
6. _______ April ist regnerisch.
7. _______ Norden ist flach.
8. _______ Winter ist eine kalte Jahreszeit.
9. _______ November und _______ Dezember sind Wintermonate.
10. _______ Montag ist der erste Wochentag.

Feminine Nouns

Names of most trees

die Tanne *fir*
die Linde *linden tree*

Names of most fruits

die Banane *banana*
die Pflaume *plum*
BUT: **der Apfel** *apple*

Names of most flowers

die Orchidee *orchid*
die Lilie *lily*

3. Supply the appropriate definite article.

1. _______ Zitrone und _______ Orange sind sauer.
2. _______ Geranie und _______ Begonie blühen.
3. _______ Birke ist ein Laubbaum.
4. _______ Banane ist süss.
5. _______ Orchidee ist teuer.
6. Wo ist _______ Apfel?
7. _______ Lilie ist weiss.
8. _______ Tanne ist ein Nadelbaum.
9. _______ Pflaume ist sauer.
10. _______ Linde ist gross.

Neuter Nouns

The names of cities

das historische München *historical Munich*
das übervölkerte Hongkong *overpopulated Hongkong*

The names of most countries

das neutrale Schweden *neutral Sweden*
das moderne Deutschland *modern Germany*

NOTE: The neuter article for cities and countries is used only if the noun is modified. Without a modifier one simply uses **München, Berlin, Italien,** etc.

The names of the following countries are not neuter but feminine:

die Schweiz *Switzerland*
die Türkei *Turkey*
die Tschechoslowakei *Czechoslovakia*

Masculine are:

der Iran *Iran*
der Irak *Iraq*

The following are only used in the plural:

die Niederlande *Netherlands*
die Vereinigten Staaten *United States*

The above exceptions are always used with their articles, whether they are modified or not.
Wir besuchen die Schweiz.

4. Supply the appropriate definite article when necessary.

1. Wir besuchen _______ Türkei.
2. Wo liegt _______ Iran?
3. _______ Köln ist eine alte Stadt.
4. _______ Vereinigten Staaten sind gross.
5. _______ historische Wien ist malerisch.
6. _______ Schweiz ist neutral.
7. _______ Niederlande sind flach.
8. _______ Deutschland ist modern.
9. Wir besuchen _______ alte Heidelberg.
10. _______ Tschechoslowakei liegt im Osten.

The names of metals and chemical elements are generally neuter:

das Gold *gold* **das Helium** *helium*
das Kupfer *copper* BUT: **der Stahl** *steel*

5. Supply the appropriate definite article.

1. _______ Aluminium ist ein leichtes Metall.
2. _______ Chlor riecht scharf.
3. Wo wird _______ Stahl produziert?
4. _______ Silber glitzert in der Sonne.
5. _______ Radium ist radioaktiv.
6. _______ Neon ist ein Edelgas.
7. _______ Kupfer ist rot.
8. _______ Gold ist teuer.
9. _______ Helium ist leicht.
10. _______ Eisen ist ein Schwermetall.

REVIEW

6. Complete the following with the appropriate definite article.

1. _______ Fräulein kauft nichts.

2. Wir besuchen _______ sonnige Italien.
3. _______ Apfel ist grün.
4. _______ Sommer ist die schönste Jahreszeit.
5. _______ Vater bringt etwas.
6. _______ Februar ist der kürzeste Monat.
7. _______ Junge spielt.
8. _______ Dienstag ist der zweite Wochentag.
9. _______ Gold ist ein Edelmetall.
10. _______ Lehrer fährt durch _______ Niederlande.
11. _______ Rose blüht.
12. _______ Mädchen lacht.
13. Wo ist _______ Katze?
14. _______ Westen ist reich.
15. _______ Januar ist ein Wintermonat.
16. _______ Banane ist gelb.
17. _______ Tanne is gross.
18. _______ Schweiz ist neutral.
19. _______ historische München ist interessant.
20. _______ Mai ist der schönste Monat.

GENDER IDENTIFICATION BY WORD ENDINGS

Masculine Endings

Nouns ending in **-el, -en, -er, -ig, -ich** and **-ling** are usually masculine.

der Schlüssel	*key*	**der Zucker**	*sugar*
der Löffel	*spoon*	**der Honig**	*honey*
der Wagen	*car, wagon*	**der Pfennig**	*penny*
der Boden	*floor*	**der Teppich**	*rug*
der Teller	*plate*	**der Lehrling**	*apprentice*

Important exceptions to the above rule are:

die Butter	*butter*	**das Fenster**	*window*
die Mutter	*mother*	**das Wetter**	*weather*
die Tochter	*daughter*	**das Leder**	*leather*
das Messer	*knife*	**das Kissen**	*pillow*
das Zimmer	*room*	**die Gabel**	*fork*

7. Supply the appropriate form of the definite article.

1. _______ Mantel liegt hier.
2. Warum ist _______ Fenster offen?
3. _______ Sperling ist ein Vogel.
4. _______ Gabel, _______ Löffel und _______ Messer sind aus Stahl.
5. _______ Himmel ist blau.
6. _______ Käfer fliegt durch _______ Zimmer.
7. _______ Rettich schmeckt scharf.
8. _______ Essig ist sauer, aber _______ Honig ist süss.
9. _______ Teppich ist alt.

10. Wo ist ______ Teller?
11. ______ Wetter ist schön.
12. ______ Wagen ist in der Garage.
13. ______ Lehrling ist jung.
14. Wo ist ______ Butter?
15. ______ Zucker ist weiss.
16. ______ Mutter und ______ Tochter sind hübsch.
17. ______ Leder ist weich.
18. Wo ist ______ Kissen?

Feminine Endings

Nouns ending in **-age, -e, -ei, -heit, -keit, -schaft, -ie, -ik, -in, -ion, -tät, -ung, -ur** are almost always femine. Nouns ending in **-e** are usually feminine.

die Courage *courage*
die Liebe *love*
die Partei *party (political)*
die Krankheit *illness*
die Schönheit *beauty*
die Freundlichkeit *friendliness*
die Freundschaft *friendship*
die Melodie *melody*
die Familie *family*
die Politik *politics*
die Musik *music*
die Fabrik *factory*
die Köchin *cook (female)*
die Nation *nation*
die Rarität *rarity*
die Universität *university*
die Wohnung *apartment*
die Rechnung *bill, invoice*
die Diktatur *dictatorship*
die Literatur *literature*

8. Supply the appropriate definite article.

1. ______ Pille ist bitter.
2. Er gibt ______ Hoffnung auf.
3. ______ Kultur dieses Volkes ist primitiv.
4. ______ Universität ist bekannt.
5. ______ Technik ist progressiv.
6. ______ Kopie ist unklar.
7. ______ Krankheit ist gefährlich.
8. ______ Bäckerei ist geschlossen.
9. Er sagt ______ Wahrheit.
10. ______ Schneiderin macht das Kleid.
11. ______ Fabrik ist im Zentrum.
12. ______ Wohnung ist modern.
13. ______ Familie ist zu Hause.
14. ______ Maschine ist neu.
15. ______ Schönheit vergeht.
16. Wo ist ______ Rarität?
17. ______ Köchin kocht.
18. ______ Nation ist stark.
19. ______ Garage ist klein.
20. ______ moderne Musik ist interessant.

Neuter Endings

Nouns ending in **-tum, -ment, -ium, -um** are usually neuter.

das Christentum *christianity*
das Instrument *instrument*
das Gymnasium *type of secondary school in Germany*
das Museum *museum*
das Datum *date*

Infinitives used as nouns are always neuter.

das Hören *hearing*
das Sehen *seeing*

9. Supply the appropriate form of the definite article.

1. ______ Lachen des Kindes ist ansteckend.
2. Wir besuchen ______ Gymnasium.
3. ______ Ornament ist pompös.
4. Wo ist ______ Heiligtum?
5. ______ Aquarium ist hier.
6. ______ Instrument ist teuer.
7. Wo ist ______ Museum?
8. ______ Datum steht hier.
9. ______ Christentum ist eine Religion.
10. ______ Arbeiten macht müde.

REVIEW

10. Supply the appropriate definite article.

1. ______ Explosion zerstört ______ Gymnasium.
2. ______ Gabel, ______ Messer und ______ Löffel liegen hier.
3. ______ Strasse ist breit.
4. ______ Lehrling arbeitet.
5. ______ Konditorei ist geschlossen.
6. ______ Dokument ist gefälscht.
7. ______ Honig und ______ Zucker sind süss.
8. Wir hören ______ Melodie.
9. ______ ganze Familie hat ______ Krankheit.
10. ______ Wohnung ist teuer.
11. ______ Lesen und ______ Schreiben lernte er zu Hause.
12. ______ Vogel sitzt dort.
13. ______ Rakete umkreist ______ Erde.
14. Warum liegen ______ Hammer und ______ Nagel hier?
15. ______ Sinfonie ist lang.
16. ______ Zentrum ist modern.
17. ______ Datum steht hier.
18. ______ Fabrik produziert viel.
19. ______ Teller ist weiss.
20. ______ Schlüssel ist aus Metall.

WORDS WITH DIFFERENT MEANINGS IN MASCULINE, FEMININE AND NEUTER FORMS

The following pairs of words have different meanings for masculine, feminine and neuter forms.

der Golf	*gulf*	**das Golf**	*golf*
der Junge	*boy*	**das Junge**	*young animal*
der Leiter	*leader, manager*	**die Leiter**	*ladder*
die Mark	*DM (German currency)*	**das Mark**	*marrow*
der See	*lake (inland)*	**die See**	*sea (ocean)*
der Tor	*fool*	**das Tor**	*gate*

11. Supply the appropriate definite article.

1. ______ Golf von Mexiko ist warm.
2. ______ Junge steigt auf ______ Leiter.
3. ______ Königsee liegt in Süddeutschland.
4. ______ neue Geschäftsleiter ist sympathisch.
5. ______ Golf ist ein Rasenspiel.
6. Wo wird ______ Knochenmark produziert?
7. ______ Deutsche Mark wird aufgewertet.
8. ______ Löwin schleppt ______ Junge herum.
9. ______ Nordsee ist oft stürmisch.
10. ______ Mondsee ist in Österreich.
11. ______ Tor war offen.
12. ______ Tor tötete den Hund.

COMPOUND NOUNS

Formation

Compound nouns in German are formed by combining two or more nouns. Often two singular nouns are joined to form one compound noun:

das Hotel, das Zimmer	**das Hotelzimmer**	*hotelroom*
der Motor, das Boot	**das Motorboot**	*motorboat*
der Winter, der Mantel	**der Wintermantel**	*winter coat*
das Auto, der Bus	**der Autobus**	*bus*
der Zahn, die Bürste	**die Zahnbürste**	*toothbrush*
das Wasser, die Farbe	**die Wasserfarbe**	*water color*

Another group of compound nouns is formed by joining a plural and a singular noun:

die Tannen, der Baum	**der Tannenbaum**	*fir tree*
die Kranken, der Wagen	**der Krankenwagen**	*ambulance*
die Kinder, das Zimmer	**das Kinderzimmer**	*children's room*
die Tage, das Buch	**das Tagebuch**	*diary*
die Strassen, die Lampe	**die Strassenlampe**	*streetlamp*
die Blumen, die Vase	**die Blumenvase**	*vase*

Some compound nouns are formed by two singular nouns connected by an **-s**.

der Staat, das Examen	**das Staatsexamen**	*state exam*
der Sport, der Mann	**der Sportsmann**	*sportsman*
der Geburtstag, der Kuchen	**der Geburtstagskuchen**	*birthday cake*
das Mitglied, die Karte	**die Mitgliedskarte**	*membership card*
der Liebling, die Melodie	**die Lieblingsmelodie**	*favorite melody*
die Universität, der Professor	**der Universitätsprofessor**	*university professor*

Gender

The last component of the compound noun determines the gender of the noun:

der Stahl, die Industrie	**die Stahlindustrie**
die Suppen, der Löffel	**der Suppenlöffel**
der Lehrer, die Hand, das Buch	**das Lehrerhandbuch**

12. Form compound nouns with the indicated nouns and fill in the blanks. Supply the appropriate definite articles.

1. _______ _________________ ist süss. *Geburtstag, Kuchen*
2. _______ _________________ ist warm. *Winter, Mantel*
3. _______ _________________ kommt. *Auto, Bus*
4. _______ _________________ ist modern. *Hotel, Zimmer*
5. _______ _________________ hat Courage. *Sport, Mann*
6. _______ _________________ ist alt. *Blume, Vase*
7. _______ _________________ ist klein. *Kind, Zimmer*
8. _______ _________________ kommt. *Kranke, Wagen*
9. _______ _________________ ist hell. *Strasse, Lampe*
10. _______ _________________ ist intelligent. *Universität, Professor*
11. _______ _________________ liegt hier. *Tag, Buch*
12. _______ _________________ ist klein. *Mitglied, Karte*
13. _______ _________________ ist dunkel. *Wasser, Farbe*
14. _______ _________________ ist schwer. *Staat, Examen*
15. _______ _________________ ist dort. *Zahn, Bürste*

NOUNS USED ONLY IN THE SINGULAR

The following nouns are used only in the singular:

die Liebe	*love*	**die Musik**	*music*
der Schmuck	*jewelry*	**das Leder**	*leather*
das Vieh	*cattle*	**der Wein**	*wine*
die Milch	*milk*	**das Fleisch**	*meat*
die Butter	*butter*	**der Honig**	*honey*
das Gold	*gold*		

13. Form sentences from the following. Follow the model:

Schmuck / sein / teuer / **Der Schmuck ist teuer.**

1. Wein / sein / alt /
2. Musik / sein / modern /
3. Fleisch / sein / frisch /
4. Butter / sein / teuer /
5. Honig / sein / süss /
6. Milch / sein / sauer /
7. Vieh / sein / hungrig /
8. Gold / sein / kostbar /

PLURAL FORMS OF NOUNS

Almost all English nouns form their plurals by adding *-s* or *-es* to the singular forms, such as *cat, cats; glass, glasses.* Only few nouns have irregular plural forms, such as *mouse, mice; woman, women.* In German, nouns rarely form their plural forms by adding **-s.** Some plural forms are identical to the singular. Many other nouns are made plural by adding various endings, with or without umlaut. Regardless of the gender of the noun, the nominative plural form of the definite article is always **die.** Although there are no definite rules for the formation of the plural noun forms, nouns can be grouped in the following way.

Group I

The nominative plural form is identical to the singular. Some plural forms add umlaut. Neuter nouns ending in **-chen** and **-lein** and masculine and neuter nouns ending in **-er, -el, -en** belong to this group. Only two feminine nouns belong to this group.

Masculine Nouns

Singular		*Plural*
der Bruder	*brother*	**die Brüder**
der Dichter	*poet*	**die Dichter**
der Finger	*finger*	**die Finger**
der Koffer	*suitcase*	**die Koffer**
der Lehrer	*teacher*	**die Lehrer**
der Schüler	*student*	**die Schüler**
der Teller	*plate*	**die Teller**
der Vater	*father*	**die Väter**
der Braten	*roast*	**die Braten**
der Wagen	*car, wagon*	**die Wagen**
der Apfel	*apple*	**die Äpfel**
der Löffel	*spoon*	**die Löffel**
der Mantel	*coat*	**die Mäntel**
der Onkel	*uncle*	**die Onkel**
der Schlüssel	*key*	**die Schlüssel**

Neuter Nouns

Singular		*Plural*
das Fenster	*window*	**die Fenster**
das Messer	*knife*	**die Messer**
das Theater	*theater*	**die Theater**
das Zimmer	*room*	**die Zimmer**
das Segel	*sail*	**die Segel**
das Becken	*basin*	**die Becken**
das Kissen	*pillow*	**die Kissen**
das Fräulein	*Miss*	**die Fräulein**
das Mädchen	*girl*	**die Mädchen**

Feminine Nouns

Singular		*Plural*
die Mutter	*mother*	**die Mütter**
die Tochter	*daughter*	**die Töchter**

14. Rewrite the following, changing all nouns to the plural. Make all necessary changes.

1. Das Kissen ist weich.
2. Der Onkel kommt.
3. Die Tochter ist klein.
4. Das Zimmer ist kalt.
5. Der Bruder raucht.
6. Der Mantel ist neu.
7. Das Fenster ist geschlossen.
8. Der Apfel ist rot.
9. Der Lehrer ist alt.
10. Der Koffer ist aus Leder.
11. Das Messer ist rostig.
12. Das Segel ist weiss.
13. Der Teller steht dort.
14. Der Schlüssel ist alt.
15. Das Fräulein ist hübsch.
16. Die Mutter wartet.
17. Der Wagen steht hier.
18. Das Theater ist modern.
19. Der Löffel ist teuer.
20. Der Schüler lernt.

Group II

These nouns add **-e** to the singular to form the plural. Some nouns also add umlaut. Masculine, feminine and neuter nouns belong to this group. Most of these nouns have only one syllable.

Masculine Nouns

Singular		*Plural*
der Arm	*arm*	**die Arme**
der Berg	*mountain*	**die Berge**
der Brief	*letter*	**die Briefe**
der Freund	*friend*	**die Freunde**
der Hund	*dog*	**die Hunde**
der Krieg	*war*	**die Kriege**
der Monat	*month*	**die Monate**
der Schuh	*shoe*	**die Schuhe**
der Sohn	*son*	**die Söhne**
der Tag	*day*	**die Tage**
der Tisch	*table*	**die Tische**
der Zug	*train*	**die Züge**

Feminine Nouns

Singular		*Plural*
die Hand	*hand*	**die Hände**
die Nacht	*night*	**die Nächte**
die Stadt	*city, town*	**die Städte**
die Wurst	*sausage*	**die Würste**

Neuter Nouns

Singular		*Plural*
das Gedicht	*poem*	**die Gedichte**
das Jahr	*year*	**die Jahre**
das Tier	*animal*	**die Tiere**

15. Rewrite the following, changing all nouns to the plural. Make all necessary changes.

1. Die Wurst schmeckt gut.
2. Der Monat ist lang.
3. Die Hand ist nass.
4. Das Gedicht ist kurz.
5. Der Hund ist braun.
6. Der Zug kommt an.
7. Der Tisch ist aus Holz.
8. Die Stadt ist modern.
9. Der Berg ist hoch.
10. Das Tier ist verletzt.
11. Der Krieg ist brutal.
12. Der Sohn ist gross.
13. Der Brief ist interessant.
14. Der Schuh ist aus Leder.
15. Der Tag ist kurz.
16. Der Freund lacht.
17. Die Nacht ist kalt.
18. Das Jahr geht vorüber.

Group III

These nouns add **-er** to the singular to form the plural. All nouns containing **a, o, u, au** in the stem add umlaut. Most of these nouns are neuter. Some are masculine, none are feminine.

Masculine Nouns

Singular		*Plural*
der Gott	*god*	**die Götter**
der Mann	*man*	**die Männer**
der Wurm	*worm*	**die Würmer**

Neuter Nouns

Singular		*Plural*
das Bild	*picture*	**die Bilder**
das Blatt	*leaf*	**die Blätter**
das Buch	*book*	**die Bücher**
das Ei	*egg*	**die Eier**
das Glas	*glass*	**die Gläser**
das Haus	*house*	**die Häuser**
das Kind	*child*	**die Kinder**
das Kleid	*dress*	**die Kleider**
das Land	*country*	**die Länder**
das Lied	*song*	**die Lieder**
das Volk	*people*	**die Völker**

16. Rewrite the following, changing all nouns to the plural. Make all necessary changes.

1. Der Wurm ist lang.
2. Das Buch ist interessant.
3. Das Ei schmeckt gut.
4. Das Land ist neutral.
5. Das Glas ist kalt.
6. Das Blatt ist grün.
7. Der Mann raucht.
8. Das Haus ist teuer.
9. Das Kleid passt nicht.
10. Das Kind weint.
11. Das Volk ist hungrig.
12. Das Bild ist billig.
13. Das Lied ist melodisch.
14. Der Gott ist alt.

Group IV

These nouns add **-(e)n** to the singular. Nouns belonging to this group never add umlaut. Most of these nouns are feminine. Feminine nouns ending in **-in** add **-nen** in the plural—e.g. **die Lehrerin, die Lehrerinnen.**

Masculine Nouns

Singular		*Plural*
der Hase	*rabbit*	**die Hasen**
der Junge	*boy*	**die Jungen**
der Name	*name*	**die Namen**
der Held	*hero*	**die Helden**
der Herr	*Mr., gentleman*	**die Herren**
der Mensch	*human being*	**die Menschen**
der Präsident	*president*	**die Präsidenten**

Neuter Nouns

Singular		*Plural*
das Herz	*heart*	**die Herzen**

Feminine Nouns

Singular		*Plural*
die Blume	*flower*	**die Blumen**
die Dame	*lady*	**die Damen**

die Katze	*cat*	**die Katzen**
die Minute	*minute*	**die Minuten**
die Schule	*school*	**die Schulen**
die Schwester	*sister*	**die Schwestern**
die Strasse	*street*	**die Strassen**
die Stunde	*hour*	**die Stunden**
die Tante	*aunt*	**die Tanten**
die Tasse	*cup*	**die Tassen**
die Woche	*week*	**die Wochen**
die Antwort	*answer*	**die Antworten**
die Fabrik	*factory*	**die Fabriken**
die Frau	*woman*	**die Frauen**
die Nation	*nation*	**die Nationen**
die Tür	*door*	**die Türen**
die Universität	*university*	**die Universitäten**
die Wohnung	*apartment*	**die Wohnungen**
die Zeitung	*newspaper*	**die Zeitungen**
die Freundin	*girl friend*	**die Freundinnen**
die Studentin	*female student*	**die Studentinnen**

17. Rewrite the following, changing all nouns to the plural. Make all necessary changes.

1. Der Herr ist alt.
2. Die Dame ist freundlich.
3. Die Katze ist schwarz.
4. Die Nation ist progressiv.
5. Der Junge ist hier.
6. Die Studentin lernt.
7. Die Tür ist offen.
8. Die Strasse ist breit.
9. Der Student ist arm.
10. Die Freundin ist krank.
11. Der Hase ist weiss.
12. Die Blume blüht.
13. Die Fabrik ist grau.
14. Die Tasse ist gelb.
15. Die Wohnung ist kalt.
16. Der Präsident ist alt.
17. Der Name ist lang.
18. Die Antwort ist falsch.
19. Der Held ist stark.
20. Die Zeitung liegt hier.

Group V

These nouns add **-s** to the singular. Mostly nouns of foreign origin belong to this group.

Masculine Nouns

Singular		*Plural*
der Job	*job*	**die Jobs**
der Park	*park*	**die Parks**

Feminine Nouns

Singular		*Plural*
die Bar	*bar*	**die Bars**
die Kamera	*camera*	**die Kameras**

Neuter Nouns

Singular		*Plural*
das Auto	*car*	**die Autos**

das Foto	*photo*	**die Fotos**
das Hotel	*hotel*	**die Hotels**
das Radio	*radio*	**die Radios**
das Sofa	*sofa*	**die Sofas**

18. Rewrite the following, changing all nouns to the plural. Make all necessary changes.

1. Die Kamera ist teuer.
2. Die Bar ist geschlossen.
3. Das Radio ist kaputt.
4. Das Hotel ist teuer.
5. Das Sofa ist weich.
6. Der Park ist gross.
7. Der Job ist interessant.
8. Das Foto ist alt.

Irregular Plural Nouns

Masculine Nouns

Singular		*Plural*
der Bus	*bus*	**die Busse**

Feminine Nouns

Singular		*Plural*
die Firma	*firm, company*	**die Firmen**

Neuter Nouns

Singular		*Plural*
das Drama	*drama*	**die Dramen**
das Gymnasium	*secondary school*	**die Gymnasien**
das Museum	*museum*	**die Museen**
das Zentrum	*center*	**die Zentren**

A few nouns have the same singular form. However, they have two plurals with different meanings.

die Bank	*bench*	**die Bänke**
die Bank	*bank*	**die Banken**
das Wort	*word*	**die Wörter** (disconnected words on a list)
das Wort	*word*	**die Worte** (connected words in a sentence)

Some nouns are used only in the plural in German.

die Eltern	*parents*
die Ferien	*vacation*
die Geschwister	*brothers and sisters*
die Leute	*people*

19. Rewrite the following in the plural. Make all necessary changes.

1. Die Firma ist bekannt.
2. Ist das Wort auf der Liste?
3. Die Bank ist im Park.
4. Das Drama ist interessant.
5. Das Museum ist modern.
6. Der Bus kommt.
7. Die Bank ist geschlossen.
8. Das Zentrum ist gross.

REVIEW

20. Rewrite the following, changing the nouns to the singular whenever possible. Make all the necessary changes.

1. Die Teller sind weiss.	12. Die Sofas sind rot.
2. Die Lehrerinnen sind hübsch.	13. Die Mütter sind freundlich.
3. Die Gläser sind leer.	14. Die Segel sind weiss.
4. Die Mäntel hängen hier.	15. Die Städte sind übervölkert.
5. Die Zimmer sind warm.	16. Die Radios sind kaputt.
6. Die Studenten lernen.	17. Die Zeitungen sind alt.
7. Die Geschäfte sind geschlossen.	18. Die Männer sind krank.
8. Die Nächte sind lang.	19. Die Hände sind schmutzig.
9. Die Helden sind bekannt.	20. Die Theater sind modern.
10. Die Bars sind billig.	21. Die Eltern sind zu Hause.
11. Die Gymnasien sind progressiv.	22. Die Leute sind im Zentrum.

21. Rewrite the following, changing the nouns to the plural whenever possible. Make all necessary changes.

1. Das Vieh ist im Stall.	11. Das Auto ist neu.
2. Der Schuh ist schwarz.	12. Der Brief ist lang.
3. Die Freundin ist nett.	13. Die Hand ist nass.
4. Das Fleisch ist teuer.	14. Das Zimmer ist gross.
5. Der Apfel ist sauer.	15. Das Tier ist wild.
6. Der Schlüssel ist rostig.	16. Das Glas ist teuer.
7. Das Mädchen ist freundlich.	17. Das Buch ist interessant.
8. Der Bus ist rot.	18. Die Strasse ist eng.
9. Die Mutter schreibt.	19. Der Freund ist reich.
10. Die Wurst ist lang.	20. Das Lied ist kurz.

CASES OF NOUNS

There are four cases of nouns in German: nominative, accusative, dative and genitive. These cases correspond to the English subject, direct object, indirect object and the possessive.

Most German nouns do not change their ending in the various cases. However, words preceding the noun do change forms and identify the particular case used. The definite articles **der, die, das** precede the nouns. Other words that function the same as the definite article are referred to as **"der"** words. They are:

dieser	*this*	**mancher**	*many (a)*
jeder	*each, every*	**solcher**	*such*
jener	*that*	**welcher**	*which*

The indefinite articles are **ein, eine, ein.** Other words that function the same as the indefinite article are referred to as **"ein"** words. They are:

kein	*no, not any*	**ihr**	*her* or *their*
mein	*my*	**unser**	*our*
dein	*your*	**euer**	*your*
sein	*his* or *its*	**Ihr**	*your*

The possessives **euer** and **unser** often drop the final **e** when an ending is added—e.g., **eure** Mutter; **unsre** Stadt. (For additional exercises on the use of the possessive adjectives, see Chapter 3.)

Nominative Case

Singular and Plural

The nominative forms of the definite and indefinite articles and of the **"der"** and **"ein"** words are as follows.

	SINGULAR			*PLURAL*
	Masculine	*Feminine*	*Neuter*	*All Genders*
Definite article:	**der**	**die**	**das**	**die**
"der" words	**dieser**	**diese**	**dieses**	**diese**
	jener	**jene**	**jenes**	**jene**
	welcher	**welche**	**welches**	**welche**
Indefinite article:	**ein**	**eine**	**ein**	(no plural)
"ein" words	**mein**	**meine**	**mein**	**meine**
	ihr	**ihre**	**ihr**	**ihre**
	unser	**unsre**	**unser**	**unsre**
Negative article:	**kein**	**keine**	**kein**	**keine**

The nominative case is used in German in the following ways:

As Subject of the Verb

Der Mann **spielt Golf.**	*The man is playing golf.*
Die Freundin **kommt.**	*The girl friend is coming.*
Das Auto **ist kaputt.**	*The car is broken.*
Die Kinder **weinen.**	*The children are crying.*
Dieser Apfel **ist sauer.**	*This apple is sour.*
Diese Stadt **ist bekannt.**	*This city is well known.*
Dieses Zimmer **ist gross.**	*This room is large.*
Diese Bücher **sind interessant.**	*These books are interesting.*
Ein Hund **bellt.**	*A dog is barking.*
Eine Kopie **ist hier.**	*A copy is here.*
Ein Mädchen **singt.**	*A girl is singing.*
Mein Bruder **ist krank.**	*My brother is ill.*
Meine Katze **ist weiss.**	*My cat is white.*
Mein Messer **ist rostig.**	*My knife is rusty.*
Meine Eltern **sind dort.**	*My parents are there.*
Kein Wagen **ist billig.**	*No car is inexpensive.*
Keine Fabrik **ist sauber.**	*No factory is clean.*
Kein Hotel **ist so modern.**	*No hotel is as modern.*
Keine Museen **sind geschlossen.**	*No museums are closed.*

As Predicate Nominative (a noun which is identical to the subject)

(The predicate nominative usually follows such verbs as **sein**—to be—and **werden**—to become.)

Die Frau ist *seine Mutter.*	*The woman is his mother.*
Martin ist *unser Freund.*	*Martin is our friend.*
Gisela wird *keine Lehrerin.*	*Gisela will not become a teacher.*

As a Noun of Address

Bitte, nehmen Sie es, *Frau Breu!*	*Please take it, Mrs. Breu.*
Herr Müller, **kommen Sie?**	*Mr. Müller, are you coming?*

22. Complete the following with **der, die, das.**

1. _______ Universität ist alt.
2. _______ Mann schreibt.
3. Ist _______ Mädchen krank?
4. _______ Junge studiert.
5. _______ Wohnung ist kalt.
6. _______ Wetter ist schön.
7. Warum schreit _______ Kind?
8. _______ Frau ist hübsch.
9. _______ Lehrer ist jung.
10. _______ Vogel singt.

23. Rewrite the above sentences with **dieser, diese, dieses.**

24. Rewrite the following, changing the nouns to the plural. Make all necessary changes.

1. Dieses Land ist reich.
2. Welcher Mann kommt?
3. Jenes Haus ist alt.
4. Wo ist die Zeitung?
5. Welche Studentin ist hübsch?
6. Jene Frau ist krank.
7. Dort liegt der Apfel.
8. Dieses Mädchen lernt.
9. Diese Stadt ist modern.
10. Wo ist das Buch?

25. Complete the following with **ein, eine, ein.**

1. Dort ist _______ Junge.
2. _______ Gabel ist aus Silber.
3. Das ist _______ Käfer.
4. _______ Mädchen kommt.
5. Dort steht _______ Museum.
6. Ist das _______ Lilie?
7. Dort liegt _______ Pille.
8. _______ Wohnung ist teuer.
9. Das ist _______ Pfennig.
10. Dort liegt _______ Apfel.

26. Complete the previous sentences with **kein, keine, kein.**

27. Complete the following with the appropriate endings, when necessary.

1. Sein_____ Freundin ist hier.
2. Wo ist euer_____ Haus?
3. Mein_____ Vater ist alt.
4. Ihr_____ Tochter lacht.
5. Dein_____ Auto ist teuer.
6. Wo ist Ihr_____ Hotel?
7. Hier ist sein_____ Mantel.
8. Unser_____ Kind ist klein.
9. Wo ist mein_____ Mutter?
10. Unsr_____ Kopie liegt dort.

28. Rewrite the following, changing the definite article to the possessive **sein.**

1. Ist das die Firma?
2. Der Job ist schwer.
3. Das Glas ist leer.
4. Der Hund bellt.
5. Wo ist die Frau?
6. Das Auto ist neu.
7. Der Bus kommt.
8. Das Drama ist lang.
9. Wo ist der Junge?
10. Die Freundin ist hübsch.

29. Rewrite the following, changing the nouns to the plural. Make all necessary changes.

1. Meine Freundin lacht.
2. Ihr Bruder ist krank.
3. Wo ist sein Lehrer?
4. Dein Messer liegt dort.
5. Wo ist unser Schlüssel?
6. Ist das euer Haus?
7. Wo ist Ihre Zeitung?
8. Dort ist mein Onkel.
9. Ist das dein Kind?
10. Wo ist eure Lehrerin?

30. Complete the following with the appropriate endings when necessary.

1. Dies____ Frau ist ihr____ Mutter.
2. Das ist doch kein____ Hund!
3. Solch____ Menschen sind beliebt.
4. Wann kommt euer____ Vater?
5. Jen____ Museum ist bekannt.
6. Dies____ Männer sind wichtig.
7. Welch____ Junge ist dein____ Bruder?
8. Er wird kein____ Doktor.
9. Ist das dein____ Pille?
10. Unsr____ Eltern sind dort.

Accusative Case

Singular and Plural

The accusative forms of the definite and indefinite article and of the **"der"** and **"ein"** words are as follows.

	SINGULAR			*PLURAL*
	Masculine	*Feminine*	*Neuter*	*All Genders*
Definite article:	**den**	**die**	**das**	**die**
"der" words	**diesen**	**diese**	**dieses**	**diese**
	welchen	**welche**	**welches**	**welche**
Indefinite article:	**einen**	**eine**	**ein**	(no plural)
"ein" words	**meinen**	**meine**	**mein**	**meine**
	ihren	**ihre**	**ihr**	**ihre**
Negative article	**keinen**	**keine**	**kein**	**keine**

The accusative case is used in the following ways:

As the Direct Object of the Verb

Wir kaufen *den Wagen.*	*We are buying the car.*
Ich nehme *die Zeitung.*	*I take the newspaper.*
Kennst du *das Drama?*	*Do you know the drama?*
Ich habe *die Bücher.*	*I have the books.*
Wir kennen *ihren Bruder.*	*We know her brother.*
Sie braucht *ihre Tasche.*	*She needs her purse.*
Sie verkaufen *ihr Auto.*	*They are selling their car.*
Sie hat *ihre Karten.*	*She has her tickets.*
Ich kenne *keinen Dichter.*	*I don't know any poet.*
Schreibst du *keine Karte?*	*Aren't you writing a card?*
Hast du *kein Geld?*	*Do you have no money?*
Er kauft *keine Schuhe.*	*He is not buying shoes.*

With Expressions of Definite Time and Duration of Time

Er bleibt *eine Woche* **in Bonn.**	*He is staying one week in Bonn.*
Sie besucht mich *jeden Tag.*	*She visits me every day.*

The accusative form of **der** is used when dating a letter: **Köln, *den* 13.8.1983**

With Prepositions

The accusative case is used as object of certain prepositions which are discussed in Chapter 2.

31. Complete the following with the appropriate form of **der, die, das.**

1. Kaufst du ______ Mantel?
2. Wir besuchen ______ Museum.
3. Kennst du ______ Frau?
4. Ich nehme ______ Banane.
5. Brauchst du ______ Buch?
6. Er kennt ______ Mädchen.
7. Hast du ______ Zeitung?
8. Ich esse ______ Apfel.
9. Wir kaufen ______ Haus.
10. Sie sehen ______ Mann.

32. Complete the above sentences with the appropriate form of **dieser, diese, dieses.**

33. Rewrite the following sentences, changing the nouns to the plural. Make all necessary changes.

1. Wir kennen den Dichter.
2. Ich bekomme den Brief.
3. Er kauft die Wurst.
4. Ich sehe das Tier.
5. Sie treffen den Freund.
6. Wir besuchen die Stadt.
7. Ich kenne den Berg.
8. Er schreibt das Gedicht.
9. Ich kaufe die Blume.
10. Wir singen das Lied.

34. Complete the following with the appropriate form of **ein, eine, ein.**

1. Ich habe ______ Koffer.
2. Er besucht ______ Universität.
3. Wir kaufen ______ Bild.
4. Ich nehme ______ Ei.
5. Wir besuchen ______ Freund.
6. Er bringt ______ Vase.
7. Sie brauchen ______ Tisch.
8. Wir haben ______ Hund.
9. Schreibst du ______ Gedicht?
10. Hast du ______ Freundin?

35. Complete the above sentences with the appropriate form of **kein.**

36. Rewrite the following sentences, changing the definite article to the possessive **unser.**

1. Kaufst du das Auto?
2. Ich sehe die Katze.
3. Wir besuchen das Kind.
4. Er ruft den Lehrer.
5. Ich nehme den Schlüssel.
6. Wir kennen die Lehrerin.

37. Complete the following with the appropriate endings when necessary.

1. Er nimmt mein____ Wagen.
2. Er besucht sein____ Mutter.
3. Besuchst du ihr____ Bruder?
4. Braucht ihr euer____ Zimmer?
5. Ich kenne ihr____ Schwester.
6. Habt ihr eur____ Zeitung?
7. Er kennt unsr____ Stadt.
8. Sie verkaufen ihr____ Haus.
9. Ich brauche mein____ Auto.
10. Kennst du sein____ Tante?

38. Rewrite the following, changing the nouns to the plural. Make all necessary changes.

1. Hat er mein Bild?
2. Brauchst du dein Buch?
3. Seht ihr unsre Freundin?
4. Ich nehme seine Zeitung.
5. Hast du deinen Mantel?
6. Wir kennen ihr Kind.

7. Ich habe ihren Schuh.
8. Verkaufst du unsren Wagen?
9. Sie brauchen ihren Freund.
10. Treffen Sie Ihren Lehrer?

Noun Endings in the Accusative Case

Singular

The accusative singular noun form of most German nouns is identical with the nominative singular. A few masculine nouns add **-e(n)** in the accusative singular.

The following nouns belong to this group:

Nominative Singular		*Accusative Singular*
der Hase	*rabbit*	**den Hasen**
der Herr	*gentleman*	**den Herrn**
der Junge	*boy*	**den Jungen**
der Held	*hero*	**den Helden**
der Mensch	*human being*	**den Menschen**
der Präsident	*president*	**den Präsidenten**
der Student	*student*	**den Studenten**

Wir treffen *den Studenten.* *We meet the student.*
Kennst du *einen Helden?* *Do you know a hero?*

39. Complete the following with the appropriate endings.

1. Sie liebt d____ Student____.
2. Wir sehen kein____ Mensch____.
3. Ich kenne d____ Präsident____.
4. Er ruft mein____ Junge____.
5. Ich kaufe kein____ Hase____.
6. Wer sieht jen____ Herr____?
7. Kennst du unsr____ Präsident____?
8. Sie treffen kein____ Held____.
9. Welch____ Hase____ kaufst du?
10. Sie haben ein____ Junge____.

REVIEW

40. Complete the following with the appropriate endings when necessary.

1. Sein____ Frau fährt jed____ Montag nach Köln.
2. Wann verkauft ihr euer____ Haus?
3. Er füttert d____ Hase____.
4. Welch____ Junge____ kennst du?
5. Dies____ Herr____ schreibt ein____ Brief.
6. Unsr____ Mutter kauft kein____ Mantel.
7. Jen____ Student____ besucht sein____ Freundin.
8. D____ Kind hat mein____ Bücher.
9. Ihr____ Freundin bleibt ein____ Tag hier.
10. Welch____ Mann hat Ihr____ Auto?
11. Mein____ Bruder kauft dies____ Bild.
12. Mein____ Schwester kennt d____ Präsident____.
13. Besucht ihr eur____ Kinder jed____ Tag?
14. Unser____ Junge____ kann solch____ Romane lesen.
15. Dies____ Katze trinkt kein____ Milch.
16. Welch____ Museen besucht er?

17. Manch____ Eltern sind streng.
18. Kennen Sie dies____ Herr____?
19. Welch____ Kleider kauft jen____ Mädchen?
20. München, d____ 6.5.1982.

Dative Case

Singular and Plural

The dative case of the definite and indefinite article and of the **"der"** and **"ein"** words are as follows.

	SINGULAR			*PLURAL*
	Masculine	*Feminine*	*Neuter*	*All Genders*
Definite article:	**dem**	**der**	**dem**	**den**
"der" words	**diesem**	**dieser**	**diesem**	**diesen**
	jenem	**jener**	**jenem**	**jenen**
Indefinite article:	**einem**	**einer**	**einem**	(no plural)
"ein" words	**meinem**	**meiner**	**meinem**	**meinen**
	ihrem	**ihrer**	**ihrem**	**ihren**
Negative article	**keinem**	**keiner**	**keinem**	**keinen**

The dative case is used in the following ways:

As the Indirect Object of the Verb

In English this is expressed by the prepositions *to* or *for*. The person or animal to whom something is given, shown, told, etc., is in the dative case.

Ich hole *dem Hund* **das Futter.**	*I am getting the food for the dog.*
Er kauft *der Frau* **die Karte.**	*He is buying the ticket for the woman.*
Wir zeigen *dem Kind* **das Boot.**	*We are showing the boat to the child.*
Wir geben *einem Mann* **Geld.**	*We are giving money to a man.*
Ich schicke *meiner Freundin* **nichts.**	*I am sending nothing to my girl friend.*
Sie kauft *unsrem Kind* **Schokolade.**	*She is buying chocolate for our child.*

The following verbs are frequently used with the dative case:

antworten	*to answer*	**Ich antworte** *dem Herrn.* *I answer the gentleman.*
bringen	*to bring, take*	**Er bringt** *seiner Freundin* **Blumen.** *He brings flowers to his girl friend.*
geben	*to give*	**Wir geben** *der Katze* **Milch.** *We are giving milk to the cat.*
holen	*to get*	**Ich hole** *meinem Bruder* **den Schlüssel.** *I am getting the key for my brother.*
kaufen	*to buy*	**Sie kauft** *ihrer Mutter* **ein Auto.** *She is buying a car for her mother.*
schicken	*to send*	**Sonja schickt** *ihrer Tante* **ein Geschenk.** *Sonja is sending a gift to her aunt.*
sagen	*to say, to tell*	**Sie sagt** *ihrem Mann* **die Wahrheit.** *She is telling her husband the truth.*
zeigen	*to show*	**Er zeigt** *dem Mädchen* **das Museum.** *He is showing the museum to the girl.*

The following verbs are always used with the dative case:

danken	*to thank (for)*	**Wir danken** *unsrem Lehrer.* *We thank our teacher.*
helfen	*to help*	**Ich helfe** *dem Kind.* *I am helping the child.*
gehören	*to belong to*	**Dieses Buch gehört** *ihrem Sohn.* *This book belongs to her son.*
gefallen	*to be pleasing to, to like*	**Jener Hut gefällt** *seiner Frau.* *His wife likes that hat.*

The verb **glauben** is used with the dative when followed by a person. The accusative is used when it is followed by a thing.

Ich glaube *dem Kind.*	*I believe the child.*
Ich glaube *die Geschichte.*	*I believe the story.*

With Prepositions

The dative case is used with certain prepositions which are presented in Chapter 2.

41. Complete the following sentences with the appropriate form of **der, die, das.**

1. Er holt ______ Lehrer Kaffee.
2. Ich schreibe ______ Freundin.
3. Wir helfen ______ Mann.
4. Dankst du ______ Kind?
5. Ich schicke ______ Studentin Geld.
6. Er sagt ______ Mädchen alles.
7. Wir kaufen ______ Onkel das Buch.
8. Es gehört ______ Dame.
9. Ich glaube ______ Fräulein.
10. Ich gebe ______ Katze Wasser.

42. Complete the above sentences with the appropriate form of **jener.**

43. Complete the following sentences with the appropriate form of **ein.**

1. Wir danken ______ Frau.
2. Ich kaufe ______ Studentin das Buch.
3. Wir helfen ______ Tier.
4. Sie geben es ______ Dame.
5. Wir glauben ______ Mann.
6. Ich helfe ______ Familie.
7. Es gehört ______ Dichter.
8. Ich schreibe ______ Freund.
9. Sie schickt es ______ Kind.
10. Er antwortet ______ Mädchen.

44. Complete the preceding sentences with the appropriate form of **kein.**

45. Complete the following with the appropriate endings.

1. Er gibt sein____ Frau Blumen.
2. Ich sage mein____ Onkel nichts.
3. Wir danken unsr____ Mutter.
4. Sie hilft ihr____ Mann.
5. Es gehört dein____ Freund.
6. Zeigst du ihr____ Tante den Brief?
7. Ich glaube ihr____ Bruder.
8. Holen Sie Ihr____ Sohn Milch?
9. Zeigt ihr eur____ Tochter das Geschenk?
10. Es gehört unsr____ Vater.

46. Complete the following with the dative form of the indicated word.

1. Ich zeige ______ Lehrer dieses Buch. *kein*
2. Wir geben ______ Vater ein Geschenk. *unser*
3. Es gehört ______ Studentin. *dies__*
4. Sie gefällt ______ Bruder. *mein*
5. Ich kaufe ______ Mutter etwas. *euer*
6. Wir schreiben ______ Tante eine Karte. *unser*
7. Er sagt ______ Mann die Neuigkeit. *jen__*
8. Ich bringe ______ Kind ein Bonbon. *jed__*
9. Er holt ______ Freundin Limonade. *sein*
10. Helfen Sie ______ Frau? *Ihr*

Noun Endings in the Dative Case

Singular

The dative singular noun form of most German nouns is identical with the nominative singular. The same nouns that add **-e(n)** in the accusative singular add **-e(n)** in the dative singular. (See section on accusative case.)

Ich gebe *dem Herrn* **die Zeitung.** *I am giving the newspaper to the gentleman.*
Wir bringen *dem Studenten* **ein Buch.** *We are bringing a book to the student.*

47. Complete the following with the appropriate endings.

1. Wir danken d____ Held____.
2. Es gehört jen____ Student____.
3. Sie glaubt unsr____ Präsident____.
4. Es gefällt dies____ Herr____.
5. Er zeigt es sein____ Junge____.
6. Ich gebe ein____ Hase____ die Karotte.
7. Wir helfen kein____ Mensch____.
8. Welch____ Junge____ gehört das Auto?

Plural

The dative plural noun always adds **-n**, unless the nominative plural form already ends in **-n.**

Ich schicke *den Kindern* **Geschenke.** *I am sending presents to the children.*
Wir geben *den Mädchen* **nichts.** *We are giving nothing to the girls.*

Nouns ending in **-s** in the nominative plural retain the **-s** in the dative plural and do not add **-n.**

Er zeigt *den Babys* **das Tier.** *He is showing the animal to the babies.*

48. Rewrite the following sentences, changing the dative nouns to the plural. Make all necessary changes.

1. Schreibst du deiner Freundin?
2. Er hilft jenem Kind.
3. Es gefällt seinem Lehrer.
4. Sie zeigt es ihrem Bruder.
5. Er antwortet dem Mann.
6. Ich hole dem Baby Milch.
7. Es gehört diesem Jungen.
8. Wir glauben der Frau.
9. Sie dankt ihrem Freund.
10. Es gehört eurem Studenten.

49. Complete the following with the appropriate form of the dative of the indicated word.

1. Ich helfe ______ Frauen. *jen__*
2. Ich danke ______ Vater. *mein*

3. Sie hilft ______ Kindern. *unser*
4. Wir kaufen es ______ Mann. *ihr.*
5. Gehört es ______ Freundinnen? *dein*
6. Er dankt ______ Frau. *dies__*
7. ______ Kind gefällt es? *welch__*
8. Sie antwortet ______ Herrn. *kein*
9. Ich bringe es ______ Baby. *ein*
10. Wir schicken ______ Studenten Geld. *jed__*

REVIEW

50. Complete the following with the correct endings when necessary:

1. Unser__ Junge hilft sein__ Freund.
2. Wer hat mein__ Tante d__ Wohnung gezeigt?
3. Man kann solch__ Leuten nicht helfen.
4. Wer glaubt dies__ Frau?
5. Jen__ Auto gefällt mein__ Tochter.
6. Welch__ Kellnerin holt dies__ Gast d__ Braten?
7. Warum hast du jed__ Kind dies__ Buch gekauft?
8. Wir danken unsr__ Eltern.
9. D__ Enkel holt sein__ Grossvater d__ Pfeife.
10. Kein__ Mensch hat d__ Invalidin geholfen.
11. Warum schreibt er sein__ Geschwister__ kein__ Brief?
12. Jen__ Hund gehört ihr__ Bruder.
13. Antwortet ihr eur__ Freundinnen__?
14. Wann sagst du dein__ Mann d__ Wahrheit?
15. Wer hat d__ Kinder__ mein__ Puppe gegeben?

Genitive Case

Singular and Plural

The genitive forms of the definite and indefinite article and of **"der"** and **"ein"** words are as follows.

	SINGULAR			*PLURAL*
	Masculine	*Feminine*	*Neuter*	*All Genders*
Definite article:	**des**	**der**	**des**	**der**
"der" words	**dieses**	**dieser**	**dieses**	**dieser**
	jenes	**jener**	**jenes**	**jener**
Indefinite article:	**eines**	**einer**	**eines**	(no plural)
"ein" words	**meines**	**meiner**	**meines**	**meiner**
	ihres	**ihrer**	**ihres**	**ihrer**
Negative article	**keines**	**keiner**	**keines**	**keiner**

The genitive case is used as follows.

To Show Possession or Relationships Between Two Nouns

In English these are expressed by the preposition *of* or with *'s*. No apostrophe is used in German.

Dort liegt das Buch *des Lehrers.*	*There lies the teacher's book.*
Wo ist das Auto *der Frau?*	*Where is the woman's car?*
Der Griff *des Messers* **ist rostig.**	*The handle of the knife is rusty.*
Das ist die Frau *meines Sohnes.*	*That is my son's wife.*
Wo ist die Tasche *meiner Tochter?*	*Where is my daughter's purse?*
Hier ist ein Foto *unsres Hauses.*	*Here is a picture of our house.*
Frau Schnabels **Mann ist hier.**	*Mrs. Schnabel's husband is here.*
Die Eltern *dieser Kinder* **sind hier.**	*The parents of these children are here.*

With Expressions of Indefinite Time

In English these are expressed with *one day, some day* (night, evening, etc.).

Eines Tages **wird sie ihren Freund sehen.**	*Some day she'll see her friend.*
Eines Morgens **kam er zu Besuch.**	*One morning he came for a visit.*

By way of anology the feminine noun **Nacht** also adds **-s** in such time expressions.

Eines Nachts **war er wieder gesund.**	*One night he was well again.*

With Prepositions

The genitive case is used with certain prepositions which are presented in Chapter 2.

Noun Endings in the Genitive Case

Singular

-s or **-es** ending

Most masculine and neuter nouns add **-(e)s** in the singular. No apostrophe is used.

An **-s** is added if the masculine or neuter noun has more than one syllable, such as **meines Bruder*s*, dieses Zimmer*s*.**

An **-es** is added if the masculine or neuter noun has only one syllable, such as **des Buch*es*.** If the last syllable is accented, the genitive ending is also **-es,** such as **des Gedícht*es*.**

-en endings

Those nouns that take **-(e)n** in the accusative and dative singular also add **-(e)n** in the genitive singular.

Die Frau *des Präsidenten* **ist krank.**	*The wife of the president is ill.*

-(e)ns endings

Some nouns add **-ens** to form the genitive singular, such as **des Herz*ens*, des Nam*ens*. des Fried*ens*.**

Traurigen Herzens **zog er in den Krieg.**	*With a heavy heart he went to war.*

-ens or apostrophe

When a masculine name ends in an **s** sound, the genitive can be formed by adding **-ens** or apostrophe.

Maxens Geburtstag **ist am 11. Mai.** *Max's birthday is May 11th.*
Max' Geburtstag **ist am 11. Mai.** *Max's birthday is May 11th.*

However, the **von** construction is preferred in such cases.

Der Geburtstag *von Max* **ist am 11. Mai.** *Max's birthday is May 11th.*

Feminine nouns

No ending is added to feminine nouns in the genitive case.

Proper names

An **-s** is added to proper names in the genitive case.

Fräulein Bauers **Hut war teuer.** *Miss Bauer's hat was expensive.*

Plural

The genitive plural noun form is identical to the nominative plural noun form.

51. Complete the following with the appropriate form of **der, die, das** and the appropriate noun endings when necessary.

1. Die Fabrik ______ Familie____ ist gross.
2. Das Auto ______ Doktor____ ist kaputt.
3. Die Farbe ______ Wagen____ ist schön.
4. Der Bau ______ Haus____ beginnt bald.
5. Der Mantel ______ Frau____ ist aus Leder.
6. Der Preis ______ Bild____ ist zu hoch.
7. Die Buchstabierung ______ Name____ ist schwer.
8. Der Vater ______ Junge____ ist hier.
9. Der Titel ______ Gedicht____ ist kurz.
10. Die Freundin ______ Student____ wartet.

52. Complete the above sentences with the appropriate form of **dieser.**

53. Complete the following sentences with the appropriate forms of **ein** and the appropriate noun endings when necessary.

1. Das Leben ______ Held____ ist interessant.
2. Es ist die Geschichte ______ Junge____.
3. Ich höre das Lachen ______ Kind____.
4. Das ist die Wohnung ______ Student____.
5. Die Frau ______ Arbeiter____ ist krank.
6. Die Mutter ______ Mädchen____ ist hier.
7. Die Politik ______ Nation____ ist wichtig.
8. Ich esse die Hälfte ______ Apfel____.
9. Wo ist das Bild ______ Herr____?
10. Ich höre den Motor ______ Maschine____.

54. Complete the following with the appropriate genitive form of the indicated word. Supply the appropriate noun endings when necessary.

1. Das ist das Buch ______ Lehrer____. *sein*
2. Ich nehme den Wagen ______ Mutter____. *mein*
3. Wo ist die Frau ______ Präsident____? *unser*
4. Dort ist das Zimmer ______ Junge____. *euer*
5. Das Leben ______ Vater____ ist schwer. *ihr*
6. Wo ist der Mantel ______ Tante____? *dein*
7. Wir sehen das Gymnasium ______ Tochter____. *ihr*
8. Dort hängt das Foto ______ Kind____. *mein*
9. Die Freundin ______ Sohn____ kommt. *sein*
10. Wo ist die Katze ______ Grossmutter____? *Ihr*

55. Rewrite the following, changing the genitive nouns to the plural. Make all necessary changes.

1. Die Kinder jener Frau sind krank.
2. Die Sitze seines Autos sind bequem.
3. Das sind die Fotos unsrer Tochter.
4. Die Bücher jenes Studenten liegen hier.
5. Wann beginnt der Bau eures Hauses?
6. Die Museen dieser Stadt sind modern.
7. Die Kleider meiner Freundin sind neu.
8. Der Wagen des Herrn steht dort.
9. Die Betonung des Namens ist schwer.
10. Die Gemälde jenes Museums sind bekannt.

Substitute for the Genitive Case

The preposition **von** with the dative case is frequently used instead of the genitive construction.

Das Kleid *meiner Tochter* **war teuer.**	*My daughter's dress was expensive.*
Das Kleid *von meiner Tochter* **war teuer.**	*My daughter's dress was expensive.*
Das Auto *meines Bruders* **ist kaputt.**	*My brother's car is broken.*
Das Auto *von meinem Bruder* **ist kaputt.**	*My brother's car is broken.*

56. Rewrite the following. Substitute the **von** dative construction for the genitive. Make all necessary changes.

1. Die Schneide dieses Messers ist scharf.
2. Die Dokumente unsres Präsidenten sind im Museum.
3. Wir haben die Hälfte des Gedichtes gelesen.
4. Hier ist ein Bild meiner Freunde.
5. Der Preis des Autos ist zu hoch.

57. Rewrite the following. Substitute the genitive for the dative **von** construction.

1. Das Wasser von jenem See ist eiskalt.
2. Der Hund von Peter bellt.
3. Die Ohren von solchen Hasen sind sehr lang.
4. Die Mutter von dem Mädchen steht dort.
5. Die Produkte von dieser Fabrik sind teuer.

REVIEW

58. Complete the following with the appropriate endings when necessary.

1. Wo ist d____ Wohnung dein____ Tante____?
2. Das ist d____ Geschäft sein____ Eltern____.
3. D____ Götter jen____ Volk____ waren nicht gütig.
4. Ein____ Nachmittag____ besuchten sie uns.
5. Ist d____ Krankheit eur____ Bruder____ ansteckend?
6. D____ Blätter dies____ Baum____ sind schon abgefallen.
7. Frau Schneider____ Mann ist schon angekommen.
8. D____ Titel dies____ Roman____ ist zu lang.
9. D____ Freunde mein____ Tochter____ sind hier.
10. D____ Mutter jen____ Junge____ ist krank.
11. D____ Hand d____ Frau____ ist kalt.
12. Wo ist d____ Foto dein____ Haus____?
13. D____ Kinder ihr____ Freundin____ sind hier.
14. Ich kenne d____ Professor jen____ Student____.
15. Sie kauft d____ Wagen mein____ Grossvater____.

SPECIAL USES OF THE DEFINITE ARTICLE

With General or Abstract Nouns

***Die Katze* ist ein Haustier.**	*A cat is a domestic animal.*
***Die Liebe* ist eine Himmelsmacht.**	*Love is a heavenly power.*
***Das Leben* ist kurz.**	*Life is short.*

59. Complete the following with the appropriate definite article.

1. ______ Panther ist eine Wildkatze.
2. ______ Technik ist progressiv.
3. ______ Leben ist kompliziert.
4. ______ Gravitation ist eine Kraft.
5. ______ Chemie ist eine Wissenschaft.
6. ______ Mensch ist sterblich.
7. ______ Hund ist ein Haustier.
8. ______ Schule ist wichtig.

With Names of Streets, Lakes, Mountains and Countries

***Die Brennerstrasse* ist im Süden.**	*Brenner Street is in the south.*
***Der Bodensee* ist tief.**	*Lake Constance is deep.*
***Der Tafelberg* ist in Südafrika.**	*Table Mountain is in South Africa.*

The definite article is required with names of countries that are feminine, masculine or plural. (See the section "Neuter Nouns" for gender of countries.)

***Die Schweiz* ist neutral.**	*Switzerland is neutral.*
***Der Iran* ist im Osten.**	*Iran is in the east.*
***Die Vereinigten Staaten* sind gross.**	*The United States is large.*

The definite article is not used with countries that are neuter, unless the name of the country is modified.

***Deutschland* produziert viel.**	*Germany produces much.*
***Das moderne Deutschland* ist progressiv.**	*Modern Germany is progressive.*

60. Complete the following with the appropriate definite article when necessary.

1. ______ Vesuv ist ein Vulkan.
2. Wo ist ______ Bergstrasse?
3. ______ Niederlande sind im Norden.
4. Hier liegt ______ Türkei.
5. ______ Tegernsee ist klein.
6. ______ Irak ist im Osten.
7. Wie hoch ist ______ Montblanc?
8. ______ historische Italien ist bekannt.
9. Dort ist ______ Alpenstrasse.
10. ______ Vereinigten Staaten sind reich.
11. ______ Afrika ist gross.
12. ______ heutige Deutschland ist modern.

With Weights, Measures and Expressions of Time

The accusative case of the definite article is used in German with expressions of weight, measure and time. In English the indefinite article is used in the sense of *per.*

Das kostet 2 Mark *das Pfund.*	*That costs 2 Marks a pound.*
Es kostet 50 Pfennig *das Meter.*	*It costs 50 Pfennig a meter.*
Er kommt einmal *die Woche.*	*He comes once a week.*
Wir bezahlen zweimal *den Monat.*	*We pay twice a month.*

61. Complete the following with the appropriate definite article.

1. Er kommt einmal ______ Jahr.
2. Es kostet 20 Pfennig ______ Pfund.
3. Ich sehe Peter einmal ______ Woche.
4. Sie schreit zweimal ______ Sekunde.
5. Das kostet 3 Mark ______ Meter.
6. Es klingelt fünfmal ______ Stunde.

With Parts of the Body or Articles of Clothing

The definite article is used in German to refer to parts of the body or articles of clothing, unless there is doubt as to the identity of the possessor. In English the possessive is used.

Er zieht sich *den Mantel* **an.**	*He is putting on his coat.*
Ich wasche mir *das Gesicht.*	*I am washing my face.*

62. Complete the following with the correct form of the definite article.

1. Er zieht sich ______ Hose an.
2. Sie waschen sich ______ Hände.
3. Wir putzen uns ______ Schuhe.
4. Ich ziehe mir ______ Mantel an.
5. Wäschst du dir ______ Gesicht?
6. Sie setzt sich ______ Hut auf.
7. Ich wasche mir ______ Kopf.
8. Putzt du dir ______ Zähne?

REVIEW

63. Complete the following with the appropriate form of the definite article.

1. Ich fahre 100 Kilometer ______ Stunde.
2. Er wäscht sich ______ Hände.
3. ______ Vogesenstrasse ist dort.
4. Das kostet 50 Pfennig ______ Pfund.
5. ______ Zugspitze ist in Deutschland.
6. ______ Ammersee ist malerisch.
7. Sie besucht uns zweimal ______ Monat.
8. ______ Vierwaldstättersee ist im Süden.
9. Er putzt sich ______ Zähne.

10. ______ Niederlande sind flach.
11. Sie kommt einmal ______ Woche.
12. ______ Schweiz ist reich.
13. ______ Leben ist schön.
14. ______ Biologie ist wichtig.
15. ______ industrielle Österreich ist modern.
16. Wo ist ______ Schwanseestrasse?
17. Wir ziehen uns ______ Schuhe an.
18. ______ Hauptstrasse ist breit.

OMISSION OF THE INDEFINITE OR DEFINITE ARTICLE

The indefinite or definite article is omitted in the following cases:

Before a Predicate Nominative

Sie ist ***Russin.***	*She is a Russian.*
Er wird ***Zahnarzt.***	*He will become a dentist.*

If the predicate nominative is modified, the article is expressed:

Er ist ***ein bekannter Pianist.***	*He is a well-known pianist.*
Er ist ***der beste Lehrer.***	*He is the best teacher.*

With Certain Set Phrases

Sie hat ***Fieber.***	*She has a fever.*
Wir haben ***Kopfweh.***	*We have a headache.*
Hast du ***Zahnweh?*** **(*****Halsweh,*** **etc.)**	*Do you have a toothache? (a sore throat, etc.)*

After the Preposition ***als,*** *Meaning* "as a(n)"

Er arbeitet dort als ***Ingenieur.***	*He works there as an engineer.*
Sie ist als ***Studentin*** **in Bonn.**	*She is in Bonn as a student.*

64. Write the German for the following.

1. I have a fever.
2. He is a teacher.
3. She is a good teacher.
4. Does he have a toothache?
5. He is in Berlin as a student.
6. He is a professor.
7. She will become a pianist.
8. We have a sore throat.

REVIEW

65. Complete the following with the appropriate endings when necessary.

1. D____ Tochter mein____ Freund____ hat dies____ Brief geschrieben.
2. Ein____ Tag____ kaufte er sein____ Frau____ ein____ Pelzmantel.
3. D____ Eltern dies____ Mädchen____ sind dort.
4. Unser____ Sohn ist dies____ Woche hier.
5. Welch____ Blumen hat d____ Junge sein____ Mutter____ gekauft?
6. Solch____ Tiere fressen kein____ Blätter.
7. Mein____ Freundinnen geben unsr____ Eltern____ kein____ Geschenk.
8. D____ Wagen jen____ Herr____ ist teuer.

9. Sie gibt ihr____ Sohn jed____ Tag ein____ Apfel.
10. Welch____ Auto gehört d____ Frau d____ Lehrer____?

66. Rewrite the following sentences, changing all nouns to the plural. Make all necessary changes.

1. Wir haben kein Foto.
2. Wo ist sein Bruder?
3. Wer hat jenes Bild genommen?
4. Welches Lied soll ich singen?
5. Wer hilft dem Baby?
6. Das gefällt dem Mädchen.
7. Meine Freundin kommt.
8. Unser Auto ist rot.
9. Wann kommt Ihre Tochter?
10. Das Kind unsres Lehrers ist hier.
11. Wo ist unser Hotel?
12. Manches Land ist arm.
13. Wo ist das Museum?
14. Das Buch des Studenten liegt hier.
15. Wird diese Geschichte eurem Freund gefallen?

67. Complete the following with the appropriate article when necessary.

1. ______ Deutschland ist modern.
2. Sie ist ______ Engländerin.
3. Hast du ______ Kopfweh?
4. Äpfel kosten 2 Mark ______ Pfund.
5. ______ Bergstrasse ist im Zentrum.
6. ______ Tschechoslowakei ist im Osten.
7. Er ist ______ reicher Amerikaner.
8. ______ Königsee ist malerisch.
9. Ich wasche mir ______ Hände.
10. ______ Löwe ist eine Wildkatze.
11. Er zieht sich ______ Mantel an.
12. Ich bin einmal ______ Woche hier.
13. ______ Vesuv ist bekannt.
14. ______ heutige China ist übervölkert.
15. Sie ist ______ beste Sängerin.
16. Sie arbeitet als ______ Sekretärin.

Chapter 2

Prepositions

In German, unlike in English, the noun following a preposition is always in a particular case other than the nominative. Some prepositions are followed by the accusative, some by the dative and some by the genitive case. In English the noun that follows a certain preposition is the same form for all prepositions.

PREPOSITIONS GOVERNING THE ACCUSATIVE CASE

The following prepositions are always followed by the accusative case:

durch—*through, by* (used in a passive construction (see Chapter 5) to express the means by which something is done)

Er läuft *durch* das Haus.	*He is running* through *the house.*
Wir gehen *durch* die Zimmer.	*We are walking* through *the rooms.*
Er wurde *durch* einen Schuss getötet.	*He was killed* by *a shot.*

entlang—*along* (this preposition follows the accusative object)

Wir gehen die Strasse *entlang.*	*We are walking* along *the street.*

für—*for*

Warum kaufte er nichts *für* seinen Freund?	*Why didn't he buy anything* for *his friend?*
Sie arbeitet *für* meine Eltern.	*She is working* for *my parents.*

gegen—*against, toward, about*

Er kämpfte *gegen* den Weltmeister.	*He fought* against *the world champion.*
Ich gehe *gegen* die Tür.	*I am going* toward *the door.*
Es waren *gegen* zehn Frauen im Zimmer.	*There were* about *ten women in the room.*

ohne—*without*

***Ohne* seine Frau geht er nicht.**	*He is not going* without *his wife.*
Wir können *ohne* unsre Kinder nicht kommen.	*We can't come* without *our children.*

um—*around*

Warum fährst du *um* das Haus? *Why are you driving* around *the house?*

If the article is not stressed, the following prepositions contract with **das**, especially in everyday speech.

durch das = durchs

Er läuft *durchs* Geschäft. *He is running through the store.*

für das = fürs

Ich bringe es *fürs* Baby. *I am bringing it for the baby.*

um das = ums

Wir stehen *ums* Auto. *We are standing around the car.*

1. Complete with the appropriate accusative preposition.

1. Der Ball fliegt _______ die Luft.
2. Das Auto fährt die Strasse _______.
3. Sie laufen _______ die Ecke.
4. Er stösst den Stuhl _______ die Wand.
5. Ich muss _______ meine Freundin gehen, weil sie krank ist.
6. Es sind _______ zehn Busse auf der Strasse.
7. Ich kaufe es _______ meinen Vater, weil er Geburtstag hat.
8. Bringst du es _______ deinen Lehrer?
9. Sie wandern _______ die Museen dieser Stadt.
10. Der Blinde kann _______ seinen Hund nicht gehen.

2. Fill in the appropriate ending or contraction.

1. Das Fahrrad fährt gegen ein_____ Baum.
2. Ich schaue durch_____ Teleskop.
3. Wir fahren ein_____ Fluss entlang.
4. Kaufst du es für dein_____ Grossmutter?
5. Wir sind um unsr_____ Garten gelaufen.
6. Ohne mein_____ Töchter kann ich nicht kommen.
7. Warum stehen die Leute um_____ Auto?
8. Das Haus wurde durch ein_____ Bombe zerstört.
9. Warum läufst du gegen d_____ Wand?
10. Habt ihr etwas für_____ Kind mitgebracht?
11. Wir fahren um_____ Museum.
12. Ich komme ohne mein_____ Freundin.
13. Er wurde durch ein_____ Explosion getötet.
14. Wer macht es für d_____ Lehrer?
15. Sie gehen gegen d_____ Fenster.
16. Warum geht ihr durch_____ Kaufhaus?
17. Die Kinder tanzen um ein_____ Linde.
18. Er geht d_____ Strasse entlang.
19. Sie kämpfen gegen d_____ Diktatur.
20. Ich kaufe es für mein_____ Schwester.

3. Complete with the appropriate form of the indicated word.

1. Ich komme ohne _____ Frau. *mein*
2. Sie bauen einen Zaun um _____ Garten. *ihr*
3. Wir haben den Brief für _____ Grossmutter. *unser*
4. Kurt wurde nicht durch _____ Schuss getötet. *sein*
5. Geht nicht _____ Berg entlang! *jen*____
6. Viele waren gegen _____ Revolution. *dies*____
7. Sie kaufte es für _____ Jungen. *ihr*
8. Der Wagen rollte gegen _____ Auto. *euer*

PREPOSITIONS GOVERNING THE DATIVE CASE

The following prepositions are always followed by the dative case.

aus—*out of, from* (point of origin—used to denote coming from place of birth or domicile), *of* (usually used without an article)

Das Mädchen kommt *aus* dem Hotel.	*The girl is coming* out of *the hotel.*
Kommen Sie auch *aus* Deutschland?	*Do you also come* from *Germany?*
Das Messer ist *aus* Stahl.	*The knife is (made)* of *steel.*

ausser—*except, besides*

***Ausser* meiner Mutter waren wir alle da.**	Except *for my mother, we were all there.*
***Ausser* diesem Volkswagen besitze ich nichts.**	*I own nothing* besides *this Volkswagen.*

bei—*with* (at the home of), *near, at*

Ich bleibe *bei* meinen Grosseltern.	*I am staying* with *my grandparents.*
Wohnst du *bei* der Schule?	*Do you live* near *school?*
Ich treffe dich *bei* der Universität.	*I'll meet you* at *the university.*

gegenüber—*across* (usually follows the dative object)

Wir wohnen dem Park *gegenüber.*	*We live* across *from the park.*
Er sitzt seinen Eltern *gegenüber.*	*He sits* across *from his parents.*

mit—*with*

Er arbeitet *mit* einem Hammer.	*He is working* with *a hammer.*
Ich reise *mit* diesen Leuten.	*I am traveling* with *these people.*

nach—*after, according to* (with this meaning, the preposition usually follows the noun), *to* (used with neuter geographical names; no article is expressed)

***Nach* dem Abendessen gehen wir aus.**	*We are going out* after *dinner.*
Der Geschichte *nach* wurde er 100 Jahre alt.	According to *the story, he became 100 years old.*
Der Flug *nach* Kanada war lang.	*The flight* to *Canada was long.*

seit—*since, for*

***Seit* seiner Kindheit wohnt er in Ulm.**	*He has been living in Ulm* since *his childhood.*
Ich habe die Krankheit *seit* einem Jahr.	*I have had the illness* for *one year.*

von—*from, by*

Er weiss nichts *von* seinen Töchtern.	*He knows nothing* about *his daughters.*

Das Geschenk kommt *von* meiner Grossmutter. — *The present is* from *my grandmother.*
Ist das ein Drama *von* Goethe? — *Is that a drama* by *Goethe?*

from (coming from a certain direction as opposed to origin)

Das Flugzeug kommt *von* Frankfurt. — *The airplane is coming* from *Frankfurt.*

by (used in the passive construction (see Chapter 5) to express the personal agent)

Das Essen wurde *von* meiner Mutter gekocht. — *The dinner was cooked* by *my mother.*

zu—*to* (indicates direction to people and places when no geographical name is used)

Wir gehen *zu* keiner Vorlesung. — *We are going* to *no lecture.*

The following prepositions contract with the dative definite article, unless the article is stressed.

bei + dem = *beim*

Ich bin *beim* Doktor. — *I am* at the *doctor's office.*

von + dem = *vom*

Kommt er schon *vom* Kino? — *Is he already coming* from the *movies?*

zu + dem = *zum*

Wir gehen *zum* Museum. — *We are going* to the *museum.*

zu + der = *zur*

Warum fährt er *zur* Schule? — *Why is he driving* to *school?*

4. Complete with the appropriate preposition or contraction.

1. Ich fahre ______ dem Auto ______ Hamburg.
2. Ich wohne ______ meinen Schwestern.
3. Er geht ______ Lehrer.
4. Wir wohnen ______ einem Jahr hier.
5. Die Universität ist dem Park ______ .
6. ______ dem Frühstück gehe ich ______ Schule.
7. Dieser Brief kommt ______ meiner Freundin.
8. Gehst du ______ deinem Bruder ins Kino?
9. Der Zug kommt ______ Augsburg.
10. Das Fenster wurde ______ unsrem Jungen zerschlagen.

5. Complete with the correct endings or contractions when necessary.

1. Der Arzt kommt aus d____ Schlafzimmer.
2. Nach d____ Schule besuche ich dich.
3. Ich kenne sie seit jen____ Tag.
4. Bist du zu____ Doktor gegangen?
5. Sie wurde von kein____ Menschen gefragt.
6. Dies____ Park gegenüber wohnt unser Onkel.
7. Er steht bei____ Hotel.
8. Wann fahren wir nach ____ Österreich?
9. Kommt sie schon von d____ Universität?
10. ____ Sage nach wurde er König.

11. Seit ein____ Monat ist sie in der Schweiz.
12. Ausser jen____ Herrn war niemand da.
13. Ich fahre mit mein____ Freunden nach ____ Bremen.
14. Sie ist seit ihr____ Abreise dort.
15. Sie bekam von jed____ Kind eine Orchidee.
16. Ich bleibe bei mein____ Geschwistern.
17. Sie kommt von____ Garten.
18. Sie wurde von dies____ Hund gebissen.
19. Arbeitest du bei dies____ Firma?
20. Das Paket kommt von mein____ Eltern.

6. Complete the following with the appropriate form of the indicated word.

1. Er läuft zu ______ Tante. *sein*
2. Sie werden von ______ Mädchen gefragt. *ein*
3. Er ist bei ______ Kaufhaus. *jen__*
4. Ich wohne seit ______ Jahr hier. *ein*
5. ______ Geschichte nach ist er reich. *dies__*
6. Sie sprechen mit ______ Lehrer. *unser*
7. Kommt ihr von ______ Haus? *euer*
8. Er wohnt ______ Park gegenüber. *kein*
9. Nach ______ Vorlesung essen wir. *die*
10. Sie kommt aus ______ Museum. *das*
11. Ich wohne seit ______ Kindheit hier. *mein*
12. Er kam aus ______ Hotelzimmer. *jen____*
13. Sie sitzt ______ Brüdern gegenüber. *ihr*
14. Was machst du mit ______ Mitgliedskarte? *dein*

PREPOSITIONS GOVERNING EITHER THE ACCUSATIVE OR THE DATIVE CASE

A group of German prepositions can be used with either the accusative or the dative case.

The accusative case is used when the verb in combination with the preposition expresses change of place or direction toward a place.

The dative case is used when the verb in combination with the preposition expresses location or motion within a fixed location.

in (accusative)—*into*

Er springt *in* den Fluss. *He is jumping* into *the river.*

in (dative)—*in*

Er schwimmt *in* dem *(im)* Fluss. *He is swimming* in *the river.*

in (followed by names of countries and cities)
(accusative) *to*

The accusative form of the definite article is required with names of countries that are feminine, masculine or plural.

Fliegst du *in* die Türkei? *Are you flying* to *Turkey?*
Er fährt *in* die Vereinigten Staaten. *He is going* to *the United States.*

(dative) *in*

The preposition is followed by the name of the country or the city. If the name of the country is feminine, masculine or plural the dative form of the definite article is expressed.

Wir sind *in* Australien.	*We are* in *Australia.*
Wohnst du *in* München?	*Do you live* in *Munich?*
Er bleibt *in der* Schweiz.	*He is staying* in *Switzerland.*
Ist sie *im* Iran?	*Is she* in *Iran?*

in (followed by dative time expressions)–*in, during*

The contraction *im* **(in dem)** precedes the names of seasons and months.

Er kommt *im* Herbst.	*He is coming* in *fall.*
***Im* Sommer ist es heiss.**	*It is hot* in *summer.*

an (accusative)–*to, onto*

Wir laufen *an* die Tür.	*We are running* to *the door.*
Ich schreibe *an* die Tafel.	*I am writing* onto *the blackboard.*

an (dative)–*at, on*

Mein Onkel steht *am (an dem)* Fenster.	*My uncle is standing* at *the window.*
Das Bild hängt *an* der Wand.	*The picture is hanging* on *the wall.*

an (followed by dative time expressions)–*in, on*

The contraction *am* **(an dem)** precedes dates, the names of days and times of day.

Sie besuchen uns *am* 10. Mai.	*They are visiting us May 10.*
Ich komme *am* Montag.	*I am coming* on *Monday.*
Er geht *am* Morgen nach Bonn.	*He is going to Bonn* in *the morning.*

auf (accusative)–*onto*

Er legt das Messer *auf* den Tisch.	*He is putting the knife* onto *the table.*

auf (dative)–*on*

Sie sitzt *auf* meinem Stuhl.	*She is sitting* on *my chair.*

hinter

(accusative) *behind*

Stellst du die Schuhe *hinter* die Tür?	*Are you putting the shoes* behind *the door?*

(dative) *behind*

Er steht *hinter* seinem Klavierlehrer.	*He is standing* behind *his piano teacher.*

neben

(accusative) *beside*

Setz dich *neben* diese Herren!	*Sit down* beside *these gentlemen.*

(dative) *beside*

Wer steht *neben* Ihrem Wagen?	*Who is standing* beside *your car?*

über (accusative)–*over, above, across*

Ich hänge die Lampe *über* den Tisch.	*I am hanging the lamp* over (above) *the table.*
Lauf nicht *über* die Strasse!	*Don't run* across *the street!*

(dative)–*over, above*

Das Flugzeug ist *über* den Häusern.	*The plane is* above (over) *the houses.*

unter

(accusative) *under, below*

Der Ball rollt *unter* den Sessel.	*The ball is rolling* under *the easy chair.*

(dative) *under, below*

Ich liege *unter* den Bäumen.	*I am lying* under *the trees.*

vor

(accusative) *in front of*

Ich habe mich *vor* die Frau gesetzt.	*I sat down* in front of *the woman.*

(dative) *in front of, ago, before*

Wir stehen *vor* den Bildern.	*We are standing* in front of *the pictures.*
***Vor* einem Jahr besuchten sie uns.**	*A year* ago *they visited us.*
Kommt ihr *vor* meinem Geburtstag?	*Are you coming* before *my birthday?*

zwischen

(accusative) *between*

Sie hat den Brief *zwischen* das Buch und die Zeitung gelegt.	*She placed the letter* between *the book and the newspaper.*

(dative) *between*

Wer sitzt *zwischen* jenem Herrn und jener Dame?	*Who is sitting* between *that gentleman and that lady?*

Contractions

The following contractions are usually made unless the definite article is emphasized.

an + das = *ans*

Sie geht *ans* Fenster.	*She is going* to the *window.*

an + dem = *am*

Er stand *am* Bett.	*He stood* at the *bed.*

auf + das = *aufs*

Er setzt sich *aufs* Sofa.	*He is sitting down* on the *sofa.*

in + das = *ins*

Geht ihr *ins* Kino?	*Are you going* to the *movies?*

in + dem = *im*

Sitzt sie *im* Garten?	*Is she sitting* in the *garden?*

hinter + das = *hinters*

Wir gehen *hinters* Haus.	*We are going* behind the *house.*

über + das = *übers*

Es fliegt *übers* Nest.	*It is flying* over the *nest.*

unter + das = *unters*

Leg es nicht *unters* Bett!	*Don't put it* under the *bed!*

vor + das = ***vors***

Stell dich ***vors*** **Mädchen!** — *Stand* in front of the *girl!*

Combinations with Verbs of Direction

The following verbs denote direction. When they are used in combination with one of the preceding prepositions, they require the accusative case.

legen—*to lay, to put, to place*

Ich ***lege*** **die Zeitung aufs Sofa.** — *I am putting the newspaper on the sofa.*

setzen—*to place, to set, to sit down*

Er ***setzte*** **sich neben das Fräulein.** — *He sat down beside the young woman.*

stellen—*to put, to place, to set*

Stell **den Stuhl hinter den Tisch!** — *Place the chair behind the table!*

Combinations with Verbs of Location

The following verbs denote location. When they are used in combination with one of the preceding prepositions, they require the dative case.

liegen—*to lie, to rest*

Warum ***liegst*** **du unter deinem Bett?** — *Why are you lying under your bed?*

sitzen—*to sit*

Du ***sitzt*** **auf ihrem Mantel.** — *You are sitting on her coat.*

stehen—*to stand*

Warum ***steht*** **er neben meinem Bruder?** — *Why is he standing next to my brother?*

7. Complete with the appropriate form of the indicated word. Make contractions when possible.

1. Wir sitzen schon in _______ Auto. *das*
2. Er geht über _______ Strasse. *die*
3. Stell die Schuhe unter _______ Bett! *das*
4. Wir sitzen vor _______ Kindern. *unser*
5. Wer kommt in _______ August? *der*
6. Sie wohnt in _______ Schweiz. *die*
7. An _______ Mittwoch fliege ich ab. *der*
8. Geh in _______ Haus! *das*
9. Schwimmt ihr immer in _______ Fluss? *dieser*
10. Wann fährst du in _______ Türkei? *die*
11. In _______ Sommer haben wir Ferien. *der*
12. Er besuchte uns vor _______ Monat. *ein*
13. Warum gehst du an _______ Küchenfenster? *das*
14. Ich legte den Löffel neben _______ Teller. *dein*
15. Er steht zwischen _______ Brüdern. *sein*
16. Sie steht hinter _______ Fabrik. *jene*
17. An _______ Abend bin ich müde. *der*
18. Dürfen wir in _______ Theater? *das*

19. Stell dich neben ______ Eltern! *dein*
20. Sein Kopf ist unter ______ Kissen. *das*
21. Warst du schon in ______ Irak? *der*
22. Setz dich nicht auf ______ Koffer! *mein*
23. Es liegt zwischen ______ Zeitungen. *ihr*
24. In ______ Mai wird es wieder warm. *der*
25. Warum geht er hinter ______ Museum? *das*
26. Er legte es auf ______ Tisch. *der*
27. Ich bin in ______ Kaufhaus. *ein*
28. Es liegt unter ______ Bett. *euer*
29. Sie sitzt auf ______ Mantel. *mein*
30. Setz dich hinter ______ Freundin! *dein*
31. Das Haus ist neben ______ Park. *jener*
32. Stell es vor ______ Garage! *unser*
33. Setzt euch in ______ Auto! *das*
34. Wir sind in ______ Vereinigten Staaten. *die*
35. Bist du in ______ Küche? *die*

Da- Compounds with Accusative and Dative Prepositions

Da- compounds are used when referring to things or ideas, discussed in a previous sentence. They are used the same way as the English pronoun *it* or *them* with prepositions. In German the **da-** form is used regardless as to whether the noun it replaces is masculine, feminine, neuter, singular or plural. If the preposition starts with a vowel, **dar-** is prefixed (e.g. **darin, darüber, darauf,** etc.). Note that **da(r)-** is never used to refer to people. (See Chapter 8 on pronouns.)

Bist du gegen *den Plan?*	*Are you against the plan?*
Ja, ich bin *dagegen.*	*Yes, I am against it.*
Denkst du *an die Ferien?*	*Are you thinking about your vacation?*
Nein, ich denke nicht *daran.*	*No, I am not thinking about it.*
Was macht ihr *mit den Bleistiften?*	*What are you doing with the pencils?*
Wir schreiben *damit.*	*We are writing with them.*
Steht sie *neben dem Bild?*	*Is she standing beside the picture?*
Ja, sie steht *daneben.*	*Yes, she is standing beside it.*

All accusative, dative and accusative/dative prepositions can be prefixed by **da(r)-** with the exceptions of **entlang, ohne, ausser, gegenüber.**

8. Complete the answers with the appropriate **da-** compounds.

1. Sitzt ihr schon im Bus? Ja, wir sitzen schon ______.
2. Spielst du mit der Puppe? Ja, ich spiele ______.
3. Stellt ihr euch neben die Bank? Ja, wir stellen uns ______.
4. Bist die schon bei der Arbeit? Ja, ich bin schon ______.
5. Legt ihr euch unter die Bäume? Ja, wir legen uns ______.
6. Ist er hinter dem Geschäft? Ja, er ist ______.
7. Glaubst du an seine Schuld? Ja, ich glaube ______.
8. Setzt ihr euch aufs Sofa? Ja, wir setzen uns ______.
9. Unterhaltet ihr euch über den Roman? Ja, wir unterhalten uns ______.
10. Brauchst du Mehl zum Backen? Ja, wir brauchen es ______.

11. Geht ihr nach der Arbeit spazieren? Ja, wir gehen ______ spazieren.
12. Hast du ihm von unsrer Reise erzählt? Ja, ich habe ihm ______ erzählt.

When **dar-** *Is Not Used*

hinein, herein

When the preposition **in** expresses direction rather than location, it is not prefixed by **dar-** but has the following distinct forms.

Motion away from the speaker:

Gehst du schon ins Haus?	*Are you going into the house already?*
Ja, ich gehe schon *hinein.*	*Yes, I am already going in. (into it)*

Motion toward the speaker:

Kommt sie ins Wohnzimmer?	*Is she coming into the living room?*
Ja, sie kommt *herein.*	*Yes, she is coming in. (into it)*

hinaus, heraus

Similarly, the dative preposition **aus** has distinct forms.

Motion away from the speaker:

Steigt er aus dem Fenster?	*Is he climbing out of the window?*
Ja, er steigt *hinaus.*	*Yes, he is climbing out. (of it)*

Motion toward the speaker:

Kommt sie aus der Garage?	*Is she coming out of the garage?*
Ja, sie kommt *heraus.*	*Yes, she is coming out. (of it)*

9. Complete the following with **hinein, herein, hinaus** or **heraus.**

1. Kommt sie ins Zimmer? Ja, sie kommt ______.
2. Geht sie aus der Küche? Ja, sie geht ______.
3. Läufst du ins Esszimmer? Ja, ich laufe ______.
4. Kommt er ins Haus? Ja, er kommt ______.
5. Kommen sie aus dem Museum? Ja, sie kommen ______.
6. Kommt sie ins Hotel? Ja, sie kommt ______.
7. Geht sie in die Kirche? Ja, sie geht ______.
8. Gehen sie aus dem Haus? Ja, sie gehen ______ .
9. Wandern sie in den Wald? Ja, sie wandern ______ .
10. Läuft sie aus der Fabrik? Ja, sie läuft ______ .

Wo- Compounds with Accusative and Dative Prepositions

In German the question word *was* (referring to things) is usually avoided after an accusative or dative preposition. Instead, **wo-** is prefixed to the preposition. If the preposition starts with a vowel, **wor-** is used.

Womit **kann ich helfen?**	*What can I help you with?*
Wovon **soll er denn leben?**	*What is he supposed to live off?*
Worüber **sprecht ihr?**	*What are you talking about?*
Worauf **wartest du?**	*What are you waiting for?*

These **wo-** compounds are used only in questions referring to things or ideas. They cannot be used when referring to people.

Wo- can be prefixed to accusative, dative and accusative/dative prepositions, with the exception of **entlang, ohne, ausser, gegenüber, seit, hinter, neben, zwischen.**

10. Complete the questions with the appropriate **wo-** compound, to the cue provided in the answer.

1. _______ fährt er nach Köln? Mit dem Auto.
2. _______ sitzen sie? Auf dem Kissen.
3. _______ schwimmt sie? Im See.
4. _______ denkst du? An die Prüfung.
5. _______ kommt er? Aus dem Hotel.
6. _______ erzählt ihr? Von der Reise.
7. _______ handelt es sich? Um Geld.
8. _______ sprechen sie? Über Chemie.
9. _______ hat er Angst? Vor der Bombe.
10. _______ brauchst du den Bleistift? Zum Schreiben.
11. _______ liegt er? Auf dem Bett.
12. _______ ist er? Bei der Arbeit.
13. _______ ist sie? Gegen die Reise.
14. _______ schreibt er? Mit dem Kugelschreiber.
15. _______ interessierst du dich? Für Musik.

PREPOSITIONS GOVERNING THE GENITIVE CASE

The following prepositions are always followed by the genitive case:

(an)statt—*instead of*

***(An)statt* seiner Schwester ist seine Tante gekommen.** — *His aunt came* instead of *his sister.*

ausserhalb—*outside of*

Die Kinder spielen *ausserhalb* des Gartens. — *The children are playing* outside of *the garden.*

innerhalb—*inside of, within*

***Innerhalb* dieser Mauern stehen die Ruinen.** — Inside of *these walls are the ruins.*

Er beendet sein Studium *innerhalb* eines Jahres. — *He is finishing his studies* within *a year.*

oberhalb—*on the upper side of, above*

Wir wohnen *oberhalb* jenes Dorfes. — *We live* on the upper side of *that village.*

unterhalb—*on the lower side, below*

***Unterhalb* unsres Hauses ist ein See.** — Below *our house there is a lake.*

diesseits—*on this side of*

Die Stadt ist *diesseits* der Berge. — *The city is* on this side of *the mountains.*

jenseits—*on the other side of*

Der Park ist *jenseits* dieses Sees. — *The park is* on the other side of *this lake.*

trotz—*in spite of, despite*

Er kam *trotz* seiner Krankheit zur Schule. *He came to school* in spite of *his illness.*

während—*during*

***Während* unsrer Ferien fahren wir nach Spanien.** *We are going to Spain* during *our vacation.*

wegen—*because of*

Wir konnten *wegen* ihrer Verspätung nicht gleich abfahren. *We could not depart immediately* because of *her delay.*

um . . . willen—*for the sake of*

***Um* seiner Mutter *willen* hat er abgesagt.** *He cancelled* for the sake of *his mother.*

11. Complete the following with the appropriate endings.

1. Wir wohnen ausserhalb d____ Stadt.
2. Er ist während d____ Nacht angekommen.
3. Innerhalb ein____ Monats ist er wieder gesund.
4. Trotz d____ Kälte kommt er mit.
5. Liegt das Haus innerhalb dies____ Dorfes?
6. Ich bleibe diesseits d____ Grenze.
7. Ich habe es um mein____ Brüder willen getan.
8. Was liegt jenseits dies____ Berge?
9. Statt ein____ Autos hat er ein Pferd gekauft.
10. Er blieb wegen jen____ Warnung zu Hause.
11. Das Haus steht oberhalb d____ Kirche.
12. Während d____ Sommers gehen wir oft baden.
13. Unterhalb d____ Waldes liegt eine Wiese.
14. Wegen mein____ Erkältung darf ich nicht ausgehen.
15. Statt ein____ Zeitung habe ich diese Zeitschrift gekauft.
16. Während d____ Ferien bin ich in Kanada.
17. Wir sind diesseits d____ Berges.
18. Ich arbeite trotz d____ Hitze im Garten.
19. Der See ist ausserhalb d____ Parks.
20. Er kommt wegen sein____ Krankheit nicht.

REVIEW

12. Complete the following with the appropriate ending, preposition or contraction when necessary.

1. Warum schaust du hinter d____ Tür?
2. Wir fahren _____ Herbst _____ Deutschland.
3. Ich fahre zu mein____ Eltern.
4. Innerhalb ein____ Stunde hatte er kein Kopfweh mehr.
5. Die Tasse steht in jen____ Küchenschrank.
6. Er hatte wegen d____ Glatteises den Unfall.
7. Sie lief in ihr____ Schlafzimmer.
8. Der Bus fährt unter d____ Brücke.

9. Das Auto fährt um d____ Stadt.
10. Sitzt du gern in d____ Sonne?
11. Wir fahren d____ Nordsee entlang.
12. Nach d____ Essen gehen wir spazieren.
13. Während d____ Krieges waren viele Leute arm.
14. Liegt das Buch schon auf mein____ Schreibtisch?
15. Er wohnt bei sein____ Schulfreund.
16. Hast du soviel für jed____ Bild bezahlt?
17. Sie soll a____ Mittwoch ankommen.
18. Wohnt ihr auch in dies____ Strasse?
19. Ich hänge das Bild an d____ Wand.
20. Wir unterhalten uns mit d____ Zimmermädchen.
21. Hat er etwas für sein____ Kinder gekauft?
22. Warum bist du gegen unsr____ Freunde?
23. Er wollte trotz sein____ Alters bergsteigen.
24. Sie tanzten um d____ Goldene Lamm.
25. Sie sind ohne ihr____ Sohn ______ Bonn geflogen.

13. Complete the following with the appropriate **wo-** compound.

1. ______ liegt das Geld? In der Schachtel.
2. ______ brauchst du es? Zum Lesen.
3. ______ fährt er weg? Mit dem Zug.
4. ______ bist du? Gegen den Plan.
5. ______ unterhaltet ihr euch? Über seine Erfindungen.
6. ______ wartest du? Auf den Bus.
7. ______ fiel das Kind? Vom Pferd.
8. ______ hast du Angst? Vor dem Hund.

14. Complete the following with the appropriate **da-** compound when necessary.

1. Liegt die Wäsche im Korb? Ja, sie liegt ______.
2. Ist das Ei neben dem Teller? Ja, es ist ______.
3. Steht ihr vor der Kamera? Ja, wir stehen ______.
4. Setzt du dich aufs Sofa? Ja, ich setze mich ______.
5. Gehst du ins Gebäude? Ja, ich gehe ______.

Chapter 3

Adjectives and Adverbs

DEMONSTRATIVE ADJECTIVES

In German the definite article **der, die, das** can also function as a demonstrative adjective, corresponding to the English *this* (plural, *these*) and *that* (plural, *those*). The demonstrative adjective, like the definite article, agrees with the noun it modifies in gender, number and case. The demonstrative adjective, therefore, has the same endings as the definite article. When used as demonstrative adjectives, the various forms of **der, die, das** are stressed.

When **hier** is used with the demonstrative adjective, it corresponds to the English *this* (*these*). When **da** or **dort** is used, it corresponds to *that* (*those*). The words **hier, da** and **dort** follow the noun that is modified by the demonstrative adjective.

Die **Jacke hier ist teuer.**	*This jacket is expensive.*
Sie kam aus *dem* **Haus dort.**	*She came out of that house.*
Helfen Sie *dem* **Jungen da!**	*Help that boy!*

1. Complete with the appropriate demonstrative adjective.

1. Ich kaufe ______ Auto hier.
2. Wieviel kostet ______ Teppich da?
3. Sie wohnten in ______ Strasse dort.
4. Warum kaufst du nicht ______ Mantel hier?
5. Er will aus ______ Glas da trinken.
6. ______ Schuhe hier sind bequem.
7. Wie findest du ______ Wein hier?
8. Er ist gegen ______ Baum dort gefahren.
9. Ich wohne bei ______ Leuten da.
10. Kennt ihr ______ Studentin dort?

Another demonstrative adjective is **dieser.** Like **der, die, das,** it agrees with the noun it modifies. Any form of **dieser** can be made to correspond to the English *this* by adding **hier. Da** and **dort** make it correspond to *that.* **Dieser** has the same endings as the definite article.

Diese **Häuser da sind sehr alt.**	*Those houses are very old.*

Willst du *diesen* Pullover hier? *Do you want this sweater?*
Ich fahre mit *diesem* Bus dort. *I am taking that bus.*

2. Form sentences from the following. Supply the appropriate form of the demonstrative adjective **dieser.**

    1. Mantel / dort / gehören / mir /
    2. Wir / holen / etwas / für / Mädchen / hier /
    3. Ich / helfen / Mann / da /
    4. Es / liegen / unter / Bücher / da /
    5. Mit / Wagen / hier / fahren / wir / nicht /
    6. Ursula / haben / Kamera / da /
    7. Ich / schlafen / nicht / in / Bett / da /
    8. Kennen / du / Mann / dort / ? /
    9. Frauen / hier / kaufen / nichts /
    10. Er / kaufen / Blumen / hier /

DESCRIPTIVE ADJECTIVES

Descriptive adjectives are words that denote the qualities of people and things, e.g. *thin, green, good.* In German, as well as in English, descriptive adjectives can be used in the following way:

Predicate Nominative

When the adjective follows the noun and is preceded by a form of **sein, werden, bleiben** it is used as a predicate adjective.

Der Kaffee war *bitter.* *The coffee was bitter.*
Sein Haar wird schon *grau.* *His hair is already getting grey.*

The predicate adjective never receives an ending.

The following are some common German adjectives:

alt	*old*	**gross**	*big, tall*
amerikanisch	*American*	**gut**	*good*
arm	*poor*	**hässlich**	*ugly*
bequem	*comfortable*	**heiss**	*hot*
bitter	*bitter*	**hübsch**	*pretty*
billig	*inexpensive*	**intelligent**	*intelligent*
blond	*blond*	**interessant**	*interesting*
böse	*bad*	**jung**	*young*
deutsch	*German*	**kalt**	*cold*
dick	*heavy, thick*	**klein**	*small, short*
dünn	*skinny, thin*	**klug**	*clever, smart*
dunkel	*dark*	**krank**	*ill*
eng	*narrow*	**kurz**	*short*
faul	*lazy*	**lang**	*long*
fleissig	*industrious*	**langsam**	*slow*
fremd	*strange*	**leer**	*empty*
frisch	*fresh*	**leicht**	*easy*
gesund	*healthy*	**nah**	*near*
glücklich	*happy*	**nett**	*nice*

neu	*new*	**schnell**	*fast*
reich	*rich*	**schwach**	*weak*
sauer	*sour*	**süss**	*sweet*
sauber	*clean*	**teuer**	*expensive*
scharf	*sharp, pungent*	**voll**	*full*
schmutzig	*dirty*	**weit**	*far*

3. Complete the following sentences with the opposite predicate adjective.

1. Das Wetter ist nicht ______, sondern kalt.
2. Der Tee ist nicht ______, sondern bitter.
3. Der Schüler ist nicht ______, sondern fleissig.
4. Die Strasse ist nicht ______, sondern kurz.
5. Meine Tochter ist nicht ______, sondern gesund.
6. Sein Bruder ist nicht ______, sondern arm.
7. Ihre Hände sind nicht ______, sondern sauber.
8. Diese Aufgabe ist nicht ______, sondern schwer.
9. Sein Mädchen ist nicht ______, sondern hübsch.
10. Dieser Mantel war nicht ______, sondern teuer.
11. Sie ist nicht ______, sondern dünn.
12. Er ist nicht ______, sondern schnell.
13. Es ist nicht ______, sondern gut.
14. Es ist nicht ______, sondern neu.
15. Sie ist nicht ______, sondern gross.

Attributive Adjective–Preceded by *"der"* Words or Definite Articles

When the adjective precedes the noun, it is used as an attributive adjective. An attributive adjective in German always takes an ending. The adjective ending is determined by the number (singular or plural), gender (masculine, feminine, neuter) and the case of the noun it modifies. Another factor that determines the ending of the adjective is the presence or absence of a **der** or **ein** word.

The following words have the same endings as the definite article; therefore, they are referred to as **"der"** words.

dieser	*this*
jeder	*each, every* (used only in the singular)
jener	*that*
mancher	*many (a)*
solcher	*such* (usually occurs only in the plural)
welcher	*which*
alle	*all* (used only in the plural)

Adjectives preceded by the definite article or **"der"** words require a special set of endings.

Nominative Case, Singular

When the attributive adjective modifies a noun that is in the nominative case singular, and when the adjective is preceded by the definite article or a **"der"** word, it receives the following endings:

Masculine	*Feminine*	*Neuter*
der billig*e* Koffer	**die alt*e* Tasche**	**das hübsch*e* Mädchen**

Der alte **Tisch ist kaputt.**	*The old table is broken.*
Die nette **Frau hilft uns.**	*The nice woman is helping us.*
Das kleine **Kind schreit.**	*The small child is screaming.*
Dieser deutsche **Wagen ist schnell.**	*This German car is fast.*
Jene grosse **Maschine ist teuer.**	*That large machine is expensive.*
Welches leere **Glas gehört dir?**	*Which empty glass belongs to you?*

If the noun is modified by two or more adjectives in succession, they all have the same endings.

Wo ist die *kleine, schwarze* Katze? *Where is the small, black cat?*

4. Complete with the appropriate endings.

1. Dies____ breit____ Fluss ist die Donau.
2. Wo ist d____ neu____, blau____ Kleid?
3. Welch____ deutsch____ Lied ist das?
4. Wann ist d____ hübsch____ Studentin wieder zu Hause?
5. Wieviel kostet dies____ warm____ Mantel?
6. Welch____ bekannt____, amerikanisch____ Dichter hat den Roman geschrieben?
7. Manch____ fremd____ Student hat Heimweh.
8. Dies____ alt____ Schlüssel ist rostig.

5. Complete with the appropriate forms of the indicated words.

1. ______ ______ Stadt ist das? *welche, deutsch*
2. ______ ______ Kind weint. *jenes, klein*
3. ______ ______ Gymnasium ist modern. *jedes, neu*
4. Wo ist ______ ______ Lehrerin? *die, jung*
5. Wieviel kostet ______ ______ Wagen? *dieser, amerikanisch*
6. Wie heisst ______ ______ Student? *jener, blond*
7. Wo ist ______ ______ ______ Buch? *das, dünn, rot*
8. Was macht ______ ______ Mensch? *jeder, gesund*
9. Dort steht ______ ______ Glas. *das, leer*
10. Wieviel kostet ______ ______ Lampe? *jene, gross*
11. Wann kommt ______ ______ Professor? *der, interessant*
12. ______ ______ Limonade schmeckt gut. *diese, kalt*

6. Form sentences from the following.

1. Jen____ / französich / Dichter / ist / weltbekannt/
2. Der / rot / Bus / wartet /
3. Manch / deutsch / Drama / ist / lang /
4. Wieviel / kostet / jen____ / schnell / Auto / ? /
5. Jed____ / modern / Museum / braucht / Geld /
6. Welch / alt / Maschine / ist / kaputt / ? /
7. Wo / ist / die / weiss / Katze / ? /
8. Wo / steht / die / frisch / Milch / ? /

Accusative Case, Singular

When the attributive adjective modifies a noun in the accusative singular and when the adjective is preceded by the definite article or by a **"der"** word, it receives the following endings:

Masculine	*Feminine*	*Neuter*
den klein*en* Schlüssel	**die reich*e* Sängerin**	**das voll*e* Glas**

Ich kenne *den deutschen* Studenten. *I know the German student.*
Sie läuft in *die alte* Fabrik. *She is running into the old factory.*
Er kauft *das schnelle* Auto. *He is buying the fast car.*
Brauchst du *diesen langen* Stock? *Do you need this long stick.*
***Welche billige* Uhr hat er?** *Which cheap watch does he have?*
Wir nehmen *jenes dünne* Papier. *We are taking that thin paper.*

Note, the accusative singular adjective endings are identical to the nominative singular, except for the masculine.

7. Complete with the correct endings.

1. Setzt euch auf dies____ bequem____ Sofa!
2. Er bleibt d____ ganz____ Woche in Bonn.
3. Wir sammeln für jen____ krank____ Jungen.
4. Er hat manch____ interessant____ Gedicht geschrieben.
5. Hast du d____ weiss____ Kater gesehen?
6. Wer hat dir jen____ wunderbar____, blau____ Orchidee gekauft?
7. Welch____ neu____ Handschuh hast du verloren?
8. Er kämpft gegen d____ bekannt____ Weltmeister.

8. Complete with the appropriate forms of the indicated words.

1. Wir gehen ______ ______ Strasse entlang. *die, lang*
2. Ich besuche ______ ______ Gymnasium. *jenes, modern*
3. Wir laufen um ______ ______ Park. *dieser, gross*
4. ______ ______ Roman liest du? *welcher, interessant*
5. Ich brauche ______ ______ Messer. *das, scharf*
6. Leg es auf ______ ______ Platte! *die, klein*
7. Kennst du ______ ______ ______ Mädchen? *jenes, fremd, jung*
8. Ich kaufe es für ______ ______ Kind. *jedes, krank*
9. Wir nehmen ______ ______ Wagen. *der, schmutzig*
10. Setz dich neben ______ ______ Ofen! *jener, heiss*
11. Sie stellte sich hinter ______ ______ ______ Mann. *der, gross, blond*
12. Er kennt ______ ______ Helden. *jener, klug*

9. Form sentences from the following.

1. Er / restaurierte / manch / historisch / Haus /
2. Wer / hat / der / alt / Lederkoffer / ? /
3. Bring / dies / schmutzig / Glas / in / die / Küche / ! /
4. Wir / kaufen / jen____ / schnell / Motorboot /
5. Welch / rot / Apfel / möchtest / du / ? /
6. Wir / wandern / durch / die / klein / Stadt /
7. Sie / bringt / Blumen / für / das / nett / Kindermädchen /
8. Ich / brauche / jed / neu / deutsch / Briefmarke /

Dative Case, Singular

When the attributive adjective modifies a noun that is in the dative singular and when the adjective is preceded by a definite article or by a **"der"** word, it receives the following endings:

Masculine	*Feminine*	*Neuter*
dem alt*en* Herrn	**der krank*en* Mutter**	**dem neu*en* Haus**

Wir helfen *diesem kranken* Herrn. *We are helping this ill gentleman.*
Er wohnt bei *jener netten* Familie. *He is staying with that nice family.*
***Welchem kleinen* Kind gibst du das Spielzeug?** *Which small child are you giving the toy?*

10. Complete with the correct endings.

1. Ich habe mich mit d____ scharf____ Messer geschnitten.
2. Er kam aus jen____ eng____ Strasse.
3. Sie hat uns von dies____ hoh____ Baum erzählt.
4. Er dankt d____ klein____, freundlich____ Mädchen.
5. Ich gebe jed____ klug____ Studentin ein Buch.
6. Warum sitzt du in d____ kalt____ Zimmer?
7. Ich helfe dies____ krank____ Frau.
8. Wir wohnen d____ gross____ Park gegenüber.

11. Complete with the appropriate form of the indicated words.

1. Sie kam aus ______ ______ Hotel. *jenes, international*
2. Wir gehen zu ______ ______ Vorlesung. *jede, interessant*
3. Wohnst du bei ______ ______ Familie? *diese, nett*
4. Sie sitzt auf ______ ______ Boden. *der, schmutzig*
5. Schreib nicht mit ______ ______ Bleistift! *jener, kurz*
6. Sie sitzen in ______ ______ ______ Wagen. *der, gross, amerikanisch*
7. Aus ______ ______ Land kommt er? *welches, fremd*
8. Er spricht mit ______ ______ Studentin. *die, hübsch*
9. Sie erzählt von ______ ______ Mann. *jener, reich*
10. Der Ballon gefällt ______ ______ Kind. *das, klein*
11. Ich gebe ______ ______ Patientin eine Pille. *jede, krank*
12. Sie sitzt auf ______ ______ Teppich. *der, hässlich*

12. Form sentences from the following.

1. Wir / schlafen / in / der / modern / Schlafwagen /
2. Mit / welch / neu / Schreibmaschine / soll / ich / schreiben / ? /
3. Er / wohnt / bei / jen____ / nett / Dame /
4. Der / Ball / liegt / unter / der / blau / Sessel /
5. Trink / nicht / aus / jen____ / rot / Glass / ! /
6. Wir / gehen / bei / dies / kalt / Wetter / nicht / aus /
7. Wer / sitzt / auf / die / alt / rostig / Bank / ? /
8. Wir / bekamen / von / manch / amerikanisch / Studenten / Post /

Genitive Case, Singular

When the attributive adjective modifies a noun that is in the genitive singular and when the adjective is preceded by a definite article or by a **"der"** word, it receives the following endings:

Masculine	*Feminine*	*Neuter*
des jung*en* Lehrers	**der dick*en* Katze**	**des bös*en* Kindes**

Er wohnt jenseits ***dieses hohen*** **Berges.**	*He lives on the other side of this high mountain.*
Wir wohnen ausserhalb ***jener grossen*** **Stadt.**	*We live outside of that large city.*
Dort ist die Mutter ***des kleinen*** **Kindes.**	*There is the mother of the small child.*

13. Complete with the appropriate endings.

1. Wo ist die Tochter dies____ arm____ Mannes?
2. Dort steht das Haus d____ reich____ Familie.
3. Ich kenne die Melodie jen____ deutsch____ Liedes.
4. Die Zimmer dies____ neu____ Hauses sind gross.
5. Wir waren während jen____ kalt____ Nacht zu Hause.
6. Jenseits dies____ klein____ Dorfes ist die Grenze.
7. Sie kommen um d____ interessant____ Professors willen.
8. Wir sind innerhalb jen____ alt____ Stadt.

14. Complete the following with the appropriate form of the indicated words.

1. Der Preis ______ ______ Mantels ist zu hoch. *der, blau*
2. Sie sind innerhalb ______ ______ Gartens. *jener, exotisch*
3. Die Frau ______ ______ Technikers ist hier. *der, deutsch*
4. Die Farbe ______ ______ Kleides ist hässlich. *dieses, billig*
5. Er kommt um ______ ______ Frau willen. *die, krank*
6. Die Kissen ______ ______ Sofas sind weich. *dieses, bequem*
7. Die Studenten ______ ______ Universität sind hier. *jene, bekannt*
8. Die Strassen ______ ______ Stadt sind eng. *diese, klein*
9. Der Mann ______ ______ Sängerin ist dort. *die, dick*
10. Das ist die Mutter ______ ______ Babys. *das, gesund*
11. Sie wohnt diesseits ______ ______ Sees. *jener, gross*
12. Dort ist der Besitzer ______ ______ Sammlung. *jene, interessant*

15. Form sentences from the following.

1. Wo / ist / der / Besitzer / dies / schmutzig / Mantel / ? /
2. Die / Gedichte / manch / deutsch / Dichter / sind / kompliziert /
3. Die / Mutter / jen____ / krank / Kind / ist / hier /
4. Der / Park / ist / jenseits / das / gross / Monument /
5. Trotz / dies / lang / Explosion / gab / es / kein / Verwundete /
6. Die / Strassen / jen____ / alt / Stadt / sind / eng /
7. Die / Zimmer / die / neu / Wohnung / sind / modern /

Plural, All Cases, All Genders

When the attributive adjective modifies a plural noun and is preceded by the plural forms of the definite article or of a **"der"** word, the adjective ending is **-en** for all cases. The plural form of **jeder** is **alle.** The plural form of **manche** is not followed by adjectives ending in **-en.** (See section "Attributive Adjectives–Not Preceded by **"der"** or **"ein"** Words," the discussion of plurals.)

Nominative	**die deutsch*en* Zeitungen**
Accusative	**die alt*en* Männer**
Dative	**den gesund*en* Kindern**
Genitive	**der hoh*en* Berge**

Diese frischen **Eier kosten viel.**	*These fresh eggs are expensive.*
Ich habe *alle leeren* **Flaschen.**	*I have all empty bottles.*
Mit *solchen neuen Autos* **kann man schnell fahren.**	*One can drive fast with such new cars.*
Das Leben *jener alten Leute* **ist traurig.**	*The life of those old people is sad.*

16. Rewrite the following, changing the nouns to the plural. Make all necessary changes.

1. Welche deutsche Stadt hat er besucht?
2. Ohne dieses warme Kleid fahre ich nicht.
3. Wir steigen auf jenen bekannten Berg.
4. Es gehört jener interessanten, jungen Frau.
5. Er schenkt etwas in jedes leere Glas.
6. Ich liege unter dem schattigen Baum.
7. Er erzählt dem kleinen Mädchen eine Geschichte.
8. Ich komme um des kranken Lehrers willen.
9. Jeder gesunde Patient darf nach Hause.
10. Sie hat den grünen Apfel.

Special Adjective Forms

A few adjectives omit certain letters when they receive an attributive adjective ending. Study the following changes. Adjectives ending in **-el** always drop the **e** in the final syllable when an ending is added.

Das Zimmer ist *dunkel.*	*The room is dark.*
Wir sind in dem *dunklen* **Zimmer.**	*We are in the dark room.*

Adjectives ending in **-er** can drop or retain the **-e** when the attributive adjective ending is added.

Das Haus ist *teuer.*	*The house is expensive.*
Ich ziehe in jenes *teure (teuere)* **Haus.**	*I am moving into that expensive house.*
Die Orange ist *sauer.*	*The orange is sour.*
Wer kauft diese *sauren (saueren)* **Orangen?**	*Who is buying these sour oranges?*
Der Kaffee ist *bitter.*	*The coffee is bitter.*
Warum trinkst du den *bittren (bitteren)* **Kaffee?**	*Why are you drinking the bitter coffee?*

The adjective **hoch** drops the **c** when an attributive adjective ending is added.

Der Turm ist *hoch.*	*The tower is high.*
Er steigt auf jenen *hohen* **Turm.**	*He is climbing that high tower.*

17. Complete the following with the appropriate form of the indicated words.

1. Was machst du in ______ ______ Haus? *das, dunkel*
2. Sie nehmen ______ ______ Pille. *die, bitter*
3. Er kauft ______ ______ Mantel. *jener, teuer*
4. Wir wohnen jenseits ______ ______ Berges. *dieser, hoch*
5. Wo ist ______ ______ Wäsche? *die, sauber*
6. Trink nicht ______ ______ Milch! *die, sauer*
7. Wo ist ______ ______ Zimmer? *das, sauber*
8. Warum kaufst du ______ ______ Spielzeug? *dieses, teuer*

9. Wo sind ______ ______ Äpfel? *der, sauer*
10. Wie heisst ______ ______ Berg? *dieser, hoch*

REVIEW

There are only two different sets of endings for adjectives following the definite articles or a **"der"** word, namely **-e** or **-en.** The **-en** ending predominates, except for the three nominative singular forms and the accusative singular, feminine and neuter.

	SINGULAR			*PLURAL*
	Masculine	*Feminine*	*Neuter*	*All Genders*
Nominative	**e**	**e**	**e**	**en**
Accusative	**en**	**e**	**e**	**en**
Dative	**en**	**en**	**en**	**en**
Genitive	**en**	**en**	**en**	**en**

18. Complete with the correct endings.

1. Hast du d____ deutsch____ Zeitungen auf jen____ rund____ Tisch gelegt?
2. Dies____ gelb____ Mantel habe ich in d____ neu____ Geschäft gekauft.
3. In d____ eng____ Strassen dies____ alt____ Stadt gibt es viel Verkehr.
4. Wer ist d____ dick____ Dame neben d____ schlank____ Herrn?
5. Wegen dies____ schlecht____ Wetters bleibe ich zu Hause.
6. D____ amerikanisch____ Studentin kam aus jen____ modern____, weiss____ Haus.
7. All____ dunkl____ Strassen werden i____ nächst____ Monat beleuchtet.
8. Mit solch____ schmutzig____ Händen kannst du d____ neu____ Buch nicht anfassen.
9. D____ freundlich____ Kellnerin hat gleich jed____ leer____ Glas mit Bier gefüllt.
10. Hat jen____ deutsch____ Dichter auch dies____ traurig____ Gedicht geschrieben?

19. Complete with the appropriate form of the indicated words.

1. ______ ______ Fräulein wohnt bei ______ ______ Familie. *dieses, deutsch; jene, nett*
2. ______ ______ Männer kaufen ______ ______ Mäntel. *alle, elegant; dies____, kurz*
3. ______ ______ Student braucht ______ ______ Buch. *jener, blond; dieses, teuer*
4. ______ ______ Frau hilft ______ ______ Herrn. *die, hübsch; der, dick*
5. ______ ______ Besitzer ______ ______ Wagens ist hier. *der, neu; der, teuer*
6. Wir waschen ______ ______ Hände ______ ______ Kindes. *die, schmutzig; das, klein*
7. ______ ______ Tourist kauft ______ ______ Kamera. *jener, amerikanisch; diese, billig*
8. ______ ______ Hund liegt unter ______ ______ Tisch. *der, schwarz; der, rund*
9. ______ ______ Leute essen auf ______ ______ Terrasse. *die, jung; die, dunkel*
10. ______ ______ Dame kauft ______ ______ Kuchen. *die, hungrig; der, gross*

Attributive Adjective–Preceded by the Indefinite Article and "ein" Words

The negative article **kein** and all the possessives are called **"ein"** words, because they receive the same endings as the indefinite article (see section "Possessive Adjectives" and Chapter 1).

Adjectives preceded by the indefinite article or an **"ein"** word require a special set of endings.

Nominative Case, Singular

When the attributive adjective modifies a noun that is nominative singular, and when the adjective is preceded by the indefinite article or an **"ein"** word, it receives the following endings:

Masculine	*Feminine*	*Neuter*
ein blau*er* Hut	**eine lang*e* Reise**	**ein bequem*es* Sofa**

Ein alter **Herr wartet.** — *An old gentleman is waiting.*
Das ist *eine billige* **Tasche.** — *That is a cheap purse.*
Ein kleines **Kind kommt.** — *A small child is coming.*
Wo ist *dein neuer* **Freund?** — *Where is your new friend?*
Dort ist *seine hübsche* **Freundin.** — *There is his pretty girl friend.*
Hier ist *unser altes* **Radio.** — *Here is our old radio.*

20. Complete with the appropriate endings when necessary. Make all necessary changes.

1. Wo ist mein____ weiss____ Hase?
2. Ihr____ alt____, amerikanisch____ Freundin kommt.
3. Dein____ hell____ Bluse ist doch schmutzig.
4. Er ist kein____ gut____ Freund.
5. Wann besucht euch eur____ reich____ Tante?
6. Der Löwe ist ein____ wild____ Tier.
7. Nur ein____ rot____ Apfel liegt im Korb.
8. Das ist kein____ hübsch____ Melodie.
9. Das ist ein____ schön____, weiss____ Lilie.
10. Mein____ deutsch____ Buch liegt dort.
11. Wo ist dein____ alt____ Onkel?
12. Es ist sein____ neu____ Auto.
13. Das ist unser____ teuer____ Schmuck.
14. Wo ist mein____ weich____ Kissen?
15. Das ist kein____ sauer____ Milch.
16. Dort kommt ein____ französisch____ Tourist.

21. Rewrite the following, changing the definite article to the indefinite article. Make all necessary changes.

1. Wo ist das weiche Kissen?
2. Der alte Freund ist hier.
3. Wann schläft das wilde Tier?
4. Die neue Maschine steht dort.
5. Hier ist der schmutzige Teller.
6. Wo ist das kleine Buch?
7. Hier liegt die deutsche Zeitung.
8. Wieviel kostet das schnelle Auto?

22. Form sentences from the following. Make all necessary changes.

1. Mein / alt / Radio / ist / kaputt /
2. Wo / wohnt / dein / nett / Freundin / ? /
3. Wieviel / kostet / Ihr / neu / Wagen / ? /
4. Wann / kommt / sein / reich / Onkel / ? /
5. Das / ist / kein / eng / Strasse /

6. Ist / unser / deutsch / Foto / interessant / ? /
7. Wo / ist / euer / schmutzig / Wäsche / ? /
8. Hier / ist / ihr / alt / Wein /

Accusative Case, Singular

When the attributive adjective modifies a noun that is accusative singular, and when the adjective is preceded by the indefinite article or an **"ein"** word, it receives the following endings:

Masculine	*Feminine*	*Neuter*
einen alt*en* Mann	**eine blau*e* Jacke**	**ein süss*es* Getränk**

Er schreibt *einen langen* Brief.	*He is writing a long letter.*
Wir besuchen *unsre gute* Freundin.	*We are visiting our good friend.*
Habt ihr *kein scharfes* Messer?	*Don't you have a sharp knife?*

Note that the accusative singular adjective endings are identical with the nominative singular, except for the masculine.

23. Complete with the correct endings when necessary.

1. Möchtest du kein____ heiss____ Tee?
2. Setz dich auf unser____ weich____ Sofa!
3. Wir kaufen kein____ teur____ Kamera für unsr____ klein____ Tochter.
4. Er geht durch sein____ schmutzig____ Fabrik.
5. Sucht ihr eur____ klein____, schwarz____ Hund?
6. Warum besucht sie nicht ihr____ krank____ Grossmutter?
7. Wer braucht ein____ gross____, modern____ Wagen?
8. Ich suche ein____ rot____ Auto.
9. Er hat kein____ hübsch____ Freundin.
10. Wir treffen unsr____ neu____ Lehrerin.
11. Nehmt euer____ alt____ Bild!
12. Wir gehen ohne mein____ klein____ Kind.

24. Rewrite the following, changing the definite article to the indefinite article. Make all necessary changes.

1. Er kauft den hässlichen Teppich.
2. Wann bekommst du den neuen Mantel?
3. Wir besuchen die historische Stadt.
4. Siehst du das rote Auto?
5. Ich kaufe es für das kranke Kind.
6. Er geht durch den langen Tunnel.
7. Der Bus fuhr gegen die alte Mauer.
8. Ich möchte das weisse Bonbon.

25. Form sentences from the following. Make all necessary changes.

1. Sie / geht / in / ihr / dunkel / Wohnung /
2. Wir / verkaufen / unser / blau / Sofa /
3. Haben / Sie / ein / billig / Zimmer / ? /
4. Ich / habe / ein / bequem / Stuhl /
5. Brauchst / du / dein / neu / Kamera / ? /
6. Wir / gehen / durch / ein / lang / Tunnel /
7. Ich / schreibe / ein / kurz / Brief /
8. Kennst / du / kein / hübsch / Studentin / ? /

Dative Case, Singular

When the attributive adjective modifies a noun that is in the dative singular, and when the adjective is preceded by the indefinite article or an **"ein"** word, it requires the following endings:

Masculine	*Feminine*	*Neuter*
einem scharf*en* Messer	**einer rot*en* Blume**	**einem dunkl*en* Zimmer**

Das Buch liegt auf *einem runden* Tisch.	*The book is lying on a round table.*
Er erzählt von *seiner langen* Reise.	*He is talking about his long trip.*
Wir wohnen in *keinem alten* Haus.	*We are not living in an old house.*

26. Complete with the correct endings.

1. Sie schrieb ihr____ lieb____ Mann eine Karte.
2. Warum sitzt du in dein____ klein____, kalt____ Zimmer?
3. Ausser unsr____ reich____ Tante kam niemand.
4. Wir fahren mit ein____ schnell____ Wagen.
5. Ich trinke aus ein____ neu____, weiss____ Tasse.
6. Seit sein____ traurig____ Kindheit ist er melancholisch.
7. Es gehört ihr____ alt____ Onkel.
8. Ich helfe mein____ klein____ Schwester.
9. Ich bleibe bei mein____ krank____ Mutter.
10. Sie wurde von ein____ wild____ Hund gebissen.
11. Er arbeitet bei kein____ gross____ Firma.
12. Sie geht zu ihr____ weiss____ Auto.

27. Rewrite the following, changing the definite article to the indefinite article.

1. Er sitzt auf dem harten Stuhl.
2. Sie wohnt in dem modernen Haus.
3. Ich bin bei der netten Frau.
4. Sie spielt mit dem süssen Baby.
5. Wir stehen neben dem grossen Mann.
6. Ich liege auf dem weichen Bett.
7. Hilfst du dem fremden Mann?
8. Sie kommt von der langen Reise zurück.

28. Form sentences from the following. Make all necessary changes.

1. Er / kam / mit / ein / interessant / Freund /
2. Wir / kennen / uns / seit / unser / glücklich / Kindheit /
3. Er / schnitt / das / Brot / mit / sein / scharf / Messer /
4. Warum / sitzt / du / auf / ein / unbequem / Stuhl / ? /
5. Die / Katze / liegt / auf / mein / schwarz / Mantel /
6. Sie / kommt / aus / ihr / dunkel / Zimmer /
7. Was / steht / in / sein / lang / Brief / ? /
8. Sie / sitzt / in / mein / neu / Auto /

Genitive Case, Singular

When the attributive adjective modifies a noun that is in the genitive singular, and when the adjective is preceded by the indefinite article or an **"ein"** word, it requires the following endings:

Masculine	*Feminine*	*Neuter*
eines nett*en* Mannes	**einer alt*en* Dame**	**eines bittr*en* Getränks**

Er liegt im Schatten ***eines hohen*** **Baumes.**	*He is lying in the shade of a tall tree.*
Hier ist das Zentrum ***unsrer kleinen*** **Stadt.**	*Here is the center of our small town.*
Wann beginnt der Bau ***eures neuen*** **Hauses?**	*When does the construction of your new house start?*

29. Complete the following with the appropriate form of the indicated words.

1. Er ist während _______ _______ Nacht verunglückt. *ein, dunkel*
2. Die Farbe _______ _______ Autos ist hässlich. *mein, alt*
3. Wegen _______ _______ Krankheit kann er nicht kommen. *sein, schlimm*
4. Sie ist die Tochter _______ _______ Arztes. *ein, amerikanisch*
5. Trotz _______ _______ Arbeit macht sie Urlaub. *ihr, wichtig*
6. Sie tat es um _______ _______ Jungen willen. *euer, krank*
7. Wie hoch war der Preis _______ _______ Waschmaschine? *dein, neu*
8. Statt _______ _______ Radios kaufte ich eine Kamera. *ein, teuer*

30. Rewrite the following, changing the genitive definite article to the indefinite article.

1. Das ist die Frau des bekannten Dichters.
2. Es ist die Geschichte des fremden Volkes.
3. Der Preis des antiken Perserteppichs ist hoch.
4. Ich singe die Melodie des deutschen Liedes.
5. Der Direktor der grossen Fabrik kommt.

31. Form sentences from the following. Make all necessary changes.

1. Trotz / mein / lang / Reise / war / ich / nicht / müde /
2. Die / Farbe / dein / neu / Pullover / ist / hübsch /
3. Sie / ist / die / Frau / ein / amerikanisch / Präsident /
4. Hier / ist / das / Foto / sein / bekannt / Bruder /
5. Wo / ist / das / Haus / Ihr / reich / Onkel / ? /
6. Wir / konnten / wegen / sein / lang / Verspätung / nicht / essen /
7. Der / Bus / ist / jenseits / ein / hoch / Turm /

Plural, All Cases, All Genders

When the attributive adjective modifies a plural noun, and when it is preceded by the plural forms of **"ein"** words, the adjective ending is **-en** for all cases. There is no plural form of the indefinite article **ein.**

Nominative	**keine leer*en* Gläser**
Accusative	**keine leer*en* Gläser**
Dative	**keinen leer*en* Gläsern**
Genitive	**keiner leer*en* Gläser**

Ihre deutschen **Freundinnen fliegen ab.**	*Her German friends are departing.*
Hast du ***keine amerikanischen*** **Zigaretten?**	*Don't you have American cigarettes?*
Wir trinken aus ***keinen schmutzigen*** **Tassen.**	*We don't drink out of dirty cups.*
Die Lehrerin ***unsrer kleinen*** **Kinder ist hier.**	*The teacher of our small children is here.*

32. Rewrite the following, changing the nouns to the plural. Make all necessary changes.

1. Er hat keinen teuren Ring gekauft.
2. Er glaubt seinem kleinen Sohn.
3. Ich telefonierte mit meiner deutschen Freundin.

4. Unsre neue Nähmaschine war teuer.
5. Wer hat meinen roten Bleistift?
6. Wegen seines faulen Bruders darf er nicht kommen.
7. Wir trinken kein kaltes Getränk.
8. Wo ist ihre warme Jacke?
9. Willst du deinen alten Lehrer besuchen?
10. Wo ist euer progressives Gymnasium?

REVIEW

The **-en** adjective ending predominates after the indefinite article or **"ein"** words. As was the case with adjectives following **"der"** words, the exceptions to the **-en** endings occur in the nominative singular masculine, feminine and neuter, and in the accusative singular, feminine and neuter.

Compare the two sets of endings:

After **"der"** *Words*

	SINGULAR			*PLURAL*
	Masculine	*Feminine*	*Neuter*	*All Genders*
Nominative	**e**	**e**	**e**	**en**
Accusative	**en**	**e**	**e**	**en**
Dative	**en**	**en**	**en**	**en**
Genitive	**en**	**en**	**en**	**en**

After **"ein"** *Words*

	SINGULAR			*PLURAL*
	Masculine	*Feminine*	*Neuter*	*All Genders*
Nominative	**er**	**e**	**es**	**en**
Accusative	**en**	**e**	**es**	**en**
Dative	**en**	**en**	**en**	**en**
Genitive	**en**	**en**	**en**	**en**

33. Complete the following with the correct endings when necessary.

1. Mein____ amerikanisch____ Freund hat dies____ herrlich____ Sinfonie komponiert.
2. In unsr____ neu____ Wohnung ist auch ein____ elektrisch____ Ofen.
3. D____ kaputt____ Maschine wurde mit ein____ leicht____ Metall repariert.
4. Sie war wegen ihr____ exotisch____ Schönheit bekannt, nicht wegen ihr____ gross____ Talents.
5. In d____ eng____ Strassen d____ historisch____ Innenstadt können kein____ gross____ Wagen fahren.
6. Ein____ melancholisch____ Melodie kam aus d____ offen____ Fenster.
7. Er brachte mir ein____ rot____ Rose in jen____ klein____ Glasvase.
8. D____ nagelneu____ Auto fuhr gegen unsr____ rostig____ Gartentür.
9. Er hat kein____ einzig____ Geschenk von sein____ bekannt____ Geschwistern bekommen.
10. Mit dies____ schmutzig____ Schuhen könnt ihr nicht in d____ saubr____ Küche kommen.

11. Machen dein____ reich____ Eltern schon wieder ein____ lang____ Reise?
12. In jen____ rund____ Korb sind d____ frisch____ Eier.

34. Complete the following with the appropriate form of the indicated word.

1. Er gibt ______ ______ Studentin ______ ______ Job. *die, jung; ein, interessant*
2. ______ ______ Onkel liegt auf ______ ______ Sofa. *mein, krank; unser, gut*
3. Sie fährt mit ______ ______ Volkswagen durch ______ ______ Stadt. *ihr, klein; die, leer*
4. Wo hat ______ ______ Tante ______ ______ Bild gekauft? *dein, reich; dieses, teuer*
5. Wegen ______ ______ Vorlesung konnte ich ______ ______ Freunde nicht treffen. *jene, lang; ihr, neu*
6. Wo ist ______ ______ Foto ______ ______ Sängers? *das, neu; der, bekannt*
7. ______ ______ Gäste trinken ______ ______ Kaffee. *mein, amerikanisch; kein, bitter*
8. Er fährt ______ ______ Auto in ______ ______ Garage. *sein, kaputt; die, dunkel*
9. Sie macht mit ______ ______ Geschwistern ______ ______ Reise. *ihr, nett; eine, kurz*
10. ______ ______ Leute sitzen in ______ ______ Wohnung. *die, arm; ihr, kalt*

Attributive Adjective—Not Preceded by *"der"* or *"ein"* Words

When the attributive adjective is not preceded by a **"der"** or **"ein"** word, the adjective requires an ending to indicate the number, gender and case of the noun it modifies. The adjective endings coincide with the endings of the definite article except in the genitive singular, masculine and neuter.

One of the following words may precede such adjectives. They themselves do not add any endings in the singular, nor do they require endings on the attributive adjectives.

manch	*many a*	**viel**	*much*
solch	*such (a)*	**wenig**	*little*
welch	*what*		

Sie hat *viel* Talent. — *She has much talent.*
***Solch* schönes Wetter!** — *Such nice weather!*

35. Complete with the appropriate German word.

1. ______ schönes Wetter! *what*
2. Er hat ______ Geld. *much*
3. Wir haben ______ Wein. *little*
4. ______ kleines Kind hat Angst. *many a*
5. Das ist ______ gute Wurst. *such*
6. Ich habe ______ grossen Hunger. *such*
7. Dort liegt ______ Gold. *much*
8. Er braucht ______ Essen. *little*

Nominative Case, Singular

When the attributive adjective modifies a nominative singular noun, and when it is not preceded by a **"der"** or **"ein"** word, it receives the following endings:

Masculine	*Feminine*	*Neuter*
schwarz*er* Kaffee	**frisch*e* Milch**	**schön*es* Wetter**

***Alter* Wein ist teuer.**	*Old wine is expensive.*
***Frische* Luft ist gesund.**	*Fresh air is healthful.*
Das ist *deutsches* Geld.	*That is German money.*
***Welch guter* Kaffee!**	*What good coffee!*
Hier ist *viel moderne* Kunst.	*Here is much modern art.*
***Manch armes* Land braucht Hilfe.**	*Many a poor country needs help.*

The nominative adjective endings are frequently used in forms of address.

***Lieber* Onkel Franz!**	*Dear uncle Franz,*
***Liebe* Tante!**	*Dear aunt,*
Du *armes* Kind!	*You poor child!*

36. Complete the following with the appropriate form of the indicated words.

1. ______ ______ Hitze! *welch, gross*
2. Das ist ______ ______ Arznei! *solch, bitter*
3. ______ Tante Anni! *lieb*
4. Dort liegt ______ ______ Wäsche. *viel, schmutzig*
5. ______ Grossvater! *lieb*
6. Dort liegt ______ ______ Geld. *wenig, deutsch*
7. ______ ______ Wein! *welch, süss*
8. Du ______ Kind! *gut*
9. Hier ist Ursulas ______ Kleid. *neu*
10. ______ ______ Luft! *welch, kalt*
11. ______ Onkel Herbert. *lieb*
12. Du ______ Hund! *arm*
13. Das ist ______ Bier. *teuer*
14. ______ ______ Student arbeitet. *manch, fleissig*

37. Form sentences from the following. Make all necessary changes.

1. Welch / interessant / Gedicht / ! /
2. Das / ist / teuer / Leder /
3. Frisch / Butter / schmeckt / gut /
4. Modern / Musik / ist / schnell /
5. Ist / das / billig / Schmuck / ? /
6. Manch / französisch / Wein / ist / teuer /
7. Du / süss / Baby / ! /

Accusative Case, Singular

When the attributive adjective modifies a noun in the accusative singular, and when it is not preceded by a **"der"** or **"ein"** word, it receives the following endings:

Masculine	*Feminine*	*Neuter*
weiss*en* Flieder	**bittr*e* Schokolade**	**gelb*es* Papier**

Trinkt ihr *viel schwarzen* Kaffee?	*Do you drink much black coffee?*
Er bestellt *kalte* Milch.	*He orders cold milk.*

Ich brauche ***wenig deutsches*** **Geld.** *I need little German money.*
Wir trinken ***heissen*** **Tee.** *We drink hot tea.*
Hast du ***saubre*** **Wäsche?** *Do you have clean laundry?*
Er isst ***viel weisses*** **Brot.** *He eats much white bread.*

Salutations are in the accusative case.

Guten **Morgen!** ***Guten*** **Tag!** ***Guten*** **Abend!** *Good morning! Hello! Good evening!*
Gute **Nacht!** *Good night!*

38. Complete the following with the appropriate form of the indicated words.

1. Ich trinke ______ ______ Limonade. *viel, sauer*
2. Wir essen ______ ______ Brot. *wenig, schwarz*
3. ______ Abend! ______ Nacht! ______ Tag! *gut*
4. Er hat ______ Hoffnung. *gross*
5. Was hast du gegen ______ Zucker? *weiss*
6. Ich trinke ______ ______ Tee. *wenig, süss*
7. Hattet ihr ______ Wetter? *schön*
8. Sie bestellt ______ Kaffee. *schwarz*
9. Ich kaufe ______ Papier. *dünn*
10. ______ ______ Butter esse ich gerne. *solch, frisch*
11. Wo finde ich ______ ______ Käse? *solch, französisch*
12. Wir geben uns ______ Mühe. *gross*
13. Er hat ______ ______ Geld. *viel, amerikanisch*
14. Ich brauche ______ ______ Wasser. *viel, heiss*

39. Form sentences from the following. Make all necessary changes.

1. Was / hast / du / gegen / klassisch / Musik / ? /
2. Leg / es / in / kalt / Wasser / ! /
3. Ich / esse / frisch / Brot /
4. Wir / brauchen / deutsch / Geld /
5. Er / hat / solch / gross / Hunger /
6. Warum / trinkst / du / kalt / Kaffee / ? /
7. Sie / nimmt / braun / Zucker /
8. Sie / hat / viel / teuer / Schmuck /

Dative Case, Singular

When the attributive adjective modifies a dative singular noun, and when it is not preceded by a **"der"** or **"ein"** word, it receives the following endings:

Masculine	*Feminine*	*Neuter*
rostfrei*em* Stahl	**heiss*er* Milch**	**kalt*em* Wasser**

Bei ***starkem*** **Wind gehen wir nicht segeln.** *We don't go sailing in strong wind.*
Ich bin in ***grosser*** **Not.** *I am in great need.*
Nach ***langem*** **Leiden ist sie verschieden.** *She passed away after long suffering.*
Ausser ***viel heissem*** **Tee trinkt er nichts.** *He drinks nothing besides much hot tea.*
Sie stammt aus ***solch alter*** **Familie.** *She comes from such an old family.*
Sie helfen ***manch armem*** **Kind.** *They help many a poor child.*

40. Complete the following with the appropriate form of the indicated words.

1. Das Auto fährt mit ______ ______ Geschwindigkeit. *solch, gross*
2. Nach ______ Zeit kam er wieder. *lang*
3. Sie kommt aus ______ Familie. *gut*
4. Ich trinke Tee mit ______ ______ Milch. *viel, warm*
5. Er lebte auf ______ Fuss. *gross*
6. Bei ______ ______ Wetter gehen wir aus. *solch, schön*
7. Es ist aus ______ Stahl. *rostfrei*
8. Ich mache es mit ______ Freude. *gross*
9. Es ist aus ______ ______ Gold. *wenig, weiss*
10. Er wäscht sich mit ______ ______ Wasser. *viel, heiss*
11. Bei ______ ______ Kälte sind wir drinnen. *solch, bitter*
12. Der Turm ist aus ______ Metall. *hart*

41. Form sentences from the following. Make all necessary changes.

1. Bei / solch / schlecht / Wetter / fliege / ich / nicht /
2. Wer / schreibt / mit / grün / Kreide / ? /
3. Nach / kurz / Zeit / wurde / es / still /
4. Das / Messer / ist / aus / rostfrei / Stahl /
5. Warum / schwimmst / du / in / solch / tief / Wasser / ? /
6. Sie / wohnt / bei / solch / nett / Familie /
7. Ich / kenne / ihn / seit / lang / Zeit /
8. Er / trank / nichts / ausser / viel / stark / Kaffee /

Genitive Case, Singular

When the attributive adjective modifies a noun in the genitive singular, and when it is not preceded by a **"der"** or **"ein"** word, it receives the following endings:

Masculine	*Feminine*	*Neuter*
stark*en* Windes	**gut*er* Qualität**	**schlecht*en* Wetters**

Trotz *starken* Regens ging er spazieren.	*He took a walk despite heavy rain.*
Sie war wegen viel *anstrengender* Arbeit müde.	*She was tired because of much taxing work.*
***Schweren* Herzens nahm er Abschied.**	*He took leave with a heavy heart.*

42. Complete the following with the appropriate forms of the indicated words.

1. Er ist Kenner ______ ______ Kunst. *solch, alt*
2. Wegen ______ Nebels konnte er uns nicht finden. *dicht*
3. Trotz ______ Hilfe war sie einsam. *freundlich*
4. ______ Herzens reiste sie ab. *traurig*
5. Die Lagerung ______ Weines ist riskant. *alt*
6. Es ist eine Geschichte ______ Liebe. *wahr*
7. Trotz ______ Krankheit war sie lebensfroh. *lang*
8. Er hat eine Quantität ______ Materials gekauft. *neu*
9. Trotz ______ ______ Mühe kann sie es nicht. *solch, gross*
10. Innerhalb ______ Zeit kam sie heraus. *kurz*

43. Form sentences from the following. Make all necessary changes.

1. Trotz / bitter / Kälte / spielten / die / Kinder / im / Schnee /
2. Er / ist / Liebhaber / modern / Musik /
3. Der / Preis / manch / alt / Wein / ist / hoch /
4. Wegen / schlecht / Wetter / hat / er / Verspätung /
5. Trotz / solch / gut / Schulung / fand / er / keine / Position /
6. Trotz / nett / Hilfe / kam / sie / nicht / vorwärts /

REVIEW

44. Complete the following with the correct endings.

1. Wir haben nun wieder schön____, sonnig____ Wetter.
2. Bei grün____ Licht darf man fahren.
3. Ich werde dich in nächst____ Zeit besuchen.
4. Solch billig____ Wein schmeckt mir nicht.
5. Welch schön____ Farbe!
6. Lieb____ Maria! Lieb____ Johann!
7. Der Schrank ist aus teur____ Holz.
8. Welch dünn____ Papier!
9. Hast du etwas gegen warm____ Bier?
10. Trotz gross____ Müdigkeit kann sie nicht schlafen.
11. Ihm gefällt wenig modern____ Musik.
12. Trinkst du viel stark____ Kaffee?
13. Gut____ Nacht! Gut____ Tag! Gut____ Abend!
14. Es ist eine gelbe Schachtel mit braun____ Deckel.
15. Ich brauche viel kalt____ Wasser.

Plural

When the attributive adjective modifies a plural noun, and when it is not preceded by a **"der"** or **"ein"** word, it has the same endings as the plural definite article. One of the following indefinite adjectives may precede the attributive adjective. In that case, they both have the endings of the plural definite article.

andere	*other*	**mehrere**	*several*
einige	*some*	**viele**	*many*
manche	*many*	**wenige**	*few*

Mehrere **Leute waren krank.**	*Several people were ill.*
Viele **Metalle sind teuer.**	*Many metals are expensive.*

45. Complete the following with the appropriate German word.

1. Dort sind ______ Studenten. *some*
2. ______ Leute machen das nicht. *other*
3. ______ Kinder hatten Angst. *several*
4. Dort stehen ______ Menschen. *many*
5. ______ Hunde sind wild. *few*
6. ______ Bücher sind interessant. *many*

Nominative and Accusative Case, All Genders

The plural attributive adjective that may or may not be preceded by an indefinite adjective receives the following endings in the nominative and accusative plural, when it is not preceded by a **"der"** or **"ein"** word:

Nominative **gross*e* Hunde** Accusative **gross*e* Hunde**

***Alte* Perserteppiche sind teuer.**	*Old Persian rugs are expensive.*
Ich fahre gerne durch *historische* Städte.	*I like to travel through historical cities.*
***Mehrere alte* Leute warten dort.**	*Several old people are waiting there.*
Ich habe *viele deutsche* Briefmarken.	*I have many German stamps.*

46. Complete with the appropriate form of the indicated words.

1. Unser Esszimmer hat ______ Wände. *gelb*
2. Sie hat ______ ______ Freunde. *viele, gut*
3. Wir besuchen ______ ______ Museen. *einige, bekannt*
4. Ich esse gern ______ Eier. *braun*
5. Jetzt sind ______ ______ Wolken am Himmel. *einige, grau*
6. ______ ______ Lastwagen bringen ______ Produkte. *mehrere, gross; frisch*
7. Sie kauft noch ______ ______ Kleider. *andere, neu*
8. ______ Menschen sind oft traurig. *alt*
9. Ich brauche ______ ______ Sachen. *wenige, teuer*
10. ______ ______ Kinder freuen sich über ______ Spielsachen. *manche, klein; automatisch*

Dative Case, All Genders

When the attributive adjective modifies a dative plural noun, and when it is not preceded by a **"der"** or **"ein"** word, it receives the following ending: **hoh*en* Bäumen.**

Sie wird mit *roten* Rosen empfangen.	*She is welcomed with red roses.*
Sie spricht mit *einigen alten* Freunden.	*She is talking with several old friends.*
Ich sitze auf *mehreren weichen* Kissen.	*I am sitting on several soft pillows.*

47. Complete the following with the appropriate form of the indicated words.

1. Er fand die Antwort in ______ Büchern. *alt*
2. Das Buch hat ______ ______ Lesern nicht gefallen. *einige, deutsch*
3. Ich wohne jetzt bei ______ Leuten. *nett*
4. Sie unterhält sich mit ______ ______ Studenten. *einige, amerikanisch*
5. Sie waren in ______ ______ Käfigen. *mehrere, klein*
6. Komm nicht mit ______ Schuhen ins Haus! *schmutzig*
7. Wir sitzen neben ______ Männern. *dick*
8. Sie hilft ______ ______ Studentinnen. *viele, intelligent*
9. Es liegt unter ______ ______ Zeitungen. *andere, alt*
10. Sie kommt mit ______ ______ Menschen zusammen. *wenige, fremd*

Genitive Case, All Genders

When the attributive adjective modifies a genitive plural noun, and when it is not preceded by a **"der"** or **"ein"** word, it receives the following ending: **klein*er* Kinder.**

Trotz ***guter*** **Freunde war sie einsam.**	*Despite good friends she was lonely.*
Der Preis ***mehrerer amerikanischer*** **Wagen ist hoch.**	*The price of several American cars is high.*
Die Qualität ***vieler billiger*** **Sachen ist schlecht.**	*The quality of many cheap things is poor.*

48. Complete the following with the appropriate form of the indicated words.

1. Die Blätter _______ _______ Bäume sind abgefallen. *einige, hoch*
2. Das Aussterben _______ _______ Tiere ist ein Problem. *mehrere, wild*
3. Der Wert _______ Münzen steigt. *alt*
4. Innerhalb _______ _______ Städte gibt es historische Funde. *viele, alt*
5. Die Häuser _______ _______ Leute sind wie Paläste. *einige, reich*
6. Die Götter _______ _______ Völker sind furchterregend. *manche, primitiv*
7. Das Dorf liegt jenseits _______ Berge. *hoch*
8. Das Leben _______ Studenten ist schwer. *faul*
9. Die Farben _______ Blätter sind schön. *herbstlich*
10. Die Titel _______ _______ Romane sind interessant. *einige, modern*

REVIEW

The following is a summary of the endings of attributive adjectives not preceded by a **"der"** or **"ein"** word.

	SINGULAR			*PLURAL*
	Masculine	*Feminine*	*Neuter*	*All Genders*
Nominative	**er**	**e**	**es**	**e**
Accusative	**en**	**e**	**es**	**e**
Dative	**em**	**er**	**em**	**en**
Genitive	**en**	**er**	**en**	**er**

49. Complete the following with the correct endings.

1. Trotz schnell_____ Hilfe wurde sie nicht gerettet.
2. Ich kenne mehrer_____ bekannt_____ Schauspieler.
3. Das Messer ist aus rostfrei_____ Stahl.
4. Lieb_____ Vater! Lieb_____ Fräulein Binder! Lieb_____ Grossmutter!
5. Krank_____ Leute brauchen frisch_____ Luft.
6. Gut_____ Morgen! Gut_____ Tag! Gut_____ Nacht!
7. Er will es mit rot_____ Farbe anmalen.
8. Welch hoh_____ Berg!
9. Wir sind schon seit lang_____ Zeit gut_____ Freunde.
10. Warum trinkst du kalt_____ Wasser?
11. Er erzählt von alt_____ Ruinen.
12. Ich brauche stark_____, schwarz_____ Kaffee.
13. Bei schlecht_____ Wetter spiele ich nicht Golf.
14. Der Preis französisch_____ Weines ist sehr hoch.
15. Ich kaufte viel_____ halbreif_____ Bananen.
16. Einig_____ deutsch_____ Studenten fuhren nach England.

17. Sie fragte nach weiss_____ Brot.
18. Die Sprachkenntnisse viel_____ ausländisch_____ Arbeiter sind gering.
19. Mit schnell_____ Autos muss man aufpassen.
20. Er schickte rot_____ Rosen.

WORDS SIMILAR TO ATTRIBUTIVE ADJECTIVES

Adjectives Used as Nouns

In German many adjectives can be used as nouns. They differ from the attributive adjectives only in that they are capitalized. In English the use of an adjectival noun is much more limited and usually occurs in the plural sense. The *rich* should help the *poor*. In German, however, the adjectival noun can be used in the singular or plural in all cases.

Ein *Toter* lag auf der Strasse.	*A dead (man) lay in the street.*
Sie erzählte von dem *Alten*.	*She was telling about the old one (man).*
Wer hilft der *Kleinen*?	*Who is helping the little one (female)?*
Die *Kranken* sind im Krankenhaus.	*The sick are in the hospital.*

50. Complete with the appropriate form of the indicated word.

1. Er spricht mit der _______. *Klein__*
2. Wo ist die _______? *Blond__*
3. Der _______ ist besser. *Schnell__*
4. Die _______ warten. *Alt__*
5. Der Akzent des _______ ist melodisch. *Fremd__*
6. Er bekommt es von den _______. *Reich__*
7. Sie bringt es für jene _______. *Arm__*
8. Wir helfen einem _______. *Krank__*
9. Die _______ singt. *Hübsch__*
10. Wo sind die _______? *Glücklich__*

Nouns with Adjective Endings

The following German words are used as nouns, but take the endings of attributive adjectives.

die Elektrische	*trolley*
die Illustrierte	*picture magazine*
der Beamte	*civil servant, official*
der/die Bekannte	*acquaintance*
der/die Deutsche	*the German*
der/die Gefangene	*prisoner*
der/die Reisende	*traveler, traveling salesperson*
der/die Verwandte	*relative*

Der/die Deutsche is the only noun of nationality that has an adjectival ending.

Ist das *eine Deutsche*?	*Is that a German (woman)?*
***Der Deutsche* lacht.**	*The German (man) is laughing.*
Er spricht mit *einer Deutschen*.	*He is talking with a German (woman).*
Wo liegt *meine Illustrierte*?	*Where is my picture magazine?*
Das ist *mein Verwandter*.	*That is my relative (male).*
Wir fragen *den Beamten*.	*We are asking the official.*

51. Complete the following with the appropriate endings.

1. Warum ist der Gefangen____ nicht hier?
2. Er spricht zum Beamt____.
3. Wann kommt die Elektrisch____?
4. Ich sehe viele Reisend____ im Zug.
5. Dort steht ein Deutsch____.
6. Meine Verwandt____ ist krank.
7. Dort ist das Auto meiner Bekannt____.
8. Die Deutsch____ spricht schnell.
9. Der Beamt____ ist nett.
10. Ich besuche meinen Verwandt____.
11. Es liegt unter der Illustriert____.
12. Ist das deine Bekannt____?
13. Der Reisend____ sitzt im Bus.
14. Dort ist eine Gefangen____.
15. Unsre Bekannt____ kommen.
16. Wir fahren mit der Elektrisch____.

Present Participle Used as Adjective

In both English and German the present participle can be used as an attributive adjective. In English the present participle ends in *-ing.* In German the present participle is formed by the infinitive plus **-d**: **lachend** (*laughing*), **singend** (*singing*). When used attributively, the appropriate adjective endings are added in German.

Das ***weinende*** **Kind tut mir leid.**	*I feel sorry for the crying child.*
Er ist in der ***brennenden*** **Fabrik.**	*He is in the burning factory.*
Wie heisst der ***regierende*** **König?**	*What is the name of the reigning king?*

52. Complete with the appropriate form of the indicated word.

1. Wirf die Nudeln ins ______ Wasser! *kochend*
2. Hört ihr den ______ Hund? *bellend*
3. Viel Glück im ______ Jahr! *kommend*
4. Wo ist das ______ Baby? *weinend*
5. Der ______ Holländer ist eine Oper. *Fliegend*
6. Ich brauche ein Zimmer mit ______ Wasser. *fliessend*
7. Sie hilft der ______ Alten. *sterbend*
8. Er ist im ______ Haus. *brennend*
9. Er sieht die ______ Katze. *leidend*
10. Wir suchen jene ______ Frau. *schreiend*

Past Participle Used as Adjective

The past participle of both weak and strong verbs can be used as adjectives. (See Chapter 5 on the formation of past participles.) When used attributively, adjective endings are added to the **-(e)t** suffix of weak verbs, and to the **-(e)n** suffix of strong verbs.

Gib das ***gestohlene*** **Geld zurück!**	*Return the stolen money.*
Ich nehme ein ***weichgekochtes*** **Ei.**	*I'll take one soft boiled egg.*
Wir stehen vor der ***geschlossenen*** **Tür.**	*We are standing in front of the closed door.*

53. Complete with the appropriate form of the indicated word.

1. Wo ist die ______ Suppe? *gekocht*
2. Sie ist am ______ Fenster. *geöffnet*
3. Wo ist der ______ Brief? *geschrieben*
4. Er steht auf dem ______ Wasser. *gefroren*
5. Dort steht der ______ Wagen. *repariert*
6. Wo sind die ______ Blumen? *geschnitten*
7. Wir sind in den ______ Staaten. *Vereinigt*

8. Ich rieche die ______ Wurst. *angebrannt*
9. Hast du die ______ Rechnung? *bezahlt*
10. Wo ist die ______ Tasse? *zerbrochen*

Adjectives Derived from Names of Cities

Adjectives derived from names of cities add **-er** and are capitalized. Regardless of the noun it modifies, the adjective always ends in **-er.**

Wie hoch ist der *Kölner* Dom?	*How high is Cologne Cathedral?*
Wir essen *Wiener* Schnitzel.	*We are eating Wiener Schnitzel.*

Neuter Adjectives Preceded by *etwas, nichts, viel, wenig*

Neuter adjectives following **etwas** (*something*), **nichts** (*nothing*), **viel** (*much*), **wenig** (*little*) are capitalized.

Er macht viel *Gutes.*	*He does much good.*
Weisst du etwas *Interessantes?*	*Do you know something interesting?*

54. Complete the following with the appropriate German word.

1. Ich kaufe nichts ______. *cheap*
2. Wir erfahren wenig ______. *new*
3. Ich esse gern ______ Lebkuchen. *Nürnberg*
4. Wir besuchen die ______ Messe. *Frankfurt*
5. Sie kocht etwas ______. *good*
6. Das ist ______ Bier. *Dortmund*
7. Sie bringt etwas ______. *old*
8. Ich habe viel ______. *modern*
9. Er trinkt eine ______ Weisse. *Berlin*
10. Wie hoch ist das ______ Münster? *Strassburg*

POSSESSIVE ADJECTIVES

Possessive adjectives are used to denote ownership or possession. The German possessive adjectives are as follows:

Singular		*Plural*	
mein	*my*	**unser**	*our*
dein	*your*	**euer**	*your*
sein	*his*	**ihr**	*their*
ihr	*her*	**Ihr**	*your*
sein	*its*		
Ihr	*your*		

Ihr (*your*–singular and plural formal address) is always capitalized. **Dein** and **euer** are capitalized only when used as a form of address in a letter or note.

Lieber Hans! Vielen Dank für *Deinen* Brief. *Dear Hans, many thanks for your letter.*

The possessive adjectives have the same endings as the indefinite article (see Chapter 1). The endings of the possessive adjectives are determined by the noun they modify, not by the possessor.

ihr (*her*) is the masculine form of the possessive adjective, because it agrees with the masculine noun *brother*.
seine (*his*) is the feminine form, because it agrees with *mother*.
The possessive **euer** is shortened to **eur** when an ending is added.

Wo ist *ihr* Bruder?	*Where is her brother?*
Ist das *seine* Mutter?	*Is that his mother?*
Wo ist *eure* Schwester?	*Where is your sister?*

The possessive **unser** can also be shortened to **unsr-** when endings are added.

Unsre (Unsere) **Nachbarn sind hier.** *Our neighbors are here.*

55. Complete the following with the appropriate forms.

1. (*His*) ______ Mutter ist krank.
2. (*Our*) ______ Bücher liegen dort.
3. (*Her*) ______ Bruder ist klug.
4. Das ist (*my*) ______ Kätzchen.
5. Wo ist (*your*–familiar singular) ______ Freund?
6. Herr Walter, (*your*) ______ Wagen steht dort.
7. (*Their*) ______ Eltern sind reich.
8. Wo sind (*your*–familiar plural) ______ Schuhe?
9. (*Our*) ______ Haus ist sehr alt.
10. Herr und Frau Müller, (*your*) ______ Tochter steht dort.

56. Complete the following with the appropriate form of the indicated word.

1. Er läuft durch ______ Garten. *unser*
2. Sie kennt ______ Freundin. *mein*
3. Hast du ______ Buch? *dein*
4. Ich habe ______ Mäntel. *euer*
5. Gehen Sie ohne ______ Frau? *Ihr*
6. Das ist für ______ Onkel. *ihr*
7. Kaufst du ______ Haus? *sein*
8. Kennen Sie ______ Grossmutter? *mein*
9. Er setzt sich in ______ Auto. *unser*
10. Ich nehme ______ Kamera. *euer*

57. Complete the following with the appropriate endings.

1. Er kommt von sein____ Freundin.
2. Ich wohne bei ihr____ Tante.
3. Sie kommen aus unsr____ Haus.
4. Ich gehe mit mein____ Eltern.
5. Sie steht hinter dein____ Wagen.
6. Wir gehen zu eur____ Lehrer.
7. Es liegt unter Ihr____ Zeitung.
8. Ausser sein____ Freundinnen war niemand da.
9. Sie ist in mein____ Zimmer.
10. Er ist bei sein____ Professor.

58. Complete the following with the appropriate genitive forms of the indicated word.

1. Die Farbe ______ Autos ist hässlich. *sein*
2. Die Haare ______ Mutter sind grau. *ihr*
3. Die Frau ______ Lehrers ist hier. *unser*
4. Während ______ Ferien fahre ich nach Berlin. *mein*
5. Trotz ______ Alters spielt sie Tennis. *ihr*
6. Warst du wegen ______ Bruders dort? *dein*
7. Wo ist die Brille ______ Vaters? *euer*
8. Wo wohnt die Tochter ______ Schwester? *Ihr*
9. Der Fluss ist jenseits ______ Gartens. *unser*
10. Die Geschwister ______ Eltern sind dort. *ihr*

59. Complete the following with the appropriate form of the possessive.

1. Wer hat (*his*) ______ Frau gesehen?
2. Dort steht (*my*) ______ Lehrer.
3. Gerda, (*your*) ______ Freunde warten.
4. (*Her*) ______ Geschwister kommen auch.
5. Wo sind (*our*) ______ Bücher?
6. Dort ist das Haus (*of her*) ______ Tante.
7. Er spielt mit (*his*) ______ Bruder.
8. Was bringt ihr für (*your*) ______ Kinder?
9. Herr Fischer, wer ist in (*your*) ______ Haus?
10. Kinder, sind das (*your*) ______ Hunde?
11. (*My*) ______ Familie wohnt hier.
12. Wo ist das Auto (*of his*) ______ Eltern?

COMPARISON OF ADJECTIVES AND ADVERBS

In German, as in English, adjectives have three degrees of comparison:

Comparison of equality	**klein**	*small, short*
Comparative	**kleiner**	*smaller, shorter*
Superlative	**kleinst-**	*smallest, shortest*
	am kleinsten	*the smallest*

The comparative of the adjective is formed by adding **-er** to the adjective.

Helga ist *kleiner* als Gisela. *Helga is shorter than Gisela.*

The superlative is formed by adding **-st** to the adjective. Note that **-est** is added to adjectives ending in **-d, -t, -ss, -z-** or **-sch.** The superlative form always requires an ending. The superlative form **am** ______ **(e)sten** is used with a predicate adjective.

Gertrud ist *am kleinsten*. *Gertrud is the shortest.*
Die Geschichte ist *am interessantesten*. *The story is the most interesting.*

The use of *more* and *most* in the comparative and superlative is not possible in German.

In German, unlike in English, the adverb derived from an adjective is identical with the adjective. In English *-ly* is usually added to an adjective to make it an adverb. No change is necessary in German. The superlative form **am** ______**(e)sten** is always used as the superlative of adverbs.

Sie singt *schön*. *She sings beautifully.*
Sie singt *am schönsten*. *She sings most beautifully.*

Er läuft *langsam.*	*He runs slowly.*
Er läuft *am langsamsten.*	*He runs most slowly.*

Vowel Change in Monosyllabic Adjectives

The stem vowel of the following monosyllabic adjectives adds an umlaut in the comparative and superlative.

Adjective/adverb		*Comparative*	*Superlative*	
alt	*old*	**älter**	**ältest-**	**am ältesten**
arm	*poor*	**ärmer**	**ärmst-**	**am ärmsten**
hart	*hard*	**härter**	**härtest-**	**am härtesten**
jung	*young*	**jünger**	**jüngst-**	**am jüngsten**
kalt	*cold*	**kälter**	**kältest-**	**am kältesten**
klug	*smart*	**klüger**	**klügst-**	**am klügsten**
krank	*sick*	**kränker**	**kränkst-**	**am kränksten**
kurz	*short*	**kürzer**	**kürzest-**	**am kürzesten**
lang	*long*	**länger**	**längst-**	**am längsten**
oft	*often*	**öfter**	**öftest-**	**am öftesten**
scharf	*sharp*	**schärfer**	**schärfst-**	**am schärfsten**
schwach	*weak*	**schwächer**	**schwächst-**	**am schwächsten**
stark	*strong*	**stärker**	**stärkst-**	**am stärksten**
warm	*warm*	**wärmer**	**wärmst-**	**am wärmsten**

Irregular Adjectives

Adjectives ending in **-el** or **-er** drop the **e** in the comparative.

bitter	*bitter*	**bittrer**	**bitterst-**	**am bittersten**
teuer	*expensive*	**teurer**	**teuerst-**	**am teuersten**
dunkel	*dark*	**dunkler**	**dunkelst-**	**am dunkelsten**

The adjective **hoch** drops the **c** in the comparative.

hoch	*high*	**höher**	**höchst-**	**am höchsten**

The adjective **nah** adds **c** in the superlative.

nah	*near*	**näher**	**nächst-**	**am nächsten**

Other irregular adjectives and adverbs are as follows.

gern	*(to) like (to)*	**lieber**	**liebst-**	**am liebsten**
gross	*big, tall*	**grösser**	**grösst-**	**am grössten**
gut	*good*	**besser**	**best-**	**am besten**
viel	*much*	**mehr**	**meist-**	**am meisten**

60. Follow the model.

Die Bluse ist billig. Das Hemd ist ______. Der Schal ist ______.
Die Bluse ist billig. Das Hemd ist billiger. Der Schal ist am billigsten.

1. Der Bleistift ist lang. Das Lineal ist ______. Der Stock ist ______.
2. Das Brot ist teuer. Die Butter ist ______. Der Käse ist ______.
3. Das Zimmer ist gross. Die Wohnung ist ______. Das Haus ist ______.
4. Ute spricht schnell. Maria spricht ______. Frau Weber spricht ______.
5. Die Uhr kostet viel. Der Ring kostet ______. Die Brosche kostet ______.

6. Der Stein ist hart. Der Marmor ist ______. Das Metall ist ______.
7. Ich sehe Rolf oft. Ich sehe Heinz ______. Ich sehe Paul ______.
8. Der Käse riecht scharf. Das Gas riecht ______. Die Säure riecht ______.
9. Er trinkt Wasser gern. Er trinkt Milch ______. Er trinkt Limonade ______.
10. Das Gebäude ist hoch. Der Turm ist ______. Der Berg ist ______.

Use of the Comparison of Adjectives and Adverbs

Comparison of Inequality

Comparisons implying inequality are expressed with the comparative followed by **als** (*than*).

Erich ist *grösser als* ich.	*Erich is taller than I.*
Der Ring ist *teurer als* die Kette.	*The ring is more expensive than the necklace.*
Er isst *mehr als* sein Vater.	*He is eating more than his father.*

61. Follow the model.

Moritz ist intelligent, aber Thomas ist ______ Moritz.
Moritz ist intelligent, aber Thomas ist intelligenter als Moritz.

1. Inge spricht viel, aber ich spreche ______ Inge.
2. Sie ist dick, aber er ist ______ sie.
3. Köln ist gross, aber Frankfurt ist ______ Köln.
4. Der BMW ist teuer, aber der Mercedes ist ______ der BMW.
5. Ich trinke Tee gern, aber ich trinke Milch ______ Tee.
6. Der Brocken ist hoch, aber die Zugspitze ist ______ der Brocken.
7. Christian ist nett, aber du bist ______ Christian.
8. Du bist jung, aber ich bin ______ du.
9. Gestern war es dunkel, aber heute ist es ______ gestern.
10. Eisen ist hart, aber Stahl ist ______ Eisen.

62. Follow the model.

Der Brief ist interessant. der Artikel
Der Brief ist interessanter als der Artikel.

1. Der Februar ist kurz. der Januar
2. Das Kleid ist teuer. die Bluse
3. Der Vater isst viel. das Baby
4. Ute kann gut Spanisch. Marianne
5. Im Haus ist es warm. im Garten
6. Das Auto fährt schnell. das Motorrad
7. Robert ist arm. Manfred
8. Mein Vater ist stark. mein Bruder
9. Die Lilie ist schön. die Geranie
10. Die Limonade ist kalt. das Wasser
11. Der Kaffee ist bitter. der Tee
12. Die Schule ist nah. die Kirche

Immer *plus Comparative Form*

Immer followed by the comparative form expresses an increase in degree.

Es wird *immer kälter.*	*It is getting colder and colder.*
Sie werden *immer reicher.*	*They are getting richer and richer.*
Er spricht *immer schneller.*	*He is talking faster and faster.*

63. Write the German.

1. It is getting darker and darker.
2. She is getting older and older.
3. He is driving faster and faster.
4. The days are getting longer and longer.
5. It is coming closer and closer.

The Superlative

The superlative form **am ______(e)sten** is always used as the superlative of adverbs. It is also used with predicate adjectives.

Dieses Auto ist *am teuersten.*	*This car is the most expensive.*
Ich laufe *am schnellsten.*	*I am running fastest.*
Dieses Messer schneidet *am besten.*	*This knife cuts best.*

64. Follow the model.

Karl und Hans sind stark. Gustav
Gustav ist am stärksten.

1. Inge und Pia springen hoch. ich
2. Peter und Josef sind gross. Karl
3. Ursel und Bärbel singen gut. wir
4. Laura und Christl sprechen schnell. meine Mutter
5. Renate und Rosa sind krank. Sabine
6. Jochen und Rolf sparen viel. mein Bruder
7. Das Rathaus und das Museum sind nah. die Kirche
8. Gerda und Georg gehen langsam. Klaus und ich
9. Meine Eltern sind reich. unsre Nachbarn
10. Der Mantel und das Kleid sind kurz. der Rock

65. Follow the model.

Das Fahrrad, das Motorrad, das Auto, fährt schnell.
Das Fahrrad fährt schnell. Das Motorrad fährt schneller. Das Auto fährt am schnellsten.

1. Der Brocken, das Matterhorn, die Zugspitze, ist hoch.
2. Wasser, Limonade, Bier, Ich trinke ______ gern.
3. Das Gedicht, die Geschichte, der Roman, ist lang.
4. Der Vogel, der Hubschrauber, das Düsenflugzeug, fliegt schnell.
5. Der Apfel, die Orange, die Zitrone, ist sauer.
6. Das Brot, der Kuchen, die Torte, schmeckt gut.
7. Hans, Josef, Franz, arbeitet viel.
8. Das Wollkleid, die Jacke, der Wintermantel, ist warm.

Comparison of Equality

Comparisons implying equality are expressed by **so . . . wie** (*as . . . as*).

Karl ist *so gross wie* **Gerhard.**	*Karl is as tall as Gerhard.*
Der Mantel kostet *so viel wie* **das Kleid.**	*The coat costs as much as the dress.*
Sie fahren *so schnell wie* **wir.**	*They are driving as fast as we.*

66. Follow the model.

Die Bank ist hoch. Stuhl
Die Bank ist so hoch wie der Stuhl.

1. Deine Nägel sind lang. Katzenkrallen
2. Pia ist gross. Inge
3. Die Jacke ist nicht warm. Mantel
4. Deine Augen sind blau. Himmel
5. Heute ist es kalt. Im Winter
6. Peter ist stark. Max
7. Die Hose ist teuer. Pullover
8. Grossmutter ist alt. Grossvater
9. Renate schreit laut. ich
10. Mein Bruder schreibt viel. sein Freund

The Comparative and Superlative Forms as Attributive Adjectives

The comparative and superlative forms of adjectives take the same endings as the positive forms of the adjectives.

Dort ist der billiger*e* Mantel.	*There is the cheaper coat.*
Ist das die teuerst*e* Kamera?	*Is that the most expensive camera?*
Das ist ein grösser*er* Wagen.	*That is a larger car.*
Ich kaufe den grösser*en* Koffer.	*I'll buy the larger suitcase.*
Sie hat das grösst*e* Zimmer.	*She has the largest room.*
Sie nehmen meine best*e* Jacke.	*They are taking my best jacket.*
Wir sind im modernst*en* Theater.	*We are in the most modern theater.*
Er hilft einer jünger*en* Frau.	*He is helping a younger woman.*
Das ist der Mann meiner jüngst*en* Schwester.	*That's the husband of my youngest sister.*

mehr *and* **weniger**

The comparative forms of **mehr** and **weniger** do not add adjective endings in the singular or plural.

Sie hat *mehr* **Bücher als du.**	*She has more books than you.*
Hast du *weniger* **Geld?**	*Do you have less money?*

67. Complete with the comparative form of the indicated adjective.

1. Das ist der ______ Mantel. *schön*
2. Dort liegt die ______ Tasche. *teuer*
3. Hier ist das ______ Messer. *scharf*
4. Das ist eine ______ Frau. *arm*
5. Sein ______ Freund kommt. *jung*
6. Ihr ______ Kind spielt. *klein*
7. Wo ist euer ______ Teppich? *gut*
8. Wann kommt ______ Wetter? *kalt*

68. Complete with the appropriate German form of the adjective.

1. Ich kaufe den ______ Mantel. *warmer*
2. Wir brauchen einen ______ Wind. *stronger*
3. Hast du ein ______ Messer? *sharper*

4. Ich kaufe eine ______ Tasche. *larger*
5. Er hat die ______ Kamera. *better*
6. Ich brauche ______ Geld. *more*
7. Wir gehen ins ______ Zimmer. *smaller*
8. Das ist für ______ Leute. *older*

69. Rewrite in German. Change the definite article to the indefinite article.

1. Wir sind in der kleineren Wohnung.
2. Er kommt aus dem bekannteren Museum.
3. Er fährt mit dem schnelleren Wagen.
4. Wir helfen dem kränkeren Patienten.
5. Sie erzählt von der besseren Zeit.
6. Er spricht mit der kleineren Frau.

70. Complete the following with the appropriate comparative form of the indicated word.

1. Es liegt jenseits des ______ Berges. *hoch*
2. Sie konnte wegen ihres ______ Bruders nicht gehen. *jung*
3. Er kam um der ______ Frau willen. *alt*
4. Trotz des ______ Windes segeln wir nicht. *stark*
5. Es ist innerhalb des ______ Parks. *klein*
6. Wir tragen wegen des ______ Wetters Mäntel. *kalt*

71. Complete the following with the appropriate superlative form of the indicated adjective.

1. Das ist der ______ Weg. *nah*
2. Wie heisst der ______ Berg? *hoch*
3. Das ist meine ______ Jacke. *warm*
4. Wo ist dein ______ Bild? *teuer*
5. Hier ist das ______ Papier. *dünn*
6. Wie heisst das ______ Metall? *hart*
7. Das ist ihr ______ Freund. *gut*
8. Wo ist unsre ______ Tochter? *alt*

72. Complete the following with the appropriate German word.

1. Ich kenne seinen (*youngest*) ______ Sohn.
2. Wir gehen ins (*most modern*) ______ Theater.
3. Er kämpft gegen den (*strongest*) ______ Mann.
4. Ich habe die (*most expensive*) ______ Kette.
5. Er nimmt seine (*best*) ______ Maschine.
6. Sie haben die (*most*) ______ Kinder.
7. Das ist für den (*most intelligent*) ______ Studenten.
8. Ich setze mich neben das (*smallest*) ______ Kind.

73. Complete with the appropriate superlative form of the indicated word.

1. Er wohnt in der ______ Wohnung. *teuer*
2. Sie schreibt mit ihrem ______ Bleistift. *kurz*
3. Wir helfen dem ______ Fräulein. *arm*
4. Ich sitze im ______ Zimmer. *warm*
5. Sie glaubt der ______ Frau. *jung*
6. Er arbeitet mit seiner ______ Maschine. *neu*
7. Wir sind im ______ Hotel. *teuer*
8. Sie segeln bei ______ Wind. *stark*

74. Complete with the appropriate German word.

1. Die Frau meines (*best*) _______ Freundes ist hier.
2. Was ist der Preis des (*most expensive*) _______ Instruments?
3. Wir sind innerhalb der (*oldest*) _______ Stadt.
4. Er macht es um des (*youngest*) _______ Kindes willen.
5. Was war das Thema des (*longest*) _______ Romans?
6. Der Freund ihrer (*prettiest*) _______ Tochter kommt.

REVIEW

75. Complete with the appropriate endings when necessary.

1. Kennst du seine älter_____ Schwester?
2. Dort steht das grösst_____ Kaufhaus.
3. Wir sind im billigst_____ Zimmer.
4. Ich habe mehr_____ Zeit.
5. Zieh deinen wärmer_____ Mantel an!
6. Ist das der best_____ Wein?
7. Habt ihr weniger_____ Bücher?
8. Ich brauche das schärfer_____ Messer.
9. Ich trinke keinen bittrer_____ Kaffee.
10. Es ist jenseits des höher_____ Berges.
11. Das war der schönst_____ Tag meines Lebens.
12. Wie heisst der Mann seiner älter_____ Schwester?
13. Sie spricht mit der ärmer_____ Frau.
14. Ich fahre mit dem teurer_____ Auto.
15. Das war die dunkelst_____ Nacht.
16. Die grösser_____ Jungen bleiben hier.
17. Wir sehen den kürzest_____ Film.
18. Trag das länger_____ Kleid!
19. Nimm den nächst_____ Weg!
20. Das war der kältest_____ Winter.

ADVERBS

The adverb **sehr** (*very*) precedes an adjective or adverb to express a high degree of a certain quality.

Dieses Auto fährt *sehr* schnell.	*This car goes very fast.*
Im Sommer ist es *sehr* heiss.	*It is very hot in summer.*
Sie ist eine *sehr* hübsche Frau.	*She is a very pretty woman.*
Hier gibt es *sehr* hohe Berge.	*There are very high mountains here.*

76. Write the German.

1. He is very old.
2. They have very good teachers.
3. He is a very intelligent man.
4. It is very cold.
5. She sings beautifully.

Many German adverbs do not have a corresponding adjective form. Such adverbs can refer to time, manner or place. A few of these adverbs are listed as follows:

Adverbs Referring to Time

abends	*in the evening*	**morgens**	*in the morning*
bald	*soon*	**nachts**	*at night*
damals	*at that time*	**nie**	*never*
gestern	*yesterday*	**nun**	*now*
heute	*today*	**oft**	*often*
immer	*always*	**selten**	*seldom, rarely*
jetzt	*now*	**spät**	*late*
manchmal	*at times, sometimes*	**täglich**	*daily, every day*

77. Complete with the appropriate German word.

1. Wo ist er ______? *now*
2. Er ist ______ in der Schule. *today*
3. Wir sind ______ zu Hause. *rarely*
4. Was war ______? *yesterday*
5. Sie sind ______ krank. *never*
6. Ich bin ______ müde. *in the evening*
7. Wo waren Sie ______? *at that time*
8. Wir besuchen ihn ______. *every day*
9. Kommen Sie ______? *soon*
10. Sie ist ______ beschäftigt. *always*
11. Er hilft uns ______. *sometimes*
12. Er fährt ______ ins Büro. *in the morning*

Adverbs Referring to Manner

gern	*gladly, like to*	**sicherlich**	*certainly*
hoffentlich	*hopefully*	**so**	*so*
leider	*unfortunately*	**vielleicht**	*perhaps, maybe*
natürlich	*naturally*	**wirklich**	*really*
nicht	*not*	**ziemlich**	*rather*
schon	*already*	**zu**	*to*

78. Complete with the appropriate German word.

1. Er ist ______ reich. *naturally*
2. Ich lese ______. *like to*
3. Wir können ______ nicht kommen. *unfortunately*
4. Sie ist ______ hier. *not*
5. Warum trinkst du ______ viel. *so*
6. Es ist ______ heiss. *really*
7. Du bist ______ klein. *too*
8. Er ist ______ alt. *rather*
9. War er ______ hier? *already*
10. ______ hat sie Kopfweh. *perhaps*

Adverbs Referring to Place

da	*there*	**drinnen**	*inside*
dort	*there*	**hier**	*here*
draussen	*outside*	**hinten**	*in the back*

links	*on the left*	**überall**	*everywhere*
oben	*above, upstairs*	**weg**	*away*
rechts	*on the right*		

79. Complete with the appropriate German word.

1. Was macht er ______? *there*
2. Sie arbeitet ______. *upstairs*
3. Wir sind ______. *inside*
4. Ich war ______. *outside*
5. War er ______? *here*
6. Sie sind ______. *away*
7. Müssen wir uns ______ halten? *on the left*
8. Wir bleiben ______. *in the back*
9. Geht immer ______! *on the right*
10. Es gab ______ Blumen. *everywhere*

POSITION OF ADVERBS

In German the adverb usually follows the verb and pronoun (if one is present). If more than one adverb occurs in a sentence, the following word order is observed: time, manner, place. **Nicht** precedes an adverb of place.

Wir sind *immer* **krank.**	*We are always ill.*
Er sagt mir *nie* **die Wahrheit.**	*He never tells me the truth.*
Sie ist *jetzt leider draussen.*	*She is unfortunately outside now.*
Er ist *heute wirklich nicht hier.*	*He is really not here today.*

80. Form sentences from the following.

1. hier, er, natürlich, bleibt
2. Maria, wohnt, unten, nicht
3. uns, Karl, sieht, täglich
4. drinnen, gestern, waren, wir, wirklich
5. nicht, arbeite, ich, abends, draussen
6. Vater, suchte, überall, dich, damals
7. sitzen, gern, wir, dort, manchmal
8. Hunger, ich, wirklich, morgens, habe, grossen
9. dick, ziemlich, sie, ist, jetzt
10. heute, weg, sie, leider, sind

81. Write the German.

1. We never drink wine.
2. She was already here today.
3. I am not there in the evening.
4. They are unfortunately upstairs now.
5. She is always inside in the morning.
6. He was here at that time.
7. I always sit outside.
8. He is perhaps in the back.
9. I am rarely away.
10. She is certainly everywhere.

ADVERB IDIOMS

Some German adverbs are used to convey the speaker's attitude or feelings. In English this is usually accomplished by voice. As a result there are no direct translations for the following:

denn

Denn usually expresses impatience, curiosity or interest. It is used in questions.

Wo ist er *denn?* *Well, where is he?*

doch

This adverb occurs both stressed and unstressed. When it is stressed, it expresses that something happened despite expectations to the contrary. It is also used instead of **ja** (*yes*) as an answer to a negative question.

Ich habe es *doch* verkauft.	*I sold it after all.*
Trinkst du nichts? *Doch,* ich trinke Tee.	*Aren't you drinking anything? Yes, (sure) I am drinking tea.*

When **doch** is unstressed it expresses that the opposite is not expected to be true. In an imperative construction, **doch** corresponds to the English "*why don't you . .*"

Sie ist *doch* nicht in Köln!	*She isn't in Cologne, is she!*
Kauf ihm *doch* etwas!	*Why don't you buy him something?*

ja

This adverb reinforces an idea, observation or fact.

Sie ist *ja* verrückt.	*Why, she is crazy.*
Wir sind *ja* schon zu Hause.	*We are already home, you know.*
Ich war *ja* krank.	*After all, I was ill.*

noch

Noch corresponds to the English *still, yet.* It indicates that an action is still continuing.

Sie ist *noch* im Krankenhaus.	*She is still in the hospital.*
Das Kind kann *noch* nicht sprechen.	*The child can't talk yet.*

Noch ein frequently means *another.*

Sie wollen *noch ein* Kind.	*They want another child.*
Möchtest du *noch eine* Tasse Tee?	*Would you like another cup of tea?*

82. Complete the following with the correct German adverb.

1. Wir haben (*still*) ______ Zeit.
2. Was habt ihr ______ bekommen?
3. Schreib uns ______ bald!
4. Wir sind (*after all*) ______ nicht dumm.
5. Hat sie keine Eltern? ______, sie sind aber verreist.
6. Habt ihr (*another*) ______ Bleistift?
7. Wir wissen es ______ schon. (*you know*)
8. Sie hat uns (*after all*) ______ besucht.

Chapter 4

Numbers, Dates, Time

NUMBERS

Cardinal Numbers

The cardinal numbers in German are as follows:

0	**null**	16	**sechzehn**	90	**neunzig**
1	**eins**	17	**siebzehn**	100	**hundert**
2	**zwei**	18	**achtzehn**	101	**hunderteins**
3	**drei**	19	**neunzehn**	102	**hundertzwei**
4	**vier**	20	**zwanzig**	120	**hundertzwanzig**
5	**fünf**	21	**einundzwanzig**	123	**hundertdreiundzwanzig**
6	**sechs**	22	**zweiundzwanzig**	143	**hundertdreiundvierzig**
7	**sieben**	30	**dreissig**	200	**zweihundert**
8	**acht**	31	**einunddreissig**	300	**dreihundert**
9	**neun**	35	**fünfunddreissig**	400	**vierhundert**
10	**zehn**	40	**vierzig**	999	**neunhundertneunundneunzig**
11	**elf**	50	**fünfzig**	1000	**tausend**
12	**zwölf**	60	**sechzig**	1001	**tausendeins**
13	**dreizehn**	70	**siebzig**	1110	**tausendeinhundertzehn**
14	**vierzehn**	80	**achtzig**	1976	**tausendneunhundertsechsundsiebzig**
15	**fünfzehn**			in dates:	**neunzehnhundertsechsundsiebzig**

The final **-s** is dropped from **sechs** and the final **-en** from **sieben** in 16 (**sechzehn**), 60 (**sechzig**), 17 (**siebzehn**) and 70 (**siebzig**). **Eins** drops the final **-s,** when followed by **und,** e.g. **einundvierzig.** However, when the word **eins** occurs at the end of a number, the final **-s** is always retained: **hunderteins, tausendeins.**

The word **ein** is not usually expressed before **hundert** and **tausend.** When it occurs within a numeral it is expressed, e.g. **tausendeinhundert.** Numbers from 1–999 999 are written as one word:

345 890 **(dreihundertfünfundvierzigtausendachthundertneunzig)**

Numbers over 1,000,000

1 000 000	**eine Million**
2 000 000	**zwei Millionen**
1 000 000 000	**eine Milliarde**
1 000 000 000 000	**eine Billion**

Eine Million, eine Milliarde and **eine Billion** are capitalized and have plural forms, because they are nouns. There is a difference between the German **Billion** and the American *billion.* The German **Billion** is equivalent to 1,000,000 millions. The American *billion* is equivalent to 1,000 millions.

With large numbers a period or spacing is used in German, whereas in English a comma is used.

Measurements and Prices

Numbers stating measurements and prices are set off by commas in German, whereas in English a period is used.

	German	*English*
2,3	**zwei komma drei**	2.3
4,45	**vier komma fünfundvierzig**	4.45
1,00 DM	**eine Mark**	DM 1.00
6,01 DM	**sechs Mark eins**	DM 6.01

The numeral **eins** is treated as an adjective when it is followed by a noun. It has the ending of the indefinite article: **eine Mark.** When the German noun **Mark** refers to the German currency, it does not have a plural form; e.g. **Es kostet nur 10,00 DM (zehn Mark).** The abbreviation **DM (Deutsche Mark)** usually follows the amount in nonofficial use.

1. Write the following numbers in German.

1. 8	6. 56	11. 101	16. 10 million
2. 16	7. 70	12. 936	17. 8.9
3. 21	8. 89	13. 1274	18. 17.61
4. 34	9. 91	14. 1980 (date)	19. 20.30 DM
5. 51	10. 100	15. 2031	20. 191.67 DM

Ordinal Numbers

Ordinal numbers *up to nineteenth* are formed by adding **-t** plus adjective endings to the cardinal numbers. Ordinals from *twentieth upwards* add **-st** plus adjective endings to the cardinals. Note that *first, third,* and *eighth* are irregular in German. A period following the number indicates that is an ordinal number in German.

1.	**der, die, das erste**	19.	**der, die, das neunzehnte**
2.	**der, die, das zweite**	20.	**der, die, das zwanzigste**
3.	**der, die, das dritte**	25.	**der, die, das einundzwanzigste**
4.	**der, die, das vierte**	40.	**der, die, das vierzigste**
7.	**der, die, das siebente (**or **siebte)**	100.	**der, die, das hundertste**
8.	**der, die, das achte**	1000.	**der, die, das tausendste**
11.	**der, die, das elfte**		

Ordinal numbers are treated like adjectives in German; therefore, they require adjective endings. Ordinal numbers are used in titles of rulers.

Nominative: **Wilhelm I. Wilhelm der Erste**

Wilhelm I (der Erste) **wohnte hier.**	*Wilhem I lived here.*

Accusative: **Wilhelm I. Wilhelm den Ersten**

Er kämpfte gegen *Wilhelm I. (den Ersten)*	*He fought against Wilhelm I.*

Dative: **Wilhelm I. Wilhelm dem Ersten**

Das Schloss gehörte *Wilhelm I. (dem Ersten)*	*The castle belonged to Wilhelm I.*

Genitive: **Wilhelms I. Wilhelms des Ersten**

Wo ist die Krone *Wilhelms I? (des Ersten)*	*Where is the crown of Wilhelm I?*

2. Complete the following with the correct form of the ordinal number.

 1. Wir wohnen im (*8.*) ______ Stock.
 2. Ich habe ein (*2.*) ______ Haus gekauft.
 3. Das ist seine (*4.*) ______ Frau.
 4. Ich bin der (*1.*) ______.
 5. Er wohnt in der (*3.*) ______ Strasse links.
 6. Heinrich (*VIII.*) ______ ______ hatte viele Frauen.
 7. Sie kommen jede (*5.*) ______ Woche.
 8. Wann regierte Friedrich (*I.*) ______ ______?
 9. Er lebte in der Zeit Ludwigs (*XV.*) ______ ______.
 10. Wir besuchen ein Schloss von Ludwig (*II.*) ______ ______.

Fractions

Fractions are formed by adding **-el** to the ordinal numbers. Fractions can be used as neuter nouns or as adjectives. No adjective endings are required for fractions. When $^3/_4$ is used as an adjective, the numerator and denominator are frequently written as one word. The same is true for fractions following whole numbers.

Fraction	*Noun*	*Adjective*
$^1/_3$	**ein (das) Drittel**	**ein drittel**
$^1/_4$	**ein (das) Viertel**	**ein viertel**
$^1/_5$	**ein (das) Fünftel**	**ein fünftel**
$^3/_4$	**drei Viertel**	**dreiviertel**
$^5/_6$	**fünf Sechstel**	**fünf sechstel**
$10^1/_3$		**zehn eindrittel**

Ein Viertel **der Klasse ist abwesend.**	*One-quarter of the class is absent.*
Er hat *ein Drittel* **des Kuchens gegessen.**	*He ate one-third of the cake.*
Ich habe *drei Viertel* **des Schatzes.**	*I have three-quarters of the treasure.*
Wir brauchen *ein viertel* **Pfund Butter.**	*We need one-quarter pound of butter.*
Es wiegt *dreiviertel* **Pfund.**	*It weighs three-quarter pounds.*
Wir müssen noch *fünf einzehntel* **Kilometer gehen.**	*We still have to walk five and one-tenth kilometers.*

Special Forms of "Half"

The fraction $^1/_2$ has the following special forms in German:

Fraction	*Noun*	*Adjective*
$\frac{1}{2}$	**die (eine) Hälfte**	**halb**

The adjectival form **halb** requires adjective endings.

Er hat ***eine halbe*** **Stunde gewartet.** *He waited for a half hour.*
Ich trinke nur ***ein halbes*** **Glas.** *I only drink half a glass.*
Sie gibt dir ***eine Hälfte.*** *She is giving you one-half.*

Special Forms of $1\frac{1}{2}$

The fraction $1\frac{1}{2}$ can be written the following ways:

eineinhalb **Pfund**
anderthalb **Kilo**
ein und ein halbes **Gramm**

3. Write the German for the following.

1. Who has my half?
2. $\frac{3}{4}$ pound
3. $\frac{1}{2}$ glass
4. $\frac{1}{3}$ of the work
5. $2\frac{1}{4}$ hours
6. $\frac{5}{8}$ of the population
7. $1\frac{1}{2}$ pounds
8. $\frac{1}{20}$
9. $\frac{1}{4}$ of the bread
10. $\frac{1}{2}$ pound

DATES

Days of the Week

The days of the week are always masculine. They are as follows:

der Montag	*Monday*
der Dienstag	*Tuesday*
der Mittwoch	*Wednesday*
der Donnerstag	*Thursday*
der Freitag	*Friday*
der Samstag or **Sonnabend**	*Saturday*
der Sonntag	*Sunday*

The Contraction **am**

In German time expressions, the contraction **am (an dem)** is used with the names of the days. **Am** corresponds to the English *on.* The contraction **am** precedes the name of the day, unless a particular day is to be emphasized. In that case, **an dem** (*on that*) is used.

Am Sonntag **haben wir keine Schule.** *We don't have school on Sunday.*
Er kommt ***am Dienstag.*** *He arrives on Tuesday.*
Sie war ***an dem*** **Montag hier.** *She was here on that Monday.*

Months

All months are masculine in gender. They are as follows:

der Januar	*January*	**der April**	*April*
der Februar	*February*	**der Mai**	*May*
der März	*March*	**der Juni**	*June*

der Juli	*July*	**der Oktober**	*October*
der August	*August*	**der November**	*November*
der September	*September*	**der Dezember**	*December*

Seasons

All seasons are masculine. They are as follows:

der Frühling	*spring*	**der Herbst**	*fall*
der Sommer	*summer*	**der Winter**	*winter*

The Contraction **im**

In German time expressions, the contraction **im (in dem)** precedes the name of the month or the season, corresponding to the English *in.* When referring to a particular month or season, **in dem** (*in that*) is used.

Ich habe ***im Juli*** **Geburtstag.**	*My birthday is in July.*
Im August **haben wir Sommerferien.**	*We have our summer vacation in August.*
Im Winter **ist es sehr kalt.**	*It is very cold in winter.*
Er kam ***in dem*** **Herbst.**	*He came (in) that fall.*

4. Write the German.

1. on Wednesday
2. in fall
3. in August
4. on Tuesday
5. in winter
6. in May
7. on that Thursday
8. on Friday
9. in spring
10. on Monday
11. on Saturday
12. in summer
13. in July
14. in that September
15. on that Monday
16. on Sunday

Days of the Month and Year

The definite article is expressed in German with dates. A period following the date indicates that the number is an ordinal number. Note that ordinal numbers receive adjective endings.

Der wievielte ist heute?	*What is today's date?*
Heute ist ***der 1. (erste)*** **Mai 1983.**	*Today is May 1, 1983.*
Den wievielten haben wir heute?	*What is today's date?*
Heute haben wir ***den 5. (fünften)*** **Juni 1985.**	*Today is June 5, 1985.*
Wann hast du Geburtstag?	*When is your birthday?*
Ich habe ***am 4. (vierten)*** **Juli Geburtstag.**	*My birthday is July 4.*
Wann kommst du an?	*When are you arriving?*
Ich komme ***am 6. (sechsten)*** **März an.**	*I'll arrive March 6.*
Ich komme ***am Montag, den 10. (zehnten)*** **August an.**	*I'll arrive on Monday, August 10.*

ist geboren, wurde geboren (was born)

In German there is a distinction between **ist geboren** and **wurde geboren.** A form of **sein + geboren** implies that the person is still alive. A form of **wurde + geboren** implies that the person is deceased.

Wann ***ist*** **sie** ***geboren?***	*When was she born? (she is still alive)*
Sie ***ist*** **1950** ***geboren.***	*She was born in 1950.*
Wann ***wurde*** **er** ***geboren?***	*When was he born? (he is deceased)*
Er ***wurde*** **1710** ***geboren.***	*He was born in 1710.*

Omission of **in**

The preposition **in** is not expressed in German when referring to a certain year, unless the numeral is preceded by the word **Jahr(e)** (*year*). In that case, the dative contraction **im** precedes **Jahr(e)**.

Der Krieg war *1918* **vorbei.**	*The war was over in 1918.*
Er schrieb es *im Jahre* **1935.**	*He wrote it in the year 1935.*

Dating a Letter

Dates in the headings of letters, notes, etc. are preceded by the accusative form of the accusative definite article **den.** In German the name of the place of origin of the writing may precede the date.

München, *den 14. (vierzehnten) Juni 1986*	*June 14, 1986*
Bonn, *den 20. November 1983*	*November 20, 1983*

Reversal of Numbers

In German, unlike in English, the first number in a date refers to the day, the second to the month.

Köln, den *9.3.1988*	*3/9/1988*
Sie starb am *22.12.1964.*	*She died 12/22/1964.*
Wir kommen am *13.8.1985* **an.**	*We'll arrive 8/13/1985.*

5. Write the German for the following.

1. His birthday is January 20.
2. Today is October 13, 1977.
3. I'll arrive Friday, March 9.
4. He died in 1970.
5. My birthday is December 10.
6. In the year 1980.
7. 5/30/1978.
8. She was born April 4, 1966. (She is still alive)
9. He was born in 1822. (He is dead)
10. Her birthday is August 10.
11. I'll arrive February 2.
12. He was born in 1974. (He is still alive)
13. Today is March 3, 1984.
14. He died in 1975.

TIME

The following expressions answer the question: **Wieviel Uhr ist es?** (*What time is it?*)

Colloquial German

1:00	**Es ist eins (ein Uhr).**	**1.00**
3:00	**Es ist drei Uhr (nachmittags, nachts).**	**3.00**
3:05	**Es ist fünf (Minuten) nach drei.**	**3.05**
3:15	**Es ist (ein) Viertel nach drei.**	**3.15**
3:20	**Es ist zwanzig (Minuten) nach drei.** **Es ist zehn vor halb vier.**	**3.20**
3:25	**Es ist fünfundzwanzig (Minuten) nach drei.** **Es ist fünf vor halb vier.**	**3.25**
3:30	**Es ist halb vier.**	**3.30**
3:35	**Es ist fünf nach halb vier.**	**3.35**
3:45	**Es ist (ein) Viertel vor vier.** **Es ist drei Viertel vier.**	**3.45**

3:50	**Es ist zehn (Minuten) vor drei.**	**3.50**
12:00 (noon)	**Es ist zwölf Uhr (mittags).**	**12.00**
12:00 (midnight)	**Es ist zwölf Uhr (mitternachts).**	**12.00**
9:00	**Es ist neun Uhr (vormittags, abends).**	**9.00**

In colloquial speech, the words **Uhr** and **Minuten** do not have to be expressed: **Es ist eins (zwei, sechs, neun).** Note that the **-s** of **eins** is dropped when **Uhr** is expressed: **Es ist ein Uhr.** In colloquial speech, adverbs of time are used to clarify a.m. and p.m. when necessary.

Der Zug kommt *um zwei Uhr (nachts, nachmittags)* **an.**

The half hour is expressed by **halb** plus the next hour:

Es ist *halb zehn.* *It is 9:30.*

Fifteen minutes before the hour are expressed by **drei Viertel** or **ein Viertel vor** plus the next hour.

Es ist *drei Viertel zehn.* *It is 9:45.*
Es ist *ein Viertel vor zehn.* *It is 9:45.*

Twenty and twenty-five minutes before or after the hour can be expressed by referring to 10 (5) minutes before or after the half hour:

Es ist *fünf vor halb acht.* *It is 7:25.*
Es ist *zehn nach halb sechs.* *It is 5:40.*

6. Write the German.

1. It is 8:00 p.m.
2. It is 10:30 a.m.
3. It is 5:15.
4. It is 7:35.
5. It is 6:25.
6. It is 4:45.
7. It is 11:20.
8. It is 3:10.
9. It is 1:00 p.m.
10. It is 12:00 noon.

Official Time

Official time in Germany is based on the 24-hour system. The word **Uhr** is always expressed. However, **Minuten** is omitted. Official time is used at railroad stations, at airports and in public media.

midnight	**vierundzwanzig Uhr**	**24.00**
12:20 a.m.	**null Uhr zwanzig**	**0.20**
1:00 a.m.	**ein Uhr**	**1.00**
3:30 a.m.	**drei Uhr dreissig**	**3.30**
11:15 a.m.	**elf Uhr fünfzehn**	**11.15**
12:20 p.m.	**zwölf Uhr zwanzig**	**12.20**
1:00 p.m.	**dreizehn Uhr**	**13.00**
2:40 p.m.	**vierzehn Uhr vierzig**	**14.40**
8:00 p.m.	**zwanzig Uhr**	**20.00**

7. Write the German, expressing the times officially.

1. It is 8:30 p.m.
2. 1:00 p.m.

3. 1:00 a.m.
4. midnight.
5. 12:35 a.m.
6. 9:25 p.m.
7. 12:40 p.m.
8. 10:45 a.m.
9. 2:00 p.m.
10. 11:00 p.m.

The Use of *um . . . Uhr*

The idiom **um . . . Uhr** corresponds to the English *at . . . o'clock.*

***Um wieviel Uhr* bist du dort?**	*At what time are you there?*
Ich bin *um 10 Uhr* dort.	*I am there at 10 o'clock.*

8. Write the German, expressing the times colloquially.

1. At 5 o'clock.
2. At 2 o'clock.
3. At 3:30.
4. At 7 o'clock.
5. At 11:00.

Periods of the Day

The periods of the day are preceded by the contraction **am,** corresponding to the English *in* or *at.*

am Morgen	*in the morning*
am Vormittag	*in the forenoon (morning)*
am Mittag	*at noon*
am Nachmittag	*in the afternoon*
am Abend	*in the evening*
BUT: **in der Nacht**	*at night*
Ich gehe *am Nachmittag* gern spazieren.	*I like to take a walk in the afternoon.*
Wir besuchen dich *am Abend.*	*We'll visit you in the evening.*
Wo bist du *in der Nacht?*	*Where are you at night?*

9. Complete the following with the appropriate German phrase.

1. Er kommt ______ ______. *(in the morning)*
2. ______ ______ trinken wir Tee. *(in the afternoon)*
3. ______ ______ ______ schlafen wir. *(at night)*
4. Wir treffen ihn ______ ______. *(at noon)*
5. Ich mache es ______ ______. *(in the evening)*

Customary Action

When the adverb of time denotes customary or habitual action, the days of the week and the periods of the day add **-s** and are not capitalized.

Wir gehen *dienstags* zum Kegeln.	*We go bowling on Tuesdays.*
Ich bin *vormittags* zu Hause.	*I am home in the mornings.*

10. Express habitual action. Follow the model.

Kommst du am Montag an?
Ja, ich komme immer montags an.

1. Bist du am Abend hier?
2. Hast du am Sonntag Zeit?

3. Gehst du am Mittwoch mit?
4. Schreibst du am Nachmittag?
5. Fährst du am Morgen zur Schule?

Other Adverbs of Time

The following adverbs of time are not capitalized when used singly or in combination:

heute	*today*
morgen	*tomorrow*
übermorgen	*the day after tomorrow*
gestern	*yesterday*
vorgestern	*the day before yesterday*
heute morgen	*this morning*
gestern abend	*last night*
morgen nachmittag	*tomorrow afternoon*
Wir haben *gestern nachmittag* **Tennis gepielt.**	*We played tennis yesterday afternoon.*

11. Write the German.

1. He is coming tomorrow evening.
2. He was home yesterday afternoon.
3. Otto, did you sleep last night?
4. They are coming the day after tomorrow.
5. She departed this morning.
6. He is coming tomorrow afternoon.

Time Expressions in the Accusative Case

Time expressions referring to a definite time or a duration of time require the accusative case.

Ich gehe *jeden Tag* **zur Arbeit.**	*I go to work every day.*
Letzten Sommer **war ich in Spanien.**	*I was in Spain last summer.*
Diesen Monat **ist er zu Hause.**	*He is home this month.*
Wir bleiben *ein ganzes Jahr.*	*We'll stay one entire year.*

12. Complete with the appropriate endings.

1. Ich bleibe ein____ Tag dort.
2. Letzt____ Herbst war ich in Deutschland.
3. Dies____ Woche bleibe ich dort.
4. Er arbeitet d____ ganz____ Abend.
5. Er trinkt jed____ Stunde Kaffee.
6. Wir singen ein____ ganz____ Stunde lang.

Time Expressions in the Dative Case

Time expressions containing the prepositions **an, in, vor** require the dative case. The prepositions **an** and **in** are usually contracted to **am** and **im** when they precede the names of days, months, seasons and periods of the day, unless a certain day, month, etc. is to be emphasized. *Ago* is expressed by the preposition **vor.** Unlike in English, the preposition **vor** (*ago*) precedes the time expression.

Wir gehen *am Morgen.*	*We are going in the morning.*
Warst du *an jenem Abend* **dort?**	*Were you there on that evening?*
Sie fahren *am Montag* **ab.**	*They'll depart on Monday.*
Im Sommer **gehen wir schwimmen.**	*We go swimming in summer.*
Er hat *im Dezember* **Geburtstag.**	*His birthday is in December.*

Sie kommt heute *in vierzehn Tagen.*	*She'll come two weeks from today.*
In acht Tagen **bist du wieder gesund.**	*You'll be well again in one week.*
Er war *vor einer Woche* **in Afrika.**	*A week ago he was in Africa.*
Sie war *vor acht Tagen* **hier.**	*She was here a week ago.*

13. Complete the following with the appropriate endings.

1. Er war vor ein____ Woche in Kanada.
2. Er war an jen____ Tag krank.
3. Ich war vor ein____ Jahr dort.
4. Ich erwarte sie in acht Tag____.
5. Wir haben euch an jen____ Abend gesehen.
6. Wo war er in jen____ Nacht?
7. Sie besuchte uns vor vierzehn Tag____.
8. Wir spielten an jen____ Samstag Golf.
9. Sie schrieb es vor ein____ Jahr.
10. Sie heirateten in jen____ Mai.

Time Expressions in the Genitive Case

Expressions of indefinite time require the genitive case in German. In English *someday* (night, morning, etc.) is used to refer to future time, and *one day* (night, etc.) is used for past time.

Eines Tages **erzählte sie die Geschichte.**	*One day she told the story.*
Ich zeige es dir *eines Tages.*	*I'll show it to you someday.*
Eines Abends **brachte er das Auto.**	*He brought the car one evening.*

By way of anology, the feminine noun **Nacht** also adds **-s** in such indefinite time expressions.

Ich traf ihn *eines Nachts* **im Park.**	*I met him in the park one night.*

14. Complete the following with the appropriate German expression.

1. Ich werde dich ______ ______ besuchen. *someday*
2. Sie wird ______ ______ mitgehen. *some night*
3. Er brachte es ______ ______. *one evening*
4. Ich besuchte sie ______ ______. *one afternoon*
5. Sie wird es ______ ______ lesen. *one morning*

REVIEW

15. Complete the following with the appropriate endings, prepositions or time expressions.

1. Wir fahren jed____ Winter nach Italien.
2. Ein____ Abend____ wurde er krank.
3. Der Lehrer kommt ______ acht Uhr.
4. Ich bleibe (*this evening*) ______ ______ zu Hause.
5. Ich gehe ______ Sommer gerne baden.
6. Warum arbeitest du d____ ganz____ Nacht?
7. Ich kaufe es ______ Dienstag.
8. Er besucht uns nächst____ Jahr.

9. (*At night*) ______ ______ ______ scheint der Mond.
10. (*Tomorrow afternoon*) ______ ______ fliege ich ab.
11. Kommen Sie doch heute ______ ______ ______! (*in one month*)
12. ______ wieviel Uhr essen wir?
13. (*In the morning*) ______ ______ war ich in der Schule.
14. Er war ______ ______ ______ (*a week ago*) in der Schweiz.
15. Ich gehe ______ (*Sundays*) nicht zur Arbeit.
16. Du bist ja ______ ______ (*at noon*) im Büro!
17. (*In two weeks*) ______ ______ ______ haben wir Ferien.
18. Wir kaufen ______ ______ (*someday*) ein Auto.
19. Ich warte schon ein____ ganz____ Stunde auf dich.
20. Sie war (*this morning*) ______ ______ in der Stadt.

Chapter 5

Verbs

WEAK AND STRONG VERBS

In German, as in other languages, verbs have a tense. The tense indicates time, such as present, past, future. Moreover, German verbs are divided into two categories, weak and strong verbs. A weak verb has no vowel change in its various forms. An example of a weak verb is **spielen.**

Infinitive	**spielen**
Past Tense	**spielte**
Past Participle	**gespielt**

A strong verb has a vowel change. Compare the various forms of **singen:**

Infinitive	**singen**
Past Tense	**sang**
Past Participle	**gesungen**

Such differences in verb forms also exist in English: *play, played, played; sing, sang, sung.* The rules for the formation of the various tenses are discussed in this chapter.

FORMAL VERSUS FAMILIAR FORMS

In German, there are three ways to express the pronoun *you.* When addressing a friend, relative, child or animal, one uses the pronoun **du.** This is referred to as the familiar singular form. The familiar plural form **ihr** is used to address two or more friends, relatives, children or animals. When addressing an acquaintance or a stranger, or people whom one would address with **Herr, Frau, Fräulein,** the formal pronoun **Sie** is used. **Sie** is used in the formal singular and plural and is always capitalized. The third person singular pronoun **man** is an indefinite pronoun meaning *one, they, people.*

PRESENT TENSE

Weak and Strong Verbs

Both weak and strong verbs use the stem of the infinitive to form the present tense. The German infinitive usually ends in **-en.** A few end in **-eln, -ern, -n.** The infinitive stem is derived from dropping **-en** or **-n** from the infinitive. The present tense is formed by adding to the stem the following endings: **-e, -st, -t, -en, -t, -en.**

ich denke	**wir denken**
du denkst	**ihr denkt**
er, sie, es denkt	**Sie, sie denken**

Wir *kaufen* **einen Wagen.**	*We are buying a car.*
Er *singt* **zu laut.**	*He is singing too loudly.*
Ich *kenne* **den Mann.**	*I know the man.*
Sagst **du die Wahrheit?**	*Are you telling the truth?*
Sie *studieren* **Englisch.**	*They study English.*
Trinkt **ihr nichts?**	*Aren't you drinking anything?*
Suchen **Sie den Hund?**	*Are you looking for the dog?*

In German there is only one form of the present tense. The German present tense corresponds to three forms in English: *I think, I do think, I am thinking.*

A partial list follows of weak and strong verbs whose infinitives end in **-en.** They form the present tense as just described. All verbs ending in **-ieren** also belong to this group.

bauen	*to build*	**leben**	*to live*
beginnen	*to begin*	**legen**	*to place, to lay*
bellen	*to bark*	**lernen**	*to learn*
besichtigen	*to view*	**lieben**	*to love*
bestellen	*to order*	**liegen**	*to lie*
besuchen	*to visit*	**machen**	*to do*
bezahlen	*to pay*	**malen**	*to paint*
bleiben	*to stay*	**nennen**	*to call, to name*
brauchen	*to need*	**operieren**	*to operate*
brennen	*to burn*	**parken**	*to park*
bringen	*to bring*	**probieren**	*to try*
buchstabieren	*to spell*	**rauchen**	*to smoke*
danken	*to thank*	**reisen**	*to travel*
denken	*to think*	**rennen**	*to run*
drehen	*to turn*	**reparieren**	*to repair*
empfangen	*to receive*	**riechen**	*to smell*
empfehlen	*to recommend*	**rufen**	*to call*
entdecken	*to discover*	**sagen**	*to say, to tell*
erklären	*to explain*	**schauen**	*to look*
erzählen	*to tell*	**schenken**	*to give*
fliegen	*to fly*	**schicken**	*to send*
fragen	*to ask*	**schreiben**	*to write*
gehen	*to go, walk*	**schreien**	*to scream*
gehören	*to belong to*	**schwimmen**	*to swim*
glauben	*to believe*	**senden**	*to send*
holen	*to get*	**singen**	*to sing*
hören	*to hear*	**springen**	*to jump*
kämmen	*to comb*	**stehen**	*to stand*
kauen	*to chew*	**steigen**	*to climb*
kaufen	*to buy*	**stellen**	*to place, to put*
kennen	*to know (to be acquainted with)*	**stören**	*to disturb*
		studieren	*to study*
klettern	*to climb*	**suchen**	*to look for*
kommen	*to come*	**tanzen**	*to dance*

telefonieren	*to telephone*	**wissen**	*to know a fact*
träumen	*to dream*	**wohnen**	*to live*
trinken	*to drink*	**zahlen**	*to pay*
vergessen	*to forget*	**zählen**	*to count*
verkaufen	*to sell*	**zeigen**	*to show*
wandern	*to wander, hike*	**zerstören**	*to destroy*
weinen	*to cry*	**ziehen**	*to pull*

1. Complete the following with the appropriate form of the present tense of the indicated verb.

1. ______ du Musik? *hören*
2. Wir ______ nichts. *trinken*
3. Wann ______ er? *kommen*
4. Ich ______ etwas. *schicken*
5. Die Sängerin ______. *singen*
6. Die Fabrik ______. *brennen*
7. Ich ______ nach Amerika. *fliegen*
8. Dieser Hund ______. *bellen*
9. Das Baby ______ hier. *bleiben*
10. ______ du an sie? *denken*
11. Warum ______ ihr? *weinen*
12. Die Touristen ______ vor der Kirche. *stehen*
13. Wann ______ die Vorstellung? *beginnen*
14. Man ______ Bier. *bringen*
15. Ich ______ schnell. *rennen*
16. Peter ______ das Auto. *parken*
17. Warum ______ ihr so? *schreien*
18. ______ Sie schon wieder? *rauchen*
19. ______ ihr seine Schwester? *kennen*
20. ______ du Richard? *lieben*
21. Pia ______ immer. *studieren*
22. Seine Eltern ______ ihn. *besuchen*
23. Wann ______ ihr das Buch? *holen*
24. Der Sportler ______ hoch. *springen*
25. Man ______ uns. *rufen*
26. Es ______ scharf. *riechen*
27. Wir ______ den Brief. *schreiben*
28. ______ ihr aufs Dach? *steigen*
29. Man ______ ihm. *glauben*
30. Ich ______ die Suppe. *probieren*
31. Das Kind ______ nicht. *telefonieren*
32. Ich ______ etwas. *hören*
33. Die Kinder ______ nichts. *brauchen*
34. Wo ______ er? *wohnen*
35. Wir ______ es. *holen*
36. Die Leute ______ nach Hause. *gehen*

Variations in Personal Endings

Additional **e**

When the stem of the infinitive ends in **-d, -t, -dn, -tm, -chn, -fn, -gn,** the present tense is formed with the following endings: **-e, -est, -et, -en, -et, -en.** The additional **-e** in the second and third person singular and in the second person plural facilitates pronunciation.

ich arbeite	**wir arbeiten**
du arbeitest	**ihr arbeitet**
er arbeitet	**sie arbeiten**

Sie ***badet*** **das Kind.**	*She is bathing the child.*
Er ***blutet*** **sehr stark.**	*He is bleeding very severely.*
Ordnest **du die Karten?**	*Are you putting the cards in order?*
Er ***atmet*** **langsam.**	*He is breathing slowly.*
Zeichnet **ihr oft?**	*Do you draw often?*
Warum ***öffnest*** **du die Tür?**	*Why are you opening the door?*
Sie ***begegnet*** **Peter.**	*She meets Peter.*

The following verbs receive this additional **e:**

antworten	*to answer*	**atmen**	*to breathe*
arbeiten	*to work*	**baden**	*to bathe*

begegnen	*to meet*	**reden**	*to talk*
beobachten	*to observe*	**reiten**	*to ride*
bitten	*to ask for*	**retten**	*to save*
bluten	*to bleed*	**schneiden**	*to cut*
finden	*to find*	**senden**	*to send*
öffnen	*to open*	**warten**	*to wait*
ordnen	*to put in order*	**wenden**	*to turn*
rechnen	*to figure* (arithmetic)	**zeichnen**	*to draw*

2. Complete the following with the appropriate form of the present tense of the indicated verb.

1. Cornelia _______ auf den Bus. *warten*
2. _______ du ins Brot? *schneiden*
3. Man _______ auch sonntags hier. *arbeiten*
4. Warum _______ du? *bitten*
5. _______ du Inge oft? *begegnen*
6. Ute _______ gut. *reiten*
7. _______ ihr alles? *finden*
8. _______ ihr gerne? *rechnen*
9. Du _______ zu viel. *reden*
10. Warum _______ ihr die Katze nicht? *retten*
11. Er _______ das Fenster. *öffen*
12. _______ der Spion das Haus? *beobachten*
13. Warum _______ du so schnell? *atmen*
14. Er _______ die Briefmarken. *ordnen*
15. Es _______ stark. *bluten*
16. _______ du alles? *senden*
17. Warum _______ du nicht? *antworten*
18. Paula _______ das Blatt. *wenden*
19. _______ du? *arbeiten*
20. _______ du das Baby? *baden*

No Additional **s** *Sound*

When the stem of the infinitive ends in **-s, -x, -z,** the personal ending for the second person singular is **-t.** No additional **s** sound is required. All other endings are regular.

Warum ***hasst*** **du ihn?**	*Why do you hate him?*
Tanzt **du gern?**	*Do you like to dance?*

The following verbs belong to this group:

beissen	*to bite*	**reisen**	*to travel*
grüssen	*to greet*	**setzen**	*to set, place*
hassen	*to hate*	**sitzen**	*to sit*
heissen	*to be called*	**tanzen**	*to dance*
mixen	*to mix*		

3. Form sentences from the following, using the present tense of the verb.

1. Wie / heissen / du?
2. Was / mixen / du?
3. Du / tanzen / gut
4. Warum / grüssen / du / mich / nicht?

5. Wohin / reisen / du?
6. Was / hassen / du?
7. Wo / sitzen / du?
8. Beissen / du / in den Apfel?

Infinitives Ending in **-eln, -ern**

When the infinitive ends in **-eln,** the **e** preceding the **-ln** is dropped in the first person singular. All other forms retain the **e.**

Ich ***klingle.***	*I am ringing.*

When the infinitive ends in **-eln** or **-ern,** the ending in the first and third persons plural is **-n.** They are like the infinitive form.

Wir ***füttern*** **den Hund.**	*We are feeding the dog.*
Sie ***klettern*** **auf den Baum.**	*They are climbing the tree.*

ich klingle	**wir klingeln**	**ich füttere**	**wir füttern**
du klingelst	**ihr klingelt**	**du fütterst**	**ihr füttert**
er klingelt	**sie klingeln**	**er füttert**	**sie füttern**

The following infinitives end in **-eln** or **-ern:**

behandeln	*to treat*	**ändern**	*to change*
klingeln	*to ring*	**bewundern**	*to admire*
lächeln	*to smile*	**füttern**	*to feed*
sammeln	*to collect*	**klettern**	*to climb*
		wandern	*to hike*

4. Complete the following with the appropriate form of the present tense.

1. Das Kind ______ auf den Tisch. *klettern*
2. Wohin ______ wir? *wandern*
3. Ich ______ seine Courage. *bewundern*
4. Man ______ Sie sofort. *behandeln*
5. Wann ______ du die Katze? *füttern*
6. Wir ______ nichts. *ändern*
7. Ich ______ doch nicht. *lächeln*
8. Die Ärzte ______ sie schon. *behandeln*
9. Das Telefon ______. *klingeln*
10. Wir ______ alles. *sammeln*
11. Ich ______ den Patienten. *behandeln*
12. Die Kinder ______ den Hund. *füttern*
13. Ich ______ nichts. *sammeln*
14. Wir ______ auf den Berg. *klettern*

Vowel Modification in Strong Verbs

Many German verbs that are considered strong have a vowel change in the stem of the present tense. This vowel change takes place in the second and third person singular. Those strong verbs containing **a, au** or **e** undergo a vowel change. They can be grouped according to the changes that take place.

***Changes from* a, au *to* ä, äu**

Verbs whose stem vowel is **a** or **au** change the same to **ä** or **äu** in the second and third person singular.

ich fahre	**wir fahren**	**ich laufe**	**wir laufen**
du fährst	**ihr fahrt**	**du läufst**	**ihr lauft**
er fährt	**sie fahren**	**er läuft**	**sie laufen**

The following verbs function in the same way as **fahren:**

backen	*to bake*	**lassen**	*to allow, to cause*
blasen	*to blow*	**schlafen**	*to sleep*
empfangen	*to receive*	**schlagen**	*to hit, beat*
fallen	*to fall*	**tragen**	*to wear, carry*
fangen	*to catch*	**wachsen**	*to grow*
graben	*to dig*	**waschen**	*to wash*
halten	*to hold, stop*		

The following verbs change **au** to **äu**:

laufen	*to run*
saufen	*to drink* (animals, people in excess)

5. Rewrite the following, changing the plural to the singular.

1. Schlaft ihr die ganze Nacht?
2. Sie wachsen schnell.
3. Wascht ihr die Wäsche?
4. Wir halten die Ballons.
5. Was tragen sie zum Ball?
6. Lasst ihr mich gehen?
7. Wir backen Brot.
8. Warum graben sie ein Loch?
9. Sie schlagen das Kind.
10. Die Tiere saufen Wasser.
11. Sie blasen ins Feuer.
12. Wohin lauft ihr?
13. Sie fallen.
14. Fangt ihr den Ball?
15. Wir schlafen schon.
16. Was tragt ihr?

Changes from **e** *to* **i** *or* **ie**

Strong verbs with an **e** in the infinitive stem change the same to **i** or **ie** in the second and third person singular.

Study the following forms:

ich breche	**wir brechen**	**ich lese**	**wir lesen**
du brichst	**ihr brecht**	**du liest**	**ihr lest**
er bricht	**sie brechen**	**er liest**	**sie lesen**

The following verbs function like **brechen:**

erschrecken	*to frighten*	**sprechen**	*to speak, talk*
essen	*to eat*	**stechen**	*to stick*
fressen	*to eat* (animals, people in excess)	**sterben**	*to die*
		treffen	*to meet*
geben	*to give*	**vergessen**	*to forget*
helfen	*to help*		

The following verbs function like **lesen:**

empfehlen	*to recommend*	**sehen**	*to see*	**stehlen**	*to steal*

Important Exceptions

gehen and **stehen**

Although **gehen** and **stehen** are strong verbs containing **e** in their stem, they do not have the preceding changes in the present tense **(du gehst, er geht; du stehst, er steht)**.

nehmen

Note that the verb **nehmen** (*to take*) has an irregular spelling pattern. Study the following forms:

ich nehme	**wir nehmen**
du nimmst	**ihr nehmt**
er nimmt	**sie nehmen**

6. Rewrite the following, changing the plurals to the singular.

1. Helft ihr mir?
2. Sie sterben bald.
3. Seht ihr uns?
4. Wir essen Suppe.
5. Die Hunde fressen.
6. Was gebt ihr ihm?
7. Wir sprechen gern.
8. Sie sehen uns.
9. Sie stehen beim Haus.
10. Geht ihr auch?
11. Was nehmt ihr?
12. Wann trefft ihr uns?
13. Was lesen sie?
14. Warum erschreckt ihr?
15. Was brechen sie?
16. Was stehlt ihr?
17. Was stechen sie?
18. Warum helfen sie nicht?
19. Was vergessen sie?
20. Empfehlt ihr dieses Hotel?

Irregular Verbs

The present tense of **sein** (*to be*), **haben** (*to have*), **werden** (*to get, to become*), **wissen** (*to know*) and **tun** (*to do*) are irregular. Study the following:

sein	**haben**	**werden**	**wissen**	**tun**
ich bin	ich habe	ich werde	ich weiss	ich tue
du bist	du hast	du wirst	du weisst	du tust
er ist	er hat	er wird	er weiss	er tut
wir sind	wir haben	wir werden	wir wissen	wir tun
ihr seid	ihr habt	ihr werdet	ihr wisst	ihr tut
sie sind	sie haben	sie werden	sie wissen	sie tun

7. Complete the following with the correct form of the present tense of **sein.**

1. Ich ______ zwanzig Jahre alt.
2. Er ______ in Afrika.
3. Wir ______ jetzt in der Schule.
4. Die Kinder ______ hungrig.
5. Ihr ______ freundlich.
6. ______ Sie auch Schauspielerin?
7. Meine Tante ______ leider krank.
8. ______ du denn glücklich?

8. Complete the following with the present tense of **haben.**

1. Meine Eltern ______ kein Auto.
2. Ich ______ keine Angst.
3. ______ du Kopfweh?
4. Die Studenten ______ jetzt Ferien.
5. ______ ihr Durst?
6. Er ______ ja Geld.
7. Wir ______ Besuch.
8. Wann ______ du denn Zeit?

9. Complete the following. Supply the correct form of the present tense of **werden.** Follow the model.

Wir werden schon wieder gesund.

1. Ich . . .
2. Ihr . . .
3. Du . . .
4. Barbara . . .
5. Fräulein Sommer, Sie . . .
6. Die Kinder . . .
7. Er . . .
8. Wir . . .

10. Complete the following with the appropriate form of **wissen.**

1. Wir ______ ja die Antwort.
2. Die Mädchen ______ es nicht.
3. ______ ihr es?
4. Ich ______, dass er hier ist.
5. Man ______ es schon.
6. ______ du es vielleicht?
7. Er ______ alles.
8. Die Leute ______ es.

11. Supply the correct form of the present tense of **tun.**

1. Was ______ du?
2. Ich ______ immer alles.
3. Wir ______ nichts.
4. Er ______ viel.
5. ______ ihr etwas?
6. ______ Sie nichts?
7. Peter und Sonja ______ wenig.
8. Brigitte ______ etwas.

Special Use of the Present Tense

Future Meaning

As in English, the present tense in German can be used to indicate that an event will take place in the future. The future meaning is conveyed by the context or by an adverbial expression indicating future time.

Ich *gehe* morgen in die Stadt.	*I am going downtown tomorrow.*
***Hilfst* du mir nächste Woche?**	*Are you helping me next week?*

12. Answer the following questions affirmatively. Write a complete sentence, using the present tense.

1. Kommst du morgen?
2. Hat er übermorgen Geburtstag?
3. Geht ihr morgen abend ins Theater?
4. Fliegen Sie im Juli nach Frankfurt?
5. Fährst du nächstes Jahr nach Regensburg?
6. Besuchst du mich heute in acht Tagen?
7. Sind Sie nächsten Monat in Deutschland?
8. Bist du morgen abend zu Hause?
9. Habt ihr nächste Woche Zeit?
10. Spielt sie nächsten Samstag Golf?

Continued Action

The present tense is used in German to express the fact that an action is started in the past and continues into the present. In English a past tense is used to express continued action. In German the time element is usually introduced by **schon** or **seit,** corresponding to the English *for.*

Ich *wohne* schon zwei Monate hier.	*I have been living here for two months.*
Er *ist* seit einer Woche in Paris.	*He has been in Paris for one week.*

13. Complete the following with the appropriate form of the indicated verb.

1. Ich_______ schon seit einem Monat. *warten*
2. Ute _______ seit zehn Jahren hier. *wohnen*
3. Er _______ schon eine Stunde dort. *sein*
4. Wir _______ schon den ganzen Tag. *arbeiten*
5. _______ du schon seit einer Stunde? *singen*
6. Ich _______ Robert seit einem Jahr. *kennen*
7. Wir _______ seit zehn Minuten hier. *sein*
8. Der Pilot _______ schon drei Stunden. *fliegen*
9. Es _______ schon zwei Tage. *regnen*
10. _______ ihr schon eine Stunde? *schreiben*

14. Answer the following questions with a complete sentence, using the cue.

1. Seit wann liest du schon? *eine Stunde*
2. Wie lange studiert er schon? *zehn Tage*
3. Seit wann bist du hier? *fünf Minuten*
4. Wie lange kennst du ihn schon? *sechs Jahre*
5. Wie lange telefonierst du schon? *zwanzig Minuten*

REVIEW

15. Complete the following with the correct form of the present tense of the indicated verb.

1. Warum _______ du ein Loch? *graben*
2. Ich _______ sofort. *kommen*
3. Man _______ hier nicht. *laufen*
4. Was _______ du daran? *ändern*
5. Wir _______ die Vögel. *füttern*
6. _______ ihr auch krank? *sein*
7. Georg _______ Beamter. *werden*
8. Wohin _______ du? *reisen*
9. Hilde _______ schon den ganzen Tag. *arbeiten*
10. _______ du die Zeitung? *lesen*
11. Wir _______ sehr leise. *atmen*
12. Das Tier _______. *fressen*
13. Wohin _______ ihr? *fahren*
14. Das Kind _______ den Ball. *fangen*
15. Ich _______ das Auto. *waschen*
16. Wir _______ ihn nicht. *grüssen*
17. _______ Sie hungrig? *sein*
18. Meine Geschwister _______ die Antwort. *wissen*
19. Warum _______ du so lange? *schlafen*
20. Es _______ schon wieder kalt. *werden*
21. Helga _______ dort. *stehen*
22. Was _______ die Studenten? *studieren*
23. Wo _______ du? *bluten*
24. Ich _______. *klingeln*
25. Wie _______ du? *heissen*
26. Was _______ er? *essen*

27. Wann ______ du Franz das Auto? *geben*
28. Manfred ______ seine Freundin. *sehen*
29. Wir ______ den Kranken. *behandeln*
30. Wo ______ du? *sitzen*

PRESENT PERFECT TENSE

The present perfect tense of most German verbs consists of the present tense of the auxiliary verb **haben** and the past participle. German verbs are grouped as weak and strong verbs. A regular weak verb has no vowel change in the stem of the past tense. Its past participle is prefixed by **ge-** and ends in **-t** or **-et.** A strong verb usually has a vowel change in the stem of the past tense. Its past participle is prefixed by **ge-** and ends in **-en.**

Regular Weak Verbs

The present perfect tense of most regular weak verbs is formed with the present tense of **haben** and the past participle. The past participle of regular weak verbs consists of the prefix **ge-** and the third person singular verb form.

Verb	*Third Person Singular*	*Past Participle*
machen	**er macht**	**gemacht**
lieben	**er liebt**	**geliebt**
arbeiten	**er arbeitet**	**gearbeitet**
öffnen	**er öffnet**	**geöffnet**

Study the following conjugation:

ich habe gemacht	**wir haben gemacht**
du hast gemacht	**ihr habt gemacht**
er, sie, es hat gemacht	**Sie, sie haben gemacht**

Wir ***haben*** **einen Wagen** ***gekauft.***	*We bought a car.*
Er ***hat*** **die Wahrheit** ***gesagt.***	*He told the truth.*
Ich ***habe*** **den Lehrer** ***gefragt.***	*I asked the teacher.*
Habt **ihr auch** ***gearbeitet?***	*Did you also work?*
Er weiss, dass ich den Brief ***geschickt habe.***	*He knows that I sent the letter.*

Note that the past participle is in last position of the sentence, unless it occurs in a dependent clause.

Weak Verbs Ending in **-ieren**

The past participle of weak verbs ending in **-ieren** is not prefixed by **ge-**.

Infinitive	*Past Participle*
studieren	**studiert**
probieren	**probiert**
telefonieren	**telefoniert**

Additional Verbs Without **ge-** *Prefix*

Verbs with the following prefixes do not take the additional **ge-** prefix in the past participle: **be-, emp-, ent-, er-, ge-, ver-, zer-** (see section on inseparable prefix verbs).

Infinitive	*Past Participle*
bestellen	**bestellt**
entdecken	**entdeckt**
erklären	**erklärt**
gehören	**gehört**
verkaufen	**verkauft**

Study the following conjugation:

ich habe zerstört	**wir haben zerstört**
du hast zerstört	**ihr habt zerstört**
er hat zerstört	**sie haben zerstört**

16. Complete the following with the appropriate present perfect form of the indicated verb.

1. Wir ______ den Kellner ______. *fragen*
2. Wo ______ Sie ______? *wohnen*
3. Wir ______ alles ______. *glauben*
4. ______ du den Mantel ______? *kaufen*
5. Gisela ______ ihren Freund ______. *lieben*
6. Die Leute ______ die Geschichte ______. *hören*
7. Ich ______ den Hund ______. *suchen*
8. Die Männer ______ viel ______. *rauchen*
9. Wo ______ ihr das Auto ______? *parken*
10. Warum ______ du ______? *weinen*
11. ______ du es auf den Tisch ______? *legen*
12. Was ______ er dir ______? *schenken*
13. Ich ______ das Baby ______. *kümmen*
14. Was ______ ihr ______? *lernen*
15. Was ______ Sie ______? *sagen*

17. Complete the following with the appropriate present perfect form of the indicated verb.

1. Warum ______ ihr ______? *bezahlen*
2. ______ du die Maschine ______? *verkaufen*
3. Die Jungen ______ das Auto ______. *reparieren*
4. Unsre Lehrerin ______ alles ______. *erzählen*
5. Ich ______ die ganze Nacht ______. *studieren*
6. Wir ______ die Suppe ______. *probieren*
7. Wer ______ die Stadt ______? *zerstören*
8. ______ dir der Fussball ______? *gehören*
9. ______ du ______? *telefonieren*
10. Meine Eltern ______ schon ______. *bestellen*
11. Er ______ uns ______. *besuchen*
12. Wann ______ Kolumbus Amerika ______? *entdecken*
13. Wer ______ das Problem ______? *erklären*
14. Warum ______ du es ______? *zerstören*
15. Inge ______ sich schon ______. *entschuldigen*

18. Rewrite in the present perfect.

1. Wir studieren viel.
2. Brauchst du Geld?
3. Warum bellt der Hund?
4. Er arbeitet viel.
5. Man zerstört das Haus.
6. Suchen Sie den Jungen?
7. Träumt ihr oft?
8. Sie atmet sehr laut.
9. Ich blute stark.
10. Die Kinder baden gerne.
11. Wo wohnt ihr?
12. Ich hole Papier.
13. Wir legen die Bücher auf den Tisch.
14. Sie telefoniert oft.
15. Die Katze gehört dem Mädchen.
16. Wer bezahlt dafür?

Irregular Weak Verbs

Some weak verbs have a vowel change in the past stem. Study the past participles of the following irregular weak verbs.

Infinitive		*Past Participle*
bringen	*to bring*	**gebracht**
denken	*to think*	**gedacht**
brennen	*to burn*	**gebrannt**
kennen	*to know (a person)*	**gekannt**
nennen	*to name*	**genannt**
senden	*to send*	**gesandt**
wenden	*to turn*	**gewandt**
wissen	*to know (a fact)*	**gewusst**

19. Write sentences from the following, using the present perfect tense.

1. Er / kennen / meine Schwester.
2. Die Kinder / wissen / die Antwort.
3. Ich / bringen / Blumen.
4. Denken / du / daran?
5. Die Häuser / brennen.
6. Wir / senden / das Paket.
7. Nennen / ihr / den höchsten Berg?
8. Ich / wenden / das Blatt.

Intransitive Verbs

The present perfect tense of some German verbs is formed with the present tense of the auxiliary verb **sein** instead of **haben.** Such verbs are referred to as intransitive verbs (verbs that do not take a direct object). Such verbs usually denote a change of location or condition. The following weak verbs are conjugated with **sein.**

Infinitive		*Past Participle*
begegnen	*to meet*	**ist begegnet**
klettern	*to climb*	**ist geklettert**
reisen	*to travel*	**ist gereist**
rennen	*to run*	**ist gerannt**
wandern	*to wander*	**ist gewandert**

Note that the irregular weak verb **rennen** has a vowel change in the past participle. Intransitive verbs are conjugated as follows:

ich bin gereist	**wir sind gereist**
du bist gereist	**ihr seid gereist**
er ist gereist	**sie sind gereist**

Wir *sind* **auf den Baum** *geklettert.*	*We climbed the tree.*
Ich *bin* **nach Deutschland** *gereist.*	*I traveled to Germany.*
Bist **du deinem Freund** *begegnet?*	*Did you meet your friend?*

20. Complete the following with the appropriate present perfect form of the indicated verb.

1. Wir ______ sehr schnell ______. *rennen*
2. Wohin ______ ihr ______? *reisen*
3. Ich ______ auf den Berg ______. *klettern*
4. ______ er durch die Schweiz ______? *reisen*
5. ______ ihr ins Dorf ______? *wandern*
6. Ich ______ nicht ______. *rennen*
7. Die Kinder ______ ihrem Lehrer ______. *begegnen*
8. Meine Mutter ______ nach München ______. *reisen*
9. ______ du auch auf den Baum ______? *klettern*
10. Ich ______ ihrem Freund ______. *begegnen*

Strong Verbs

The present perfect tense of most strong verbs is formed with the auxiliary verb **haben.** Some are conjugated with **sein.** The past participle of strong verbs is prefixed by **ge-,** unless the verb already has one of the following prefixes: **be, emp-, ent-, er-, ge-, ver-, zer-** (see section on inseparable prefix verbs). The past participle of strong verbs ends in **-en.**

ich habe gesehen	**wir haben gesehen**
du hast gesehen	**ihr habt gesehen**
er hat gesehen	**sie haben gesehen**

ich habe empfangen	**wir haben empfangen**
du hast empfangen	**ihr habt empfangen**
er hat empfangen	**sie haben empfangen**

Ich ***habe*** **das Flugzeug** ***gesehen.***	*I saw the airplane.*
Hast **du den Brief** ***empfangen?***	*Did you receive the letter?*
Wir ***haben*** **uns die Hände** ***gewaschen.***	*We washed our hands.*
Fritz ***hat*** **den Apfel** ***gegessen.***	*Fritz ate the apple.*

Past Participles Without Vowel Change

The past participle of the following strong verbs consists of the prefix **ge-** and the infinitive form of the verb. Note the extra **g** in **gegessen.**

Infinitive		*Past Participle*
backen	*to bake*	**gebacken**
essen	*to eat*	**gegessen**
fahren	*to drive, go*	**(ist) gefahren**
fallen	*to fall*	**(ist) gefallen**
fangen	*to catch*	**gefangen**
fressen	*to eat (animals)*	**gefressen**
geben	*to give*	**gegeben**
graben	*to dig*	**gegraben**
halten	*to hold*	**gehalten**
kommen	*to come*	**(ist) gekommen**
lassen	*to let*	**gelassen**
laufen	*to run*	**(ist) gelaufen**
lesen	*to read*	**gelesen**
messen	*to measure*	**gemessen**
schlafen	*to sleep*	**geschlafen**
schlagen	*to hit*	**geschlagen**

sehen	*to see*	**gesehen**
tragen	*to carry, wear*	**getragen**
treten	*to step*	**(ist) getreten**
vergessen	*to forget*	**vergessen**
wachsen	*to grow*	**(ist) gewachsen**
waschen	*to wash*	**gewaschen**

Note that the past participles preceded by **ist** are conjugated with **sein** in the present perfect tense.

ich bin gewachsen	**wir sind gewachsen**
du bist gewachsen	**ihr seid gewachsen**
er ist gewachsen	**sie sind gewachsen**

Er ***ist*** **nach Hamburg** ***gefahren.***	*He drove (went) to Hamburg.*
Ich ***bin*** **ins Zimmer** ***getreten.***	*I stepped into the room.*
Sie ***sind*** **schnell** ***gewachsen.***	*They grew fast.*

21. Complete with the appropriate present perfect form of the indicated verb.

1. ______ du den Roman ______? *lesen*
2. Er ______ den Jungen ______. *schlagen*
3. Ich ______ es meinem Lehrer ______. *geben*
4. Wann ______ ihr den Film ______? *sehen*
5. Wir ______ einen Kuchen ______. *backen*
6. Ich ______ die Strecke ______. *messen*
7. Was ______ das Tier ______? *fressen*
8. Die Männer ______ nach Gold ______. *graben*
9. Die Frau ______ keinen Hut ______. *tragen*
10. Ich ______ mir die Hände ______. *waschen*
11. ______ ihr den Tiger ______? *fangen*
12. Wer ______ die Bananen ______? *essen*
13. ______ du den Mantel zu Hause ______? *lassen*
14. Warum ______ ihr nicht ______? *schlafen*

22. Write sentences from the following using the present perfect tense.

1. Mein Bruder / fahren / schnell.
2. Treten / du / ins Haus?
3. Wir / wachsen / schon wieder.
4. Fahren / ihr / nach Bremen?
5. Die Kinder / wachsen / immer.
6. Ich / fahren / gestern.
7. Laufen / ihr / ins Haus?
8. Wann / du / kommen?
9. Die Leute / laufen / schnell.
10. Ich / ins Wasser / fallen.

Past Participles with Vowel Change

Many strong verbs change their stem vowels in the past participle. The participles of such verbs can be grouped according to the vowel changes taking place. The following groups may facilitate learning these past participles.

Changes from **ei** ***to*** **(i)e**

The **ei** of the infinitive stem is changed to **(i)e** in the past participle of the following verbs:

Infinitive		*Past Participle*
ei		*ie*
bleiben	*to stay*	**(ist) geblieben**
leihen	*to loan*	**geliehen**
scheinen	*to shine, to seem*	**geschienen**
schreiben	*to write*	**geschrieben**
schreien	*to scream*	**geschrien**
schweigen	*to be silent*	**geschwiegen**
steigen	*to climb*	**(ist) gestiegen**
ei		*i*
beissen	*to bite*	**gebissen**
leiden	*to suffer*	**gelitten**
reiten	*to ride*	**(ist) geritten**
schneiden	*to cut*	**geschnitten**

23. Rewrite the following in the present perfect tense.

1. Reitest du oft?
2. Wir schreien laut.
3. Warum schreibt ihr nicht?
4. Die Sonne scheint.
5. Warum beisst er?
6. Bleibt ihr lange?
7. Die Kranken leiden.
8. Warum schweigt ihr?
9. Steigst du auf die Leiter?
10. Ich leihe dir Geld.
11. Er schneidet dem Kind das Haar.
12. Leidet ihr nicht?
13. Ich schreie nicht.
14. Schreibst du den Brief?

***Changes from* ie, au *to* o *or* e**

The **ie, au** of the infinitive stem is changed to **o** or **e** in the past participles of the following verbs.

Infinitive		*Past Participle*
ie		*o*
biegen	*to bend*	**gebogen**
fliegen	*to fly*	**(ist) geflogen**
fliehen	*to flee*	**(ist) geflohen**
fliessen	*to flow*	**(ist) geflossen**
frieren	*to freeze*	**gefroren**
riechen	*to smell*	**gerochen**
schiessen	*to shoot*	**geschossen**
schliessen	*to shut*	**geschlossen**
verlieren	*to loose*	**verloren**
wiegen	*to weigh*	**gewogen**
ziehen	*to pull*	**gezogen**
au		*o*
saufen	*to drink* (animals)	**gesoffen**
ie		*e*
liegen	*to lie*	**gelegen**

24. Complete the following with the correct present perfect form of the indicated verb.

1. _______ du den Schlüssel _______? *verlieren*
2. Er _______ den Braten _______. *riechen*
3. _______ ihr nach Nürnberg _______? *fliegen*
4. Ein Beamter _______ den Koffer _______. *wiegen*
5. Warum _______ du auf den Hasen _______? *schiessen*
6. Er _______ sie an den Haaren _______. *ziehen*
7. Ein Gefangener _______ gestern _______. *fliehen*
8. Wohin _______ das Wasser _______? *fliessen*
9. Warum _______ du die Augen _______? *schliessen*
10. Wir _______ an den Beinen _______. *frieren*
11. Der Wind _______ die Bäume _______. *biegen*
12. Er _______ im Schatten _______. *liegen*
13. Der Hund _______ das Wasser _______. *saufen*
14. Ich _______ das Geld _______. *verlieren*

Changes from **i** *to* **u, o** *or* **e**

The **i** of the infinitive stem is changed to **u, o** or **e** in the past participles of the following verbs:

Infinitive		*Past Participle*
i		*u*
binden	*to bind*	**gebunden**
finden	*to find*	**gefunden**
singen	*to sing*	**gesungen**
sinken	*to sink*	**(ist) gesunken**
springen	*to jump*	**(ist) gesprungen**
stinken	*to stink*	**gestunken**
trinken	*to drink*	**getrunken**
i		*o*
beginnen	*to begin*	**begonnen**
gewinnen	*to win*	**gewonnen**
schwimmen	*to swim*	**(ist) geschwommen**
i		*e*
bitten	*to ask*	**gebeten**
sitzen	*to sit*	**gesessen**

25. Form sentences from the following, using the present perfect tense.

1. Die Sonne / sinken / ins Meer.
2. Die Vorlesung / beginnen.
3. Springen / ihr / von der Brücke?
4. Ich / singen / das Lied.
5. Schwimmen / du / über die Nordsee?
6. Er / gewinnen / den Preis.
7. Das Gas / stinken.
8. Binden /du / den Hund / an den Baum?
9. Die Männer / springen / über die Hürde.
10. Singen / ihr / oft?
11. Ich / trinken / Wasser.
12. Wir / beginnen / gestern.
13. Er / sitzen / auf dem Sofa.
14. Bitten / ihr / die Frau?
15. Wer / finden / den Schmuck?
16. Er / trinken / kaltes Bier.

Changes from **e** *or* **u** *to* **o** *or* **a**

The **e** or **u** of the infinitive stem is changed to **o** or **a** in the past participles of the following verbs:

Infinitive		*Past Participle*
e		*o*
brechen	*to break*	**gebrochen**
empfehlen	*to recommend*	**empfohlen**
heben	*to lift*	**gehoben**
helfen	*to help*	**geholfen**
nehmen	*to take*	**genommen**
sprechen	*to talk, speak*	**gesprochen**
stehlen	*to steal*	**gestohlen**
sterben	*to die*	**(ist) gestorben**
treffen	*to meet*	**getroffen**
werfen	*to throw*	**geworfen**
e		*a*
gehen	*to go*	**(ist) gegangen**
stehen	*to stand*	**gestanden**
u		*a*
tun	*to do*	**getan**

26. Rewrite the following in the present perfect tense.

1. Trefft ihr sie?
2. Sie werfen den Ball.
3. Warum brichst du es in Stücke?
4. Ich helfe ihr.
5. Das Kind nimmt nichts.
6. Der Verletzte stirbt.
7. Warum stiehlst du?
8. Fräulein Knauer, Sie sprechen zu schnell.
9. Wir helfen dem Kranken.
10. Sprichst du viel?
11. Gehst du ins Kino?
12. Ich stehe hier.
13. Wir empfehlen die Suppe.
14. Der Kran hebt das Auto.
15. Was tust du?

The Verbs *sein, haben, werden*

The present perfect tense of the verbs **sein, haben** and **werden** is as follows:

sein	**haben**	**werden**
ich bin gewesen	ich habe gehabt	ich bin geworden
du bist gewesen	du hast gehabt	du bist geworden
er ist gewesen	er hat gehabt	er ist geworden
wir sind gewesen	wir haben gehabt	wir sind geworden
ihr seid gewesen	ihr habt gehabt	ihr seid geworden
sie sind gewesen	sie haben gehabt	sie sind geworden

Wir *sind* in Japan *gewesen.*	*We were in Japan.*
Ich *bin* müde *geworden.*	*I became tired.*
Hast* du Geld *gehabt?	*Did you have money?*
Seid* ihr krank *geworden?	*Did you become ill?*
Er *ist* in der Schule *gewesen.*	*He was in school.*

27. Rewrite the following, changing the verbs to the present perfect.

1. Hast du Hunger?
2. Ich bin krank.
3. Wir haben Hunger.
4. Sie werden immer dicker.
5. Er wird wieder gesund.
6. Wann sind Sie dort?
7. Ich habe Kopfweh.
8. Wir werden nass.
9. Bist du auch müde?
10. Ich werde böse.
11. Habt ihr Geld?
12. Ich habe Sorgen.
13. Sie ist unglücklich.
14. Die Pferde sind unruhig.
15. Wirst du nervös?
16. Seid ihr krank?

Use of the Present Perfect

The German present perfect tense is also referred to as conversational past, because it is always used in conversation. It is used to relate or ask about *single* past events. This tense is not interchangeable with any other German past tense, such as the imperfect tense, which is used in narrating or reporting about a *series* of past events. No such distinction is made in English. For this reason, the German present perfect tense corresponds to several past forms in English. Study the following examples:

Was *habt* **ihr gestern** *gemacht?*	*What* did *you do* yesterday?
Wir *sind* **in die Stadt** *gegangen.*	*We* went *downtown.*
Hast **du den Roman** *gelesen?*	Did (Have) *you* read *the novel?*
Ja, ich *habe* **ihn schon** *gelesen.*	*Yes I* have *already* read *it.*
Was *hat* **er** *gemacht?*	*What* was *he* doing?
Er *hat gegessen.*	*He* was eating.

REVIEW

28. Complete the following with the appropriate form of the present perfect tense.

1. ______ Sie den Turm ______? *besichtigen*
2. Er ______ mir nichts ______. *geben*
3. Wie lange ______ du dort ______? *wohnen*
4. Otto ______ etwas ______. *kaufen*
5. Die Leute ______ mich ______. *kennen*
6. Was ______ du ______? *backen*
7. ______ ihr ihn ______? *sehen*
8. Die Kinder ______ laut ______. *schreien*
9. Er ______ vor einer Stunde ______. *telefonieren.*
10. Ich ______ den ganzen Tag ______. *arbeiten*
11. ______ ihr schon ______? *bestellen*
12. Wem ______ du ______? *begegnen*
13. Warum ______ er ______? *schweigen*
14. Wir ______ nichts ______. *verloren*
15. Die Katze ______ es ______. *fressen*
16. Du ______ aber ______! *wachsen*
17. ______ ihr auch ins Wassser ______? *springen*
18. Ich ______ von dir ______. *träumen*
19. Man ______ es ganz ______. *zerstören*

20. ______ du schon ______? *studieren*
21. Wann ______ du ______? *kommen*
22. Ich ______ alles ______. *erzählen*
23. ______ ihr den Kuchen ______? *essen*
24. ______ Sie lange ______? *warten*
25. Die Kinder ______ Limonade ______. *trinken*
26. Wir ______ das Haus ______. *verkaufen*
27. ______ du stark ______? *bluten*
28. Ich ______ auf die Leiter ______. *steigen*
29. Er ______ alles ______. *sagen*
30. Der Mechaniker ______ den Wagen ______. *reparieren*
31. ______ du die Suppe ______? *empfehlen*
32. Warum ______ das Boot ______? *sinken*
33. Wen ______ ihr nach der Arbeit ______? *treffen*
34. Wie lange ______ du ______? *schlafen*
35. Die Kinder ______ die Tür ______. *schliessen*

IMPERFECT TENSE

The imperfect tense is also referred to as the narrative past because it is used to narrate or report a chain of events that took place in the past. The imperfect tense has restricted use in conversation in German. For this reason the **du, ihr** and **Sie** forms are used infrequently.

Weak Verbs

The imperfect tense of weak verbs is formed by adding the following endings to the stem of the infinitive: **-te, -test, -te, -ten, -tet, -ten.** Study the following conjugation:

ich bestellte	**wir bestellten**
du bestelltest	**ihr bestelltet**
er bestellte	**sie bestellten**

Wir *tanzten* den ganzen Abend.	*We danced the whole night.*
Ich *machte* damals eine Reise.	*I made a trip at that time.*
Sie *fragten* den Lehrer.	*They asked the teacher.*
Er *bestellte* Schweinebraten.	*He ordered pork roast.*

29. Rewrite the following in the imperfect tense.

1. Sie spielen.
2. Er wohnt in Köln.
3. Wir glauben daran.
4. Ich studiere gern.
5. Der Hund bellt.
6. Ich bezahle die Rechnung.
7. Man gratuliert ihm.
8. Wir brauchen Milch.
9. Meine Eltern bauen es.
10. Das Telefon klingelt.

30. Complete the following with the correct imperfect form of the indicated verb.

1. Du ______ damals ein Bild. *malen*
2. Wir ______ das Rathaus. *besichtigen*
3. Die Mädchen ______ ihn. *fragen*
4. Ich ______ ihm etwas. *schenken*
5. Wir ______ damals Französisch. *lernen*

6. Konrad ______ den Wagen. *reparieren*
7. Die Herren ______ mir den Weg. *zeigen*
8. Ihr ______ uns damals. *besuchen*
9. Unsre Eltern ______ eine Kamera. *kaufen*
10. Man ______ sie. *stören*

Variation in Personal Endings

Additional **e**

When the stem of the infinitive ends in **-d, -t, -dn, -tm, -chn, -fn** or **-gn,** an additional **e** occurs between the stem and the personal imperfect endings to facilitate pronunciation. Study the following conjugation:

ich arbeitete	**wir arbeiteten**
du arbeitetest	**ihr arbeitetet**
er arbeitete	**sie arbeiteten**

Er *öffnete* die Tür.	*He opened the door.*
Wir *badeten* das Kind.	*We bathed the child.*
Sie *ordneten* Briefmarken.	*They put stamps in order.*
Ich *begegnete* dem Mädchen.	*I met the girl.*

31. Rewrite the following in the imperfect tense.

1. Ich atme ganz regelmässig.
2. Man tötet ihn.
3. Wir retten den Verunglückten.
4. Du öffnest die Tür.
5. Sie begegnen ihren Eltern.
6. Paul beobachtet den Vogel.
7. Ich arbeite gern.
8. Er ordnet die Bücher.
9. Sie antwortet nicht.
10. Sie bluten stark.

Irregular Weak Verbs

The following weak verbs are irregular in the imperfect. Study the imperfect forms:

Infinitive	*Imperfect*	*Infinitive*	*Imperfect*
brennen	**brannte**	**senden**	**sandte**
kennen	**kannte**	**wenden**	**wandte**
nennen	**nannte**	**bringen**	**brachte**
rennen	**rannte**	**denken**	**dachte**
		wissen	**wusste**

Er *brachte* mir Blumen.	*He brought me flowers.*
Wir *rannten* ins Haus.	*We ran into the house.*
Ich *kannte* den Künstler.	*I knew the artist.*

32. Rewrite the following in the imperfect tense.

1. Er weiss das nicht.
2. Ich sende ihm einen Brief.
3. Es brennt dort.
4. Wir bringen Geschenke.
5. Sie denken daran.
6. Die Kinder rennen.
7. Man nennt es.
8. Ich kenne ihn auch.
9. Er wendet das Heu.
10. Du kennst uns.

Strong Verbs

Unlike weak verbs, all strong verbs have a vowel change in the imperfect stem. The personal imperfect endings of strong verbs also differ from those of weak verbs. Study the following imperfect forms of the strong verb **bleiben:**

ich blieb	**wir blieben**
du bliebst	**ihr bliebt**
er blieb	**sie blieben**

Note that the first and third person singular of strong verbs never receive an ending in the imperfect. The other personal endings are **-st, -en, -t, -en.**

Vowel Changes in the Stem

To facilitate learning the different vowel changes taking place in the imperfect stems of strong verbs, the following groupings can be made:

***Changes from* a, au, ei *to* ie *or* i**

The following verbs change to **ie** or **i** in the imperfect:

Infinitive		*Imperfect*
a		*ie*
fallen	*to fall*	**fiel**
halten	*to stop, hold*	**hielt**
lassen	*to let*	**liess**
schlafen	*to sleep*	**schlief**
au		*ie*
laufen	*to run*	**lief**
ei		*ie*
bleiben	*to stay*	**blieb**
leihen	*to loan*	**lieh**
scheinen	*to shine*	**schien**
schreiben	*to write*	**schrieb**
schreien	*to scream*	**schrie**
schweigen	*to be silent*	**schwieg**
steigen	*to climb*	**stieg**
ei		*i*
beissen	*to bite*	**biss**
leiden	*to suffer*	**litt**
reiten	*to ride*	**ritt**
schneiden	*to cut*	**schnitt**
e		*i*
gehen	*to go, walk*	**ging**
a		*i*
fangen	*to catch*	**fing**

Variations in Personal Endings

When the imperfect stem ends in **-d, -t, -ss, -chs,** an **e** is added between the stem and the personal endings of the second person singular and plural. However, these forms as well as the second person singular and plural of other verbs in the imperfect are rarely used. For example, **du schnittest, ihr schnittet.**

When the imperfect stem ends in **-ie,** the ending of the first and third persons plural is **-n** instead of **-en.**

Wir *schrien* sehr laut.	*We screamed very loudly.*
Warum *schrien* sie nicht?	*Why didn't they scream?*

33. Rewrite in the imperfect tense.

1. Sie leidet.
2. Er schläft schon.
3. Sie schreiben Briefe.
4. Wir reiten gerne.
5. Ich schreie laut.
6. Das Buch fällt auf den Boden.
7. Der Zug hält dort.
8. Ludwig bleibt dort.
9. Sie schweigen immer.
10. Wir leiden sehr.
11. Er schreibt die Aufgabe.
12. Sie schweigt nicht.
13. Ihr schneidet ins Papier.
14. Die Sonne scheint.
15. Man leiht dem Kind das Buch.
16. Der Hund beisst das Mädchen.

34. Write sentences from the following, using the imperfect tense.

1. Ich / lassen / Gudrun / gehen.
2. Das Pferd / laufen / am schnellsten.
3. Hubert / reiten / den ganzen Tag.
4. Wir / leihen / Gisela / das Buch.
5. Der Rattenfänger / fangen / Ratten.
6. Ich / schneiden / ins Fleisch.
7. Meine Eltern / schreiben / den Brief.
8. Wir / schreien / nicht.

***Changes from* e, ie, au *to* o**

The following verbs change to **o** in the imperfect:

Infinitive		*Imperfect*
ie		*o*
biegen	*to bend*	**bog**
fliegen	*to fly*	**flog**
fliehen	*to flee*	**floh**
fliessen	*to flow*	**floss**
frieren	*to freeze*	**fror**
riechen	*to smell*	**roch**
schiessen	*to shoot*	**schoss**
schliessen	*to shut*	**schloss**
verlieren	*to lose*	**verlor**
wiegen	*to weigh*	**wog**
ziehen	*to pull*	**zog**
au		*o*
saufen	*to drink*	**soff**
e		*o*
heben	*to lift*	**hob**

35. Complete the following with the appropriate imperfect form.

1. Er ______ nach Spanien. *fliegen*
2. Ich ______ mein Gepäck. *verlieren*

3. Es ______ stark. *riechen*
4. Wir ______ die Fensterläden. *schliessen*
5. Der Jäger ______ auf das Reh. *schiessen*
6. Du ______ an den Händen. *frieren*
7. Man ______ das Gold. *wiegen*
8. Die Kinder ______ das Spielzeug. *ziehen*
9. Wohin ______ das Wasser? *fliessen*
10. Ihr ______ damals nach Frankreich. *fliehen*
11. Die Tiere ______ Wasser. *saufen*
12. Ich ______ in die Schweiz. *fliegen*
13. Er ______ den Sack vom Wagen. *heben*
14. Die Männer ______ das Metall. *biegen*

Changes from **e, i, ie, o, u** *to* **a**

The following verbs change to **a** in the imperfect tense:

Infinitive		*Imperfect*
e		*a*
brechen	*to break*	**brach**
empfehlen	*to recommend*	**empfahl**
essen	*to eat*	**ass**
fressen	*to eat*	**frass**
geben	*to give*	**gab**
helfen	*to help*	**half**
lesen	*to read*	**las**
messen	*to measure*	**mass**
nehmen	*to take*	**nahm**
sehen	*to see*	**sah**
sprechen	*to speak*	**sprach**
stehen	*to stand*	**stand**
stehlen	*to steal*	**stahl**
sterben	*to die*	**starb**
treffen	*to meet*	**traf**
treten	*to step*	**trat**
vergessen	*to forget*	**vergass**
werfen	*to throw*	**warf**
i		*a*
beginnen	*to begin*	**begann**
binden	*to bind*	**band**
bitten	*to ask*	**bat**
finden	*to find*	**fand**
gewinnen	*to win*	**gewann**
schwimmen	*to swim*	**schwamm**
singen	*to sing*	**sang**
sinken	*to sink*	**sank**
sitzen	*to sit*	**sass**
springen	*to jump*	**sprang**
stinken	*to stink*	**stank**
trinken	*to drink*	**trank**

ie		*a*
liegen	*to lie*	**lag**
o		*a*
kommen	*to come*	**kam**
u		*a*
tun	*to do*	**tat**

36. Complete the following with the appropriate imperfect form of the indicated verb.

1. Wir ______ Schokolade. *essen*
2. Ich ______ viel Geld. *gewinnen*
3. Er ______ über die Hürde. *springen*
4. Wir ______ das Haus. *sehen*
5. Er ______ am Abend. *kommen*
6. Ich ______ das Gedicht. *lesen*
7. Er ______ die Zeitung. *nehmen*
8. Die Hunde ______ ins Wasser. *springen*
9. Ich ______ nichts. *tun*
10. Das Schiff ______ schnell. *sinken*
11. Der Bandit ______ uns die Hände. *binden*
12. Die Frau ______ an Krebs. *sterben*
13. Meine Tanten ______ mir nichts. *geben*
14. Wir ______ auf dem Sofa. *sitzen*
15. Ich ______ die Bilder. *sehen*
16. Er ______ die Lektüre. *beginnen*
17. Die Leute ______ im Bodensee. *schwimmen*
18. Es ______ nach faulen Eiern. *stinken*
19. Ihr ______ uns im Zentrum. *treffen*
20. Ich ______ Ursel. *bitten*
21. Das Kind ______ den Ball. *werfen*
22. Du ______ darüber. *sprechen*
23. Wir ______ den Film. *sehen*
24. Otto ______ das Geld. *stehlen*
25. Ich ______ deine Schwester. *treffen*
26. Wir ______ dem Kranken. *helfen*
27. Die Leute ______ dort. *stehen*
28. Herr Kraus ______ seine Aktentasche. *vergessen*
29. Der Ingenieur ______ den Wasserstand. *messen*
30. Wir ______ nicht auf den Teppich. *treten*

37. Form sentences from the following, using the imperfect tense.

1. Der Hund / fressen / das Futter.
2. Die Bücher / liegen / auf dem Tisch.
3. Wir / springen / aus dem Fenster.
4. Ich / sitzen / auf einem Stuhl.
5. Die Sängerin / singen / die Arie.
6. Die Kinder / trinken / keinen Wein.
7. Er / finden / die Diamantbrosche.
8. Wir / kommen / um acht Uhr.
9. Ich / sehen / Monika / im Kino.
10. Er / tun / alles.

Changes from **a** *to* **u**

The following verbs change to **u** in the imperfect tense:

Infinitive		*Imperfect*
a		*u*
fahren	*to drive, go*	**fuhr**
graben	*to dig*	**grub**
schlagen	*to hit*	**schlug**
tragen	*to carry, wear*	**trug**
wachsen	*to grow*	**wuchs**
waschen	*to wash*	**wusch**

38. Rewrite the following in the imperfect tense.

1. Die Lehrerinnen fahren in die Stadt.
2. Ich schlage ihn nicht.
3. Die Alte gräbt ein Loch.
4. Wir tragen Lederhosen.
5. Das Baby wächst schnell.
6. Tante Ida wäscht die Bettwäsche.
7. Er trägt etwas.
8. Ich fahre mit dem Zug.

Auxiliary Verbs *sein, haben, werden*

The use of the imperfect tense of the auxiliary verbs **sein, haben** and **werden** is not restricted to narration as is true with other verbs. All imperfect forms of **sein, haben** and **werden** are freely used in conversation. The imperfect forms of these verbs are irregular. Study the following:

ich war	**ich hatte**	**ich wurde**
du warst	**du hattest**	**du wurdest**
er war	**er hatte**	**er wurde**
wir waren	**wir hatten**	**wir wurden**
ihr wart	**ihr hattet**	**ihr wurdet**
sie waren	**sie hatten**	**sie wurden**

39. Complete with the correct imperfect form of **sein.**

1. Wie _____ die Oper?
2. Wo _____ du?
3. Ich _____ in Regensburg.
4. _____ du krank?
5. Wir _____ sehr müde.
6. _____ ihr zu Hause?
7. Herr Breu, _____ Sie nervös?
8. Meine Geschwister _____ schon fertig.
9. _____ ihr auch dort?
10. Mutter _____ sehr böse.

40. Complete with the correct imperfect form of **haben.**

1. _____ du Angst?
2. Die Jungen _____ Hunger.
3. Wir _____ Geld.
4. Ich _____ nichts.
5. _____ du keine Zeit?
6. _____ ihr Durst?
7. _____ du Glück?
8. Gisela _____ keinen Freund.
9. _____ ihr auch Kameras?
10. _____ Sie ein Auto?

41. Complete with the correct imperfect form of **werden.**

1. Unsre Eltern ______ immer älter.
2. Wir ______ schnell wieder gesund.
3. Es ______ sehr heiss.
4. Klaus ______ Doktor.
5. Ich ______ böse.
6. Fräulein Eber ______ nervös.
7. Wann ______ du krank?
8. ______ ihr auch hungrig?
9. ______ er böse?
10. Wann ______ ihr müde?

Use of the Imperfect Tense

Narrative Past

In German the imperfect tense (narrative past) is used mainly to narrate or report a chain of events that took place in the past. The imperfect is not interchangeable with the present perfect tense (conversational past), which is used when the speaker talks or asks about single past events. The following exemplifies the different use of these two past tenses. Note that the imperfect of **sein, haben** and **werden** is used in narration as well as in conversation.

Narration

"Ich **war** letzten Sonntag mit Bärbel in Garmisch. Wir **trafen** dort ihren Bruder und **machten** zusammen eine Radtour. Ich **wurde** schon nach einer Stunde müde. Endlich **kamen** wir zu einem Rasthaus, wo wir uns ein gutes Essen **bestellten. . . .**"

Conversation

"Was **hast** du letzten Sonntag **gemacht**?"
"Ich **war** mit Bärbel in Garmisch."
"**Habt** ihr jemand **getroffen**?"
"Ja, wir **haben** ihren Bruder **getroffen** und **haben** zusammen eine Radtour **gemacht.**"
"**Seid** ihr weit **gefahren**?"
"Ja, aber ich **wurde** schon nach einer Stunde müde."
"**Habt** ihr nicht **gerastet**?"
"Doch, endlich **sind** wir zu einem Rasthaus **gekommen,** wo wir uns ein gutes Essen **bestellt haben. . .** "

42. Rewrite the following in paragraph form, using the narrative past.

1. Peter hat mich gestern besucht.
2. Wir haben Limonade getrunken.
3. Er hat auch ein Stück Schokoladenkuchen gegessen.
4. Wir sind ins Zentrum gefahren.
5. Wir haben dort seine Freunde getroffen und wir sind ins Kino gegangen.
6. Der Film war prima. Er hat mir sehr gefallen.
7. Wir sind um acht Uhr nach Hause gekommen.
8. Wir haben eine Stunde Platten gespielt und haben über Musik gesprochen.
9. Meine Mutter hat noch Wurstbrote gemacht.
10. Peter ist danach nach Hause gegangen.

Expression of Simultaneous Past Events.

The imperfect is used to express that two actions took place at the same time. The dependent clauses are often introduced by **während** (*while, during the time which*) or **als** (*when*). Note that the verb is in last position in clauses introduced by **während** and **als.**

Sie ***trank*** **Kaffee, als er ins Zimmer** ***kam.***	*She was drinking coffee when he came into the room.*

Ich ***arbeitete*** **nicht, als ich krank** ***war.*** — *I did not work when I was ill.*
Er ***las*** **einen Roman, während ich** ***studierte.*** — *He was reading a novel while I was studying.*

43. Complete the following with the appropriate imperfect form of the indicated verbs.

1. Ich ______, während er ______. *schlafen, lesen*
2. Er ______, während Karin ______. *lächeln, singen*
3. Wir ______, während die Leute ______. *essen, tanzen*
4. Ich ______, als das Telefon ______. *schreiben, klingeln*
5. Er ______ Wein, als er mich ______. *kaufen, treffen*
6. Wir ______ nach Hause, als es kalt ______. *gehen, werden*
7. Er ______, als ich die Geschichte ______. *lachen, erzählen*
8. Wir ______ draussen, als du ______. *sein, kommen*
9. Ich ______ Klaus, als er ______. *helfen, bluten*
10. Wir ______, während er das Gras ______. *schwimmen, schneiden*

Customary Past Occurrence

The German imperfect tense is used to express habitual past action. Words like **gewöhnlich** (*usually*) and **immer** (*always*) occur in such sentences. In English the usual action is expressed by *used to.*

Wir ***besuchten*** **sie immer.** — *We always used to visit her.*
Er ***schlief*** **gewöhnlich die ganze Nacht.** — *He usually slept the whole night.*

44. Form sentences from the following, using the imperfect tense to show customary occurrence.

1. Wir / fahren / gewöhnlich / in die Schweiz.
2. Ich / sein / immer / krank.
3. Die Damen / trinken / gewöhnlich / Tee.
4. Die Schauspielerin / werden / immer / nervös.
5. Wir / gehen / sonntags / gewöhnlich / zur Kirche.
6. Er / arbeiten / immer
7. Karin / trinken / gewöhnlich / Limonade.
8. Wir / geben / den Kindern / immer / Geld.
9. Ich / helfen / Renate / immer.
10. Wir / spielen / gewöhnlich / moderne Musik.

REVIEW

45. Complete the following with the appropriate imperfect form of the indicated verb.

1. Wann ______ du krank? *werden*
2. Inge ______ an einer schlimmen Krankheit. *leiden*
3. Ich ______ dort ein ganzes Jahr. *arbeiten*
4. Er ______ das Autofenster. *öffnen*
5. Der Mechaniker ______ es. *reparieren*
6. Die Touristen ______ das Schloss. *besichtigen*
7. ______ ihr böse? *sein*
8. Ich ______ den Film. *sehen*

9. Er ______, als ich ______. *schlafen, kommen*
10. ______ du keine Zeit? *haben*
11. Herr Wimmer, ______ Sie auch dort? *sein*
12. Thomas ______ das Geld. *nehmen*
13. Ich ______ viel Wasser, während ich krank ______. *trinken, sein*
14. Wir ______ ihm das Bild. *zeigen*
15. Man ______ immer. *klingeln*
16. Das Kind ______ durch den Garten. *laufen*
17. Die Haushälterin ______ die Wäsche. *waschen*
18. Ich ______ seine Adresse. *vergessen*
19. Wir ______ gewöhnlich um zehn Uhr dort. *sein*
20. Ich ______ ein Buch, während Ulrich ______. *lesen, studieren*

FUTURE TENSE

Weak and Strong Verbs

The future tense of both weak and strong verbs is formed with the auxiliary verb **werden** and the infinitive. The infinitive is in last position, unless it occurs in a dependent clause. Study the following conjugation:

ich werde suchen	**wir werden suchen**
du wirst suchen	**ihr werdet suchen**
er wird suchen	**sie werden suchen**

Ich *werde* dich nicht *vergessen*.	*I shall not forget you.*
***Werdet* ihr auch *kommen*?**	*Will you also come?*
Wir *werden* einen Hund *kaufen*.	*We are going to buy a dog.*
Ich weiss, dass du *kommen wirst*.	*I know that you will come.*

46. Complete the following with the correct future form of the indicated verb.

1. ______ ihr hier ______? *bleiben*
2. ______ du ______? *telefonieren*
3. Die Leute ______ es nicht ______. *glauben*
4. Ich ______ die Rechnung ______. *bezahlen*
5. Er ______ es ______. *lesen*
6. Wir ______ es ______. *machen*
7. ______ ihr uns ______? *helfen*
8. Die Kinder ______ den Brief ______. *schreiben*
9. Ich ______ die Tür ______. *öffnen*
10. ______ du den Mantel ______? *kaufen*
11. Was ______ ihr ______? *bestellen*
12. Warum ______ er nicht ______? *kommen*
13. Ich ______ es nicht ______. *vergessen*
14. Wir ______ das Metall ______. *biegen*
15. Die Leute ______ laut ______. *schreien*
16. Du ______ in der Kälte ______. *frieren*

Use of the Future Tense

The future tense is most commonly used if the adverb indicating future time is not expressed. If such an adverb occurs in the sentence, the present tense is used in German, like in English. Compare the following:

Wir *werden* **unsre Freunde** *besuchen.*	*We shall visit our friends.*
Ich *fahre morgen* **nach Stuttgart.**	*I am going to Stuttgart tomorrow.*

47. Rewrite the following in the future tense, omitting the adverb of time.

1. Wir bringen morgen das Auto.
2. Ich fahre nächste Woche nach Berlin.
3. Kommst du übermorgen?
4. Er schreibt das Gedicht morgen abend.
5. Zeigt ihr euren Eltern das Haus nächsten Monat?
6. Sie arbeiten heute abend.
7. Ich esse morgen bei Inge.
8. Kaufst du es morgen nachmittag?

Probability

In German the future tense is used especially to express probability. When used in this way, the adverbs **vielleicht** (*perhaps*) and **wohl** (*probably*) occur in the sentence.

Du *wirst wohl* **müde** *sein.*	*You are probably tired.*
Sie *werden vielleicht schlafen.*	*Perhaps they are sleeping.*

48. Write the German.

1. Perhaps she is ill.
2. We are probably coming.
3. Perhaps they are crying.
4. Children, you are probably hungry. (*Hunger haben*)
5. Peter, you probably know it.
6. I am probably going.
7. He is probably working.
8. Perhaps they are helping.

PLUPERFECT TENSE

Weak and Strong Verbs

The pluperfect tense of weak and strong verbs is formed with the imperfect form of either the auxiliary **haben** or **sein** + past participle. Study the following:

ich hatte gesucht	**ich war gegangen**
du hattest gesucht	**du warst gegangen**
er hatte gesucht	**er war gegangen**
wir hatten gesucht	**wir waren gegangen**
ihr hattet gesucht	**ihr wart gegangen**
sie hatten gesucht	**sie waren gegangen**

Ich *hatte* die Geschichte *gehört*. — *I had heard the story.*
Wir *waren* zu Hause *geblieben*. — *We had stayed at home.*
Er *war* schon dort *gewesen*. — *He had already been there.*
Sie *hatten* den Hund *gefüttert*. — *They had fed the dog.*

49. Rewrite the following in the pluperfect tense.

1. Wir haben getanzt.
2. Hast du gesungen?
3. Sie sind gefahren.
4. Habt ihr gefragt?
5. Man hat es genommen.
6. Sie haben viel getrunken.
7. Hast du studiert?
8. Ich habe es repariert.
9. Wann ist er gekommen?
10. Er hat mich besucht.
11. Hast du den Wagen gewaschen?
12. Konrad ist dort geblieben.
13. Ich habe die Jacke getragen.
14. Sie ist in Rom gewesen.
15. Hat er dem Kranken geholfen?
16. Wir haben gearbeitet.

Use of the Pluperfect Tense

In German, as in English, the pluperfect is used to relate events that took place before another past event. Note that the conjunction **denn** (*for*) does not affect the word order of the clause that contains the pluperfect form of the verb. The imperfect tense is used in the main clause. Study the following examples.

Ich war müde, denn ich *hatte* den ganzen Tag *gearbeitet*.
I was tired, for I had worked the entire day.
Er hatte Hunger, denn er *hatte* nichts *gegessen*.
He was hungry, for he had not eaten anything.

50. Follow the model.

Ich bin glücklich. Ich habe Geld gewonnen.
Ich war glücklich, denn ich hatte Geld gewonnen.

1. Wir sind arm. Wir haben alles verloren.
2. Sie hat Angst. Sie ist schon oft im Krankenhaus gewesen.
3. Ich weiss alles. Ich habe viel studiert.
4. Sie bestellen viel. Sie haben den ganzen Tag nichts gegessen.
5. Laura ist traurig. Ihr Freund hat sie nicht besucht.
6. Sie sind schwach. Sie waren krank.
7. Ich bin müde. Ich habe schlecht geschlafen.
8. Wir haben Durst. Wir haben nichts getrunken.
9. Es riecht nach Gas. Er hat die Flasche zerbrochen.
10. Ich habe kein Geld. Ich habe viel gekauft.

FUTURE PERFECT TENSE

Weak and Strong Verbs

The future perfect tense is formed with the present tense of **werden** + past participle + auxiliary verb (**haben** or **sein**).

ich werde gemacht haben — **ich werde gefahren sein**
du wirst gemacht haben — **du wirst gefahren sein**
er wird gemacht haben — **er wird gefahren sein**

wir werden gemacht haben	**wir werden gefahren sein**
ihr werdet gemacht haben	**ihr werdet gefahren sein**
sie werden gemacht haben	**sie werden gefahren sein**

Use of the Future Perfect Tense

The future perfect is used mainly to express past probability. When it is used in this way, the adverbs **vielleicht** (*perhaps*) and **wohl** (*probably*) occur in the sentence. Otherwise this tense is rarely used.

Er *wird* **wohl lange** *geschlafen haben.*	*He was probably sleeping for a long time.*
Sie *werden* **vielleicht dort** *geblieben sein.*	*They probably stayed there.*

51. Rewrite the following in the future perfect tense. Add **wohl** to the sentence.

1. Ihr habt getanzt.
2. Sie sind gekommen.
3. Maria hat geschlafen.
4. Wir haben es nicht gesehen.
5. Du hast nicht gefragt.
6. Er hat das Gedicht geschrieben.
7. Der Hund hat Manfred gebissen.
8. Du hast lange gewartet.

VERBS WITH INSEPARABLE PREFIXES

Verbs whose prefix is **be-, emp-, ent-, er-, ge-, ver-, zer-** are called inseparable prefix verbs, because the prefix stays attached to the verb at all times. The inseparable prefix verbs are conjugated like other verbs, except that their past participle is not prefixed by **ge-**. The inseparable prefixes are never stressed in pronunciation, and they do not have an independent meaning. However, they do change the meaning of the verbs to which they are prefixed. Only the prefix **zer-** has a constant meaning. It denotes destruction or reduction to small parts or components: **drücken** (*to squeeze*), **zerdrücken** (*to squash*). The prefix **be** makes a verb transitive (one that can be followed by a direct object, and is conjugated with **haben.**): **Er** *ist gekommen.* But: **Er** *hat* **Geld** *bekommen.*

Note how the different prefixes alter the meaning of the verb.

stehen—*to stand*

bestehen	*to pass, persist*	**Ich** *habe* **das Examen** *bestanden.*
entstehen	*to originate*	**Wie** *entsteht* **das Gas?**
gestehen	*to confess*	**Er** *gestand* **alles.**
verstehen	*to understand*	**Sie** *werden* **das Problem** *verstehen.*

fallen—*to fall*

entfallen	*to fall out of, to slip*	**Sein Name** *ist* **mir** *entfallen.*
gefallen	*to be pleasing*	**Das Kleid** *hat* **ihr** *gefallen.*
verfallen	*to decline*	*Verfällt* **das Zentrum?**
zerfallen	*to fall apart*	**Der Kuchen** *ist zerfallen.*

52. Complete the following with the appropriate present tense form of the indicated verb.

1. Ute ______ ein Klavier. *bekommen*
2. Ich ______ alles. *zerbrechen*
3. Er ______ das Bild. *verkaufen*
4. Wir ______ die Antwort. *verstehen*
5. Ich ______ die Gäste. *empfangen*
6. Er ______ Kuchen. *bestellen*
7. ______ dir das Motorrad? *gefallen*
8. ______ ihr eure Eltern? *besuchen*
9. Ich ______ das Problem. *erklären*
10. ______ du alles? *erzählen*
11. Wir ______ das Hotel. *empfehlen*
12. Du ______ alles. *vergessen*

53. Rewrite the following in the present perfect tense.

1. Wir verstehen das Wort.
2. Es gefällt mir nicht.
3. Sie gestehen die Wahrheit.
4. Warum zerfällt es?
5. Ich bestehe das Examen.
6. Wer besucht dich?
7. Verkauft ihr das Haus?
8. Er empfängt den Brief.
9. Warum erzählst du alles?
10. Was entdeckt er?

VERBS WITH SEPARABLE PREFIXES

Certain German prefixes are called separable, because they are separated from the verb under certain conditions. Many prefixes are adverbs or prepositions, some are verbs. Such separable prefixes have definite meanings and very often denote direction. Unlike inseparable prefixes, separable prefixes are always accented. The following separable prefixes are frequently used. Their primary meanings are given.

ab	*off, down*	**abfliegen** (*to take off*), **abschreiben** (*to copy down*)
an	*at, on*	**anschauen** (*to look at*), **anziehen** (*to put on*)
auf	*up, open*	**aufstehen** (*to get up*), **aufmachen** (*to open up*)
aus	*out*	**ausbrechen** (*to break out*), **ausbrennen** (*to burn out*)
ein	*into, in*	**eintreten** (*to step into*), **einsteigen** (*to get into*)
fort	*away*	**fortgehen** (*to go away*), **fortbleiben** (*to stay away*)
heim	*home*	**heimkommen** (*to come home*), **heimgehen** (*to go home*)
her	*toward the speaker—hither*	**hersehen** (*to look toward*), **herkommen** (*to come toward*)
hin	*away from the speaker—there*	**hingehen** (*to go there*), **hinwerfen** (*to throw there*)
mit	*with, along*	**mitfahren** (*to ride along*), **mitlachen** (*to laugh along*)
nach	*after*	**nachschauen** (*to look after*), **nachkommen** (*to come after*)
nieder	*down*	**niederlegen** (*to lie down*), **niedersetzen** (*to sit down*)
vor	*before*	**vorsetzen** (*to set before*), **vorlegen** (*to put before*)
weg	*away*	**weglaufen** (*to run away*), **wegnehmen** (*to take away*)
zu	*to, close*	**zuhören** (*to listen to*), **zumachen** (*to close*)
zurück	*back*	**zurücknehmen** (*to take back*), **zurückgeben** (*to give back*)
zusammen	*together*	**zusammenkommen** (*to come together*), **zusammennähen** (*to stitch together*)

Not all German prefixes can be translated into idiomatic English by using these equivalents:

aussehen	*to look like*	**nachmachen**	*to imitate*
ausbessern	*to improve*	**zusammenlegen**	*to fold*

Three commonly used verbs with separable prefixes are as follows:

kennenlernen *to become acquainted with*

spazierengehen *to take a walk*
spazierenfahren *to go for a ride*

Position of the Separable Prefix

The separable prefix always occurs at the end of a sentence or clause, either separated or prefixed to the verb.

The prefix occurs separately at the end of the sentence in the following instances:

Present Tense

Ich *gehe* **oft** *aus.*
Kommst **du auch** *heim?*
Geht **ihr morgen** *mit?*

54. Complete the following with the correct present tense of the indicated verb.

1. Er ______ in den Zug ______. *einsteigen*
2. Wir ______ oft ______. *zusammenkommen*
3. Ich ______ auch ______. *mitfahren*
4. Warum ______ du den warmen Mantel ______? *anziehen*
5. ______ ihr euch schon ______? *niederlegen*
6. Wann ______ ihn deine Eltern ______? *kennenlernen*
7. Wann ______ du ______? *zurückkommen*
8. Ich ______ nicht gern ______. *hingehen*
9. Wann ______ ihr ______? *aufstehen*
10. Deine Freunde ______ mit uns ______. *spazierenfahren*

Imperfect Tense

Sie *ging* **abends** *spazieren.*
Warum *schaute* **sie es** *an?*

55. Form sentences from the following, using the imperfect tense.

1. Er / aufessen / alles.
2. Ich / abschreiben / das Lied.
3. Wir / kennenlernen / ihn.
4. Arnim / einsammeln / für die Armen.
5. Kinder / nachmachen / alles.
6. Wer / zumachen / das Fenster?
7. Wie / zusammennähen / er / das Leder?
8. Wann / heimgehen / die Studenten?

Imperative Mode

See the section on the imperative mode.

Geh **mit uns** *spazieren!*
Kommt **bald** *zurück!*
Lernen **Sie Arnold** *kennen!*

56. Write the imperative. Follow the model.

Irmgard, herkommen schnell.
Irmgard, komm schnell her!

1. Gisela, weglaufen nicht.
2. Frau Bayer, zumachen schnell.
3. Konrad, mitfahren bitte.
4. Ursula und Theo, eintreten leise.
5. Fräulein Breu, aufstehen langsam.
6. Helga, herkommen doch.
7. Mutter, zumachen die Schachtel.
8. Arno, anschauen es nicht.

Compound Tenses

The prefix is joined to the verb when the separable prefix verb occurs in last position, as in the following instances:

Future Tense

Er *wird* wohl *mitessen.*
Ich werde nicht ausgehen.

57. Rewrite in the future tense.

1. Wir gehen fort.
2. Ich gehe hinaus.
3. Er bringt es zurück.
4. Sie nehmen nichts weg.
5. Gehst du aus?
6. Ich schaue das Album an.

Present Perfect

Sie *sind* schon *angekommen.*

Pluperfect

Ich *hatte* es schon *aufgemacht.*

Note that the separable prefix verbs, unlike the inseparable prefix verbs, add the **ge-** prefix in the past participle. It comes between the prefix and the verb suffix.

Infinitive	*Past Participle*
ausgehen	**aus*ge*gangen**
kennenlernen	**kennen*ge*lernt**
mitkommen	**mit*ge*kommen**

58. Rewrite in the present perfect tense.

1. Sie lachten auch mit.
2. Wir schauten bei ihr nach.
3. Ich lernte ihn kennen.
4. Der Zug kam bald an.
5. Wir gingen spazieren.
6. Ich fuhr mit ihm heim.
7. Gudrun stand dann auf.
8. Sie schauten bald nach.

59. Fill in the correct pluperfect form of the indicated verb.

1. Er ______ sofort ______. *einsteigen*
2. Ich ______ das Licht ______. *ausmachen*
3. Wir ______ es ______. *abschreiben*
4. Die Kinder ______ die Bücher ______. *niederlegen*
5. ______ ihr ______? *zusammenkommen*
6. Ich ______ ihn ______. *kennenlernen*
7. Unsre Eltern ______ lange ______. *fortbleiben*
8. Wer ______ uns ______? *zuhören*

Separable Prefix Verbs in Dependent Clauses

The separable prefix is never separated from the verb when the separable prefix verb occurs in a dependent clause. Study the following.

Present — **Ich weiss, dass er bald** *ankommt.*
Imperfect — **Er lachte, als ich** *hinfiel.*
Future — **Sie weiss, warum ich** *mitgehen werde.*
Present Perfect — **Ich freue mich, dass du** *heimgekommen bist.*
Pluperfect — **Er weiss, dass er** *abgeschrieben hatte.*

60. Rewrite the following, introducing each sentence with **Ich weiss, dass. . .**

1. Er ist fortgegangen.
2. Sie wird herkommen.
3. Wir fliegen morgen ab.
4. Ihr habt Peter kennengelernt.
5. Der Zug war angekommen.
6. Ich komme nach.
7. Er ging aus.
8. Wir werden heimkommen.
9. Du fährst mit.
10. Er hatte nachgeschaut.

VERBS FOLLOWED BY SPECIAL CASES

Dative Case

The following verbs are always followed by the dative case:

antworten *to answer* **Wir antworten** *dem Lehrer.*
danken *to thank* **Er dankte** *seiner Tante.*
folgen *to obey, to follow* **Folgst du** *deiner Mutter?*
gefallen *to like, to be pleasing to* **Der Film hat** *den Kindern* **gefallen.**
gehören *to belong to* **Das gehört** *seiner Freundin.*
glauben *to believe* **Ich glaube** *meinem Freund.*
gratulieren *to congratulate* **Wir gratulieren** *ihr* **zum Geburtstag.**
schmecken *to like, to taste good* **Dieses Fleisch schmeckt** *mir.*

Dative and Accusative Case

The following verbs can be followed by both the dative and the accusative cases. The person to whom something is given, shown, etc. is in the dative case. Whatever is given, shown, etc. is in the accusative.

bringen *to bring, take* **Sie bringt** *dem Kranken Suppe.*
geben *to give* **Er gibt** *seiner Tochter das Gold.*
holen *to get* **Wir holen** *dem Hasen eine Karotte.*
kaufen *to buy* **Ich kaufte** *den Kindern das Spielzeug.*
sagen *to say, tell* **Sie sagen** *ihren Eltern die Wahrheit.*
schenken *to give, present* **Ich habe** *meinem Vater eine Krawatte* **geschenkt.**
schicken *to send* **Wer hat** *dir das Paket* **geschickt?**
schreiben *to write* **Er hat** *seiner Freundin einen Brief* **geschrieben.**
zeigen *to show* **Sie zeigten** *den Touristen den Hafen.*

61. Write sentences from the following, using the present tense of the verbs.

1. Ich / zeigen / das Kind / das Buch.
2. Er / schicken / dein Mutter / ein Karte.
3. Wir / glauben / der Mann.
4. Ich / bringen / die Studentin / der Roman.

5. Danken / du / dein Lehrer?
6. Wir / helfen / unser Grossmutter.
7. Das Haus / gehören / mein Eltern.
8. Antworten / ihr / die Lehrerin?
9. Maria / kaufen / ihr Freundin / ein Kette.
10. Der Wagen / gehören / mein Bruder.
11. Wer / holen / der Kranke / ein Pille?
12. Die Blumen / gefallen / unser Tante.
13. Warum / gratulieren / du / dein Schwester?
14. Er / schenken / das Baby / ein Puppe.
15. Wir / schicken / der Präsident / ein Protest.
16. Die Kinder / folgen / das Kindermädchen.

Prepositional Objects

Many German verbs + prepositions are followed by either the dative or accusative case. Often the German prepositions do not correspond to the prepositions used with the English verbs.

Accusative Objects after **an, auf, über**

When verbs are followed by the prepositions **an, auf, über,** the prepositions govern the accusative case. Study the following examples:

antworten auf	*to reply to something*	**Wir** *antworten auf* **seine Frage.**
denken an	*to think of*	**Ich** *denke* **oft** *an* **meine Freundin.**
glauben an	*to believe in*	**Wir** *glaubten an* **seine Unschuld.**
hoffen auf	*to hope for*	**Er** *hat auf* **gutes Wetter** *gehofft.*
lachen über	*to laugh about*	**Sie** *hat* **nicht** *über* **das Thema** *gelacht.*
sprechen über	*to talk about in detail*	*Sprecht* **ihr** *über* **das Instrument?**
warten auf	*to wait for*	**Warum** *hast* **du nicht** *auf* **deine Eltern** *gewartet?*

Dative Objects after **von, zu, nach, vor**

The dative case is used after the following verbs + prepositions.

fragen nach	*to ask about*	**Er** *fragte nach* **meiner Mutter.**
gehören zu	*to be a part or a member of*	**Otto** *gehört* **auch** *zum* **Klub.**
halten von	*to think of something or somebody*	**Was** *hältst* **du** *von* **dem Programm?**
hören von	*to hear from*	**Ich** *habe* **heute** *von* **meiner Schwester** *gehört.*
sprechen von	*to talk of*	**Er** *hat von* **seiner Reise** *gesprochen.*
suchen nach	*look for*	**Ich** *suche nach* **meinen Eltern.**
träumen von	*dream about*	**Sie** *träumte von* **ihrem Hund.**
wissen von	*to know about*	**Er** *weiss* **nichts** *von* **diesem Thema.**

62. Complete the following with the correct case endings.

1. Er fragte nach mein_____ Adresse.
2. Er weiss nichts von d_____ Thema.
3. Sie lachte über d_____ Frage.
4. Sie brachte ihr_____ Mann ein_____ Krawatte.
5. Wir glauben d_____ Kind.
6. Was hältst du von sein_____ Frau?

7. Das Buch gehört zu dies____ Sammlung.
8. Hast du dein____ Freund geholfen?
9. Warum dankst du nicht sein____ Mutter?
10. Ich habe mein____ Bruder nicht geantwortet.
11. Dieses Bild gefällt mein____ Freundin.
12. Wer wartet auf d____ Zug?
13. Sucht ihr nach d____ Schule?
14. Ich träume von mein____ Reise.
15. Wir antworten auf sein____ Brief.
16. Ich schenke mein____ Grossmutter ein____ Orchidee.
17. Hast du d____ Geburtstagskind gratuliert?
18. Die Torte schmeckte mein____ Mutter.

REFLEXIVE VERBS

The reflexive verb expresses that the action is both executed and received by the subject. A reflexive construction consists of a subject, verb and pronoun, the subject and pronoun being the same person or thing. The object pronoun used to show this relationship is called a reflexive pronoun. The reflexive pronoun may be in the accusative or dative case, depending on the verb used.

Reflexive Verbs Governing the Accusative Case

The following is a partial list of common reflexive verbs followed by accusative reflexive pronouns.

sich amüsieren	*to enjoy, amuse oneself*
sich anziehen	*to dress*
sich aufregen	*to get excited*
sich ausziehen	*to undress*
sich benehmen	*to behave*
sich bewegen	*to move*
sich entscheiden	*to decide*
sich entschuldigen	*to apologize, to excuse oneself*
sich erinnern an	*to remember*
sich erkälten	*to catch cold*
sich freuen	*to be glad*
sich freuen auf	*to look forward to*
sich freuen über	*to be glad about*
sich fürchten vor	*to be afraid of*
sich gewöhnen an	*to get used to*
sich interessieren für	*to be interested in*
sich legen	*to lie down*
sich rasieren	*to shave*
sich setzen	*to sit down*
sich stellen	*to place oneself*
sich umziehen	*to change (clothing)*
sich unterhalten	*to converse, to enjoy oneself*
sich verletzen	*to hurt oneself*
sich verspäten	*to be late*
sich vorstellen	*to introduce oneself*

sich waschen	*to wash oneself*
sich wundern über	*to be surprised at*
sich zuwenden	*to turn to*

Accusative Reflexive Pronouns

The accusative reflexive pronouns are identical with the accusative personal pronouns, except in the third person singular and plural.

ich wasche mich	**wir waschen uns**
du wäschst dich	**ihr wascht euch**
er wäscht sich	**sie waschen sich**

Er *interessiert sich* **für klassische Musik.**
Ich *fürchte mich* **vor grossen Hunden.**
Sie *werden sich* **wohl an ihn** *erinnern.*
Ich *habe mich* **schon** *rasiert.*
Sie *legte sich* **aufs Sofa.**
Warum *hast* **du** *dich* **nicht** *entschuldigt?*

The reflexive pronoun is placed as close as possible to the subject. However, it never comes between pronoun subject and verb.

Rasierst du *dich* **jeden Tag?**
Ich habe *mich* **darüber gewundert.**

Reflexive Verbs with Separable Prefixes

The separable prefixes of reflexive verbs are treated like prefixes of verbs used non-reflexively. (See section on separable prefix verbs.)

Ich *ziehe mich* **nicht** *aus.*
Er *zog sich an.*
Sie *werden sich* **wohl** *umziehen.*
Warum *hast* **du** *dich aufgeregt?*

63. Complete the following with the correct reflexive verb and pronoun. Use the present tense.

1. Ich _______ _______ für Chemie. *sich interessieren*
2. Wir _______ _______ über Politik. *sich unterhalten*
3. Du _______ _______ so _______. *sich aufregen*
4. Wohin _______ ihr _______? *sich setzen*
5. Ich _______ _______ sehr oft. *sich erkälten*
6. Wann _______ du _______ _______? *sich vorstellen*
7. Die Eltern _______ _______ _______. *sich umziehen*
8. Er _______ _______. *sich freuen*
9. Ursula _______ _______ aufs Sofa. *sich legen*
10. Wir _______ _______ über das Geschenk. *sich freuen*
11. Unser Vater _______ _______. *sich rasieren*
12. Ich _______ _______ immer. *sich amüsieren*
13. Das Tier _______ _______ schnell. *sich bewegen*
14. _______ du _______ auf die Ferien? *sich freuen*
15. _______ ihr _______? *sich waschen*
16. Er _______ _______ nicht. *sich entscheiden*

17. Ich ______ ______ oft. *sich verspäten*
18. ______ Sie ______ an meinen Onkel? *sich erinnern*
19. Der Junge ______ ______ schon ______. *sich anziehen*
20. ______ du ______ immer? *sich entschuldigen*

64. Rewrite in the present perfect tense.

1. Er fürchtet sich vor Pferden.
2. Wir interessieren uns für die Sammlung.
3. Sie benehmen sich ganz nett.
4. Freut ihr euch über das Geschenk?
5. Ich ziehe mich schon um.
6. Wir stellen uns heute vor.
7. Erkältest du dich oft?
8. Sie wäscht sich schon.
9. Die Männer rasieren sich.
10. Verspätet ihr euch?

65. Answer the following questions, using the cue.

1. Warauf hast du dich gefreut? *auf seine Ankunft*
2. Wohin legt ihr euch denn? *aufs Bett*
3. Wann hast du dich verletzt? *am Freitag*
4. Wofür interessierst du dich? *für Briefmarken*
5. Woran hast du dich schon gewöhnt? *an die Arbeit*
6. Wann hat er sich erkältet? *im Winter*
7. Worüber wundern Sie sich? *über die Explosion*
8. Wovor fürchten sich die Kinder? *vor dem Gewitter*

Imperative Forms

The reflexive pronouns are always expressed in commands. The reflexive pronoun follows a particular command form. (See section on the imperative mode.)

Setz *dich!*
Zieht *euch* **um!**
Fürchten Sie *sich* **nicht!**
Waschen wir *uns!*

66. Write the German.

1. Let's converse.
2. Children, don't be late.
3. Peter, don't catch cold.
4. Mr. Ziegler, introduce yourself.
5. Let's sit down.
6. Gisela, wash yourself.
7. Girls, excuse yourselves.
8. Mrs. Klein, amuse yourself.
9. Ute, don't be afraid of the dog.
10. Father, shave.

Reflexive Versus Nonreflexive Use of Verbs

Some German reflexive verbs can be used nonreflexively as well. The reflexive pronoun is used only when the action refers back to the subject.

Reflexive use	**Ich amüsiere mich.**	*I am amusing myself.*
Nonreflexive use	**Ich amüsiere das Baby.**	*I am amusing the baby.*

67. Complete the following with the correct reflexive pronoun when necessary.

1. Leg ______ den Mantel auf den Stuhl!
2. Er stellt ______ mich vor.
3. Ich unterhalte ______ mit ihm.
4. Sie haben ______ verletzt.
5. Er zieht ______ aus.
6. Die Mutter wäscht ______ das Kind.
7. Wir waschen ______.
8. Sie haben ______ das Tier verletzt.
9. Ich ziehe ______ das Baby an.
10. Der Barbier rasiert ______ den Mann.

Reflexive Verbs Governing the Dative Case

The dative case is required after the following reflexive verbs:

sich einbilden	*to imagine*
sich etwas vorstellen	*to imagine something*
sich weh tun	*to hurt oneself*

Dative Reflexive Pronouns

The dative reflexive pronouns are identical with the dative personal pronouns, except in the third person singular and plural. Here, as in the accusative, the reflexive pronoun is **sich.**

ich tue mir weh	**wir tun uns weh**
du tust dir weh	**ihr tut euch weh**
er tut sich weh	**sie tun sich weh**

The dative reflexive pronoun is also frequently used with such verbs as **kaufen, holen, bestellen, machen, nehmen.** Such constructions are rendered in English with *for myself* (*yourself,* etc.).

Ich ***kaufe mir*** **ein Auto.**	*I am buying a car for myself.*
Er ***holte sich*** **etwas.**	*He got something for himself.*

Dative Reflexive Pronouns with Parts of the Body

The dative reflexive pronouns are used in German to refer to parts of the body or articles of clothing, unless there is doubt as to the identity of the possessor. In English the possessive is used.

Ich habe mir die Zähne geputzt.	*I brushed my teeth.*
Ich ziehe mir die Schuhe an.	*I am putting on my shoes.*
Wäschst du dir den Kopf?	*Are you washing your hair?*

68. Complete the following with the appropriate reflexive form of the indicated verb. Use the present tense.

1. Du ______ ______ bestimmt ______. *sich weh tun*
2. Wir ______ ______ die Schuhe. *putzen*
3. Ich ______ ______ die Uhr. *kaufen*
4. Warum ______ ihr ______ nicht die Hände? *waschen*
5. Das Mädchen ______ ______ so viel ______. *sich einbilden*
6. Die Dame ______ ______ den Hut ______. *aufsetzen*
7. Er ______ ______ Bier. *bestellen*
8. Ich ______ ______ die Reise ______. *sich vorstellen*
9. Wir ______ ______ das Motorrad. *kaufen*
10. Er ______ ______ Kaffee. *holen*
11. Die Kinder ______ ______ ______. *sich weh tun*
12. Ihr ______ ______ viel ______. *sich einbilden*

13. Ich ______ ______ den Kopf. *waschen*
14. ______ ihr ______ etwas? *nehmen*
15. Wann ______ du ______ das Kleid? *machen*

69. Answer the following questions, using the cue.

1. Was stellst du dir vor? *das Haus*
2. Was haben Sie sich geholt? *das Papier*
3. Wann bestellt ihr euch das Essen? *bald*
4. Wo hast du dir weh getan? *am Fuss*
5. Wo ziehen sich die Gäste an? *im Schlafzimmer*
6. Wer bildet sich etwas ein? *Gisela*

70. Form the imperative. Follow the model.

Inge, waschen Gesicht.
Inge, wasch dir das Gesicht!

1. Herr Müller, bestellen Buch.
2. Kinder, putzen Zähne.
3. Peter und Heinz, kaufen etwas.
4. Marlene, weh tun nicht.
5. Kinder, waschen Hände.
6. Frau Wimmer, nehmen etwas.

MODAL VERBS

The following are the German modal auxiliary verbs:

dürfen	Expresses permission (*to be allowed to, may*). When used in the negative it means *must not.*
müssen	Expresses necessity (*to have to, must, to be obliged to*)
können	Expresses ability (*to be able to, can*)
mögen	Expresses the idea of (not) liking something or somebody. It is frequently used in the negative. [*(not) to like to, (not) to care for, (not) to want to*]
wollen	Expresses desire (*to want to*)
sollen	Expresses obligation (*to be supposed to, ought*)

Present Tense

The present tense of modal auxiliary verbs is irregular. Study the following forms:

dürfen		**müssen**	
ich darf	wir dürfen	ich muss	wir müssen
du darfst	ihr dürft	du musst	ihr müsst
er darf	sie dürfen	er muss	sie müssen

können		**mögen**	
ich kann	wir können	ich mag	wir mögen
du kannst	ihr könnt	du magst	ihr mögt
er kann	sie können	er mag	sie mögen

wollen		**sollen**	
ich will	wir wollen	ich soll	wir sollen
du willst	ihr wollt	du sollst	ihr sollt
er will	sie wollen	er soll	sie sollen

Note that all modals except **sollen** use a different stem vowel for the singular and the plural in the present tense. The plural stem agrees with the infinitive. The first and third person singular forms have no personal endings in the present tense.

The modal auxiliary verbs are used with the infinitive. The infinitive occurs in last position of the sentence, unless the modal + infinitive is used in a dependent clause. In a negative sentence, the **nicht** usually precedes the infinitive.

Wir *dürfen* **dem Techniker** *helfen.*	*We may help the technician.*
Darfst **du** *rauchen?*	*Are you allowed to smoke?*
Ich *darf* **mir eine Zeitung** *nehmen.*	*I am allowed to take a newspaper.*
Ihr *dürft nicht bleiben.*	*You must not stay.*
Musst **du noch** *studieren?*	*Do you still have to study?*
Ich *muss* **nach Hause** *gehen.*	*I have to go home.*
Werner *kann* **gut** *singen.*	*Werner can sing well.*
Du *kannst nicht mitkommen.*	*You cannot come along.*
Wir *mögen* **es** *nicht sehen.*	*We don't want to see it.*
Ich *mag* **es auch** *hören.*	*I like to hear it also.*
Wollt **ihr bei uns** *bleiben?*	*Do you want to stay with us?*
Ich *will* **es** *nicht machen.*	*I don't want to do it.*
Wir *sollen* **etwas** *mitbringen.*	*We ought to take something along.*
Du *sollst* **die Wahrheit** *sagen.*	*You ought to tell the truth.*

71. Complete the following with the appropriate present tense form of **dürfen.**

1. Wir _______ nicht bleiben.
2. Die Kinder _______ gehen.
3. Dieter, du _______ nicht rauchen.
4. _______ ich das Geschenk aufmachen?
5. Er _______ die Geschichte erzählen.
6. Anna, du _______ heute helfen.
7. _______ ihr das Radio kaufen?
8. Du _______ nicht gehen.

72. Rewrite the following, supplying the appropriate form of the present tense of **müssen.**

1. Er arbeitet schwer.
2. Sie holen Brot.
3. Studierst du?
4. Singen Sie heute?
5. Wir stehen auf.
6. Wann seid ihr im Büro?
7. Die Kinder bleiben zu Hause.
8. Ich bestelle das Essen.

73. Form sentences from the following, using the present tense.

1. Ich / können / glauben / die Geschichte / nicht.
2. Können / ihr / mitkommen / morgen?
3. Wir / helfen / können / unsrem Freund / nicht.
4. Max / können / gut / tanzen.
5. Können / du / langsamer / sprechen?
6. Ich / können / alles / hören.

74. Complete the following with the appropriate present tense form of **mögen.**

1. Ich _______ nicht studieren.
2. Er _______ nicht helfen.
3. Wir _______ nicht arbeiten.
4. _______ du nicht helfen?
5. _______ ihr das Auto sehen?
6. Inge _______ alles essen.
7. _______ Sie nichts anschauen?
8. Die Kinder _______ nicht schlafen.

75. Write the German, using the modal **wollen** in all instances.

1. We want to help.
2. I don't want to see it.
3. He wants to come.
4. Do they want to sleep?
5. Ursel, do you want to go?
6. She wants to study.
7. Erika and Frank, do you want to work?
8. I want to visit the museum.

76. Rewrite the following, supplying the appropriate form of the present tense of **sollen.**

1. Ich kaufe dem Kind etwas.
2. Er kommt schnell.
3. Sagst du die Wahrheit?
4. Die Studenten lernen.
5. Man stiehlt nicht.
6. Wir kommen nicht.
7. Bleibt ihr?
8. Ich repariere das Auto.

Idiomatic Expressions

In some German idiomatic expressions containing modal auxiliaries, the infinitives can be omitted. Study the following.

Er *muss* nach Hause.	*He has to go home.*
Wir *müssen* in die Stadt.	*We have to go downtown.*
***Musst* du zur Arbeit? (zur Schule)**	*Do you have to go to work? (to school)*
Gerda *kann* Deutsch.	*Gerda knows German.*
***Kannst* du Französisch?**	*Do you know French?*
Wir *mögen* keinen Kuchen.	*We don't want (to eat) any cake.*
Ich *mag* keinen Spinat.	*I don't want any spinach.*
Wir *wollen* ins Kino. (nach Hause)	*We want to go to the movies. (home)*

77. Write the German. Do not express the infinitive.

1. We know English.
2. I don't want any soup.
3. They have to go home.
4. Does he know German?
5. She has to go downtown.
6. He doesn't want any milk.

Imperfect Tense

In contrast to the present tense, the formation of the imperfect is quite regular. The following endings are added to the imperfect stems of modals: **-te, -test, -te, -ten, -tet, -ten.** The imperfect stems are as follows:

dürfen	**durf-te**	**müssen**	**muss-te**
können	**konn-te**	**sollen**	**soll-te**
mögen	**moch-te**	**wollen**	**woll-te**

Note that **dürfen, können, mögen** and **müssen** have a sound change in the imperfect stem.

Wir *konnten* die Geschichte nicht verstehen.
Er *durfte* nicht kommen.
Sie *wollte* nicht aufmachen.
Ich *musste* ihn tragen.

78. Rewrite the following in the imperfect tense.

1. Wir wollen mitmachen.
2. Ich mag keinen Reis.
3. Kannst du bleiben?
4. Dürft ihr denn rauchen?
5. Du kannst nicht heimgehen.
6. Luise will bezahlen.
7. Warum wollen Sie helfen?
8. Musst du studieren?
9. Ich will es sehen.
10. Könnt ihr das machen?

79. Write sentences from the following. Use the imperfect tense.

1. können / ihr / ihm / helfen?
2. ich / wollen / etwas / kaufen.
3. sollen / er / auch / mitmachen?
4. wir / müssen / ihn / anrufen.
5. die Kinder / mögen / kein / Gemüse.
6. dürfen / du / nicht / gehen?

Special Use of the Imperfect Tense

The imperfect tense of the modals is not restricted to narration, but is freely used in conversation and in posing questions.

80. Form questions from the following. Use the imperfect tense. Follow the model.

du abfahren? müssen
Musstest du abfahren?

1. Herr Maier, Sie schlafen? wollen
2. ihr rauchen? dürfen
3. du ausgehen? können
4. ihr Bananen? mögen
5. Fräulein Lang, Sie daran glauben? sollen
6. ihr helfen? müssen
7. du es kaufen? sollen
8. ihr fragen? wollen
9. du mitmachen? dürfen
10. ihr es sehen? können
11. Sie alles nehmen? müssen
12. ihr Bier bestellen? sollen
13. du keine Milch? mögen
14. Sie Konrad kennenlernen? wollen

Compound Tenses

Present Perfect Tense

Past Participles of Modals

The modal auxiliary verbs are unique because they have two different past participles. One is formed the conventional way with the **ge-** prefix, the other is identical to the infinitive. In either case the perfect tenses are formed with **haben.**

Past Participles Formed with* ge- *Prefix

When no infinitive is needed to convey the meaning of a particular idiomatic expression, the following past participles of the modals are used.

dürfen	**gedurft**	**müssen**	**gemusst**
können	**gekonnt**	**sollen**	**gesollt**
mögen	**gemocht**	**wollen**	**gewollt**

Ich *habe* **Französisch** *gekonnt.* — *I knew French.*
Er *hat* **nach Hause** *gemusst.* — *He had to go home.*
Wir *haben* **keinen Spinat** *gemocht.* — *We didn't like any spinach.*

81. Rewrite the following. Use the present perfect tense.

1. Ich mag ihn nicht.
2. Sie will nach Köln.
3. Darfst du das?
4. Wir müssen zur Schule.
5. Kann er das?
6. Die Leute mögen nicht.
7. Ihr könnt doch Deutsch.
8. Sie können Englisch.
9. Ich muss zur Arbeit.
10. Wir dürfen es.
11. Magst du keine Limonade?
12. Ich soll in die Stadt.

Double Infinitive Construction

When the modal is followed by the infinitive of another verb, the present perfect is then formed with a form of **haben** + infinitive of verb + infinitive of modal. This construction is called double infinitive construction, because the two infinitives occur together in last position of the sentence.

Sie *haben* **es nicht** *sehen dürfen.*	*They weren't allowed to see it.*
Ich *habe* **nicht** *arbeiten können.*	*I was not able to work.*
Hast **du den Roman** *lesen müssen?*	*Did you have to read the novel?*
Er *hat* **Gisela** *kennenlernen wollen.*	*He wanted to get acquainted with Gisela.*

82. Rewrite the following in the present perfect tense.

1. Wir sollten nicht mitfahren.
2. Ich konnte nicht schreiben.
3. Musstet ihr hier bleiben?
4. Warum wollte er anrufen?
5. Ich durfte es bringen.
6. Man konnte Musik hören.
7. Sie mochten nicht aufstehen.
8. Warum wolltest du es zerstören?
9. Er durfte es sehen.
10. Wolltet ihr dort parken?
11. Ich wollte heimgehen.
12. Musstest du zu Hause bleiben?
13. Sie konnten gut lesen.
14. Hubert musste studieren.
15. Wir wollten Maria helfen.
16. Konnten Sie schwimmen?

Pluperfect Tense

As in the formation of the present perfect tense, the pluperfect of modal auxiliaries can be formed with two different past participles. Compare the following:

Er *hatte* **Deutsch** *gekonnt.*	*He had known German.*
Wir *hatten* **es** *machen dürfen.*	*We had been allowed to do it.*

83. Rewrite the following in the pluperfect tense.

1. Wir konnten es.
2. Ich musste abfahren.
3. Er wollte es.
4. Sie mochten keinen Kuchen.
5. Sie sollte mich anrufen.
6. Durftest du sie besuchen?
7. Ich wollte nicht davon sprechen.
8. Ihr durftet es ja wissen.
9. Sie konnte das Fenster aufmachen.
10. Ich musste zur Schule.
11. Wir mochten Peter nicht.
12. Wolltest du hinausgehen?
13. Ich konnte Russisch.
14. Er musste den Wagen reparieren.

Future Tense

The future of modals is formed with a form of **werden** + infinitive + infinitive of modal.

Er *wird* **wohl nicht** *fahren können.*	*He will probably not be able to go.*
Ich *werde* **nicht** *kommen dürfen.*	*I may not be allowed to come.*

84. Change the following to the future tense.

1. Sie können nicht schlafen.
2. Wir müssen den ganzen Tag studieren.
3. Er will es sehen.
4. Ich muss klingeln.
5. Ihr dürft nichts kaufen.
6. Kannst du es schicken?
7. Gudrun will nicht mitmachen.
8. Wollt ihr die Suppe probieren?
9. Sie dürfen nicht schreien.
10. Wir können nicht arbeiten.

DEPENDENT INFINITIVES

Simple Tenses–Present and Imperfect

Like modals, the verbs **hören** (*to hear*), **sehen** (*to see*), **helfen** (*to help*) and **lassen** (*to let, to allow, to leave*) can be used either by themselves or with the infinitive of another verb. This infinitive is referred to as a dependent infinitive. Note that the verb **lassen** means *to leave* when used by itself. When used with a dependent infinitive it means *to let* or *to allow*. Compare the following:

Ich *lasse* **den Mantel hier.**	*I leave the coat here.*
Ich *lasse* **Robert** *kommen.*	*I let Robert come.*
Wir *hörten* **Musik.**	*We heard music.*
Wir *hörten* **Anita** *singen.*	*We heard Anita sing.*
Er *sah* **die Parade.**	*He saw the parade.*
Er *sah* **Inge** *kommen.*	*He saw Inge come.*
Hilfst **du Peter?**	*Are you helping Peter?*
Hilfst **du Peter** *schreiben?*	*Are you helping Peter write?*

85. Write sentences from the following, using the present tense.

1. Wir / lassen / das Bild / in der Schule.
2. Ich / helfen / Rita / den Hund / suchen.
3. Sehen / du / deine Schwester / arbeiten?
4. Hören / Sie / die Sonate?
5. Er / hören / seine Frau / schreien.
6. Lassen / ihr / Hans / gehen?
7. Die Leute / hören / uns / sprechen.
8. Ich / sehen / die Kirche.
9. Frau Berger / helfen / heute.
10. Er / lassen / Gerda / mitkommen.

Compound Tenses–Present Perfect and Pluperfect

When the verbs **hören, sehen, lassen** and **helfen** are used in the perfect tenses with a dependent infinitive, the double infinitive construction is used. If used without a dependent infinitive, the regular past participle is used. (See section on double infinitives.)

Compare the following:

Ich *habe* **das Lied** *gehört.*	*I heard the song.*
Ich *habe* **sie** *schreien hören.*	*I heard her scream.*
Wir *haben* **das Museum** *gesehen.*	*We saw the museum.*
Wir *haben* **Agnes** *malen sehen.*	*We saw Agnes paint.*
Hast **du das Buch dort** *gelassen?*	*Did you leave the book there?*
Hast **du Ute** *probieren lassen?*	*Did you let Ute try?*
Er *hatte* **auch** *geholfen.*	*He had also helped.*
Er *hatte* **auch** *waschen helfen.*	*He had also helped to wash.*

86. Rewrite the following in the present perfect tense.

1. Ich liess es liegen.
2. Wir hörten sie lachen.
3. Er sah seinen Freund.
4. Sie halfen Heinz das Auto reparieren.
5. Er hörte nichts.
6. Ich sah Pia reiten.
7. Sie hörten Sonja weinen.
8. Wir liessen die Zeitungen zu Hause.
9. Wir halfen den Kindern.
10. Vater liess uns gehen.

Future Tense

When the future tense is formed with one of the preceding verbs and a dependent infinitive, the double infinitive construction occurs at the end of the sentence.

Ich *werde* **die Sängerin** *hören.*	*I shall hear the singer.*
Ich *werde* **das Kind** *weinen hören.*	*I shall hear the child cry.*
Wir *werden* **das Bild hier** *lassen.*	*We shall leave the painting here.*
Wir *werden* **das Bild** *hängen lassen.*	*We shall let the picture hang.*

87. Rewrite the following, adding the indicated word.

1. Er wird Peter sehen. *schreiben*
2. Ich werde Otto hören. *kommen*
3. Wir werden den Kindern helfen. *zeichnen*
4. Wirst du Dieter sehen? *lachen*
5. Sie werden Rainer hören. *sprechen*
6. Werden Sie Anneliese helfen? *lesen*
7. Ich werde den Mantel hier lassen. *liegen*
8. Werdet ihr Grossmutter hören? *rufen*

Dependent Clauses

When the double infinitive construction occurs in dependent clauses, the conjugated form of the auxiliary **haben** or **werden** is not moved into last position as might be expected. Instead the auxiliary precedes the double infinitive.

Er sagt, dass er *hat kommen dürfen.*
Ich bin glücklich, weil ich Ursel *werde singen hören.*

88. Change the following main clauses to dependent clauses. Introduce the dependent clause with **Er sagt, dass. . . .** Follow the model.

Ich habe Anna lachen sehen.
Er sagt, dass ich Anna habe lachen sehen.

1. Du hast die Jacke liegen lassen.
2. Wir haben Josef studieren helfen.
3. Sie haben Franz singen hören.
4. Ich habe es machen lassen.
5. Sie hat das Geschenk öffnen dürfen.
6. Du hast den Bleistift zurückgeben wollen.
7. Wir haben Peter kommen lassen.
8. Ihr habt das Auto bringen müssen.

Preceded by *zu* (to)

Dependent infinitives are never preceded by **zu** (*to*) when used in the future tense, or when used with the modals or the verbs **sehen, hören, helfen** and **lassen.** However, dependent infinitives are preceded by **zu** (*to*) in the following instances.

After Certain Prepositions

The following prepositions introduce infinitive phrases in which the dependent infinitive is preceded by **zu** in German. Note that the gerund ending *-ing* is used in English for the first two.

(an)statt . . . zu (*instead of . . . -ing*)

Wir haben gemalt anstatt *zu studieren.*	*We were painting instead of studying.*

ohne . . . zu (*without . . . -ing*)

Er kam ins Zimmer ohne *zu klopfen.*	*He came into the room without knocking.*

um . . . zu (*in order to*)

Sie ging hinaus, um den Brief *zu lesen.*	*She went outside in order to read the letter.*

Note that the dependent infinitive is in last position in German. The infinitive phrase is set off by comma when it consists of more elements than **zu** + infinitive.

When a separable prefix verb occurs in an infinitive phrase, **zu** comes between prefix and infinitive.

Er telefonierte, um uns ein*zu*laden. *He called in order to invite us.*

89. Complete the following with the German.

1. Er geht vorbei, ______. *without seeing Norma*
2. Sie bleibt zu Hause, ______. *instead of going to school*
3. Ich bin gelaufen, ______. *in order to help Gertrud*
4. Sie sind gekommen, ______. *without calling (anrufen)*
5. Ich gehe auf mein Zimmer, ______. *in order to change*
6. Er hat telefoniert, ______. *in order to invite the children*
7. Sie gibt es ihrem Bruder, ______. *instead of bringing it to Helga*
8. Sie geht aus, ______. *without putting on a coat*
9. Wir haben sie besucht ______. *in order to ask*
10. Ich konnte das Gedicht, ______. *without learning it*

With Anticipatory **da(r)-** *Compounds Followed by* **zu** + *Dependent Infinitive*

Introductory phrases containing an anticipatory **da(r)-** compound are completed by an infinitive preceded by **zu.** In English **da(r)-** is disregarded. Note that the infinitive is in last position in the German sentence.

Ich warte darauf, das Auto *zu* sehen.	*I am waiting to see the car.*
Er hofft darauf, sein Geld wieder*zu*finden.	*He is hoping to find his money.*
Sie wartet darauf, sich *zu* setzen.	*She is waiting to sit down.*

90. Complete the following with the correct German infinitive phrase. For all sentences, use the German clause appearing in the first one.

1. Er denkt nicht daran, ______. *to excuse himself*
2. *to ask us*
3. *to help the children*
4. *to tell the story*
5. *to shave*
6. *to come along*
7. *to get it*
8. *to take money*
9. *to feed the dog*
10. *to eat the cake*

Certain Verbs Introducing **zu** + *Infinitive*

The following are some of the verbs introducing **zu** + infinitive:

anfangen	*to start, begin*
aufhören	*to stop*
bitten	*to ask*
erlauben	*to allow*
etwas schön (nett, etc.) **finden**	*to find (consider) something pretty (nice,* etc.*)*

helfen	*to help*
hoffen	*to hope*
vergessen	*to forget*
versprechen	*to promise*
vorschlagen	*to propose*
wünschen	*to wish*

Er ***hörte auf,*** **Golf** ***zu spielen.***	*He stopped to play golf.*
Ich ***hoffe,*** **euch bald** ***zu sehen***	*I hope to see you soon.*
Sie ***findet es dumm,*** **ihn** ***zu fragen.***	*She considers it stupid to ask him.*

91. Supply the correct infinitive phrase.

1. Ich verspreche dir, dich oft ______. *anrufen*
2. Er fängt an, seine Aufgaben ______. *schreiben*
3. Sie vergass, mir die Zeitung ______. *mitgeben*
4. Sie hat mich gebeten, ihn auch ______. *einladen*
5. Wir helfen dir gern, das Gras ______. *schneiden*
6. Ich finde es toll, bei euch ______. *sein*
7. Ich schlage vor, es ______. *lesen*
8. Wir hoffen, Oma ______. *besuchen*
9. Versprecht ihr, meinen Freund ______? *begleiten*
10. Er bittet, seine Mutter ______. *mitnehmen*
11. Sie finden es nett, ihren Onkel ______. *sehen*
12. Ich höre auf, die Geschichte ______. *glauben*

The Verb **brauchen + nicht zu +** *Dependent Infinitive*

The form **brauchen + nicht zu +** infinitive corresponds to the English *not to have to.* This form is usually used instead of the negative form of **müssen.**

Muss ich kommen?	*Do I have to come?*
Nein, du ***brauchst nicht zu kommen.***	*No, you don't have to come.*
Muss ich deinem Vater helfen?	*Do I have to help your father?*
Nein, du ***brauchst*** **ihm** ***nicht zu helfen.***	*No, you don't have to help him.*
Müssen wir heute abend singen?	*Do we have to sing tonight?*
Nein, ihr ***braucht*** **heute abend** ***nicht zu singen.***	*No, you don't have to sing tonight.*

Note that **nicht zu +** infinitive occurs at the end of the sentence.

92. Rewrite the following in the negative. Use the negative of **brauchen.**

1. Er muss studieren.
2. Ich muss lesen.
3. Wir müssen das Buch zurückgeben.
4. Sie muss arbeiten.
5. Ihr müsst es machen.
6. Du musst Herbert helfen.
7. Ich muss Bert besuchen.
8. Renate muss lesen.
9. Sie müssen die Geschichte erzählen.
10. Ich muss es bestellen.

VERBS AS OTHER PARTS OF SPEECH

Infinitives Used as Nouns

German infinitives used as nouns are neuter in gender and are always capitalized. They often correspond to the English gerund ending in *-ing.*

Ihr *Lachen* machte mich nervös. *Her laughing (laughter) made me nervous.*
Das viele *Rauchen* ist ungesund. *A lot of smoking is unhealthful.*

The contraction **beim +** infinitive noun means *while . . . -ing,* or *in the act of.*

Er hat sich *beim Schwimmen* verletzt. *He got hurt while swimming.*

93. Complete in German. For all sentences, use the German clause appearing in the first one.

1. Ich habe mich ______ (*while walking*) amüsiert.
2. (*while dancing*)
3. (*while singing*)
4. (*while working*)
5. (*while painting*)
6. (*while repairing*)
7. (*while studying*)
8. (*while playing*)
9. (*while telephoning*)
10. (*while swimming*)

Present Participles Used as Adjectives and Adverbs

The present participle is formed by adding **-d** to the infinitive. It can be used as an adjective or as an adverb.

Ist das *weinende* Kind krank? *Is the crying child ill?*
Er kam *lachend* ins Zimmer. *He came into the room laughing.*

94. Complete the following with the correct form of the present participle.

1. Sie sieht ______ aus. *leiden*
2. Der ______ Student wartet auf den Professor. *lesen*
3. Wir brauchen ein Zimmer mit ______ Wasser. *fliessen*
4. Hörst du den ______ Hund? *bellen*
5. ______ lief er ins Haus. *bluten*
6. Wie heisst die ______ Frau? *singen*
7. Kennst du den ______ Jungen? *weinen*
8. Dort liegt das ______ Kind. *schlafen*
9. Wer ist das ______ Mädchen? *lächeln*
10. ______ geht er vorbei. *grüssen*

Past Participles Used as Adjectives and Adverbs

Many past participles of weak and strong verbs can be used as adjectives and adverbs.

Ich möchte ein *weichgekochtes* Ei. *I would like a soft-boiled egg.*
Das Mädchen ist *verletzt.* *The girl is hurt.*

95. Fill in the correct form of the past participle.

1. Die ______ Stadt wird aufgebaut. *zerstören*
2. Die Suppe ist ______. *anbrennen*
3. Was macht ihr mit dem ______ Geld? *stehlen*
4. Hier ist deine ______ Arbeit. *schreiben*
5. Frisch ______ Brötchen schmecken herrlich. *backen*
6. Wo ist die ______ Arbeit? *beginnen*
7. Das Tier ist ______. *fangen*
8. Der ______ Hund schläft. *füttern*
9. Wo steht das ______ Auto? *reparieren*
10. Mach das ______ Fenster zu! *öffnen*

Participles Used as Nouns

Many present and past participles can be used as nouns. Such nouns are capitalized and receive adjective endings.

Seine ***Geliebte*** **ist angekommen.**	*His beloved arrived.*
Der ***Reisende*** **hatte grosse Koffer.**	*The traveler had large suitcases.*

96. Complete with the correct adjective endings.

1. Wo sind die Verletzt____?
2. Ein Gefangen____ ist ausgebrochen.
3. Der Sterbend____ liess seine Kinder kommen.
4. Eine Verwundet____ lag auf der Strasse.
5. Wo wohnt der Gesandt____?
6. Die Reisend____ sind müde.
7. Die Verliebt____ tanzen.
8. Das Gefroren____ ist gut.
9. Wie heisst der Gefallen____?
10. Das Neugeboren____ schreit.

IMPERATIVE MODE

Weak and Strong Verbs

The imperative expresses commands, requests or orders. Just as there are three different forms of address (**Sie, ihr, du**), there are three corresponding imperative forms. Commands may be preceded by **bitte** (*please*). **Bitte** can also occur within the sentence or in last position. The word **doch** softens the command, corresponding to the English *why don't you?* In German commands, an exclamation point is used.

Formal Commands (singular and plural)

The formal commands are formed by using the infinitive + **Sie.**

Kommen Sie!	*Come.*
Bitte ***parken Sie*** **hier!**	*Please park here.*
Rauchen Sie **bitte nicht!**	*Please don't smoke.*
Antworten Sie **doch!**	*Why don't you answer?*
Herr Müller, ***erzählen Sie*** **die Geschichte bitte!**	*Mr. Müller, tell the story, please.*
Meine Herren, ***nehmen Sie*** **bitte nichts!**	*Gentlemen, please don't take anything*

Familiar Commands

Plural

The familiar plural command corresponds to the **ihr** form of the present tense. Note that the pronoun **ihr** is not expressed.

Macht **die Aufgaben!**	*Do your homework.*
Lest **doch den Roman!**	*Why don't you read the novel?*
Bitte ***holt*** **die Bücher!**	*Please get the books.*
Öffnet **bitte das Fenster!**	*Please open the window.*
Sprecht **langsamer bitte!**	*Talk slower, please.*
Kommt **doch am Abend!**	*Why don't you come in the evening?*

Singular

The familiar singular command is formed by dropping the **-en** of the infinitive. Note that the pronoun **du** is not expressed.

Frag **deinen Vater!**	*Ask your father.*
Komm **mit deinem Bruder bitte!**	*Come with your brother, please.*
Gudrun, bitte *kauf* die Kamera!	*Gudrun, please buy the camera.*
Trink **doch Wasser!**	*Why don't you drink water?*
Such **das Bild bitte!**	*Look for the picture, please.*
Geh **ins Zimmer!**	*Go into the room.*

97. Answer the following questions with formal commands. Follow the model.

essen? Ja, essen Sie bitte.

1. schreiben?
2. schlafen?
3. gehen?
4. tanzen?
5. lächeln?
6. reden?
7. arbeiten?
8. erzählen?
9. essen?
10. fahren?

98. Complete the following with the familiar plural command.

1. ______ es! *finden*
2. ______ lauter! *sprechen*
3. ______ weniger! *trinken*
4. ______ den Mantel! *holen*
5. ______ gut! *schlafen*
6. ______ das Auto! *parken*
7. ______ mehr! *studieren*
8. ______ zur Schule! *gehen*
9. ______ dort! *bleiben*
10. ______ den Arzt! *rufen*
11. ______ den Braten! *essen*
12. ______ das Geld! *nehmen*
13. ______ langsamer! *reiten*
14. ______ Milch! *bestellen*
15. ______ bald! *schreiben*

99. Rewrite the following commands, changing the plural to the singular.

1. Singt lauter!
2. Kommt jetzt!
3. Sucht das Geld!
4. Bleibt hier!
5. Macht es!
6. Grüsst Tante Ida!
7. Geht ins Haus!
8. Probiert die Wurst!
9. Weint nicht!
10. Springt ins Wasser!
11. Schwimmt mehr!
12. Sagt die Wahrheit!
13. Ruft die Polizei!
14. Fragt den Lehrer!
15. Raucht nicht!

Variations of the Familiar Singular Command

***Additional* -e**

When the infinitive stem ends in **-d, -t, -dn, -tm, -chn, -fn, -gn** or **-ig,** an **-e** is added to the familiar singular command form.

Öffne **die Tür**	*Open the door.*
Entschuldige **bitte!**	*Excuse me, please.*
Antworte **bitte!**	*Answer, please.*
Wende **es!**	*Turn it.*
Atme **regelmässig!**	*Breathe normally.*

Infinitives Ending in **-eln** *and* **-ern**

When the infinitive ends in **-eln,** the **e** preceding the **-ln** is dropped and an **-e** ending is added.

Klingle **nicht!**	*Don't ring.*
Lächle **doch!**	*Why don't you smile?*
Behandle **das Kind!**	*Treat the child!*

When the infinitive ends in **-ern,** an **-e** ending is added.

Ändere **nichts!**	*Don't change anything.*
Füttere **die Katze!**	*Feed the cat.*
Wandere **nicht!**	*Don't hike.*

100. Answer the following with the familiar singular command. Follow the model.

arbeiten? Ja, arbeite!

1. warten?
2. reden?
3. lächeln?
4. es füttern?
5. ihn behandeln?
6. es öffnen?
7. antworten?
8. es ändern?
9. es beobachten?
10. rechnen?
11. es schneiden?
12. es sammeln?
13. wandern?
14. arbeiten?

Stem Vowel **e** *Changes to* **i** *or* **ie**

Those strong verbs that modify their stem vowel in the present tense from **e** to **i** or **ie** have the same change in the familiar singular command.

Gib **Gisela den Brief!**	*Give the letter to Gisela.*
Hilf **uns!**	*Help us.*
Iss **die Suppe!**	*Eat your soup.*
Sprich **langsamer!**	*Speak more slowly.*
Lies **doch das Buch!**	*Why don't you read the book?*
Nimm **nichts!**	*Don't take anything.*

101. Rewrite the following, changing the formal command to the familiar singular command.

1. Helfen Sie dem Kind!
2. Sprechen Sie lauter!
3. Geben Sie es dem Lehrer!
4. Stehlen Sie nicht!
5. Lesen Sie die Zeitung!
6. Brechen Sie es nicht!
7. Treffen Sie die Frau!
8. Sterben Sie nicht!
9. Erschrecken Sie nicht!
10. Essen Sie das Fleisch!
11. Nehmen Sie den Schmuck!
12. Vergessen Sie nichts!

Irregular Forms

The imperative forms of **haben, sein, werden** and **wissen** are slightly irregular. Study the following forms.

Formal, singular and plural	**Haben Sie! Seien Sie! Werden Sie! Wissen Sie!**
Familiar, plural	**Habt! Seid! Werdet! Wisst!**
Familiar, singular	**Hab! Sei! Werde! Wisse!**

102. Complete the following commands of the indicated verb.

1. Peter und Hans, ______ keine Angst! *haben*
2. Ilse, ______ nicht frech! *sein*
3. Herr Koch, ______ ja nicht krank! *werden*
4. Kinder, ______ morgen die Antwort! *wissen*
5. Fräulein Bucher, ______ bitte ruhig! *sein*
6. Du liebes Kind, ______ bald wieder gesund! *werden*
7. Christa, ______ nur vorsichtig! *sein*
8. Fritz, ______ doch Geduld! *haben*
9. Herr Knauer, ______ keine Angst! *haben*
10. Frau Bremer, ______ es nächste Woche! *wissen*
11. Kinder, ______ lieb! *sein*
12. Fräulein Sommer, ______ doch so nett! *sein*

First Person Command (Let's)

The idea of *let's* is expressed by using the first person plural. The pronoun **wir** follows the conjugated verb.

Singen wir!	*Let's sing.*
Gehen wir!	*Let's go.*
Fahren wir **mit dem Auto!**	*Let's go by car.*

103. Answer the following with the first person command. Follow the model.

Pferd füttern? Füttern wir das Pferd!

1. Das Abendessen kochen?
2. Den Lehrer fragen?
3. Warme Milch trinken?
4. Wein kaufen?
5. Jetzt gehen?
6. Die Aufgaben schreiben?
7. Den Hund rufen?
8. Das Buch holen?
9. Viel arbeiten?
10. Nichts ändern?

Impersonal Imperative

Instructions to the public are expressed by an infinitive command form. The exclamation point is not necessary with such instructions. The infinitive command occurs in last position.

Bitte *anschnallen.*	*Please fasten your seat belts.*
Rechts *fahren.*	*Drive on the right side.*
Nicht *aufstehen.*	*Do not get up.*
Einfahrt *freihalten.*	*Keep the driveway clear.*

CONDITIONAL MODE

Weak and Strong Verbs

The German conditional mood is a derivation of the future tense. It is formed with the auxiliary **würde** + infinitive, corresponding to the English verb pattern *would* + infinitive. The conditional expresses what would happen, if it were not for another circumstance. As in the future tense, the infinitive of the conditional is in last position, unless it occurs in a dependent clause.

ich würde sagen	**wir würden sagen**
du würdest sagen	**ihr würdet sagen**
er würde sagen	**sie würden sagen**

Sie *würden* das Haus nicht *kaufen.* — *They would not buy the house.*
Ich *würde* dem Kind *helfen.* — *I would help the child.*
Würdest* du das Geld *nehmen? — *Would you take the money?*
Er weiss, dass ich es *sagen würde.* — *He knows that I would say it.*

104. Rewrite the following in the conditional mode.

1. Wir nehmen nichts.
2. Bezahlst du?
3. Ich schwimme den ganzen Tag.
4. Sie arbeiten viel.
5. Er studiert nicht.
6. Fahrt ihr nach Deutschland?
7. Singen Sie laut?
8. Ich springe nicht ins Wasser.
9. Liest du das Buch?
10. Er repariert den Wagen.
11. Kommt ihr?
12. Sie bringen das Geschenk.
13. Helft ihr mir?
14. Ich gehe auch.
15. Tragen Sie die Jacke?
16. Laufen die Kinder?

Use of the Conditional

In both English and German the conditional is used in the conclusion of contrary-to-fact *if* clauses. (See the section on the subjunctive.)

The conditional is also used as a polite form of request.

Würden* Sie bitte einen Moment *warten?
Würdest* du mir bitte *helfen?
***Würdet* ihr *singen* bitte?**

105. Rewrite in German, changing the commands to the conditional.

1. Kommen Sie bitte!
2. Nimm das bitte!
3. Bleibt hier bitte!
4. Fahren Sie bitte schneller!
5. Gib mir bitte das Messer!
6. Sprechen Sie bitte langsamer!
7. Gehen Sie bitte!
8. Park bitte das Auto!
9. Bestellt das Essen bitte!
10. Zeigen Sie es den Kindern bitte!
11. Besuchen Sie Ihren Vater bitte!
12. Warte hier bitte!

SUBJUNCTIVE MODE

The subjunctive mode may be contrasted to the indicative mode, as follows. The indicative is used to express the fact that an action is taking, has taken or will take place. When the statement is a fact or when it implies a probability, the indicative mode, or mood, is used.

Er hat grossen Hunger. — *He is very hungry.*
Ich weiss, dass sie krank ist. — *I know that she is ill.*
Wir werden ihn besuchen. — *We will visit him.*
Er hat es genommen. — *He took it.*

The subjunctive is used to express that a certain action has not or may not take place, because it is a supposition, conjecture or desire, rather than a fact. When a statement is contrary to fact or when it implies a possibility rather than a probability, the subjunctive mood is used.

Ich wollte er *wäre* hier! — *I wish he were here.*
Er sagte, er *hätte* keine Zeit. — *He said he would have no time.*
Sie tut, als ob sie Geld *hätte*. — *She acts as if she had money.*

In German there are two types of subjunctive moods: the general subjunctive, which is used very frequently, and the special subjunctive, which has limited use. Unless otherwise indicated, this section discusses the general subjunctive.

Present Subjunctive

The present subjunctive is formed by adding the following subjunctive endings to the imperfect stem: **-e, -est, -e, -en, -et, -en.**

ich sagte	**wir sagten**
du sagtest	**ihr sagtet**
er sagte	**sie sagten**

Ich wollte, er *sagte* mir die Wahrheit. — *I wish he would tell me the truth.*

Weak Verbs

The German present subjunctive of weak verbs is identical with the imperfect indicative. In English the very same is the case. The present subjunctive of all English verbs, except of *to be,* is identical with the past indicative; e.g. *If* I had *the money* . . . ; *If* he lost *everything* . . . but: *If* we were *rich* . . .

In English, as well as in German, these present subjunctive forms are ambiguous. Only the context makes clear whether the forms are used in the past indicative or the present subjunctive. For this reason, the present conditional **würde** + infinitive is often substituted in German. (See section on the conditional mode.) The German present subjunctive corresponds to the English present conditional *would* + infinitive (*would run*) or to the present subjunctive (*ran*), depending on use. Although the present subjunctive resembles the imperfect indicative, it always refers to present or future time.

106. Rewrite the following, substituting the present subjunctive for the present conditional.

1. Sie würden uns besuchen.
2. Wir würden viel machen.
3. Würdet ihr es kaufen?
4. Ich würde es erzählen.
5. Würdest du es zerstören?
6. Würden Sie dort arbeiten?
7. Ich würde ihn fragen.
8. Wir würden zahlen.
9. Er würde es glauben.
10. Ich würde es sagen.
11. Würdest du dort wohnen?
12. Würdet ihr es hören?
13. Sie würden es lernen.
14. Wir würden nicht weinen.
15. Ich würde bezahlen.
16. Er würde studieren.
17. Würdet ihr das Haus bauen?
18. Würden Sie dort spielen?
19. Sie würden alles hören.
20. Würdest du malen?

107. Write the German, using the present subjunctive.

1. I would cry.
2. We would play.
3. They would get it.
4. He would not believe it.
5. Children, would you study?
6. Gerda, would you buy flowers?
7. Mrs. Treibl, would you live there?
8. She would work.
9. We would learn.
10. They would try the soup.

Irregular Weak Verbs

The irregular weak verbs **brennen, kennen, nennen, rennen, senden** and **wenden** do not modify the imperfect stem vowel to form the present subjunctive. They retain the vowel of the infinitive stem.

ich rennte	**wir rennten**
du renntest	**ihr renntet**
er rennte	**sie rennten**

Die Kerze *brennte* den ganzen Tag.	*The candle would burn all day.*
Ich *sendete* ihr etwas.	*I would send her something.*

The irregular weak verbs **bringen, denken** and **wissen** use the modified imperfect stem and add umlaut plus the subjunctive endings to form the present subjunctive.

ich brächte	**ich dächte**	**ich wüsste**
du brächtest	**du dächtest**	**du wüsstest**
er brächte	**er dächte**	**er wüsste**
wir brächten	**wir dächten**	**wir wüssten**
ihr brächtet	**ihr dächtet**	**ihr wüsstet**
sie brächten	**sie dächten**	**sie wüssten**

Er *dächte* nicht daran.	*He would not think of it.*
Ich *brächte* ihm nichts.	*I would not bring him anything.*
Wir *wüssten* alles.	*We would know everything.*

108. Rewrite the following, substituting the present subjunctive for the present conditional.

1. Das Hause würde brennen.
2. Würdet ihr daran denken?
3. Ich würde etwas bringen.
4. Würdest du es nennen?
5. Sie würden schnell rennen.
6. Wir würden es wissen.
7. Ich würde den Brief senden.
8. Wir würden das Blatt wenden.
9. Ich würde das wissen.
10. Würdest du das Buch bringen?

Strong Verbs

The present subjunctive of strong verbs is formed by adding the subjunctive endings **-e, -est, -e, -en, -et, -en** to the imperfect stem. Those verbs containing the vowels **a, o, u** in the imperfect stem add umlaut.

No umlaut		*Umlaut*	
ich bliebe	**wir blieben**	**ich nähme**	**wir nähmen**
du bliebest	**ihr bliebet**	**du nähmest**	**ihr nähmet**
er bliebe	**sie blieben**	**er nähme**	**sie nähmen**

Umlaut		*Umlaut*	
ich flöge	**wir flögen**	**ich führe**	**wir führen**
du flögest	**ihr flöget**	**du führest**	**ihr führet**
er flöge	**sie flögen**	**er führe**	**sie führen**

Er *käme* am Samstag.	*He would come on Saturday.*
Wir *flögen* nach Paris.	*We would fly to Paris.*
***Gingest* du nach Hause?**	*Would you go home?*
Ich *führe* in die Schweiz.	*I would go to Switzerland.*
Sie *schrieben* die Karte.	*They would write the card.*

109. Write sentences from the following, using the present subjunctive.

1. ich / schreiben / das Gedicht.
2. wir / trinken / nichts.
3. lassen / du / ihn / gehen?
4. die Alten / gehen / zur Kirche.
5. die Sonne / scheinen / nicht.
6. die Studenten / lesen / das Buch.
7. er / fliegen / auch.
8. schlafen / du / lange?
9. ich / geben / Anna / alles.
10. er / laufen / schnell.
11. die Leute / fahren / mit dem Auto.
12. wir / schreien / laut.
13. er / schneiden / das Haar.
14. ich / bleiben / hier.
15. wir / kommen / auch.
16. nehmen / du / das Papier?
17. ich / essen / Brot.
18. das Pferd / ziehen / den Schlitten.
19. er / verlieren / das Geld.
20. wir / springen / hoch.

Irregular Strong Verbs

The following strong verbs modify their imperfect stem vowels to form the present subjunctive:

helfen	**ich hülfe**	**sterben**	**ich stürbe**
stehen	**ich stünde**	**werfen**	**ich würfe**

Ich *stünde* dort.	*I would stand there.*
Wer *hülfe* dem Kind?	*Who would help the child?*
Wir *würfen* den Ball.	*We would throw the ball.*
Er *stürbe* vor Angst.	*He would die of fright.*

110. Write the German.

1. He would die.
2. They would help.
3. We would throw the ball.
4. She would stand here.
5. I would help.
6. They would die.
7. We would stand here.
8. Helga, would you help?

Auxiliaries **haben** *and* **sein**

ich hätte	**wir hätten**	**ich wäre**	**wir wären**
du hättest	**ihr hättet**	**du wärest**	**ihr wäret**
er hätte	**sie hätten**	**er wäre**	**sie wären**

Ich *hätte* kein Geld.	*I would not have any money.*
Wir *hätten* Ferien.	*We would have a vacation.*
Er *wäre* zu klein.	*He would be too small.*
***Wärest* du dort?**	*Would you be there?*

111. Change the indicative to the subjunctive.

1. Wir haben kein Auto.
2. Ich bin reich.
3. Sie haben keine Ferien.
4. Du bist nicht glücklich.
5. Ich habe keinen Hund.
6. Sie ist böse.
7. Sie sind nicht intelligent.
8. Ihr habt kein Geld.
9. Er hat nichts.
10. Habt ihr Geld?
11. Wir sind krank.
12. Hast du Angst?
13. Wir haben alles.
14. Seid ihr müde?
15. Bist du froh?
16. Ich bin arm.

Modal Verbs

Modal auxiliary verbs retain the vowel of the infinitive in the stem of the present subjunctive. Note the consonant change in **mögen.**

dürfen	**ich dürfte**	(*might, would be permitted*) used in polite questions *may I? could I?*
können	**ich könnte**	(*were able, would be able*)
mögen	**ich möchte**	(*would* or *should like*)
müssen	**ich müsste**	(*ought to, would have to*)
sollen	**ich sollte**	(*should, would have to*)
wollen	**ich wollte**	(*wanted, would want to*)

The subjunctive form of the modals are frequently used to express possibility or opinions and to phrase questions politely. In English the modals are usually expressed with *would* + meaning of the modal.

Du *solltest* zu Hause bleiben.	*You should stay at home.*
***Müsstest* du nicht arbeiten?**	*Wouldn't you have to work?*
***Möchtest* du ein Stück Kuchen?**	*Would you like a piece of cake?*
***Dürfte* ich es sehen?**	*Could I see it?*

112. Restate the following. Use the present subjunctive to form polite requests or questions.

1. Können Sie mir helfen?
2. Willst du auch zeichnen?
3. Müsst ihr nicht studieren?
4. Darf er mitgehen?
5. Sollst du Marianne besuchen?
6. Kann ich ein Stück nehmen?
7. Musst du nicht lernen?
8. Wollt ihr den Film sehen?
9. Kann sie es holen?
10. Darf ich bleiben?

113. Complete the following with the correct present subjunctive form of **mögen.**

1. ______ du noch etwas?
2. Ich ______ Schokolade.
3. Wir ______ gehen.
4. Die Kinder ______ reiten.
5. ______ Sie mitmachen?
6. ______ du dort leben?
7. ______ Sie etwas haben?
8. Ich ______ fliegen.
9. ______ ihr essen?
10. ______ du etwas bestellen?

Contrary-to-fact Wishes

Contrary-to-fact wishes may be introduced by the present subjunctive of verbs of wishing, e.g. **ich wollte, ich wünschte.** When using a contrary-to-fact wish, the speaker expresses his dissatisfaction with an actual situation and expresses how he would like it to be.

Fact	**Er ist nicht zu Hause.**	*He is not at home.*
Wish	**Ich wollte, er wäre zu Hause.**	*I wish he were at home.*

114. Rewrite the following using the present subjunctive. Change the fact to a contrary-to-fact wish. Start with **Ich wollte . . . .** Follow the model.

Sie ist krank. Ich wollte, sie wäre nicht krank.

1. Er bleibt dort.
2. Sie können abfahren.
3. Wir leben in einem Dorf.
4. Ich habe Zahnweh.
5. Ihr arbeitet so viel.
6. Ich muss studieren.
7. Wir sind nicht zu Hause.
8. Du kaufst dir nichts.

9. Sie weint.
10. Ich bin arm.
11. Wir haben es.
12. Er nimmt es.
13. Er sieht Paula.
14. Sie besuchen Oma.

Contrary-to-fact Wishes Introduced by **wenn** *(if)*

When the contrary-to-fact wish is expressed within a **wenn** (*if*) clause, the conjugated verb is in last position. Such wishes often contain the words **nur** or **doch**, corresponding to the English *only*.

Wenn sie nur daran *glaubten!*	*If only they believed in it.*
Wenn er doch nicht *rauchte!*	*If only he wouldn't smoke.*
Wenn ich es nur nicht tun *müsste!*	*If only I didn't have to do it.*

115. Form wishes from the following. Start with **Wenn.** Follow the model.

ich / nur mehr Geld / haben
Wenn ich nur mehr Geld hätte!

1. wir / nur in München / sein.
2. er / nur das Fenster / öffnen.
3. ihr / doch ein Auto / kaufen.
4. die Leute / nur nicht so laut / schreien.
5. ich / nur alles / wissen.
6. er / nur nicht krank / sein.
7. die Kinder / nur zu Hause / bleiben.
8. ich / nur Deutsch / können.
9. ihr / nur mehr / haben.
10. Georg / nur nicht / abfahren.

The introductory **wenn** of the preceding wishes can also be omitted. In that case the conjugated verb is in first position.

Hätte **ich nur mehr Zeit!**	*If only I had more time.*
Gäbe **es nur besseres Essen!**	*If only there were better food.*
Dürfte **ich nur heimgehen!**	*If only I could go home.*

116. Rewrite the following, omitting **wenn.**

1. Wenn sie nur die Wahrheit sagte!
2. Wenn ich doch schlafen könnte!
3. Wenn er nur das Auto reparierte!
4. Wenn sie nur nicht so viel tränken!
5. Wenn er doch schwiege!
6. Wenn wir nur keine Angst hätten!
7. Wenn du nur hier wärest!
8. Wenn er nur hier bliebe!
9. Wenn sie es nur glaubte!
10. Wenn ihr nur mehr lerntet!

Conditional Sentences

Contrary-to-fact Conditions

Conditional sentences consist of a conditional clause, introduced by **wenn** (*if*) and a conclusion. The verbs in a conditional sentence may be in the indicative or the subjunctive mood.

If the speaker wants to express that the condition is factual, real or fulfillable, the indicative is used.

Wenn ich Geld *habe, kaufe* **ich es.**	*If I have money, I'll buy it.*

In this sentence, the speaker does not yet have money, but there is a good probability that he'll have it in the future.

If a condition is contrary to fact, unreal or unfulfillable, the subjunctive is used.

Wenn ich Geld *hätte, kaufte* **ich es.**	*If I had money, I would buy it.*

With the use of the subjunctive mood of the verb, the speaker expresses that he does not have the money now, nor will he have it in the future. In the preceding sentence, the present subjunctive was used in both the condition and the conclusion. Variations from the above patterns are possible in German. The present conditional is frequently used to replace the ambiguous subjunctive form of weak verbs.

machte **ich eine Weltreise.**
Wenn ich reich *wäre,* or
würde **ich eine Weltreise** *machen.*

In colloquial speech, the present conditional also replaces the subjunctive of strong verbs in the conclusion of the conditional sentence.

zöge **ich den Pelzmantel an.**
Wenn es kälter *wäre,* or
würde **ich den Pelzmantel** *anziehen.*

The present subjunctive of **haben, sein** and the modal verbs is not replaced by the present conditional.

117. Replace the present subjunctive in the conclusion with the conditional. Repeat the italicized clause where indicated.

1. *Wenn ich kein Geld hätte,* arbeitete ich.
2. . . . , wohnte ich nicht hier.
3. . . . , gäbe ich dir nichts.
4. . . . , flöge ich nicht nach Hamburg.
5. . . . , bestellte ich mir nichts.
6. *Wenn er käme,* tränken wir Kaffee.
7. . . . , unterhielten wir uns.
8. . . . , freute ich mich.
9. . . . , zöge ich mich um.
10. . . . , fürchtete ich mich nicht.

118. Complete the following with the correct present subjunctive form of the indicated verb.

1. Wenn ich Zeit ______, ______ ich dir. *haben, helfen*
2. Wenn er hier ______, ______ ich glücklich. *sein, sein*
3. Wenn Ute etwas ______, ______ sie es. *brauchen, nehmen*
4. Wenn du zu Hause ______, ______ wir dich. *bleiben, besuchen*
5. Wenn ihr ______, ______ ihr es. *studieren, wissen*
6. Wenn wir Essen ______, ______ wir es. *bestellen, essen*
7. Wenn du Deutsch ______, ______ du es. *lernen, können*

Omission of wenn

The conjugated verb is in first position of the sentence when **wenn** is omitted.

Wäre **das Radio kaputt, (dann)** *würde* **er es** *reparieren.*
If the radio were broken, (then) he would fix it.
Machtest **du das Fenster** *auf,* **(dann)** *würde* **es kalt** *werden.*
If you opened the window, (then) it would get cold.

119. Rewrite the following, omitting the introductory **wenn.** Add **dann.**

1. Wenn du mir hülfest, wäre ich froh.
2. Wenn er käme, bliebe ich dort.
3. Wenn wir ihn fragten, würde er uns antworten.
4. Wenn sie es wollte, gäbe ich es ihr.
5. Wenn ich Angst hätte, würde ich schreien.

120. Write the German, using the present subjunctive in both clauses. Omit **wenn.**

1. If I were ill, I would stay at home.
2. If we knew it, we would tell Alexander.
3. If she had money, she would buy the coat.
4. If they worked, they would be happier.
5. If he arrived, I would pick him up.

Clauses Introduced by als ob

The subjunctive is used in clauses introduced by **als ob** (*as if*), because the speaker makes an unreal comparison

Er sieht aus, *als ob* er krank wäre.	*He looks as if he were ill.*
Sie tun, *als ob* sie Angst hätten.	*They act as if they were afraid.*

121. Complete the following with the correct present subjunctive form.

1. Wir tun, als ob wir Zeit ______. *haben*
2. Du tust, als ob du sie ______. *lieben*
3. Er tut, als ob er ins Haus ______. *gehen*
4. Sie tun, als ob sie krank ______. *sein*
5. Ich tue, als ob ich bleiben ______. *wollen*
6. Ich tue, als ob ich es ______. *können*
7. Sie tut, als ob sie hier ______. *bleiben*
8. Sie tun, als ob sie ______. *arbeiten*
9. Er tut, als ob er alles ______. *sehen*
10. Wir tun, als ob wir es ______. *nehmen*

Past Subjunctive

The past subjunctive is formed with a form of **hätte** or **wäre** + past participle.

ich hätte gesungen	**wir hätten gesungen**
du hättest gesungen	**ihr hättet gesungen**
er hätte gesungen	**sie hätten gesungen**
ich wäre gegangen	**wir wären gegangen**
du wärest gegangen	**ihr wäret gegangen**
er wäre gegangen	**sie wären gegangen**

The German past subjunctive corresponds to the English *had* + past participle (*had run, had gone*) or to the English past conditional *would + have* + past participle (*would have run, would have gone*), depending on use. Since the past subjunctive in German is not ambiguous, there is no need to use the past conditional.

The past subjunctive is used with contrary-to-fact wishes, contrary-to-fact conditional clauses and **als ob** clauses referring to past time.

Wenn sie nur *mitgeholfen hätte!*	*If only she had helped.*
Hätte* ich nur den Roman *gelesen!	*If only I had read the novel.*
Wenn wir *studiert hätten, hätten* wir die Antworten *gewusst.*	*If we had studied, we would have known the answers.*
Wäre* er krank *gewesen, hätte* er nicht *gearbeitet.	*If he had been ill, he wouldn't have worked.*
Sie tut, als ob sie dort *gewesen wäre.*	*She acts, as if she had been there.*

122. Write wishes in the past subjunctive. Change the fact to a contrary-to-fact wish. Follow the model.

Ich hatte keinen Schlüssel.
Wenn ich nur einen Schlüssel gehabt hätte!

1. Wir waren nicht in der Schule.
2. Du hast nicht angerufen.
3. Ich habe mich nicht gebadet.
4. Er hatte keine Angst.
5. Ihr seid nicht gekommen.

123. Rewrite the following wishes, omitting **wenn.**

1. Wenn du nur geschrien hättest!
2. Wenn wir ihr nur begegnet wären!
3. Wenn ich nur hingegangen wäre!
4. Wenn er nur nicht gestorben wäre!
5. Wenn sie nur geschrieben hätte!

124. Complete the following with the past subjunctive of the indicated verb.

1. Wenn er alles ______ ______, ______ er keinen Hunger ______. *essen, haben*
2. Wenn du es ______ ______, ______ ich es nicht ______. *zurückbringen, holen*
3. Wenn ihr das Fenster ______ ______, ______ ihr euch nicht ______. *zumachen, erkälten*
4. Wenn du mich ______ ______, ______ ich es dir ______. *anrufen, sagen*
5. Wenn das Kind nicht so ______ ______, ______ es nicht so laut ______. *bluten, schreien*

125. Rewrite the following, omitting **wenn.**

1. Wenn es geklingelt hätte, hätten wir aufgemacht.
2. Wenn du angerufen hättest, wäre ich gekommen.
3. Wenn wir es gefunden hätten, hätten wir es wieder zurückgegeben.
4. Wenn ihr geschrieben hättet, hätten wir euch dort getroffen.

126. Write the German.

1. He acts as if he had bought it.
2. They act as if they had not slept.
3. She acts as if she had been ill.
4. He acts as if he had come along.

Modal Auxiliaries

When the modal auxiliary is used with a dependent infinitive in the past subjunctive, the double infinitive construction is used.

Hätte **ich es nur** *machen können!* *If only I could have done it!*

If the double infinitive occurs in a **wenn** clause or an **als ob** clause, the auxiliary **hätte** precedes the double infinitive.

Wenn ich nur *hätte kommen dürfen!*
Wenn du es *hättest machen wollen,* **wäre ich glücklich gewesen.**
Sie tun, als ob sie alles *hätten tun dürfen.*

127. Rewrite the following, adding the indicated modals.

1. Wäre er nur geblieben! *dürfen*
2. Wenn ich doch nicht gegangen wäre! *müssen*

3. Er tut, als ob er es gesehen hätte! *können*
4. Du tust, als ob ich es geschrieben hätte. *sollen*
5. Wenn ich geritten wäre (*wollen*), hätte ich es dir gesagt.
6. Hätte er nur gesungen! *können*
7. Wenn du nur nichts gegessen hättest! *wollen*
8. Wenn wir gefragt hätten (*dürfen*), hätten wir die Antwort gewusst.
9. Hätte sie nur geholfen! *können*
10. Sie tun, als ob sie auf mich gewartet hätten. *müssen*

Indirect Statement

When the words of a speaker are quoted directly, they appear in quotation marks; e.g. *She said: "He found the keys."* This direct statement can be transformed to an indirect one, e.g. *She said that he found the keys.*

In English the indicative mood is used in both statements. The German speaker, however, usually uses the subjunctive when repeating a statement indirectly. By using the subjunctive, the German speaker indicates that he is not certain that the statement is completely factual. The use of the subjunctive implies a certain scepticism or simply that the information is second hand. If the German speaker is absolutely certain that the information is fact, he uses the indicative.

Both the general and the special subjunctive is used in indirect statements.

Special Subjunctive

Present Subjunctive of Weak and Strong Verbs

The subjunctive endings **-e, -est, -e, -en, -et, -en** are added to the infinitive stem of both weak and strong verbs.

Weak Verbs		*Strong Verbs*	
ich sage	**wir sagen**	**ich gehe**	**wir gehen**
du sagest	**ihr saget**	**du gehest**	**ihr gehet**
er sage	**sie sagen**	**er gehe**	**sie gehen**

All verbs except **sein** follow the above pattern.

Special Subjunctive of **sein**

Study the following:

ich sei	**wir seien**
du seiest	**ihr seiet**
er sei	**sie seien**

128. Rewrite the following, using the present tense of the special subjunctive. Where indicated, substitute different words for the italicized word.

1. Sie sagt, er *wäre* in Kanada.
2. . . . bliebe . . .
3. . . . wohnte . . .
4. . . . studierte . . .
5. . . . arbeitete . . .
6. Sie sagt, sie *gäbe* uns etwas.
7. . . . kaufte . . .
8. . . . brächte . . .
9. . . . holte . . .
10. . . . schickte . . .
11. . . . schenkte . . .
12. Er sagte, ich *hätte* nichts.
13. . . . wüsste . . .
14. . . . könnte . . .
15. . . . wollte . . .
16. . . . fände . . .
17. . . . tränke . . .
18. . . . ässe . . .

Past Subjunctive

The past tense of the special subjunctive is formed with a form of **sei** or **habe** + past participle.

ich habe gesehen	**wir haben gesehen**
du habest gesehen	**ihr habet gesehen**
er habe gesehen	**sie haben gesehen**
ich sei gegangen	**wir seien gegangen**
du seiest gegangen	**ihr seiet gegangen**
er sei gegangen	**sie seien gegangen**

129. Rewrite the following, changing the general to the special subjunctive. Repeat the italicized clause where indicated.

1. *Er sagt,* er hätte schon geschrieben.
2. . . . , ich wäre ins Kino gegangen.
3. . . . , sie wäre im Krankenhaus gewesen.
4. . . . , er hätte etwas geholt.
5. . . . , ich hätte es repariert.
6. . . . , er hätte nicht kommen dürfen.

Use of the Special Subjunctive

The use of the special subjunctive is rather limited. Some German speakers use it in indirect statements; others never use it. Moreover, the special subjunctive is mainly used in the first and third person singular.

Whether the present tense or the past tense of the subjunctive is used in the indirect quotation depends on the tense of the verb in the direct quotation.

When the original statement is in the present tense, the present tense of the general or the special subjunctive is used. In German, unlike in English, the tense of the introductory verb does not influence the choice of tense in the indirect statement. The verb of the introductory verb may be any tense in German. Study the following:

Direct Statement		*Indirect Statement*
„Ich *bin* krank"	**Er sagt,** **Er sagte,** **Er hat gesagt,** **Er hatte gesagt,**	**er *sei* (*wäre*) krank.**

When the verb of the original statement is in the future tense, the present tense or the present conditional may be used in the indirect statement:

„Ich *werde* ihn *fragen*"	**Sie sagt,** **Sie sagte,** **Sie hat gesagt,** **Sie hatte gesagt,**	**sie *würde* ihn *fragen.*** **sie *frage* (*fragte*) ihn.**

When the verb of the original statement is in the imperfect, present perfect or pluperfect, the past subjunctive is used:

„Ich *kam* gestern *an*" **„Ich *bin* gestern *angekommen*"** **„Ich *war* gestern *angekommen*"**	**Er sagt,** **Er sagte,** **Er hat gesagt,** **Er hatte gesagt,**	**er *sei* (*wäre*) gestern *angekommen.***

130. Change the direct statement to an indirect one. Start with **Sie sagte, ...** Use the general subjunctive.

1. „Mutter ist krank gewesen."
2. „Grossvater hatte Geld."
3. „Peter hat Angst."
4. „Sie war allein."
5. „Er hatte ihn gesehen."
6. „Christa war nach Köln gefahren."
7. „Onkel Werner ist in Hamburg."
8. „Ich hatte dich besucht."

131. Change the preceding to indirect statements, using the special subjunctive. Start with **Er hat gesagt, . . .**

PASSIVE VOICE

The German passive construction consists of a form of **werden** + past participle.

Present Tense

The present tense is formed with the present tense of **werden** + past participle. Study the following:

ich werde gefragt	**wir werden gefragt**
du wirst gefragt	**ihr werdet gefragt**
er wird gefragt	**sie werden gefragt**

Die Wäsche *wird* **von Mutter** *gewaschen.*
Die Kinder *werden* **von ihrem Vater** *abgeholt.*

The passive construction shifts emphasis from the subject of the active sentence to the object, because the direct object of the active sentence becomes the subject of the passive sentence. In an active sentence the subject initiates an action, whereas the subject of a passive construction is acted upon by an agent. This agent was the subject of the active sentence and is preceded by **von** or **durch** in German. In English the agent is introduced with *by.* If it is a personal agent, it is in the dative case because it is preceded by **von.** If the agent is the means by which something is done, it is in the accusative case, the object of the preposition **durch.**

Active	**Die Eltern fragen den Jungen.**	*The parents ask the boy.*
Passive	**Der Junge** *wird von den Eltern gefragt.*	*The boy is asked by his parents.*
Active	**Der Sturm zerstört die Ernte.**	*The storm is destroying the harvest.*
Passive	**Die Ernte** *wird durch den Sturm zerstört.*	*The harvest is destroyed by the storm.*

However, many passive sentences in German do not express an agent. They simply consist of a subject and the passive verb pattern.

Die Tür *wird geschlossen.*	*The door is (being) closed.*
Die Vorlesung *wird gehalten.*	*The lecture is (being) held.*

In German, the indirect object of the active sentence cannot become the subject of the passive sentence. It must remain the indirect object. The German passive construction does not need a subject. **Es** may be placed in first position of the sentence. It functions merely as a filler and not as a subject. Otherwise, the indirect object or other elements may be in first position, when no subject is present.

Active	**Der Arzt hilft dem Verwundeten.**	*The doctor is helping the wounded (man).*
Passive	**Dem Verwundeten wird vom Arzt geholfen.**	*The wounded man is helped by the doctor.*
	Es wird dem Verwundeten vom Arzt geholfen.	*The wounded man is helped by the doctor.*

132. Complete the following with the correct present passive and preposition and article or contraction, when necessary.

1. Das Brot ______ ______ Bäcker ______. *backen*
2. Die Kranke ______ ______ Arznei ______. *retten*
3. Das Abendessen ______ schon ______. *servieren*
4. Die Bücher ______ ______ ihm ______. *anschauen*
5. Es ______ ______ uns ______. *nehmen*
6. Dem Kranken ______ ______ Doktor ______. *helfen*
7. Die Aufgabe ______ ______ dem Mädchen ______. *schreiben*
8. Die Wäsche ______ ______ Mutter ______. *waschen*
9. Das Loch ______ ______ den Männern ______. *graben*
10. Das Hotel ______ ______ die Bombe ______. *zerstören*
11. Wir ______ ______ Vater ______. *sehen*
12. Ich ______ ______ dem Jungen ______. *schlagen*
13. Er ______ ______ seiner Freundin ______. *hören*
14. Das Haus ______ ______ den Sturm ______. *zerstören*
15. Das Auto ______ ______ dem Mechaniker ______. *reparieren*

133. Change the active to the passive voice.

1. Der Hund beisst das Kind.
2. Das Feuer zerstört das Haus.
3. Meine Freunde trinken den Kaffee.
4. Er füttert das Pferd.
5. Der Vater hilft dem Kranken.

Imperfect Tense

The imperfect passive is formed by a form of **wurde** + past participle. Study the following:

ich wurde gefragt	**wir wurden gefragt**
du wurdest gefragt	**ihr wurdet gefragt**
er wurde gefragt	**sie wurden gefragt**

Wir ***wurden*** **von ihm** ***gesehen.***	*We were seen by him.*
Die Geschichte ***wurde*** **von dem Lehrer** ***erzählt.***	*The story was told by the teacher.*
Wann ***wurdest*** **du** ***gefragt?***	*When were you asked?*

134. Change the following to the imperfect passive tense.

1. Wir werden abgeholt.
2. Die Rechnung wird von Renate bezahlt.
3. Wirst du beobachtet?
4. Das Auto wird geparkt.
5. Es wird schon von den Leuten gemacht.
6. Das Museum wird von der Klasse besucht.
7. Das Wort wird von dem Studenten buchstabiert.

8. Ich werde gesehen.
9. Die Maschine wird von dem Mechaniker repariert.
10. Das Haus wird durch die Bombe zerstört.

135. Write the German.

1. He was seen.
2. The window was opened by Marlene.
3. They were asked by their father.
4. She was heard.
5. It was washed by my aunt.
6. We were helped by the boy.
7. I was observed.
8. The city was destroyed by a bomb.

Compound Tenses, Present Perfect and Pluperfect

The auxiliary verb **sein** is used in the formation of the present perfect and the pluperfect passive. The past participle of **werden** is **geworden.** The **ge-** prefix of the past participle is dropped in these tenses. The perfect tenses in the passive consist of a form of **sein** + past participle of verb + **worden.** Study the following:

ich bin gefragt worden	**wir sind gefragt worden**
du bist gefragt worden	**ihr seid gefragt worden**
er ist gefragt worden	**sie sind gefragt worden**
ich war gefragt worden	**wir waren gefragt worden**
du warst gefragt worden	**ihr wart gefragt worden**
er war gefragt worden	**sie waren gefragt worden**

Das Auto ***ist*** **vom Mechaniker** ***repariert worden.***
The car was repaired by the mechanic.
Ich ***bin*** **von meiner Mutter** ***gefragt worden.***
I was asked by my mother.
Das Haus ***war*** **von meinem Bruder** ***verkauft worden.***
The house was sold by my brother.

136. Rewrite the following in the present perfect tense.

1. Das Museum wurde 1911 erbaut.
2. Der Löwe wurde vom Wärter gefüttert.
3. Es wurde ihr darüber erzählt.
4. Das Kleid wurde rot gefärbt.
5. Es wurde ihm gegeben.
6. Du wurdest überall gesucht.
7. Ich wurde von ihm gesehen.
8. Das Restaurant wurde durch das Feuer zerstört.
9. Er wurde vom Arzt behandelt.
10. Die Kinder wurden von den Hunden gebissen.

Future Tense

The future passive is formed by the present tense of **werden** + past participle of verb + **werden.** Study the following:

ich werde gefragt werden	**wir werden gefragt werden**
du wirst gefragt werden	**ihr werdet gefragt werden**
er wird gefragt werden	**sie werden gefragt werden**

Er *wird* **wohl** *abgeholt werden.*	*He will probably be picked up.*
Die Möbel *werden* **wohl** *gebracht werden.*	*The furniture will probably be delivered.*
Ich *werde* **von meinem Freund** *besucht werden.*	*I'll be visited by my friend.*

The future passive is used chiefly to express probability.

When an adverb of time referring to the future occurs in the sentence, the present passive is preferred.

Die Äpfel *werden morgen* **von den Männern** *gepflückt.*
The apples will be picked by the men tomorrow.

137. Rewrite the following in the future passive. Omit the adverb of time.

1. Das Haus wird nächstes Jahr von meinen Freunden gebaut.
2. Die Geschichte wird morgen erzählt.
3. Die Tiere werden übermorgen durch Gift getötet.
4. Das Geschenk wird morgen abend von den Kindern bewundert.
5. Die Rechnung wird später von meinem Vater bezahlt.
6. Der Brief wird morgen geholt.
7. Das Haus wird am Sonntag beobachtet.
8. Der Brief wird morgen vom Lehrer geschrieben.
9. Rudi wird nächsten Monat gefragt.
10. Franz wird in einer Stunde abgeholt.

Substitute for the Passive

Passive constructions are not used as frequently in German as they are in English. Especially in spoken German, the active construction is preferred. One common substitute for the passive is an active sentence containing the indefinite pronoun **man** as subject. **Man** can only be used in an active sentence. However, such sentences are often rendered into passive sentences in English. Compare the following. Note that the subject of the passive sentence becomes the direct object in the active one.

Passive	**Ich** *bin gesehen worden.*	*I was seen.*
Active	*Man hat* **mich** *gesehen.*	
Passive	**Peter** *wird gefragt.*	*Peter is asked.*
Active	*Man fragt* **Peter.**	
Passive	**Der Wagen** *wurde rapariert.*	*The car was repaired.*
Active	*Man reparierte* **den Wagen.**	
Passive	**Das Haus** *wird* **wohl** *verkauft werden.*	*The house will probably be sold.*
Active	**Man** *wird* **wohl das Haus** *verkaufen.*	

138. Rewrite the following, using **man.**

1. Die Ruine wird zerstört.
2. Wir werden angerufen.
3. Das Essen wird bestellt.
4. Die Geschichte wurde erzählt.
5. Der Doktor wurde geholt.
6. Der Katalog wurde geschickt.
7. Das Bild ist verkauft worden.
8. Der Mann ist angerufen worden.
9. Der Brief war geschrieben worden.
10. Die Limonade war getrunken worden.
11. Die Stadt wird wohl aufgebaut werden.
12. Das Auto wird wohl geparkt werden.

Actional Versus Statal Passive

In German, unlike in English, a distinction is made between the action itself and the state resulting from an action. The English sentence *It was taken* may express the action or the result of the action. In German such ambiguity is not possible. The action is expressed by the actional passive, formed by **werden** + past participle.

Es wird gekocht.	*It is (being) cooked.*
Es wurde gezählt.	*It was (being) counted.*

If the German speaker wants to express the result of that action, the verb **sein** + past participle is used. Such a construction is referred to as a statal passive.

Es ist gekocht.	*It is cooked.*
Es war gezählt.	*It was counted.*

Compare the following forms of the actional and statal passive.

	Actional	*Statal*
Present	**Es wird gebaut.**	**Es ist gebaut.**
Imperfect	**Es wurde gebaut.**	**Es war gebaut.**
Present perfect	**Es ist gebaut worden.**	**Es ist gebaut gewesen.**
Pluperfect	**Es war gebaut worden.**	**Es war gebaut gewesen.**
Future	**Es wird gebaut werden.**	**Es wird gebaut.**

139. Express the following in the actional passive.

1. It is found.
2. It was destroyed.
3. It was shown.
4. It was saved.
5. It is repaired.
6. It is begun.
7. It will be cut.
8. It had been built.
9. It was paid.
10. It is said.

140. Express the preceding in the statal passive.

SPECIAL MEANINGS OF CERTAIN VERBS

kennen, wissen, können

The verb *to know* can be expressed in German with three different verbs.

kennen—*to know people or things* (in the sense to be acquainted with)

Ich kenne diese Stadt.	*I know this city.*
Hast du ihn gut gekannt?	*Did you know him well?*

wissen—*to know a fact.* This verb frequently introduces dependent clauses.

Er wusste es schon.	*He already knew it.*
Weisst du, wo er wohnt?	*Do you know where he lives?*

können—*to know how* (in the sense of having mastered something)

Er kann gut Deutsch.	*He knows German well.*
Ich habe die Aufgabe gekonnt.	*I knew the lesson.*

141. Fill in the correct form of **kennen, wissen** or **können,** using the present tense.

1. Seit wann ______ du deinen Freund?
2. Ich ______ die Schauspielerin.
3. Wir ______ auch Englisch.
4. ______ ihr, wo er wohnt?
5. Er ______, dass sie krank ist.
6. Das Mädchen ______ uns nicht.
7. Ich ______, wo er ist.
8. ______ du Deutsch?
9. ______ ihr den Präsidenten?
10. Die Kinder ______, dass ich hier bin.

142. Write the German.

1. We know the president.
2. They know French.
3. Inge, did you know my aunt?
4. I know the answer.
5. He knows everything.

liegen, sitzen, stehen

These three verbs are used intransitively (they cannot be followed by a direct object). They denote location and if used with accusative/dative prepositions are followed by the dative case. All three are strong verbs.

liegen—*to lie*

Sie liegt stundenlang im Bett.	*She is lying in bed for hours.*
Er hat unter dem Auto gelegen.	*He was lying under the car.*

sitzen—*to sit*

Warum sitzt du hinter ihr?	*Why are you sitting behind her?*
Er hat dort gesessen.	*He was sitting there.*

stehen—*to stand*

Sie standen unter dem Apfelbaum.	*They were standing under the apple tree.*
Sie steht vor dem Bild.	*She is standing in front of the picture.*

legen, setzen, stellen

In contrast to the preceding verbs, these three verbs are followed by the accusative case when used with accusative/dative prepositions. All three are weak verbs and can be used reflexively.

legen, sich legen—*to lay, to put, to lie down*

Ich habe es auf den Tisch gelegt.	*I put it on the table.*
Er legte sich aufs Sofa.	*He lay down on the sofa.*

setzen, sich setzen—*to set, to sit down*

Setz dich auf den Boden!	*Sit down on the floor.*

stellen, sich stellen—*to place, to put (oneself), to stand*

Wer hat die Vase auf den Tisch gestellt?	*Who put the vase on the table?*
Stell dich neben mich!	*Place yourself (stand) beside me.*

143. Complete the following with the correct form of **liegen** or **legen.** Use the present tense.

1. Wo ______ das Buch?
2. Ich ______ auf dem Boden.
3. ______ er noch im Bett?
4. Warum ______ du dich nicht aufs Sofa?
5. Anna, ______ die Zeitung auf den Tisch!
6. Wir ______ unter dem Baum.
7. Er ______ das Messer neben den Teller.
8. Ich ______ das Papier auf den Tisch.

144. Complete the following with the appropriate form of **sitzen** or **setzen.** Use the present tense.

1. Er ______ sich vor Günther.
2. Wo ______ ihr?
3. Ich ______ mich ins Auto.
4. Peter ______ sich neben seine Tante.
5. Wohin ______ du dich?
6. Ich ______ auf dem Sofa.
7. Er ______ neben dem Mädchen.
8. ______ du in der Küche?

145. Complete the following with the correct form of **stehen** or **stellen.** Use the present tense.

1. Die Leute ______ an der Haltestelle.
2. Wohin ______ Mutter die Vase?
3. Ich ______ mich hinter Martin.
4. ______ du dich neben den Jungen?
5. Ich ______ den Teller auf den Tisch.
6. Wo ______ dein Freund?
7. Wir ______ den Stuhl ins Zimmer.
8. ______ du vor dem Auto?

lassen

The verb **lassen** can be used with or without a dependent infinitive. When it is used without a dependent infinitive, it has the meaning of *to leave* (*to leave something someplace*). The past participle is prefixed with **ge-** in this case.

Ich lasse den Hund zu Hause.	*I leave the dog at home.*
Er hat sein Auto in der Garage gelassen.	*He left his car in the garage.*

When **lassen** is used with a dependent infinitive, it means *to let* or *to allow* (*to let someone do something*). In this case, the double infinitive construction is used in the compound tenses.

Bitte lasst ihn doch gehen!	*Please let him go.*
Er hat mich mitkommen lassen.	*He allowed me to come along.*

146. Complete the following with the appropriate German verb form. Use the present tense.

1. Wir ______ die Kinder dort. *leave*
2. Er ______ Irene hier ______. *allows to stay*
3. Herr Weiss, bitte ______ Sie Marianne ______! *let go*
4. Ich ______ Herbert ______. *let sing*
5. ______ du das Auto in der Garage? *leave*
6. Frau Hauptmann ______ ihre Tochter ______. *allows to call*
7. Thomas, ______ den Mantel hier! *leave*
8. Ich ______ die Tasche zu Hause. *leave*

147. Rewrite the following in the present perfect tense.

1. Wir lassen die Kinder spielen.
2. Er lässt das Fahrrad dort.
3. Lässt du die Jacke zu Hause?
4. Sie lassen uns mitmachen.
5. Rudi lässt Inge mitmachen.
6. Ich lasse die Katze im Garten.

Chapter 6

Interrogative Words and Constructions

INTERROGATIVE FORMS BY INVERSION

Simple Tenses

Questions that can be answered by **ja** (*yes*) or **nein** (*no*) are formed by inverting the subject and the verb of the declarative sentence. In German any verb may be inverted with the subject to start a question

Statement	*Question*
Robert reparierte das Auto.	*Reparierte* **Robert das Auto?**
Horst, du bist krank.	**Horst,** *bist* **du krank?**
Sie fährt auch mit.	*Fährt* **sie auch mit?**
Konrad kann Deutsch.	*Kann* **Konrad Deutsch?**

1. Form questions from the following.

1. Er kommt morgen.
2. Herbert bringt es zurück.
3. Er setzte sich aufs Bett.
4. Du weisst alles.
5. Die Männer arbeiteten viel.
6. Ihr braucht es.
7. Ihr amüsiert euch.
8. Petra bestellte auch Bier.
9. Die Touristen besichtigen das Schloss.
10. Er will nicht.
11. Du hörst nichts.
12. Sie muss in die Stadt.
13. Sie bleiben dort.
14. Er rauchte viel.
15. Du schwimmst nicht.

Compound Tenses and Dependent Infinitives

In compound tenses the subject and the auxiliary verb are inverted to form a question. In sentences containing dependent infinitives, the modal or verb used in such a way as **hören, sehen, helfen** and **lassen** is inverted with the subject. The dependent infinitive is in last position in questions.

Statement	*Question*
Er würde helfen.	***Würde* er *helfen?***
Robert, du hast es gesehen.	**Robert, *hast* du es *gesehen?***
Ihr hättet gelesen.	***Hättet* ihr *gelesen?***
Sie hat sich niedergesetzt.	***Hat* sie sich *niedergesetzt?***
Du kannst es machen.	***Kannst* du es *machen?***
Sie sehen ihren Vater kommen.	***Sehen* sie ihren Vater *kommen?***

2. Form questions from the following.

1. Er hat schon geschrieben.
2. Sie haben sich gestern kennengelernt.
3. Ihr habt alles verloren.
4. Sie wird es aufmachen.
5. Du darfst es nehmen.
6. Er hat sich verletzt.
7. Ihr werdet euch umziehen.
8. Du hättest es gekauft.
9. Er ist gestorben.
10. Sie können nicht dort bleiben.
11. Du lässt Peter helfen.
12. Sie sieht die Kinder spielen.
13. Er hat die Geschichte erzählt.
14. Ihr habt die Oper gesehen.
15. Sie haben immer studiert.

Use of *doch* in Answer to Negative Questions

In answer to a negative question, **doch** is used instead of **ja. Doch** is stressed when used this way.

Hast du *kein* Buch?	***Doch,* natürlich habe ich ein Buch.**
Könnt ihr *nicht* lesen?	***Doch,* wir können lesen.**
Bist du *nicht* krank?	***Doch,* ich bin krank.**

3. Form questions from the following taking the cue from the answers. Follow the model.

Kannst du nicht schwimmen? **Doch, ich kann schwimmen.**

1. ______? Doch, er ist hier.
2. ______? Doch, ich fahre mit.
3. ______? Doch, wir dürfen nach Bonn fahren.
4. ______? Doch, ich komme mit.
5. ______? Doch, sie hilft den Kindern.

INTERROGATIVE ADVERBS AND ADVERBIAL EXPRESSIONS

The following interrogative adverbs are used to introduce questions. Again, the subject and the verb, which follow the adverb, are inverted.

Wann?	*When?*	**Wie oft?**	*How often?*
Warum?	*Why?*	**Wieviel?**	*How much? How many?*
Wie?	*How?*	**Wie viele?**	*How many?*
Wie lange?	*How long?*	**Um wieviel Uhr?**	*At what time?*

Wann *kommt* der Zug *an?*	*When is the train arriving?*
Warum *hast* du nichts *gesagt?*	*Why didn't you say anything?*
Wie *ist* das Wetter?	*How is the weather?*
Wie lange *bleibst* du dort?	*How long are you staying there?*
Wie oft *besuchst* du sie?	*How often do you visit her?*

Wieviel *kostet* **es?**	*How much does it cost?*
Wieviel (Wie viele) Hunde *habt* **ihr?**	*How many dogs do you have?*
Um wieviel Uhr *kommst* **du?**	*At what time are you coming?*

Wieviel or *wie viele*

Both **wieviel** and **wie viele** correspond to the English *how many.* **Wieviel** is generally used in colloquial speech.

Wieviel (*Wie viele*) **Planeten gibt es?**	*How many planets are there?*

4. Complete the following with the appropriate interrogative adverb or adverbial expression.

1. Sie fliegt morgen ab. ______ fliegt sie ab?
2. Peter ist klug. ______ ist Peter?
3. Er besucht uns dreimal die Woche. ______ besucht er uns?
4. Der Film war lang. ______ war der Film?
5. Ich habe zehn Minuten gewartet. ______ hast du gewartet?
6. Das Hemd kostet zehn Mark. ______ kostet das Hemd?
7. Er heisst Hans. ______ heisst er?
8. Ich habe es dreimal gesehen. ______ hast du es gesehen?
9. Ich bleibe eine Woche dort. ______ bleibst du dort?
10. Er kommt um drei Uhr. ______ kommt er?
11. Sie ist am Nachmittag gekommen. ______ ist sie gekommen?
12. Wir kommen nächste Woche. ______ kommt ihr?
13. Ich komme nicht, weil ich krank bin. ______ kommst du nicht?
14. Wir treffen Johann um zehn Uhr. ______ trefft ihr Johann?
15. Er kommt im Sommer. ______ kommt er?

Wo, woher, wohin

The interrogative adverb **wo** (*where*) implies locality. The answer usually contains a preposition followed by the dative case.

Wo **seid ihr?**	**Wir sind in der Schule.**

The interrogative adverb **woher** (*from which place*) is used in questions to determine origin.

Woher **kommst du?**	**Ich komme aus dem Wald.**

The interrogative adverb **wohin** (*to which place*) expresses movement toward a certain place. The answer usually contains a preposition followed by the accusative case.

5. Complete the following with **wo, wohin** or **woher.**

1. Bärbel ist in Düsseldorf. ______ ist Bärbel?
2. Ich komme aus Zürich. ______ kommst du?
3. Wir fahren nach England. ______ fahrt ihr?
4. Er kommt von seiner Grossmutter. ______ kommt er?
5. Wir gehen ins Kino. ______ geht ihr?
6. Ich fahre in die Stadt. ______ fährst du?
7. Wir sind in der Küche. ______ seid ihr?
8. Therese kommt aus Deutschland. ______ kommt Therese.
9. Anna läuft ins Geschäft. ______ läuft Anna.
10. Ich bin hinter dem Haus. ______ bist du?

REVIEW

6. Form questions using the interrogative word that will elicit the italicized element in the response. Follow the model.

Anna kommt *morgen.* *Wann* **kommt Anna?**

1. Sie fährt *nach Kanada.*
2. Sie bringen es *übermorgen.*
3. Alexander besuchte uns *dreimal.*
4. Heute ist es *heiss.*
5. Sie ist *in Holland.*
6. Er sieht mich *zweimal am Tag.*
7. Ella kommt *aus München.*
8. Sie bleiben *drei Monate* dort.
9. Sie sind *in Köln.*
10. Es kostet *zehn Mark.*

INTERROGATIVE PRONOUNS

Wer, wen, wem, wessen

The following interrogative pronouns are used when questions refer to people:

Nominative	**Wer?**	*Who?*
Accusative	**Wen?**	*Whom?*
Dative	**Wem?**	*Whom?*
Genitive	**Wessen?**	*Whose?*

There are no plural forms of the preceding interrogative pronouns. The answers, however, may be in the singular or the plural.

Wer **kommt?**	*Who is coming?*
Wen **hast du gesehen?**	*Whom did you see?*
Für *wen* **kaufst du es?**	*For whom are you buying it?*
Wem **gehört die Kamera?**	*To whom does the camera belong?*
Bei *wem* **bleibst du?**	*With whom are you staying?*
Wessen **Mantel ist das?**	*Whose coat is that?*

Was

The interrogative pronoun **was** is used in questions referring to things, ideas or actions. The form **was** is the same for the nominative and the accusative case. There is no dative and no genitive singular, as well as no plural. The answers, however, may be in the singular or the plural.

Was **ist das?**	*What is that?*
Was **machst du?**	*What are you doing?*

7. Complete the following with the correct interrogative pronoun.

1. _______ hat er dir gegeben?
2. _______ bringst du Blumen?
3. _______ habt ihr gegessen?
4. Bei _______ hast du gewohnt?
5. _______ arbeitet dort?
6. Mit _______ gehst du?
7. _______ besucht ihr?
8. _______ Wagen ist das?
9. Für _______ machst du das?
10. Von _______ hast du das?
11. _______ hast du geholfen?
12. _______ habt ihr getroffen?
13. _______ kann das machen?
14. _______ hat sie gedankt?
15. _______ Hut liegt dort?
16. Zu _______ geht ihr?
17. Gegen _______ bist du?
18. _______ Buch ist das?
19. _______ sagte er?
20. _______ tust du?

Wo- Compounds

The interrogative pronoun **was** is usually avoided after dative and accusative prepositions. Instead, **wo(r)-** is prefixed to the preposition to form the question. (See Chapter 2.)

***Worauf* wartest du?**	*What are you waiting for?*
***Wovor* fürchten Sie sich?**	*What are you afraid of?*
***Wofür* interessierst du dich?**	*What are you interested in?*

Wo- compounds can be used with all accusative and dative prepositions except **entlang, ohne, ausser, gegenüber, seit, hinter, neben** and **zwischen.**

Wo- compounds cannot refer to people. The interrogative pronouns must be used in such cases.

An *wen* erinnerst du dich?	**An Hedwig.**
***Woran* erinnerst du dich?**	**An letzten Sommer.**

8. Complete the following with the correct preposition + interrogative pronoun or **wo-** compound. Take your cue from the answers.

    1. _______ sprecht ihr. Von dem Sportwagen.
    2. _______ repariert er? Die Uhr.
    3. _______ fahrt ihr? Mit dem Zug.
    4. _______ habt ihr gefragt? Herrn Böll.
    5. _______ habt ihr gefragt? Nach dem Weg.
    6. _______ brauchst du Geld? Für die Karten.
    7. _______ hofft er? Auf gutes Wetter.
    8. _______ hast du das gekauft? Für Susi.
    9. _______ wundert er sich? Über Ursula.
    10. _______ brauchst du? Den Schlüssel.
    11. _______ sprecht ihr? Mit Frau Kröger.
    12. _______ interessiert er sich? Für moderne Musik.
    13. _______ liegt es? In der Schachtel.
    14. _______ brauchst du das? Zum Reparieren.
    15. _______ setzt du dich? Hinter die dicke Dame.

Welch- (which, which one)

The question word **welch-** may be used attributively as an interrogative adjective or as an interrogative pronoun. **Welch-** receives the endings of the definite article. All forms in the singular and plural are used.

Interrogative Adjective	*Interrogative Pronoun*
***Welches* Haus gehört euch?**	***Welches* möchtest du haben?**
***Welchen* Wein hat er getrunken?**	***Welchen* hat sie gekauft?**
Mit *welchem* Auto wollen wir fahren?	**Aus *welchem* ist sie gestiegen?**
***Welche* Blumen soll ich abschneiden?**	***Welche* kann er bringen?**

9. Complete the following with the correct form of **welch.**

    1. _______ Kinder haben es genommen?
    2. Bei _______ Leuten seid ihr geblieben?
    3. Nach _______ Strasse hat er gefragt?
    4. _______ Teppich habt ihr gekauft?

5. Aus _______ Land kommt er?
6. _______ Buch gehört dir?
7. Mit _______ Studentin kommst du zusammen?
8. Für _______ Roman interessierst du dich?
9. In _______ Haus wohnen Sie?
10. _______ Blume gefällt dir?
11. _______ Wagen ist kaputt?
12. _______ Kette hat er gekauft?

10. Complete the following with the correct form of the interrogative pronoun **welch-**. Take your cue from the statement. Follow the model.

Hier sind schöne Äpfel. Welchen möchtest du haben?

1. Dort sind viele Hunde. _______ gehört dir?
2. Ich habe zwei Autos. Mit _______ möchtest du fahren?
3. Wir besuchen unsre Tanten. Für _______ kaufst du ein Geschenk?
4. Dort sind viele Taschen. _______ gehört dir?
5. Dort liegen viele Bleistifte. _______ brauchst du?

11. Rewrite in the plural.

1. Welches nimmst du?
2. Welche hat er gekauft.
3. Von welcher erzählt er?
4. Welchen brauchst du?
5. Für welche kauft er es?

INTERROGATIVE ADJECTIVE

Was für ein- is usually used as an interrogative adjective. In the singular, the indefinite article **ein-** receives adjective endings. In the plural the expression is **was für. Für** does not act as a preposition in these expressions.

Was für eine **Maschine habt ihr gekauft?**	**Eine Drehmaschine.**
Mit was für einem **Herrn hast du gesprochen?**	**Mit einem alten Herrn.**
Was für **Leute sind das?**	**Das sind Gastarbeiter.**

12. Express in German.

1. What kind of car is that?
2. What kind of girl is that?
3. With what kind of people does he go to Germany?
4. In what kind of house do they live?
5. What kind of books does he write?

Chapter 7

Negative Words and Constructions

THE NEGATIVE *nicht*

Verbs are made negative with the use of **nicht** (*not*). Although **nicht** occurs in various positions in the sentence, it usually negates the entire statement. The rules for the position of **nicht** follow.

In Last Position

When a verb (except **sein**) is in the present or the imperfect tense, and the sentence consists of the following elements, **nicht** occurs in last position. In each example in this chapter, the affirmative is given first, the negative second.

Subject and Verb

Sie liest.	**Sie liest** *nicht.*
Anton fragte.	**Anton fragte** *nicht.*

Subject, Verb, and Direct Object (Noun or Pronoun)

Wir besuchten die Dame.	**Wir besuchten die Dame** *nicht.*
Gisela holte es.	**Gisela holte es** *nicht.*
Wir freuten uns.	**Wir freuten uns** *nicht.*

Subject, Verb, Direct Object (Pronoun) and Indirect Object (Noun or Pronoun)

Sie gab es dem Kind.	**Sie gab es dem Kind** *nicht.*
Ich erklärte es ihr.	**Ich erklärte es ihr** *nicht.*

Subject, Verb, Indirect Object (Noun or Pronoun) and Direct Object (Noun)

Ich gab dem Jungen die Birne.	**Ich gab dem Jungen die Birne** *nicht.*
Werner kaufte ihr die Vase.	**Werner kaufte ihr die Vase** *nicht.*

Subject, Verb, Objects, and Adverb of Time

Er besuchte uns heute.	**Er besuchte uns heute** *nicht.*

1. Rewrite the following sentences in the negative.

1. Er kennt den Herrn.
2. Wir geben es den Leuten.
3. Ich wasche mich.
4. Heinz weiss es.
5. Sie kamen vorgestern.
6. Ich kaufe den Mantel.
7. Sie nimmt es.
8. Er dankt mir.
9. Ich zeige ihr den Roman.
10. Wir rauchen.

Preceding Certain Elements

Nicht precedes the following elements in the statement it negates:

Predicate Adjectives and Nouns

Er ist krank.	**Er ist *nicht* krank.**
Das sind meine Kinder.	**Das sind *nicht* meine Kinder.**

Separable Prefixes

Das Flugzeug flog ab.	**Das Flugzeug flog *nicht* ab.**

Past Participles

Sie sind gefahren.	**Sie sind *nicht* gefahren.**

Dependent Infinitives

Wir hören sie lachen.	**Wir hören sie *nicht* lachen.**
Ich darf kommen.	**Ich darf *nicht* kommen.**
Ich hoffe, es zu sehen.	**Ich hoffe, es *nicht* zu sehen.**

Double Infinitives

Er hat es machen wollen.	**Er hat es *nicht* machen wollen.**

Adverbs of Place or Prepositional Phrases

Er wohnte hier.	**Er wohnte *nicht* hier.**
Wir sind im Wohnzimmer.	**Wir sind *nicht* im Wohnzimmer.**
Ich freue mich darauf.	**Ich freue mich *nicht* darauf.**

When a past participle and prepositional phrase or adverb of place occur in the same sentence, **nicht** precedes the prepositional phrase or adverb of place.

Ich habe im Sand gelegen.	**Ich habe *nicht* im Sand gelegen.**
Er war zu Hause gewesen.	**Er war *nicht* zu Hause gewesen.**
Sie hat dort gespielt.	**Sie hat *nicht* dort gespielt.**

In Dependent Clauses

Nicht precedes the verb or verbal complex in a dependent clause.

Ich weiss, dass er arbeitet.	**Ich weiss, dass er *nicht* arbeitet.**
Sie sagt, dass er kommen kann.	**Sie sagt, dass er *nicht* kommen kann.**
Ich hoffe, dass er es gesehen hat.	**Ich hoffe, dass er es *nicht* gesehen hat.**

2. Rewrite in the negative.

1. Sie haben gespielt.
2. Ich wollte die Rechnung bezahlen.
3. Wir haben sie schreien hören.
4. Maria hat neben dem Hotel gewartet.
5. Ich weiss, dass er fliegen will.
6. Das ist meine Tante.

7. Er sagt, dass er sie gesucht hätte.
8. Das Mädchen fährt heim.
9. Wir sind zur Schule gegangen.
10. Ich bin dort geblieben.
11. Wir sind im Kino.
12. Ich sehe sie kommen.
13. Er kommt mit.
14. Ihr könnt es sehen.
15. Sie sind reich.
16. Er hat hier gewartet.
17. Wir haben es geholt.
18. Das sind meine Bücher.
19. Ich hoffe, Inge zu besuchen.
20. Du hast sie genommen.

With *sondern*

The negative **nicht** does not always occur in fixed position. It may directly precede any element (except a conjugated verb) it negates. In this case, **nicht** is usually followed by a clause introduced by **sondern** (*but, on the contrary*).

Sie raucht *nicht* Zigaretten, *sondern* Zigarren.
She doesn't smoke cigarettes but cigars.
Er hat *nicht* sie besucht, *sondern* ihre Schwester.
He didn't visit her but her sister.

3. Rewrite the following in the negative, placing **nicht** in the appropriate position. Take your cue from the clause introduced by **sondern.** Follow the model.

Er hat das Flugzeug gesehen.
_______, sondern gehört.
Er hat das Flugzeug nicht gesehen, sondern gehört.

1. Sie ist bei ihrer Tante geblieben.
   _______, sondern bei ihrer Schwester.
2. Er hat das Auto repariert.
   _______, sondern das Fahrrad.
3. Wir haben das rote Buch gekauft.
   _______, sondern das blaue.
4. Ich brauche den Löffel.
   _______, sondern das Messer.
5. Ihr habt das Radio gewonnen.
   _______, sondern gestohlen.
6. Ich lese die Zeitung.
   _______, sondern den Roman.

In the Negative Interrogative

The rules for negation with **nicht** also apply to the position of **nicht** in a negative interrogative construction.

Arbeitest du?	**Arbeitest du *nicht?***
Gehst du mit?	**Gehst du *nicht* mit?**
Hast du ihn dort kennengelernt?	**Hast du ihn *nicht* dort kennengelernt?**

4. Rewrite the following in the negative.

1. Habt ihr ihnen geholfen?
2. Sind sie abgefahren?
3. Holt sie es?
4. Macht sie mit?
5. Darfst du bleiben?
6. Hast du ihn gefragt?
7. Ist das dein Freund?
8. Hast du mitgesungen?
9. Rasiert er sich?
10. Hat sie es vergessen?
11. Willst du ihm helfen?
12. War das seine Frau?
13. Ist sie schön?
14. Kaufst du die Blumen?
15. Kann er sich daran erinnern?

NEGATIVE AND AFFIRMATIVE QUESTIONS—*doch* AND *ja*

When answering the negative question, a stressed **doch** is used instead of **ja.**

Fährst du ***nicht*** **nach Hause?**	***Doch,*** **ich fahre nach Hause.**
Kann sie ***nicht*** **lesen?**	***Doch,*** **sie kann lesen.**

When the answer to an affirmative question is affirmative, **ja** is used.

Fährst du nach Hause?	***Ja,*** **ich fahre nach Hause.**
Kann sie lesen?	***Ja,*** **sie kann lesen.**

5. Answer the following questions, using **ja** or **doch.**

1. War er krank?
2. Ist er nicht gestorben?
3. Hast du es gekonnt?
4. Braucht ihr es nicht?
5. Hat er es nicht gefressen?
6. Ist sie nicht intelligent?

THE NEGATIVE FORM OF *brauchen*

The negative form of **brauchen (brauchen + nicht zu +** infinitive) is usually preferred to the negative form of **müssen** to express *not to have to* (see Chapter 5, "Dependent Infinitives," p. 140).

Muss er hier bleiben?
Nein, er ***braucht nicht*** **hier** ***zu*** **bleiben.**
Muss er Cornelia helfen?
Nein, er ***braucht*** **Cornelia** ***nicht zu*** **helfen.**

6. Rewrite the following in the negative.

1. Sie muss kommen.
2. Hans muss schreiben.
3. Ihr müsst abfahren.
4. Wir müssen gehen.
5. Ich muss studieren.
6. Sie müssen arbeiten.
7. Wir müssen springen.
8. Du musst den Roman lesen.

OTHER NEGATIVE WORDS

The following negatives follow the same rules for position that apply to **nicht.**

gar nicht—*not at all*

Das ist ***gar nicht*** **teuer.**	*That is not at all expensive.*

nicht mehr—*no more, no longer, any more*

Sie wohnen ***nicht mehr*** **hier.**	*They don't live here anymore.*

nie—*never*

Er hilft uns ***nie.***	*He never helps us.*

noch nicht—*not yet*

Wir haben uns ***noch nicht*** **umgezogen.**	*We haven't changed yet.*

noch nie—*not ever*

Wir waren ***noch nie*** **dort.**	*We have not ever been there.*

7. Rewrite the following, adding the German equivalent of the Eng

1. Er fragt uns. *never*
2. Wir sind müde. *not at all*
3. Sie wohnt in Bonn. *no longer*
4. Ich kann fahren. *not yet*
5. Er hat sie gesehen. *not ever*
6. Er hilft. *never*
7. Sie geht ins Kino. *no more*
8. Er war in Deutschland. *not ever*
9. Wir sind nach H
10. Sie sind freundl
11. Ich habe Schne
12. Er kennt mich.
13. Sie lernte den
14. Wir machen mit. *not at al*
15. Er hat die Sammlung verkauft. *not yet*

The Negative Article *kein-*

Kein- (*no, not any, not a*) precedes a noun object or a predicate noun. It is used when the noun in the affirmative statement is used with an indefinite article or with no article.

Er hat einen Bruder.	**Er hat *keinen* Bruder.**
Wir trinken Milch.	**Wir trinken *keine* Milch.**

When the noun in the affirmative is preceded by a definite article, a **"der"** word or a possessive adjective, the negative **nicht** is used instead.

Dieses Bier schmeckt gut.	**Dieses Bier schmeckt *nicht* gut.**
Meine Tochter ist hier.	**Meine Tochter ist *nicht* hier.**
Der Hund bellt.	**Der Hund bellt *nicht*.**

8. Rewrite the following in the negative, using **kein-** or **nicht.**

1. Er erzählte ein Märchen.
2. Wir besuchten eine bekannte Stadt.
3. Er hat unser Kind gesehen.
4. Hat sie Blumen gekauft?
5. Trinkt er Wasser?
6. Ich habe einen warmen Mantel.
7. Das sind Haselnüsse.
8. Ich habe mich auf die Ferien gefreut.
9. Wir essen Bananen.
10. Ich habe einen Freund.
11. Ich kenne den Herrn.
12. Sie singt das Lied.
13. Er hat Kinder.
14. Dieser Ring ist teuer.
15. Hier liegt ein Buch.
16. Wer isst Brot?
17. Das ist ein Tachometer.
18. Die Lehrerin schreibt.
19. Ist die Milch sauer?
20. Ich habe Zeit.

The Pronouns *nichts, niemand*

Nichts (*nothing*) and **niemand** (*nobody*) are used only in the singular. **Nichts** has no endings, and no endings are required for **niemand. Nichts** can be followed by a neuter adjective used as a noun.

Er hat *nichts* gekauft.	*He bought nothing.*
Er gab mir *nichts* Kostbares.	*He gave me nothing valuable.*
Ich kenne *niemand*.	*I know nobody.*

9. Write the German.

1. He can see nothing.
2. Nobody helps us.
3. I have nothing old.
4. They know nothing.
5. He asks nobody.

Chapter 8

Pronouns

PERSONAL PRONOUNS

Nominative Case

Singular		*Plural*	
ich	*I*	**wir**	*we*
du	*you*	**ihr**	*you*
er	*he, it*	**sie**	*they*
sie	*she, it*	**Sie**	*you*
es	*it*		

Second Person

In German there are three personal pronouns for *you.* The singular familiar pronoun **du** is used when addressing a member of the family, a child, a friend or an animal. The plural familiar pronoun **ihr** is used when addressing two or more members of the family, children, friends or animals. The pronoun of formal address is **Sie.** The same form is used for the singular and the plural. It is used when addressing an acquaintance, a stranger or someone whom one would address with **Herr, Frau, Fräulein. Sie** takes the same verb form used for the third person plural **sie** (*they*). The pronoun **Sie** as well as its possessive forms are always capitalized.

Karin, kannst ***du*** **mir helfen?**	*Karin, can* you *help me?*
Kinder, habt ***ihr*** **Zeit?**	*Children, do* you *have time?*
Fräulein Stifter, kommen ***Sie*** **auch?**	*Miss Stifter, are* you *also coming?*

In a letter or a note, the personal pronouns **du** and **ihr,** as well as the corresponding possessive forms, are capitalized.

Liebe Inge! Ich freue mich schon darauf, dass ***Du Deine*** **Ferien bei uns verbringen wirst.**

Third Person

The gender of the third person pronouns is determined by the antecedent. Masculine, feminine and neuter nouns are replaced by the pronouns that correspond to their grammatical gender. The pronouns **er, sie, es** correspond to English *it,* if they refer to things. **Er** and **sie** correspond to *he* and *she,* if the noun denotes a male or female being.

The third person plural pronoun **sie** (*they*) refers to both things and people.

Wo ist der Wagen?	***Er* ist in der Garage.**
Where is the car?	*It is in the garage.*
Wo ist der Junge?	***Er* ist im Haus.**
Where is the boy?	*He is in the house.*
Dort ist die Kirche.	***Sie* ist sehr alt.**
There is the church.	*It is very old.*
Wann kommt Mutter?	***Sie* kommt bald.**
When is mother coming?	*She is coming soon.*

The neuter noun **das Mädchen** is replaced by the personal pronoun **es,** unless the girl's name is stated. Then it is replaced by **sie.**

Wer ist das Mädchen?	***Es* ist Roberts Schwester.**
Gabi ist nicht hier.	***Sie* ist in der Stadt.**

The neuter noun **das Fräulein** is always replaced by **sie.**

Welches Fräulein hat dir geholfen?	**Dort steht *sie*.**

1. Complete the following with the correct personal pronouns.

   1. Paul war in Deutschland. Jetzt spricht ______ gut Deutsch.
   2. Petra, wohin hast ______ das Geld gelegt?
   3. Meine Herren, was brauchen ______ noch?
   4. Wo liegt die Zeitung? Dort liegt ______.
   5. Rex, ______ bist ein guter Hund.
   6. Liebe Kinder! Hoffentlich habt ______ Eure Ferien gut verbracht.
   7. Das Mädchen blutet. ______ hat sich verletzt.
   8. Wo ist Fräulein Sommer? ______ ist am Bodensee.
   9. Toni und Georg, wo seid ______ denn?
   10. Meine Kinder sind nicht hier. ______ sind in England.
   11. Die Katze schläft. ______ ist müde.
   12. Inge ist krank. ______ ist im Krankenhaus.
   13. Frau Steinhagel, sind ______ heute abend dort?
   14. Die Blätter sind abgefallen. ______ liegen unter dem Baum.
   15. Wo ist das Messer? Hier ist ______.
   16. Gudrun und Ute, was habt ______ gemacht?
   17. Meine Eltern machen Urlaub. ______ sind in der Schweiz.
   18. Günther, hast ______ den Wagen?

Accusative Case

Singular		*Plural*	
mich	*me*	**uns**	*us*
dich	*you*	**euch**	*you*
ihn	*him, it*	**sie**	*them*
sie	*her, it*	**Sie**	*you*
es	*it*		

The accusative personal pronouns are used when they are the direct object of the verb or the object of a preposition requiring the accusative case.

Er hat *mich* besucht.	*He visited* me.
Wir gehen ohne *ihn*.	*We are going without* him.
Liebst du *sie?*	*Do you love* her?

The third person singular and plural may refer to both things and people.

Kennst du nicht Herrn Krull? Doch, ich kenne *ihn*.
Hast du die Tasche? Ja, ich habe *sie*.

2. Complete the following with the correct pronouns.

 1. Schreibt Karl den Brief? Ja, ______ schreibt ______.
 2. Trifft Marlene ihre Freundinnen? Ja, ______ trifft ______.
 3. Seht ihr Helga? Ja, ______ sehen ______.
 4. Kocht Mutter das Abendessen? Ja, ______ kocht ______.
 5. Will Ute die Blumen pflücken? Ja, ______ will ______ pflücken.
 6. Kennt Konrad seine Grosseltern? Ja, ______ kennt ______.
 7. Siehst du den Beamten? Ja, ______ sehe ______.
 8. Erinnerten sich die Kinder an ihre Tante? Ja, ______ erinnerten sich an ______.
 9. Kennst du das Mädchen? Ja, ______ kenne ______.
 10. Kauft ihr den Mantel? Ja, ______ kaufen ______.
 11. Triffst du mich? Ja, ______ treffe ______.
 12. Liebt Peter seine Freundin? Ja, ______ liebt ______.
 13. Esst ihr den Kuchen? Ja, ______ essen ______.
 14. Nimmst du das Auto? Ja, ______ nehme ______.

3. Rewrite the following, substituting the italicized element with the pronoun.

 1. Renate braucht *das Buch.*
 2. Wir kaufen *den Apparat.*
 3. Ich setzte mich neben *die Alte.*
 4. Wir essen *die Bananen.*
 5. Ich darf *den Roman* lesen.
 6. Wer hat *den Hasen* gefüttert?

4. Answer the following questions with complete sentences.

 1. Hat er mich erkannt?
 2. Schreibt er euch?
 3. Hast du es für mich gekauft?
 4. Geht er ohne euch?
 5. Könnt ihr uns dort besuchen?

Dative Case

Singular		*Plural*	
mir	*me*	**uns**	*us*
dir	*you*	**euch**	*you*
ihm	*him, it*	**ihnen**	*them*
ihr	*her, it*	**Ihnen**	*you*
ihm	*it*		

The dative personal pronouns are used as the indirect object of verbs, or as the object of prepositions requiring the dative case. The accusative and the dative forms **uns, euch** are identical.

Kaufst du *ihr* etwas?	*Are you buying* her *something?*
Warum ist er neben *dir?*	*Why is he beside* you?

5. Rewrite the following, substituting the italicized noun with a personal pronoun.

1. Er gab es *seiner Freundin.*
2. Wir helfen *unsrem Lehrer.*
3. Gibst du *dem Hund* das Futter?
4. Wir unterhielten uns mit *der Dame.*
5. Er erzählte von *dem Verunglückten.*
6. Wohnst du bei *deinen Verwandten?*
7. Ich schrieb *meinen Freunden* Ansichtskarten.
8. Sie holte *dem Mädchen* Medizin.
9. Es gehört *meinen Eltern.*
10. Sie bringen *der Kranken* Essen.
11. Es gefällt *meinem Onkel.*
12. Ich kaufe *Ihrer Mutter* etwas.
13. Er kommt von *seinem Freund.*
14. Wir stehen hinter *dem Mann.*

6. Answer the following questions with complete sentences. Start with **Ja, . . .**

1. Hat er dir etwas gebracht?
2. Zeigst du uns die Stadt?
3. Sagt ihr uns die Wahrheit?
4. Hat er dir geholfen?
5. Bringst du mir etwas mit?
6. Hat er dir dafür gedankt?
7. Hat sie euch geholfen?
8. Kaufen Sie ihm etwas?
9. Gefällt dir das Bild?
10. Kauft ihr mir den Wagen?

Position of Pronoun Objects

Preceding Noun Objects

When a dative or an accusative pronoun occurs in the sentence along with a noun object, the pronoun precedes the noun, regardless of its case.

Er hat *mir* das Problem erklärt.
Er hat *sie* seinem Vater vorgestellt.

7. Rewrite the following, substituting a pronoun for the italicized element. Make changes in the word order when necessary.

1. Er gab seiner Mutter *das Geld.*
2. Ich habe *meiner Freundin* ein Paket geschickt.
3. Sie zeigte ihrem Kind *die Tiere.*
4. Sie erzählen *ihren Freunden* die Neuigkeit.
5. Sie bringen den Kranken *Blumen.*
6. Er kauft seiner Tante *die Orchidee.*
7. Ich schreibe *dem Lehrer* eine Karte.
8. Sie glaubt *dem Jungen* die Geschichte.
9. Ich gebe der Dame *die Karte.*
10. Wir kaufen *den Kindern* Geschenke.

Double Object Pronouns

When an accusative pronoun object and a dative pronoun object are used in the same sentence, the accusative pronoun always precedes the dative pronoun.

Hat er *es* dir geschrieben?
Ich habe *ihn* ihm geschenkt.
Ich habe *sie* ihr gegeben.

8. Rewrite the following, changing the noun objects to pronouns.

1. Wir bringen dem Verletzten Wasser.
2. Ich hole meinem Freund den Fussball.

3. Wir erzählten den Kindern die Geschichte.
4. Er gibt dem Kind den Hund.
5. Er hat seiner Freundin die Geschichte geglaubt.
6. Johann zeigte den Ausländern das Rathaus.
7. Der Professor erklärte den Studenten die Theorie.
8. Ich kaufe meinen Eltern die Maschine.
9. Er schreibt seinem Lehrer die Neuigkeit.
10. Dieter holt dem Hund das Wasser.

9. Answer the following questions affirmatively with complete sentences. Change the noun object to a pronoun. Make all necessary changes.

1. Hat er dir die Theaterkarten geschenkt?
2. Hast du ihnen die Aufnahme gezeigt?
3. Hat er euch die Bücher gekauft?
4. Bringst du mir den Kaffee?
5. Hat sie euch den Wagen gegeben?

In Relation to the Subject

Following the Subject

If the subject, which may be a noun or a pronoun, is in first position of the sentence, the pronoun objects follow the subject. The subject and the objects are separated only by the verb.

Peter **hat** *ihn* **gesehen.**
Ich **zeige** *dir* **nichts.**
Sie **bringen** *es uns.*

Following or Preceding the Subject

If the subject is a noun, and if it is not in first position of the sentence or clause, the pronoun objects may precede or follow the subject.

Kennt *ihn Peter?*	or	**Kennt** *Peter ihn?*	*Does Peter know him?*
Kauft *dir* **Ute etwas?**	or	**Kauft Ute** *dir* **etwas?**	*Is Ute buying you something?*

However, if the subject is a pronoun, the pronoun object must always follow the subject.

Kennt er *ihn?*
Kauft sie *dir* **etwas?**

10. Rewrite the following, changing the italicized element to a pronoun. Have the pronoun object precede the subject when possible.

1. Hilft Ellen *ihren Brüdern?*
2. Ich glaube, dass Maria *das Kleid* gekauft hat.
3. Wir wissen nicht, ob er *die Kirche* besichtigt hat.
4. Ich habe Zeit, weil Norma *unsren* Onkel abholt.
5. Morgen kauft Susi *ihrer Freundin* den Pullover.

11. Rewrite the following, changing the italicized element to a personal pronoun. Have the pronoun object follow the subject.

1. Jeden Tag holt Pia *ihrem Vater* die Zeitung.
2. Ich weiss, wann Peter *Frau Müller* geholfen hat.

3. Bringt Gabriele *das Programm?*
4. Hat er *das Geld* genommen?
5. Weisst du, wo Dieter *die Leute* getroffen hat?

Prepositional Pronouns

Prepositional pronouns may be in the accusative or the dative case.

Accusative Case

Verb phrases containing the prepositions **an, auf, über** are followed by the accusative case.

denken an	*to think of*	**Ich denke oft an** *dich.*
lachen über	*to laugh about*	**Wir lachten über** *ihn.*
sprechen über	*to talk about (in detail)*	**Sprecht ihr über** *sie?*
warten auf	*to wait for*	**Warten Sie auf** *uns?*

Dative Case

The dative case is required after verb phrases containing the prepositions **von, zu, nach** and **vor.**

Angst haben vor	*to be afraid of*	**Er hat keine Angst vor** *Ihnen.*
einladen zu	*to invite to*	**Wir laden ihn zu** *uns* **ein.**
fragen nach	*to ask about*	**Hat er nach** *mir* **gefragt?**
hören von	*to hear from*	**Hast du von** *ihr* **gehört?**
sprechen von	*to talk of*	**Wir haben von** *ihm* **gesprochen.**
wissen von	*to know about*	**Was weisst du von** *ihnen?*

12. Replace the noun with the appropriate pronoun.

1. Er lachte über die Alte.
2. Wir sprechen von den Leuten.
3. Er fragt nach meiner Schwester.
4. Was weisst du von dem Herrn?
5. Er denkt an seine Frau.
6. Warten Sie auf den Professor?
7. Warum hast du Angst vor dem Hund?
8. Wir sprechen über seinen Onkel.
9. Ich habe von meinem Bruder gehört.
10. Er lädt sie zu seinen Eltern ein.

13. Complete the following with the appropriate accusative or dative pronoun.

1. Sie haben von ______ (*du*) gesprochen.
2. Wer hat Angst vor ______ (*er*)?
3. Was weiss er von ______ (*wir*)?
4. Wir haben über ______ (*sie*) gelacht.
5. Haben Sie über ______ (*wir*) gesprochen?
6. Hast du etwas von ______ (*er*) gehört?
7. Er fragt immer nach ______ (*du*).
8. Er wartete auf ______ (*du*).
9. Ladet ihr mich zu ______ (*ihr*) ein?
10. Denkst du auch an ______ (*ich*)?
11. Wer lacht über ______ (*wir*)?
12. Wir sprechen von ______ (*du*).
13. Ich spreche über ______ (*sie*).
14. Er wartet auf ______ (*Sie*).

Da- *Compounds*

When the third person pronouns are used with prepositions, they can refer only to people.

Sprecht ihr von Klaus?	**Ja, wir sprechen** *von ihm.* *Yes, we are talking about him.*
Wartet er auf seine Frau?	**Ja, er wartet** *auf sie.* *Yes, he is waiting for her.*
Bist du bei deinen Eltern?	**Ja, ich bin** *bei ihnen.* *Yes, I am with them.*

When the pronouns refer to things or ideas, the preposition is prefixed by **da(r)-**. (See Chapter 2.)

Sprecht ihr von dem Plan?	**Ja, wir sprechen** *davon.*
	Yes, we are talking about it.
Wartest du auf den Brief?	**Ja, ich warte** *darauf.*
	Yes, I am waiting for it.

14. Answer the following questions affirmatively, using the appropriate **da-** compound or personal pronoun.

1. Denkst du an deine Reise?
2. Liegst du unter dem Auto?
3. Wartest du auf Anna?
4. Sprecht ihr über die Oper?
5. Sprichst du von Marlene?
6. Fährst du mit dem Zug?
7. Stehst du vor den Bildern?
8. Wartest du auf das Paket?
9. Steht ihr neben euren Eltern?
10. Denkt er an seine Frau?
11. Fragt sie nach deiner Schwester?
12. Sitzen Sie hinter dem Herrn?
13. Arbeitest du mit dem Hammer?
14. Fahrt ihr mit euren Freunden?
15. Weisst du etwas von dem Plan?
16. Hast du Angst vor dem Alten?

REFLEXIVE PRONOUNS

Reflexive pronouns are used when the action expressed by the verb is both executed and received by the subject. (For a complete review, see Chapter 5.)

Accusative Case

Accusative reflexive pronouns are identical with the accusative personal pronouns, except for the third person singular and plural.

	Singular		*Plural*
mich	*myself*	**uns**	*ourselves*
dich	*yourself*	**euch**	*yourselves*
sich	*him-, her-, itself*	**sich**	*themselves, yourself, yourselves*

15. Complete the following with the correct reflexive pronouns.

1. Ich verletzte ______ beim Skilaufen.
2. Er rasiert ______ jeden Tag.
3. Wir müssen ______ waschen.
4. Stellt ______ vor!
5. Fürchten Sie ______ vor dem Hund?
6. Helga kann ______ nicht daran erinnern.
7. Warum hast du ______ verspätet?
8. Freust du ______ auf Weihnachten?
9. Ich lege ______ aufs Bett.
10. Die Kinder ziehen ______ um.

Dative Case

The dative reflexive pronouns are identical with the dative personal pronouns, except in the third person singular and plural. Here, as in the accusative, the reflexive pronoun is **sich**.

Singular		*Plural*	
mir	*myself*	**uns**	*ourselves*
dir	*yourself*	**euch**	*yourselves*
sich	*him-, her-, itself*	**sich**	*themselves, yourself, yourselves*

16. Complete the following with the correct reflexive pronouns.

1. Kauft ihr ______ das Pferd?
2. Ich habe ______ das Bier bestellt.
3. Er hat ______ weh getan.
4. Nimm ______ etwas!
5. Ich wasche ______ das Gesicht.
6. Kannst du ______ das vorstellen?
7. Die Kinder kauften ______ Schokolade.
8. Ich nehme ______ das Buch.
9. Kaufst du ______ das Auto?
10. Holen wir ______ die Möbel!

Position

Reflexive pronouns are placed as close to the subject as possible. The reflexive pronoun follows a pronoun subject. However, the reflexive pronoun never comes between the pronoun subject and the verb.

Er kaufte *sich* einen Anzug.
Erinnerst du *dich* an ihn?

If the subject is a noun, the reflexive pronoun may precede or follow it. However, the noun subject cannot be in first position of the sentence or clause.

Gestern hat *sich* Erika verletzt. or **Gestern hat Erika *sich* verletzt.**

17. Answer the following questions with complete sentences. Start the answer with the cue and place the reflexive pronoun in the same position as in the original sentence.

1. Wann haben sich die Kinder weh getan? *heute morgen*
2. Worauf freut sich Max? *auf die Ferien*
3. Warum hat sich der Beamte verspätet? *wegen des Unfalls*
4. Wann hat Vater sich das Auto gekauft? *vor einer Stunde*
5. Woran erinnert sich dein Freund? *an seine Ferien*
6. Wann putzt Barbara sich die Zähne? *am Abend*
7. Was kauft sich Herr Obermeyer? *ein Motorrad*
8. Wann rasiert sich Vater? *am Morgen*

POSSESSIVE PRONOUNS

mein-	*mine*	**unsr-**	*ours*
dein-	*yours*	**eur-**	*yours*
sein-	*his, its*	**ihr-**	*theirs*
ihr-	*hers*	**Ihr-**	*yours*

The possessive pronoun receives the endings of **welcher, welche, welches** in all cases. The gender of the possessive pronoun is determined by the gender of the noun it replaces.

Possessive Used as Adjective	*Possessive Used as Pronoun*
Wann triffst du *deinen* Freund?	**Ich treffe *meinen* um zwei Uhr.**
When are you meeting your friend?	*I am meeting mine at two o'clock.*
Das ist *sein* Mantel.	***Meiner* hängt im Schrank.**
That is his coat.	*Mine is hanging in the closet.*

Eure **Kinder sind hier.**	**Wo sind** *unsre?*
Your children are here.	*Where are ours?*

18. Complete the following with the correct form of the possessive pronoun.

1. Ich habe meine Bücher. Hast du ______?
2. Wir sprechen von unsrer Reise. Sprecht ihr von ______?
3. Habt ihr schon eure Freunde gesehen? Wir haben ______ noch nicht gesehen.
4. Er hat sein Geld bekommen. Ich habe ______ noch nicht bekommen.
5. Er schreibt seinen Freunden. Schreibst du ______?
6. Das ist nicht meine Schwester, sondern ______ (*his*).
7. Ich habe nicht deinen Mann gesehen, sondern ______ (*hers*).
8. Er wohnt nicht in seinem Haus, sondern in ______ (*ours*).
9. Ich war nicht bei deinen Eltern, sondern bei ______ (*mine*).
10. Ich schreibe nicht mit seinem Bleistift, sondern mit ______ (*hers*).

DEMONSTRATIVE PRONOUNS

The nominative, accusative and dative forms of **der, die, das** and of **dieser, diese, dieses** may be used as demonstrative pronouns. The demonstrative pronouns are the same as the demonstrative adjectives. (See Chapter 3.) In the dative plural, however, the demonstrative pronoun **der** is **denen.** The genitive is rarely used.

The demonstrative pronouns **der** and **dieser** may be followed by **hier** to correspond to the English *this one* (*these*) and **da** or **dort** to mean *that one* (*those*).

Ich kaufe *den hier.*	*I'll buy this one.*
Wem gehört *dieser dort?*	*To whom does that one belong?*
Geben Sie mir *diese da!*	*Give me those.*
Bleib bei *denen hier!*	*Stay with these.*

19. Complete the following with the appropriate form of the demonstrative pronoun **der.** Follow the model.

Der Mantel hier ist wärmer als ______.
Der Mantel hier ist wärmer als der dort (da).

1. Der Film hier ist länger als ______.
2. In dem Parkhaus dort sind mehr Autos als in ______.
3. Die Frau hier ist jünger als ______.
4. Er kam aus dem Haus da, nicht aus ______.
5. Ich kaufe die Maschine dort, nicht ______.
6. Wir sprechen von den Leuten hier, nicht von ______.

20. Complete the following with the correct demonstrative pronoun **dieser.**

1. Diese Brücke hier ist breiter als ______.
2. Wir fahren mit diesem Auto dort, nicht mit ______.
3. Er kauft nicht diese Bücher hier, sondern ______.
4. Dieser Ring da ist teurer als ______.
5. Ich möchte dieses Kleid dort, nicht ______.

INDEFINITE PRONOUNS

Singular

The following indefinite pronouns refer to people. They are used only in the nominative, accusative and dative case singular.

jeder—*everyone*

Ich habe *jeden* **gefragt.**	*I asked everyone.*
Er bekommt von *jedem* **etwas.**	*He gets something from everyone.*
Jeder **muss mitmachen.**	*Everyone has to participate.*

Note that the accusative and dative forms receive the endings of the definite article **der, die, das.**

jemand—*someone*

Er hat *jemand* **gehört.**	*He heard someone.*
Sie wohnt bei *jemand.*	*She is living with someone.*

The accusative and the dative forms are identical with the nominative. No endings are required.

niemand—*no one*

Ich kenne *niemand* **hier.**	*I know no one here.*
Er geht zu *niemand.*	*He is going to no one.*

No endings are required in the accusative and dative cases.

man—*one, they, people*

Man **kann nicht alles haben.**	*One can't have everything.*
Er hilft *einem* **gern.**	*He likes to help one (people).*

The form **man** occurs only in the nominative case. In the accusative **man** becomes **einen;** in the dative, **einem.**

The following indefinite pronouns refer only to things. They have no endings.

alles—*everything*

Ich habe *alles* **gegessen.**	*I ate everything.*

etwas—*something*

Ja, er hat *etwas* **gesagt.**	*Yes, he said something.*

nichts—*nothing*

Sie hat uns *nichts* **gebracht.**	*She brought us nothing.*

viel—*much*

Wir haben *viel* **gelernt.**	*We learned much.*

wenig—*little*

Er weiss *wenig.*	*He knows little.*

Plural

The following indefinite pronouns may refer to things or to people. They receive the plural endings of the definite article.

alle—*everyone, all*

Es gehört *allen.*	*It belongs to everyone.*

andere–*others* (*other ones*)

Wir haben auch ***andere.*** — *We also have others.*

einige–*some*

Einige **haben ihn im Park getroffen.** — *Some met him in the park.*

manche–*many*

Manche **bleiben gern hier.** — *Many like to stay here.*

mehrere–*several*

Ich habe ***mehrere*** **davon gekauft.** — *I bought several of them.*

viele–*many*

Er hat mit ***vielen*** **gespielt.** — *He played with many.*

wenige–*few*

Wenige **haben das Problem verstanden.** — *Few understood the problem.*

21. Complete the following with the correct form of the German indefinite pronoun.

1. Ich habe ______ (*no one*) gesehen.
2. Er hat ______ (*something*) gesagt.
3. ______ (*Few*) haben ihn besucht.
4. Er hat sich mit ______ (*some*) unterhalten.
5. ______ (*everyone*) war zu Hause.
6. Sie kann ______ (*nothing*).
7. ______ (*one*) sollte ihm danken.
8. ______ (*Many*) haben es gewusst.
9. Ich kenne ______ (*everyone*).
10. Sie gibt ______ (*one*) ______ (*nothing*).
11. Er weiss ______ (*much*).
12. Wir haben ______ (*little*) gesehen.
13. ______ (*Someone*) ist gekommen.
14. Ich habe dann ______ (*other ones*) gesucht.
15. Hast du ______ (*several*) gekauft?
16. ______ (*Many*) haben Talent.
17. Habt ihr ______ (*everything*) gemacht?
18. ______ (*People*) hat ihn gern.

RELATIVE PRONOUNS

The relative pronoun introduces a clause that modifies a noun. In German two sets of relative pronouns are used. One is a form of **der, die, das;** the other, a form of **welcher, welche, welches.** The relative pronoun **der** is more commonly used. **Welcher** is used primarily in writing and may be used for stylistic considerations.

The relative pronoun agrees with the noun it replaces in number and gender. The case, however, is determined by its use in the relative clause. Since the relative clause is a dependent clause, the conjugated verb moves to last position in that clause. Separable prefixes are joined to the verb. The relative clause is separated by a comma from the main clause.

The endings of the relative pronouns coincide with those of the definite article, except in the genitive singular and plural and in the dative plural.

Nominative Case

SINGULAR			*PLURAL*
Masculine	*Feminine*	*Neuter*	*All Genders*
der	**die**	**das**	**die**
welcher	**welche**	**welches**	**welche**

The relative pronouns in the following examples are in the nominative case because they function as the subject of the relative clause.

Kennst du den Mann, ***der*** **dort steht?**
Do you know the man who is standing there?
Otto kommt von der Lehrerin, ***die*** **ihm das Problem erklärt hat.**
Otto is coming from the teacher who explained the problem to him.
Das Mädchen, ***das*** **dort steht, ist seine Schwester.**
The girl who is standing there is his sister.
Siehst du die Vögel, ***die*** **dort auf dem Baum sitzen?**
Do you see the birds that are sitting there on the tree?

In the following sentence the relative pronoun **welche-** is preferred to avoid repetition of **die.**

Die Dame, ***welche*** **(die) die Brosche gekauft hat, ist sehr reich.**

22. Complete the following with the appropriate form of the nominative relative pronoun **der.**

1. Wo ist das Buch, ______ dir gehört?
2. Der Junge, ______ dort steht, ist mein Bruder.
3. Wo sind die Bilder, ______ uns so gefallen?
4. Die Frau, ______ bei uns wohnt, ist keine Sängerin.
5. Wie heisst der Dichter, ______ dieses Gedicht geschrieben hat?
6. Kennst du das Mädchen, ______ dort sitzt?
7. Dort ist die Lehrerin, ______ uns geholfen hat.
8. Wir fahren mit dem Zug, ______ jetzt ankommt.

Accusative Case

The forms of the accusative relative pronouns are identical with the nominative forms, except in the masculine singular. The accusative case of the relative pronoun is used when it functions as the direct object of the verb or as the object of a preposition that is followed by the accusative. No contractions are possible.

SINGULAR			*PLURAL*
Masculine	*Feminine*	*Neuter*	*All Genders*
den	**die**	**das**	**die**
welchen	**welche**	**welches**	**welche**

Der Anzug, ***den*** **du trägst, ist altmodisch.**
The suit that you are wearing is old fashioned.
Die Geschichte, ***die*** **wir gelesen haben, war sehr lang.**
The story that we read was very long.

Das Haus, in *das* wir ziehen, ist hundert Jahre alt.
The house into which we are moving is one hundred years old.
Das sind die Freunde, für *die* ich es gekauft habe.
Those are the friends for whom I bought it.

23. Complete the following with the appropriate accusative form of the relative pronoun **der.**

1. Wo sitzt der Junge, ______ du kennengelernt hast?
2. Die Frau, neben ______ ich mich gesetzt habe, ist Schauspielerin.
3. Der Mantel, ______ er angezogen hat, gehört mir.
4. Das Mädchen, auf ______ er wartete, ist meine Freundin.
5. Die Hunde, ______ ich füttern soll, sind ja wild.
6. Die Bluse, ______ du trägst, ist sehr hübsch.
7. Hier ist das Paket, ______ er mir geschickt hat.
8. Wir kennen den Lehrer, für ______ sie es macht.

24. Combine the sentences with a nominative or accusative relative pronoun. Follow the model.

Wie heisst das Mädchen? Wir haben es kennengelernt.
Wie heisst das Mädchen, das wir kennengelernt haben?

1. Liest du das Buch? Er hat es gebracht.
2. Brauchst du die Zeitung? Sie liegt auf dem Tisch.
3. Kennst du den Herrn? Wir haben ihn getroffen.
4. Heute kam der Junge. Er hatte uns damals geholfen.
5. Kennst du die Leute? Sie gehen dort spazieren.
6. Wo sind die Blumen? Ich habe sie gekauft.

Dative Case

The dative relative pronouns are used when they function as the indirect object of the verb of the dependent clause, or when they are the object of verbs or prepositions requiring the dative case. The dative plural relative pronoun differs from the definite article. It adds **-en** to become **denen.** No contractions are possible.

SINGULAR			*PLURAL*
Masculine	*Feminine*	*Neuter*	*All Genders*
dem	**der**	**dem**	**denen**
welchem	**welcher**	**welchem**	**welchen**

Dort liegt der Hund, vor *dem* ich Angst habe.
There lies the dog of which I am afraid.
Heute besucht mich meine Freundin, von *der* ich dir erzählt habe.
My girl friend, about whom I told you, is visiting me today.
Das Mädchen, *dem* ich die Kette gegeben hatte, hat es verloren.
The girl to whom I had given the necklace lost it.
Die Studenten, neben *denen* er sitzt, sind sehr intelligent.
The students next to whom he is sitting are very intelligent.

25. Complete the following with the correct dative relative pronoun **der.**

1. Das Buch, nach ______ er fragte, gehört mir.
2. Der Deutsche, mit ______ er spricht, kommt aus Berlin.

3. Die Leute, ______ ich helfen wollte, sind weggefahren.
4. Das Haus, in ______ wir wohnen, ist modern.
5. Dort ist die Reisende, ______ ich den Weg gezeigt habe.
6. Die Dame, ______ ich es gebe, ist sehr intelligent.
7. Die Strassen, nach ______ er fragt, sind im Zentrum.
8. Das Hotel, aus ______ er kommt, ist sehr alt.

26. Combine the two sentences with the correct form of the dative relative pronoun **welcher.**

1. Dort sitzt der Tourist. Du sollst ihm das Essen bringen.
2. Kennst du meine Geschwister. Ich wohne bei ihnen.
3. Die Leiter ist kaputt. Er steht darauf.
4. Hier ist das Auto. Wir fahren damit spazieren.
5. Der Stuhl ist alt. Du sitzt darauf.

Genitive Case

All genitive relative pronouns differ from the definite article. The relative pronoun **welcher** has the same forms as **der.**

SINGULAR			*PLURAL*
Masculine	*Feminine*	*Neuter*	*All Genders*
dessen	**deren**	**dessen**	**deren**

Ich treffe meinen Freund, *dessen* **Auto ich brauche.**
I'll meet my friend whose car I need.
Dort ist die Dame, *deren* **Geld ich gefunden habe.**
There is the lady whose money I found.
Das Haus, *dessen* **Baustil mir gefällt, wurde 1910 gebaut.**
The house, the style of which I like, was built in 1910.
Die Kinder, *deren* **Katze verletzt wurde, laufen zum Tierarzt.**
The children whose cat was injured are running to the veterinarian.

27. Complete the following with the correct genitive relative pronouns.

1. Die Frau, ______ Auto kaputt ist, sucht einen Mechaniker.
2. Der Dichter, ______ Roman wir gelesen haben, hält einen Vortrag.
3. Hier kommt das Kind, ______ Eltern ich gut kenne.
4. Die Künstler, ______ Werke wir besichtigen, sind weltbekannt.
5. Die Studentin, ______ Buch ich gefunden habe, ist nett.
6. Die Museen, ______ Sammlungen ich kenne, sind reich.
7. Dort ist der Junge, ______ Vater uns geholfen hat.
8. Wo ist das Mädchen, ______ Fahrrad dort liegt?

Indefinite Relative Pronouns

Wer, was

The indefinite relative pronouns **wer** (*whoever*) and **was** (*whatever*) are used when there is no antecedent.

Wer **mitgehen will, muss um fünf Uhr hier sein.**
Whoever wants to come along has to be here at five o'clock.

Was auch passiert, ich habe keine Angst.
Whatever happens I am not afraid.

28. Complete the following with the correct indefinite relative pronouns.

1. _______ mir hilft, wird belohnt.
2. _______ er sagt, ist die Wahrheit.
3. _______ das Geld genommen hat, soll es zurückgeben.
4. _______ er auch will, bekommt er.
5. _______ das Problem löst, bekommt den Preis.

The relative pronoun **was** (*that, which*) must be used if the antecedent is an indefinite pronoun referring to things (**alles, nichts, etwas,** etc.).

Er erzählte mir etwas, _was_ ich schon wusste.
He told me something that I knew already.

Was is also used when the antecedent is an entire clause.

Er hatte das Geld gewonnen, _was_ mich sehr freute.
He had won the money, about which I was very glad.

Wo

When the antecedent is the name of a country, city or place, **wo** (*where, in which*) is substituted for the relative pronoun.

Er besucht London, _wo_ er viele Freunde hat.
He is visiting London, where he has many friends.

29. Complete the following with the correct relative pronoun or pronoun substitute.

1. Er hat nichts, _______ grossen Wert hat.
2. Wir sind in Bayern, _______ es viele Barockkirchen gibt.
3. Wir fahren in die Alpen, _______ man gut skifahren kann.
4. Er ist sehr krank, _______ mir grosse Sorgen macht.
5. Alles, _______ ich habe, hat Inge mir geschenkt.
6. Er weiss etwas, _______ sehr wichtig ist.
7. Wir landen in Frankfurt, _______ es den internationalen Flughafen gibt.
8. Er ist der beste Sportler, _______ mich sehr freut.

Wo- compounds

When relative pronouns are preceded by prepositions and when they refer to things or ideas, they may be replaced by **wo-** compounds.

Das Paket, _worauf_ (auf das) er wartet, soll heute ankommen.
The package for which he is waiting is supposed to arrive today.

30. Rewrite the following, substituting the correct **wo-** compound for the preposition + relative pronoun.

1. Der Stuhl, auf dem du sitzt, ist eine Rarität.
2. Wir besuchen das Haus, in dem Goethe geboren wurde.
3. Ist das das Spielzeug, mit dem sie sich so amüsiert?
4. Dort ist die Kirche, nach der er fragte.

5. Sind das die Bücher, für die du dich interessierst?
6. Wo ist der Brief, auf den er wartet?
7. Das Problem, über das ihr sprecht, ist schwer.
8. Wo ist die Ruine, von der er erzählt?

REVIEW

31. Complete the following with the correct relative pronouns **der, wer, was,** or the substitute **wo.**

1. Sie gab uns alles, ______ sie hatte.
2. Wo ist der Brief, ______ ich mitnehmen soll?
3. ______ er auch ist, er muss warten.
4. Dort ist der Klub, zu ______ ich gehöre.
5. Die Kinder, ______ Eltern noch nicht gekommen sind, warten noch.
6. Willst du das Auto, ______ dort steht?
7. Ist das das Flugzeug, mit ______ du geflogen bist?
8. Ich habe den Apparat, ______ er vergessen hat.
9. Wir besuchen München, ______ das Bier so gut ist.
10. Der Koffer, ______ dort steht, gehört seiner Freundin.
11. Wo ist das Buch, ______ er vergessen hat?
12. Es gab nichts, ______ er nicht machen konnte.
13. Der Komponist, ______ Oper uns so gut gefallen hat, ist tot.
14. ______ alles weiss, braucht keine Angst zu haben.
15. Kannst du das Gedicht, ______ wir lernen mussten?
16. Die Kranken, ______ dort sitzen, brauchen viel Ruhe.
17. Wir fliegen nach Holland, ______ zur Zeit die Tulpen blühen.
18. Die Kinder, ______ ich die Geschenke brachte, danken mir.
19. Kennst du die Leute, ______ Auto ich parken musste?
20. Ich sehe etwas, ______ ich kaufen will.
21. Wo ist die Kirche, ______ er besuchte?
22. Die Tasche ______ ich kaufte, ist aus Leder.
23. Der Mann, neben ______ er steht, ist bekannt.
24. Alles, ______ du brauchst ist hier.
25. Dort ist der Deutsche, ______ ich den Weg zeigte.

Chapter 9

Word Order and Conjunctions

POSITION OF THE VERB

The verb is the only element in the German sentence to have a fixed position. It may occur in three different positions depending on the particular syntax in which it is used.

Regular Word Order: Verb in Second Position

Simple Tenses

In a simple statement, the verb occurs in second position preceded by the subject and followed by objects and other sentence parts. The subject may be a noun, pronoun or other noun phrase. Words like **danke, ja, nein** and **doch** do not affect this word order.

Subject	*Verb*	*Other Sentence Parts*
Der Mann	**ist**	**unser Lehrer.**
Die Erde	**dreht**	**sich um die Sonne.**
Ja, mein kleiner Bruder	**gab**	**ihm das Buch.**

Compound Tenses

In statements containing compound tenses, the conjugated verb or the auxiliary is in second position. The dependent infinitive, the double infinitive or the past participle is in last position, preceded by the other sentence parts.

Subject	*Conjugated Verb*	*Other Sentence Parts*	*Infinitives or Past Participles*
Doch, Inge	**wird**	**ihm**	**helfen.**
Meine Eltern	**wollten**	**sich einen Ofen**	**kaufen.**
Ich	**habe**	**es ihr**	**zeigen wollen.**
Seine Schwester	**hat**	**ihm gestern das Buch**	**gekauft.**
Das rote Auto	**wurde**	**von ihm**	**gestohlen.**

Separable Prefixes

Simple Tenses

In simple tenses, the prefix is separated from the verb and occurs in last position.

Subject	*Verb*	*Other Sentence Parts*	*Prefix*
Wir	**gehen**	**jeden Sonntag**	**spazieren.**
Die Studenten	**kamen**	**mit dem Zug**	**an.**

Compound Tenses

In compound tenses, the prefix is attached to the verb and occurs in last or next-to-last position.

Subject	*Conjugated Verb*	*Other Sentence Parts*	*Infinitives or Past Participles*
Er	**wird**	**bald**	**heimgehen.**
Ich	**habe**	**das Geschenk**	**aufmachen dürfen.**
Der Junge	**ist**	**gestern abend**	**weggelaufen.**

1. Form sentences from the following. Start with the subject.

   1. vor einer Stunde / der Schnellzug / angekommen / ist.
   2. bei uns / bleibt / Norma.
   3. mitmachen / will / der kleine Junge.
   4. von ihm / wurde / zurückgebracht / die Goldkette.
   5. wir / ihn / können / haben / sehen.
   6. mit Klaus / Gerda / geht / spazieren.
   7. den Jungen / der Hund / beisst.
   8. es / ich / habe / dürfen / kaufen.
   9. die Geschichte / wird / er / erzählen.
   10. er / mich / kommen / sieht.

2. Rewrite the following sentences, using the present perfect tense.

   1. Sie mussten schneller laufen.
   2. Wir machten die Schachtel auf.
   3. Er wollte nicht heimgehen.
   4. Ich wollte es ihm zeigen.
   5. Seine Grosseltern brachten es mit.
   6. Mein Vater liess mich gehen.
   7. Er konnte gut singen.
   8. Der Alte setzte sich auf die Bank.
   9. Ich hörte die Kinder schreien.
   10. Der Zug fuhr vor einer Stunde ab.

Inverted Word Order

Verb in Second Position–Simple and Compound Tenses

In the previous sentences, the subject was in first position. However, other sentence parts, such as an object, or an adverb or any other logical unit, may occupy first place. Such a non-subject element is followed by the conjugated verb, which is then followed by the subject and other sentence parts.

The conjugated verb is still in second position. Infinitives, past participles and separable prefixes occur in last position.

Any Element	*Conjugated Verb*	*Subject*	*Other Sentence Parts*
Vor zwei Tagen	**reiste**	**mein Freund**	**nach Indien.**
Trotz des Regens	**sind**	**wir**	**mit ihm ausgegangen.**
Dadurch	**wollte**	**er**	**viel Geld gewinnen.**

Questions introduced by an interrogative adverb (**Wann? Warum? Wo? Wie? Wovon?**, etc.) follow the inverted word order pattern.

Interrogative Adverb	*Conjugated Verb*	*Subject*	*Other Sentence Parts*
Wann	**hat**	**das Konzert**	**begonnen?**
Wohin	**habt**	**ihr**	**es gelegt?**

3. Rewrite the following, starting the sentence with the italicized element.

1. Wir wollten *das Auto* in Deutschland kaufen.
2. Sie kommen *heute* zurück.
3. Er hat es *im Kino* vergessen.
4. Er ist am Abend *meistens* müde.
5. Meine Eltern waren *leider* zu Hause.
6. Ich konnte *wegen meiner Erkältung* nicht kommen.
7. Wir haben es *gestern abend* gemacht.
8. Sie fahren *mit dem Zug* in die Schweiz.
9. Das Museum ist *im Zentrum.*
10. Ich habe es *oft* hören müssen.

4. Form questions from the following, using the present tense. Start the questions with the interrogative adverbs.

1. Wann / du / zumachen / das Fenster?
2. Was / das Kind / dürfen / wissen?
3. Wieviel / die Kamera / kosten?
4. Wo / die Leute / wollen / wohnen?
5. Warum / du / nicht / niedersetzen / dich?
6. Wohin / du / fahren / mit dem Auto?
7. Worauf / die Bücher / sollen / liegen?
8. Woher / die Kinder / kommen?

Variations of Position of the Noun Subject

In sentences using inverted word order, the noun subject may be preceded by a pronoun object. An accusative, dative or reflexive pronoun may thus come between the subject and the verb. When the subject is a pronoun, this variation is not possible. Then the object pronoun must follow the subject.

Wo hat *dich* Peter kennengelernt?
or
Wo hat Peter *dich* kennengelernt?

Gestern abend hat *ihm* Anton geholfen.
or
Gestern abend hat Anton *ihm* geholfen.

Am Sonntag hat *sich* Paula schön angezogen.
or
Am Sonntag hat Paula *sich* schön angezogen.

Wo hat er *dich* gesehen?
Warum gibst du *ihm* etwas?

5. Rewrite the following. Place the pronoun before the subject when possible.

    1. Morgen bringt er mir die Leiter.
    2. Vor einer Woche hat Axel uns besucht.
    3. Im Theater hat Konrad sich amüsiert.
    4. Jeden Tag schickt Mutter ihr etwas.
    5. Wo hat Ursel dich getroffen?
    6. Wann kannst du es machen?
    7. Warum helft ihr mir nicht?
    8. Gestern hat Vater uns etwas gebracht.
    9. Um neun Uhr trifft ihr Freund sie.
    10. In der Stadt kaufte ich ihm die Krawatte.

Verb in First Position—Simple and Compound Tenses

The conjugated verb occurs in first position in the following instances.

***Questions Answered by* ja *or* nein**

When asking whether something is true or false, the question is started with the conjugated verb. The infinitives, the past participle and the separable prefix are in last position.

***Kennst* du meine Freundin?**	*Do you know my girlfriend?*
***Hat* er es nehmen dürfen?**	*Was he permitted to take it?*
***Wirst* du ihn dort treffen?**	*Will you meet him there?*
***Kommt* er bald heim?**	*Is he coming home soon?*

When the verb is in first position, the noun subject may be preceded or followed by a pronoun object.

***Hat ihn* dein Bruder gesehen?** or ***Hat* dein Bruder *ihn* gesehen?**

6. Rewrite the following, changing the statements to questions. Place the pronoun object before the subject when possible.

    1. Du hast ihm den Brief geschrieben.
    2. Peter kennt mich.
    3. Gerda wollte das Museum besuchen.
    4. Ihr helft ihm den Baum pflanzen.
    5. Herr Klein macht die Tür auf.
    6. Er kann Deutsch.
    7. Erika hat sich bei ihr entschuldigt.
    8. Du hast dir das schnelle Auto gekauft.
    9. Ihr habt es ihm genommen.
    10. Man hat dich gefragt.

Imperatives

The verb is the first element in command forms. No subject is expressed in the familiar commands. The subject follows the imperative form in the formal commands and in the **wir** form. Separable prefixes move to last position.

***Geh* hinters Haus!**	*Go behind the house.*
Steht* bitte *auf!	*Please get up.*
***Setzen* Sie *sich* bitte!**	*Please sit down.*
***Fahren* wir mit dem Motorrad!**	*Let's go by motorcycle.*
Bitte *fahren* Sie bald *ab!*	*Please depart soon.*
Macht auf!	*Open up.*

7. Complete the following with the correct forms of the familiar singular and plural commands.

1. _______ mir das Bild! *zeigen*
2. _______ uns die Tür! *öffnen*
3. _______ ihn! *fragen*
4. _______ bald _______! *heimkommen*
5. _______ es sofort _______! *nachmachen*

8. Write formal commands. Follow the model.

darauf warten? Ja, warten Sie darauf!

1. das Bier trinken?
2. das Lied singen?
3. darüber lachen?
4. es mir schicken?
5. den warmen Mantel anziehen?

Conditional Sentences

Any real or contrary-to-fact condition may start with **wenn,** or with the conjugated verb. When the conjugated verb is in first position, the infinitives, the past participle and the separable prefix move to last position.

Wenn er nach Hause käme, wäre ich froh.
or
***Käme* er nach Hause, wäre ich froh.**

Wenn sie abfahren will, rufe ich das Taxi.
or
***Will* sie abfahren, rufe ich das Taxi.**

9. Rewrite the following, omitting **wenn.**

1. Wenn ich daran denke, bestelle ich es.
2. Wenn er es gewollt hätte, hätte ich es ihm gekauft.
3. Wenn es kalt wird, heizen wir das Haus.
4. Wenn du mitmachen willst, musst du dich umziehen.
5. Wenn ich es ihr wegnehme, weint sie.

Main Clauses Following Dependent Clauses

When the main clause follows the dependent clause, the conjugated verb is in first position of that main clause.

Wenn ich Zeit hätte, *besuchte* ich sie.
Weil sie krank war, *kam* sie nicht.

10. Rewrite the following, starting with the dependent clause.

1. Ich konnte es nicht machen, da ich keine Zeit hatte.
2. Sie spielte Klavier, als er ins Zimmer kam.
3. Ich werde euch besuchen, wenn ich das Auto habe.
4. Ich musste viel schlafen, während ich krank war.
5. Du musst mir helfen, bevor du gehst.

Verb in Last Position

Simple and Compound Tenses

Dependent clauses introduced by subordinating conjunctions or words functioning as subordinating conjunctions (relative pronouns, interrogative words) have the conjugated verb in last position. Separate prefixes are always prefixed to the verb in dependent clauses.

Noun subjects may be preceded or followed by pronoun objects when the verb is in last position.

Relative Pronouns and Interrogative Words

The conjugated verb is in last position in relative clauses and in indirect questions introduced by interrogative words.

Dort steht der Student, den ich in Paris kennengelernt *habe.*
Du bekommst alles, was du *willst.*
Weisst du, wann der Zug *ankommt?*
Ich möchte wissen, wieviel du davon getrunken *hast.*

11. Rewrite the following, changing the direct questions to indirect ones. Start with **Ich weiss nicht, . . .** Follow the model.

    Warum bleibt er dort? Ich weiss nicht, warum er dort bleibt.

    1. Wo hat er gewohnt?
    2. Wieviel muss sie noch machen?
    3. Wovon lebt er?
    4. Warum bringt er es mit?
    5. Worüber wird er erzählen?

12. Combine the two sentences, using the correct form of the relative pronoun **der.** Follow the model.

    Kennst du die Leute? Du hast ihnen das Bild gezeigt.
    Kennst du die Leute, denen du das Bild gezeigt hast?

    1. Wo ist der Mantel? Ich habe ihn gekauft.
    2. Die Kinder spielen mit der Puppe. Er hat sie mitgebracht.
    3. Dort steht das Flugzeug. Ich fliege damit ab.
    4. Hilfst du dem Mädchen? Sein Vater ist gestorben.
    5. Wo sind die Karten. Er hat sie mir geschenkt.

Haben *or* **werden** *with the Double Infinitive*

If a double infinitive construction occurs in a dependent clause, the conjugated form of the auxiliary **haben** or **werden** does not move to last position. Instead the conjugated verb precedes the double infinitive.

Ich freute mich, weil er *hat* **kommen können.**
Ich weiss, dass er sie *wird* **singen hören.**

13. Rewrite the following, changing the verb to the present perfect. Follow the model.

    Weisst du, ob er schreiben wollte?
    Weisst du, ob er hat schreiben wollen?

    1. Er ist glücklich, weil er gehen durfte.
    2. Ich glaube, dass er fragen wollte.
    3. Kennst du den Mann, den ich schreien hörte?
    4. Weisst du, ob er arbeiten musste?
    5. Ich weiss, was er machen sollte.

POSITION OF THE OBJECT

Noun and pronoun objects are usually arranged in the following manner, regardless of the position of the verb:

Dative nouns precede accusative nouns.

Der Professor erklärte *den Studenten das Problem.*

Pronoun objects precede noun objects, regardless of their case.

Weisst du, ob sie *es* ihren Eltern zeigt?
Hast du *dir* die Hände gewaschen?
Sie kauft *ihm* das Auto.

14. Rewrite the following, changing the dative noun object to a pronoun.

 1. Wir zeigten der Dame die Lampe.
 2. Wann hat er dem Hasen die Karotte gegeben?
 3. Ich habe meiner Tante eine Vase geschenkt.
 4. Hat er seinem Sohn das Motorrad gekauft?
 5. Wer hat den Leuten das Geld genommen?
 6. Weisst du, ob er den Kindern Schokolade gegeben hat?

15. Rewrite the preceding exercise, changing the accusative noun object to a pronoun.

Accusative pronoun objects preceding dative pronoun objects.

Wir bestellten *es* uns.
Ich war krank, als er *sie* mir brachte.

16. Rewrite the following, changing both noun objects to pronouns.

 1. Willst du deiner Mutter das Gedicht vorlesen?
 2. Wann hat er seinen Eltern den Brief gebracht?
 3. Weisst du, ob er seinem Vater die Geschichte erzählt hat?
 4. Wann hat er den Touristen das Museum gezeigt?
 5. Ich habe Fräulein Hartmann die Zeitschrift gegeben.

Pronoun objects may precede or follow noun subjects if the subject is not in first position.

Ich glaube, dass *ihn* der Lehrer gesehen hat.
Er weiss, warum Angelika *mir* das Geschenk gegeben hat.
Kann *dir* der Junge helfen?
Hat das Mädchen *sich* verletzt?

17. Rewrite the following, placing the pronoun objects before the subject.

 1. Gibt Peter dir den Ring?
 2. Warum kann Ursula uns nicht besuchen?
 3. Kennt der Professor ihn?
 4. Hat Frau Schafft sich schon umgezogen?
 5. Sie weint, weil die Leute sie auslachten.

POSITION OF THE ADVERB

Adverbs follow pronoun objects.

Ich habe es ihr *gestern* gebracht.
Hast du sie *dort* getroffen?

Adverbs may precede or follow noun objects. The item of greater news value follows the item of less news value.

Ich weiss, dass du deinem Freund *gestern* geschrieben hast.
Ich weiss, dass du *gestern* deinem Freund geschrieben hast.

18. Rewrite the following, changing the noun objects to pronouns.

1. Er sieht täglich seine Freunde.
2. Wir geben natürlich den Leuten alles zurück.
3. Sie besucht abends ihre Freundin.
4. Ich habe wirklich den Schauspieler getroffen.
5. Er kann leider seine Eltern nicht abholen.

If more than one adverb is used in a sentence, they occur in the order of adverb of time, manner, place.

Ich bin *um acht Uhr mit dem Zug nach Bonn* gefahren.

19. Answer the following questions with complete sentences, incorporating the cue in your answer.

1. Wann bist du nach Hause gekommen? *am Nachmittag*
2. Wo trefft ihr sie um zehn Uhr? *im Hotel*
3. Wann warst du dort? *jeden Tag*
4. Mit wem gehst du heute abend spazieren? *mit Ursel*
5. Wie bist du in die Stadt gefahren? *sehr schnell*
6. Womit seid ihr gestern ins Kino gefahren? *mit dem alten Wagen*

If there are several time expressions in one sentence, the general time precedes the specific time.

Er ist *gestern vormittag um elf Uhr* gekommen.

20. Answer the following questions affirmatively. Follow the model.

War er gestern abend hier? um sieben Uhr
Ja, er war gestern abend um sieben Uhr hier.

1. Besucht ihr mich morgen? um drei Uhr
2. Fahrt ihr diesen Sommer in die Berge? im Juli
3. Gehst du nächste Woche ins Theater? am Mittwoch
4. Fliegt ihr heute abend ab? um sechs Uhr
5. Bist du morgen zu Hause? zwischen sieben und acht Uhr.

COORDINATING CONJUNCTIONS

A coordinating conjunction does not affect the regular word order of the clause it introduces. The coordinating conjunction is followed by the subject, the conjugated verb and the other sentence parts. The following are the most common coordinating conjunctions:

aber—*but*

Er musste hier bleiben, ***aber*** **ich durfte ins Kino gehen.**
He had to stay here, but I could go to the movies.

denn—*for*

Sie geht nicht mit, ***denn*** **sie ist krank.**
She isn't going along, for she is ill.

oder—*or*

Sag ihm die Wahrheit, ***oder*** **er wird sie von mir hören.**
Tell him the truth, or he'll hear it from me.

sondern—*but (on the contrary)*

Sondern follows a negative.

Sie fuhr nicht in die Stadt, ***sondern*** **sie blieb zu Hause.**
She did not go downtown, but she stayed home.

und—*and*

Ich habe im Gras gelegen, ***und*** **er hat gearbeitet.**
I was lying in the grass, and he was working.

21. Combine the following sentences with the indicated coordinating conjunction.

1. Er ist arm. Seine Eltern sind reich. *aber*
2. Ich freute mich. Er wollte sofort mit der Arbeit anfangen. *denn*
3. Wir sind nicht dort geblieben. Wir sind ausgegangen. *sondern*
4. Sei vorsichtig! Es wird kaputt. *oder*
5. Ich spiele Golf. Er spielt Tennis. *und*
6. Er ist glücklich. Er hat Geld gewonnen. *denn*
7. Wir sind nicht in Deutschland. Wir sind in Spanien. *sondern*
8. Du kannst zu Hause bleiben. Ich muss zur Schule. *aber*
9. Er trinkt Milch. Ich trinke Limonade. *und*
10. Er kommt zu uns. Wir gehen zu ihm. *oder*

SUBORDINATING CONJUNCTIONS

The following are frequently used subordinating conjunctions. All dependent clauses introduced by subordinating conjunctions are separated by a comma from the main clause. Note that the verb occurs in the last position in the dependent clause.

als—*when*

Als **er ins Zimmer** ***kam,*** **standen alle auf.**
When he came into the room, everyone got up.

als ob—*as if*

Sie sieht aus, ***als ob*** **sie krank** ***gewesen wäre.***
She looks as if she had been ill.

bevor—*before*

Bevor **du ins Kino** ***gehst,*** **musst du mir noch helfen.**
Before you go to the movies, you have to help me.

bis—*until*

Ich studierte, bis ich müde *wurde.*
I studied until I became tired.

da—*since, as*

Ich musste warten, da sie noch nicht *angezogen war.*
I had to wait since she wasn't dressed yet.

damit—*in order to, so that*

Ich rufe ihn an, damit er nicht *kommt.*
I'll call him so that he won't come.

dass—*that*

Ich weiss, dass er einen Hund *hat.*
I know that he has a dog.

je . . . . desto—*the . . . . the*

Je mehr sie *blutet,* **desto lauter schreit sie.**
The more she is bleeding, the more loudly she is screaming.

nachdem—*after*

Er grüsste mich, nachdem ich ihn *gegrüsst hatte.*
He greeted me after I had greeted him.

ob—*whether, if*

Sie wollen wissen, ob sie *rauchen dürfen.*
They want to know whether they may smoke.

obwohl—*although*

Er ging, obwohl es sein Vater *verboten hatte.*
He went although his father forbade it.

seit, seitdem—*since*

Seitdem wir weniger Benzin *haben,* **bleiben wir öfters zu Hause.**
Since we have less gasoline, we stay home more often.

während—*while*

Ich studierte, während er einen Roman *las.*
I studied while he was reading a novel.

weil—*because*

Wir konnten nichts kaufen, weil wir kein Geld *hatten.*
We couldn't buy anything because we had no money.

wenn—*when*

Wenn er nach Hause *kommt,* **gehen wir ins Theater.**
When he comes home, we go to the theater.

The English *when* has three meanings in German: **als, wenn** and **wann.** Each has a definite use in German, and they are not interchangeable.

Als refers to a single action in the past. It is used with the imperfect, the present perfect or the pluperfect tense.

Ich freute mich, *als* **er die Goldmedaille** *gewann.*
I was glad when he won the gold medal.

Wenn corresponds to English *if* in conditional clauses. In time clauses it may be rendered with *at the time when.* It is then used with the present tense, referring to the future.

> **Ich gehe schwimmen,** *wenn* **es heiss** *wird.*
> *I'll go swimming when it gets hot.*

Wenn may also be used with the imperfect tense. It then has the meaning of *whenever.*

> *Wenn* **er hier** *war,* **gingen wir spazieren.**
> *Whenever he was here, we went for a walk.*

Wann is an interrogative, meaning *when.* It is used in direct and indirect questions.

Wann **erwartest du ihn?**	*When do you expect him?*
Weisst du, *wann* **Ilse** *kommt?*	*Do you know when Ilse is coming?*

22. Write the German, using the correct form of **wenn, als** or **wann.**

    1. When are you reading the book?
    2. When she is ill, she stays home.
    3. Whenever he visited me, he brought me something.
    4. Do you know when he is arriving?
    5. When it became cold, I went into the house.

23. Rewrite the following, introducing the second sentence with the indicated subordinating conjunction.

    1. Sie hat Kopfweh. Die Kinder haben viel Lärm gemacht. *weil*
    2. Er ist in Berlin. Seine Frau ist noch hier. *während*
    3. Ich fragte ihn. Sie sind wieder gesund. *ob*
    4. Es war sehr kalt. Wir waren in Alaska. *als*
    5. Sie konnte gut Deutsch. Sie hatte in Deutschland studiert. *nachdem*
    6. Wir kauften alles. Wir hatten viel Geld gewonnen. *da*
    7. Wir blieben im Wald. Es wurde dunkel. *bis*
    8. Konrad musste mithelfen. Er konnte ausgehen. *bevor*
    9. Er trägt einen Pullover. Er erkältet sich nicht. *damit*
    10. Sie ist immer müde. Sie kann nicht gut schlafen. *seitdem*

24. Complete the following with the correct German conjunction.

    1. Ich weiss, ______ er in Köln ist. *that*
    2. ______ es kalt ist, trägt er keinen Mantel. *although*
    3. Ich wartete, ______ er fertig war. *until*
    4. Sie tut, ______ sie reich wäre. *as if*
    5. Weisst du, ______ sie dort ist? *whether*
    6. ______ wir arbeiten, haben wir keine Zeit. *since*
    7. ______ weniger sie isst, desto schlanker wird sie. *the*
    8. Er studiert, ______ er alles weiss. *so that*
    9. Ich konnte nicht kommen, ______ ich in Rom war. *since*
    10. Wir waren im Theater, ______ du studiert hast. *while*

Answers

Chapter 1

1.
1. Der
2. Das
3. Die
4. Der
5. Das
6. Die
7. Das
8. Die
9. Der
10. Die
11. Der
12. Das
13. Die
14. Die
15. Das
16. Der
17. Der
18. Das
19. Die
20. Das

2.
1. Der
2. Der
3. Der, der
4. Der
5. Der
6. Der
7. Der
8. Der
9. Der, der
10. Der

3.
1. Die, die
2. Die, die
3. Die
4. Die
5. Die
6. der
7. Die
8. Die
9. Die
10. Die

4.
1. die
2. der
3. ___
4. Die
5. Das
6. Die
7. Die
8. ___
9. das
10. Die

5.
1. Das
2. Das
3. der
4. Das
5. Das
6. Das
7. Das
8. Das
9. Das
10. Das

6.
1. Das
2. das
3. Der
4. Der
5. Der
6. Der
7. Der
8. Der
9. Das
10. Der, die
11. Die
12. Das
13. die
14. Der
15. Der
16. Die
17. Die
18. Die
19. Das
20. Der

7.
1. Der
2. das
3. Der
4. Die, der, das
5. Der
6. Der, das
7. Der
8. Der, der
9. Der
10. der
11. Das
12. Der
13. Der
14. die
15. Der
16. Die, die
17. Das
18. das

8.
1. Die
2. die
3. Die
4. Die
5. Die
6. Die
7. Die
8. Die
9. die
10. Die
11. Die
12. Die
13. Die
14. Die
15. Die
16. die
17. Die
18. Die
19. Die
20. Die

9.
1. Das
2. das
3. Das
4. das
5. Das
6. Das
7. das
8. Das
9. Das
10. Das

10.
1. Die, das
2. Die, das, der
3. Die
4. Der
5. Die
6. Das
7. Der, der
8. die
9. Die, die
10. Die
11. Das, das
12. Der
13. Die, die
14. der, der
15. Die
16. Das
17. Das
18. Die
19. Der
20. Der

11.
1. Der
2. Der, die
3. Der
4. Der
5. Das
6. das
7. Die
8. Die, das
9. Die
10. Der
11. Das
12. Der

12. 1. Der Geburtstagskuchen
2. Der Wintermantel
3. Der Autobus
4. Das Hotelzimmer
5. Der Sportsmann
6. Die Blumenvase
7. Das Kinderzimmer
8. Der Krankenwagen
9. Die Strassenlampe
10. Der Universitätsprofessor
11. Das Tagebuch
12. Die Mitgliedskarte
13. Die Wasserfarbe
14. Das Staatsexamen
15. Die Zahnbürste

13. 1. Der Wein ist alt.
2. Die Musik ist modern.
3. Das Fleisch ist frisch.
4. Die Butter ist teuer.
5. Der Honig ist süss.
6. Die Milch ist sauer.
7. Das Vieh ist hungrig.
8. Das Gold ist kostbar.

14. 1. Die Kissen sind weich.
2. Die Onkel kommen.
3. Die Töchter sind klein.
4. Die Zimmer sind kalt.
5. Die Brüder rauchen.
6. Die Mäntel sind neu.
7. Die Fenster sind geschlossen.
8. Die Äpfel sind rot.
9. Die Lehrer sind alt.
10. Die Koffer sind aus Leder.
11. Die Messer sind rostig.
12. Die Segel sind weiss.
13. Die Teller stehen dort.
14. Die Schlüssel sind alt.
15. Die Fräulein sind hübsch.
16. Die Mütter warten.
17. Die Wagen stehen hier.
18. Die Theater sind modern.
19. Die Löffel sind teuer.
20. Die Schüler lernen.

15. 1. Die Würste schmecken gut.
2. Die Monate sind lang.
3. Die Hände sind nass.
4. Die Gedichte sind kurz.
5. Die Hunde sind braun.
6. Die Züge kommen an.
7. Die Tische sind aus Holz.
8. Die Städte sind modern.
9. Die Berge sind hoch.
10. Die Tiere sind verletzt.
11. Die Kriege sind brutal.
12. Die Söhne sind gross.
13. Die Briefe sind interessant.
14. Die Schuhe sind aus Leder.
15. Die Tage sind kurz.
16. Die Freunde lachen.
17. Die Nächte sind kalt.
18. Die Jahre gehen vorüber.

16. 1. Die Würmer sind lang.
2. Die Bücher sind interessant.
3. Die Eier schmecken gut.
4. Die Länder sind neutral.
5. Die Gläser sind kalt.
6. Die Blätter sind grün.
7. Die Männer rauchen.
8. Die Häuser sind teuer.
9. Die Kleider passen nicht.
10. Die Kinder weinen.
11. Die Völker sind hungrig.
12. Die Bilder sind billig.
13. Die Lieder sind melodisch.
14. Die Götter sind alt.

17. 1. Die Herren sind alt.
2. Die Damen sind freundlich.
3. Die Katzen sind schwarz.
4. Die Nationen sind progressiv.
5. Die Jungen sind hier.
6. Die Studentinnen lernen.
7. Die Türen sind offen.
8. Die Strassen sind breit.
9. Die Studenten sind arm.
10. Die Freundinnen sind krank.
11. Die Hasen sind weiss.
12. Die Blumen blühen.
13. Die Fabriken sind grau.
14. Die Tassen sind gelb.
15. Die Wohnungen sind kalt.
16. Die Präsidenten sind alt.
17. Die Namen sind lang.
18. Die Antworten sind falsch.
19. Die Helden sind stark.
20. Die Zeitungen liegen hier.

18. 1. Die Kameras sind teuer.
2. Die Bars sind geschlossen.
3. Die Radios sind kaputt.
4. Die Hotels sind teuer.
5. Die Sofas sind weich.
6. Die Parks sind gross.
7. Die Jobs sind interessant.
8. Die Fotos sind alt.

19. 1. Die Firmen sind bekannt.
2. Sind die Wörter auf der Liste?
3. Die Bänke sind im Park.
4. Die Dramen sind interessant.

5. Die Museen sind modern.
6. Die Busse kommen.
7. Die Banken sind geschlossen.
8. Die Zentren sind gross.

20.
1. Der Teller ist weiss.
2. Die Lehrerin ist hübsch.
3. Das Glas ist leer.
4. Der Mantel hängt hier.
5. Das Zimmer ist warm.
6. Der Student lernt.
7. Das Geschäft ist geschlossen.
8. Die Nacht ist lang.
9. Der Held ist bekannt.
10. Die Bar ist billig.
11. Das Gymnasium ist progressiv.
12. Das Sofa ist rot.
13. Die Mutter ist freundlich.
14. Das Segel ist weiss.
15. Die Stadt ist übervölkert.
16. Das Radio ist kaputt.
17. Die Zeitung ist alt.
18. Der Mann ist krank.
19. Die Hand ist schmutzig.
20. Das Theater ist modern.
21. _____
22. _____

21.
1. _____
2. Die Schuhe sind schwarz.
3. Die Freundinnen sind nett.
4. _____
5. Die Äpfel sind sauer.
6. Die Schlüssel sind rostig.
7. Die Mädchen sind freundlich.
8. Die Busse sind rot.
9. Die Mütter schreiben.
10. Die Würste sind lang.
11. Die Autos sind neu.
12. Die Briefe sind lang.
13. Die Hände sind nass.
14. Die Zimmer sind gross.
15. Die Tiere sind wild.
16. Die Gläser sind teuer.
17. Die Bücher sind interessant.
18. Die Strassen sind eng.
19. Die Freunde sind reich.
20. Die Lieder sind kurz.

22.

1.	Die	6.	Das
2.	Der	7.	das
3.	das	8.	Die
4.	Der	9.	Der
5.	Die	10.	Der

23.

1.	Diese	6.	Dieses
2.	Dieser	7.	dieses
3.	dieses	8.	Diese
4.	Dieser	9.	Dieser
5.	Diese	10.	Dieser

24.
1. Diese Länder sind reich.
2. Welche Männer kommen?
3. Jene Häuser sind alt.
4. Wo sind die Zeitungen?
5. Welche Studentinnen sind hübsch?
6. Jene Frauen sind krank.
7. Dort liegen die Äpfel.
8. Diese Mädchen lernen.
9. Diese Städte sind modern.
10. Wo sind die Bücher?

25.

1.	ein	6.	eine
2.	Eine	7.	eine
3.	ein	8.	Eine
4.	Ein	9.	ein
5.	ein	10.	ein

26.

1.	kein	6.	keine
2.	Keine	7.	keine
3.	kein	8.	Keine
4.	Kein	9.	kein
5.	kein	10.	kein

27.

1.	e	6.	____
2.	____	7.	____
3.	____	8.	____
4.	e	9.	e
5.	____	10.	e

28.
1. Ist das seine Firma?
2. Sein Job ist schwer.
3. Sein Glas ist leer.
4. Sein Hund bellt.
5. Wo ist seine Frau?
6. Sein Auto ist neu.
7. Sein Bus kommt.
8. Sein Drama ist lang.
9. Wo ist sein Junge?
10. Seine Freundin ist hübsch.

29.
1. Meine Freundinnen lachen.
2. Ihre Brüder sind krank.
3. Wo sind seine Lehrer?
4. Deine Messer liegen dort.
5. Wo sind unsre Schlüssel?
6. Sind das eure Häuser?
7. Wo sind Ihre Zeitungen?
8. Dort sind meine Onkel.
9. Sind das deine Kinder?
10. Wo sind eure Lehrerinnen?

30. 1. e, e 2. ____ 3. e 4. ____ 5. es 6. e 7. er, ____ 8. ____ 9. e 10. e

31. 1. den 2. das 3. die 4. die 5. das 6. das 7. die 8. den 9. das 10. den

32. 1. diesen 2. dieses 3. diese 4. diese 5. dieses 6. dieses 7. diese 8. diesen 9. dieses 10. diesen

33.
1. Wir kennen die Dichter.
2. Ich bekomme die Briefe.
3. Er kauft die Würste.
4. Ich sehe die Tiere.
5. Sie treffen die Freunde.
6. Wir besuchen die Städte.
7. Ich kenne die Berge.
8. Er schreibt die Gedichte.
9. Ich kaufe die Blumen.
10. Wir singen die Lieder.

34. 1. einen 2. eine 3. ein 4. ein 5. einen 6. eine 7. einen 8. einen 9. ein 10. eine

35. 1. keinen 2. keine 3. kein 4. kein 5. keinen 6. keine 7. keinen 8. keinen 9. kein 10. keine

36.
1. Kaufst du unser Auto?
2. Ich sehe unsre Katze.
3. Wir besuchen unser Kind.
4. Er ruft unsren Lehrer.
5. Ich nehme unsren Schlüssel.
6. Wir kennen unsre Lehrerin.

37. 1. en 2. e 3. en 4. ____ 5. e 6. e 7. e 8. ____ 9. ____ 10. e

38.
1. Hat er meine Bilder?
2. Brauchst du deine Bücher?
3. Seht ihr unsre Freundinnen?
4. Ich nehme seine Zeitungen.
5. Hast du deine Mäntel?
6. Wir kennen ihre Kinder.
7. Ich habe ihre Schuhe.
8. Verkaufst du unsre Wagen?
9. Sie brauchen ihre Freunde.
10. Treffen Sie Ihre Lehrer?

39. 1. en, en 2. en, en 3. en, en 4. en, n 5. en, n 6. en, n 7. en, en 8. en, en 9. en, n 10. en, n

40. 1. e, en 2. ____ 3. en, n 4. en, n 5. er, ____, en 6. e, en 7. er, ____, e 8. as, e 9. e, en 10. er, ____ 11. ____, es 12. e, en, en 13. e, en 14. ____, ____, e 15. e, e 16. e 17. e 18. en, n 19. e, es 20. en

41. 1. dem 2. der 3. dem 4. dem 5. der 6. dem 7. dem 8. der 9. dem 10. der

42. 1. jenem 2. jener 3. jenem 4. jenem 5. jener 6. jenem 7. jenem 8. jener 9. jenem 10. jener

43. 1. einer 2. einer 3. einem 4. einer 5. einem 6. einer 7. einem 8. einem 9. einem 10. einem

44. 1. keiner 2. keiner 3. keinem 4. keiner 5. keinem 6. keiner 7. keinem 8. keinem 9. keinem 10. keinem

45. 1. er 2. em 3. er 4. em 5. em 6. er 7. em 8. em 9. er 10. em

46. 1. keinem 2. unsrem 3. dieser 4. meinem 5. eurer 6. unsrer 7. jenem 8. jedem 9. seiner 10. Ihrer

47.
1. em, en
2. em, en
3. em, en
4. em, n
5. em, n
6. em, n
7. em, en
8. em, n

48.
1. Schreibst du deinen Freundinnen?
2. Er hilft jenen Kindern.
3. Es gefällt seinen Lehrern.
4. Sie zeigt es ihren Brüdern.
5. Er antwortet den Männern.
6. Ich hole den Babys Milch.
7. Es gehört diesen Jungen.
8. Wir glauben den Frauen.
9. Sie dankt ihren Freunden.
10. Es gehört euren Studenten.

49.
1. jenen
2. meinem
3. unsren
4. ihrem
5. deinen
6. dieser
7. Welchem
8. keinem
9. einem
10. jedem

50.
1. ____, em
2. er, ie
3. en
4. er
5. es, er
6. e, em, en
7. em, es
8. en
9. er, em, ie
10. ____, er
11. en, n, en
12. er, em
13. en, ____
14. em, ie
15. en, n, e

51.
1. der, ____
2. des, s
3. des, s
4. des, es
5. der, ____
6. des, es
7. des, ns
8. des, n
9. des, es
10. des, en

52.
1. dieser, ____
2. dieses, s
3. dieses, s
4. dieses, es
5. dieser, ____
6. dieses, es
7. dieses, ns
8. dieses, n
9. dieses, es
10. dieses, en

53.
1. eines, en
2. eines, n
3. eines, es
4. eines, en
5. eines, s
6. eines, s
7. einer, ____
8. eines, s
9. eines, n
10. einer, ____

54.
1. seines, s
2. meiner, ____
3. unsres, en
4. eures, n
5. ihres, s
6. deiner, ____
7. ihrer, ____
8. meines, es
9. seines, es
10. Ihrer, ____

55.
1. Die Kinder jener Frauen sind krank.
2. Die Sitze seiner Autos sind bequem.
3. Das sind die Fotos unsrer Töchter.
4. Die Bücher jener Studenten liegen hier.
5. Wann beginnt der Bau eurer Häuser?
6. Die Museen dieser Städte sind modern.
7. Die Kleider meiner Freundinnen sind neu.
8. Der Wagen der Herren steht dort.
9. Die Betonung der Namen ist schwer.
10. Die Gemälde jener Museen sind bekannt.

56.
1. Die Schneide von diesem Messer ist scharf.
2. Die Dokumente von unsrem Präsidenten sind im Museum.
3. Wir haben die Hälfte von dem Gedicht gelesen.
4. Hier ist ein Bild von meinen Freunden.
5. Der Preis von dem Auto ist zu hoch.

57.
1. Das Wasser jenes Sees ist eiskalt.
2. Peters Hund bellt.
3. Die Ohren solcher Hasen sind sehr lang.
4. Die Mutter des Mädchens steht dort.
5. Die Produkte dieser Fabrik sind teuer.

58.
1. ie, er, ____
2. as, er, ____
3. ie, es, es
4. es, s
5. ie, es, s
6. ie, es, es
7. s
8. er, es, s
9. ie, er, ____
10. ie, es, n
11. ie, er, ____
12. as, es, es
13. ie, er, ____
14. en, es, en
15. en, es, s

59.
1. Der
2. Die
3. Das
4. Die
5. Die
6. Der
7. Der
8. Die

60.
1. Der
2. die
3. Die
4. die
5. Der
6. Der
7. der
8. Das
9. die
10. Die
11. ____
12. Das

61.
1. das
2. das
3. die
4. die
5. das
6. die

62.
1. die
2. die
3. die
4. den
5. das
6. den
7. den
8. die

63.
1. die
2. die
3. Die
4. das
5. Die
6. Der
7. den
8. Der
9. die
10. Die
11. die
12. Die
13. Das
14. Die
15. Das
16. die
17. die
18. Die

64.
1. Ich habe Fieber.
2. Er ist Lehrer.
3. Sie ist eine gute Lehrerin.
4. Hat er Zahnweh?
5. Er ist als Student in Berlin
6. Er ist Professor.
7. Sie wird Pianistin.
8. Wir haben Halsweh.

65.
1. ie, es, es, en
2. es, es, er, ___, en
3. ie, es, s
4. ___, e
5. e, er, er, ___
6. e, e
7. e, en, ___, ___
8. er, es, n
9. em, en, en
10. es, er, es, s

66.
1. Wir haben keine Fotos.
2. Wo sind seine Brüder?
3. Wer hat jene Bilder genommen?
4. Welche Lieder soll ich singen?
5. Wer hilft den Babys?
6. Das gefällt den Mädchen.
7. Meine Freundinnen kommen.
8. Unsre Autos sind rot.
9. Wann kommen Ihre Töchter?
10. Die Kinder unsrer Lehrer sind hier.
11. Wo sind unsre Hotels?
12. Manche Länder sind arm.
13. Wo sind die Museen?
14. Die Bücher der Studenten liegen hier.
15. Werden diese Geschichten euren Freunden gefallen?

67.
1. ___
2. ___
3. ___
4. das
5. Die
6. Die
7. ein
8. Der
9. die
10. Der
11. den
12. die
13. Der
14. Das
15. die
16. ___

Chapter 2

1.
1. durch
2. entlang
3. um
4. gegen
5. ohne
6. gegen
7. für
8. für
9. durch
10. ohne

2.
1. en
2. s
3. en
4. e
5. en
6. e
7. s
8. e
9. ie
10. s
11. s
12. e
13. e
14. en
15. as
16. s
17. e
18. ie
19. ie
20. e

3.
1. meine
2. ihren
3. unsre
4. seinen
5. jenen
6. diese
7. ihren
8. euer

4.
1. mit, nach
2. bei
3. zum
4. seit
5. gegenüber
6. Nach, zur
7. von
8. mit
9. von
10. von

5.
1. em
2. er
3. em
4. m
5. em
6. em
7. m
8. ___
9. er
10. Der
11. em
12. em
13. en, ___
14. er
15. em
16. en
17. vom
18. em
19. er
20. en

6.
1. seiner
2. einem
3. jenem
4. einem
5. Dieser
6. unsrem
7. eurem
8. keinem
9. der
10. dem
11. meiner
12. jenem
13. ihren
14. deiner

7.
1. im
2. die
3. unters
4. unsren
5. im
6. der
7. Am
8. ins
9. diesem
10. die
11. Im
12. einem
13. ans
14. deinen
15. seinen
16. jener
17. Am
18. ins
19. deine
20. dem
21. im
22. meinen
23. ihren
24. Im
25. hinters
26. den
27. einem
28. eurem
29. meinem
30. deine
31. jenem
32. unsre
33. ins
34. den
35. der

8.
1. darin
2. damit
3. daneben
4. dabei
5. darunter
6. dahinter
7. daran
8. darauf
9. darüber
10. dazu
11. danach
12. davon

9.
1. herein
2. hinaus
3. hinein
4. herein
5. heraus
6. herein
7. hinein
8. hinaus
9. hinein
10. heraus

10.
1. Womit
2. Worauf
3. Worin
4. Woran
5. Woraus
6. Wovon
7. Worum
8. Worüber
9. Wovor
10. Wozu
11. Worauf
12. Wobei
13. Wogegen
14. Womit
15. Wofür

11.
1. er
2. er
3. es
4. er
5. es
6. er
7. er
8. er
9. es
10. er
11. er
12. es
13. es
14. er
15. er
16. er
17. es
18. er
19. es
20. er

12.
1. ie
2. im, nach
3. en
4. er
5. em
6. es
7. ——
8. ie
9. ie
10. er
11. ie
12. em
13. es
14. em
15. em
16. es
17. m
18. er
19. ie
20. em
21. e
22. e
23. es
24. as (ums)
25. en, nach

13.
1. Worin
2. Wozu
3. Womit
4. Wogegen
5. Worüber
6. Worauf
7. Wovon
8. Wovor

14.
1. darin
2. daneben
3. davor
4. darauf
5. hinein

Chapter 3

1.
1. das
2. der
3. der
4. den
5. dem
6. Die
7. den
8. den
9. den
10. die

2.
1. Dieser Mantel dort gehört mir.
2. Wir holen etwas für dieses Mädchen hier.
3. Ich helfe diesem Mann da.
4. Es liegt unter diesen Büchern da.
5. Mit diesem Wagen hier fahren wir nicht.
6. Ursula hat diese Kamera da.
7. Ich schlafe nicht in diesem Bett da.
8. Kennst du diesen Mann dort?
9. Diese Frauen hier kaufen nichts.
10. Er kauft diese Blumen hier.

3.
1. heiss
2. süss
3. faul
4. lang
5. krank
6. reich
7. schmutzig
8. leicht
9. hässlich
10. billig
11. dick
12. langsam
13. schlecht
14. alt
15. klein

4.
1. er, e
2. as, e, e
3. es, e
4. ie, e
5. er, e
6. er, e, e
7. er, e
8. er, e

5.
1. Welche deutsche
2. Jenes kleine
3. Jedes neue
4. die junge
5. dieser amerikanische
6. jener blonde
7. das dünne, rote
8. jeder gesunde
9. das leere
10. jene grosse
11. der interessante
12. Diese kalte

6.
1. Jener französische Dichter ist weltbekannt.
2. Der rote Bus wartet.
3. Manches deutsche Drama ist lang.
4. Wieviel kostet jenes schnelle Auto?
5. Jedes moderne Museum braucht Geld.
6. Welche alte Maschine ist kaputt?
7. Wo ist die weisse Katze?
8. Wo steht die frische Milch?

7.
1. es, e
2. ie, e
3. en, en
4. es, e
5. en, en
6. e, e, e
7. en, en
8. en, en

8. 1. die lange
2. jenes moderne
3. diesen grossen
4. Welchen interessanten
5. das scharfe
6. die kleine
7. jenes fremde, junge
8. jedes kranke
9. den schmutzigen
10. jenen heissen
11. den grossen, blonden
12. jenen klugen

9. 1. Er restaurierte manches historische Haus.
2. Wer hat den alten Lederkoffer?
3. Bring dieses schmutzige Glas in die Küche!
4. Wir kaufen jenes schnelle Motorboot.
5. Welchen roten Apfel möchtest du?
6. Wir wandern durch die kleine Stadt.
7. Sie bringt Blumen für das nette Kindermädchen.
8. Ich brauche jede neue, deutsche Briefmarke.

10. 1. em, en 5. er, en
2. er, en 6. em, en
3. em, en 7. er, en
4. em, en, en 8. em, en

11. 1. jenem internationalen
2. jeder interessanten
3. dieser netten
4. dem schmutzigen
5. jenem kurzen
6. dem grossen, amerikanischen
7. welchem fremden
8. der hübschen
9. jenem reichen
10. dem kleinen
11. jeder kranken
12. dem hässlichen

12. 1. Wir schlafen in dem modern Schlafwagen.
2. Mit welcher neuen Schreibmaschine soll ich schreiben?
3. Er wohnt bei jener netten Dame.
4. Der Ball liegt unter dem blauen Sessel.
5. Trink nicht aus jenem roten Glas!
6. Wir gehen bei diesem kalten Wetter nicht aus.
7. Wer sitzt auf der alten, rostigen Bank?
8. Wir bekamen von manchem amerikanischen Studenten Post.

13. 1. es, en 5. er, en
2. er, en 6. es, en
3. es, en 7. es, en
4. es. en 8. er. en

14. 1. des blauen
2. jenes exotischen
3. des deutschen
4. dieses billigen
5. der kranken
6. dieses bequemen
7. jener bekannten
8. dieser kleinen
9. der dicken
10. des gesunden
11. jenes grossen
12. jener interessanten

15. 1. Wo ist der Besitzer dieses schmutzigen Mantels?
2. Die Gedichte manches deutschen Dichters sind kompliziert.
3. Die Mutter jenes kranken Kindes ist hier.
4. Der Park ist jenseits des grossen Monuments.
5. Trotz dieser langen Explosion gab es keine Verwundete.
6. Die Strassen jener alten Stadt sind eng.
7. Die Zimmer der neuen Wohnung sind modern.

16. 1. Welche deutschen Städte hat er besucht?
2. Ohne diese warmen Kleider fahre ich nicht.
3. Wir steigen auf jene bekannten Berge.
4. Es gehört jenen interessanten, jungen Frauen.
5. Er schenkt etwas in alle leeren Gläser.
6. Ich liege unter den schattigen Bäumen.
7. Er erzählt den kleinen Mädchen Geschichten.
8. Ich komme um der kranken Lehrer willen.
9. Alle gesunden Patienten dürfen nach Hause.
10. Sie hat die grünen Äpfel.

17. 1. dem dunklen
2. die bittre (bittere)
3. jenen teuren (teueren)
4. dieses hohen
5. die saubre (saubere)
6. die saure (sauere)
7. das saubre (saubere)
8. dieses teure (teuere)
9. die sauren (saueren)
10. dieser hohe

18. 1. ie, en, en, en 6. ie, e, em, en, en
2. en, en, em, en 7. e, en, m, en
3. en, en, er, en 8. en, en, as, e
4. ie, e, em, en 9. ie, e, es, e
5. es, en 10. er, e, es, e

19.

1.	Dieses deutsche	jener netten
2.	Alle eleganten	diese kurzen
3.	Jener blonde	dieses teure (teuere)
4.	Die hübsche	dem dicken
5.	Der neue	des teuren (teueren)
6.	die schmutzigen	des kleinen
7.	Jener amerikanische	diese billige
8.	Der schwarze	dem runden
9.	Die jungen	der dunklen
10.	Die hungrige	den grossen

20.
1. ____, er
2. e, e, e
3. e, e
4. ____, er
5. e, e
6. ____, es
7. ____, er
8. e, e
9. e, e, e
10. ____, es
11. ____, er
12. ____, es
13. ____, er
14. ____, es
15. e, e
16. ____, er

21.
1. Wo ist ein weiches Kissen?
2. Ein alter Freund ist hier.
3. Wann schläft ein wildes Tier?
4. Eine neue Maschine steht dort.
5. Hier ist ein schmutziger Teller.
6. Wo ist ein kleines Buch?
7. Hier liegt eine deutsche Zeitung.
8. Wieviel kostet ein schnelles Auto?

22.
1. Mein altes Radio ist kaputt.
2. Wo wohnt deine nette Freundin?
3. Wieviel kostet Ihr neuer Wagen?
4. Wann kommt sein reicher Onkel?
5. Das ist keine enge Strasse.
6. Ist unser deutsches Foto interessant?
7. Wo ist eure schmutzige Wäsche?
8. Hier ist ihr alter Wein.

23.
1. en, en
2. ____, es
3. e, e, e, e
4. e, e
5. en, en, en
6. e, e
7. en, en, en
8. ____, es
9. e, e
10. e, e
11. ____, es
12. ____, es

24.
1. Er kauft einen hässlichen Teppich.
2. Wann bekommst du einen neuen Mantel?
3. Wir besuchen eine historische Stadt.
4. Siehst du ein rotes Auto?
5. Ich kaufe es für ein krankes Kind.
6. Er geht durch einen langen Tunnel.
7. Der Bus fuhr gegen eine alte Mauer.
8. Ich möchte ein weisses Bonbon.

25.
1. Sie geht in ihre dunkle Wohnung.
2. Wir verkaufen unser blaues Sofa.
3. Haben Sie ein billiges Zimmer?
4. Ich habe einen bequemen Stuhl.
5. Brauchst du deine neue Kamera?
6. Wir gehen durch einen langen Tunnel.
7. Ich schreibe einen kurzen Brief.
8. Kennst du keine hübsche Studentin?

26.
1. em, en
2. em, en, en
3. er, en
4. em, en
5. er, en, en
6. er, en
7. em, en
8. er, en
9. er, en
10. em, en
11. er, en
12. em, en

27.
1. Er sitzt auf einem harten Stuhl.
2. Sie wohnt in einem modernen Haus.
3. Ich bin bei einer netten Frau.
4. Sie spielt mit einem süssen Baby.
5. Wir stehen neben einem grossen Mann.
6. Ich liege auf einem weichen Bett.
7. Hilfst du einem fremden Mann?
8. Sie kommt von einer langen Reise zurück.

28.
1. Er kam mit einem interessanten Freund.
2. Wir kennen uns seit unsrer glücklichen Kindheit.
3. Er schnitt das Brot mit seinem scharfen Messer.
4. Warum sitzt du auf einem unbequemen Stuhl?
5. Die Katze liegt auf meinem schwarzen Mantel.
6. Sie kommt aus ihrem dunklen Zimmer.
7. Was steht in seinem langen Brief?
8. Sie sitzt in meinem neuen Auto.

29.
1. einer dunklen
2. meines alten
3. seiner schlimmen
4. eines amerikanischen
5. ihrer wichtigen
6. eures kranken
7. deiner neuen
8. eines teuren (teueren)

30.
1. Das ist die Frau eines bekannten Dichters.
2. Es ist die Geschichte eines fremden Volkes.
3. Der Preis eines antiken Perserteppichs ist hoch.
4. Ich singe die Melodie eines deutschen Liedes.
5. Der Direktor einer grossen Fabrik kommt.

31.
1. Trotz meiner langen Reise war ich nicht müde.
2. Die Farbe deines neuen Pullovers ist hübsch.
3. Sie ist die Frau eines amerikanischen Präsidenten.
4. Hier ist das Foto seines bekannten Bruders.
5. Wo ist das Haus Ihres reichen Onkels?

6. Wir konnten wegen seiner langen Verspätung nicht essen.
7. Der Bus ist jenseits eines hohen Turmes.

32.
1. Er hat keine teuren Ringe gekauft.
2. Er glaubt seinen kleinen Söhnen.
3. Ich telefonierte mit meinen deutschen Freundinnen.
4. Unsre neuen Nähmaschinen waren teuer.
5. Wer hat meine roten Bleistifte?
6. Wegen seiner faulen Brüder darf er nicht kommen.
7. Wir trinken keine kalten Getränke.
8. Wo sind ihre warmen Jacken?
9. Willst du deine alten Lehrer besuchen?
10. Wo sind eure progressiven Gymnasien?

33.
1. ____, er, e, e
2. er, en, ____, er
3. ie, e, em, en
4. er, en, es, en
5. en, en, er, en, e, en
6. e, e, em, en
7. e, e, er, en
8. as, e, e, e
9. ____, es, en, en
10. en, en, ie, e
11. e, en, e, e
12. em, en, ie, en

34.

1.	der jungen	einen interessanten
2.	mein kranker	unsrem guten
3.	ihrem kleinen	die leere
4.	deine reiche	dieses teure (teuere)
5.	jener langen	ihre neuen
6.	das neue	des bekannten
7.	meine amerikanischen	keinen bittren (bitteren)
8.	sein kaputtes	die dunkle
9.	ihren netten	eine kurze
10.	Die armen	ihrer kalten

35.

1. Welch	5. solch
2. viel	6. solch
3. wenig	7. viel
4. Manch	8. wenig

36.
1. Welch grosse
2. solch bittre (bittere)
3. Liebe
4. viel schmutzige
5. Lieber
6. wenig deutsches
7. Welch süsser
8. gutes
9. neues
10. Welch kalte
11. Lieber
12. armer
13. teures (teueres)
14. Manch fleissiger

37.
1. Welch interessantes Gedicht!
2. Das ist teures Leder.
3. Frische Butter schmeckt gut.
4. Moderne Musik ist schnell.
5. Ist das billiger Schmuck?
6. Manch französischer Wein ist teuer.
7. Du süsses Baby!

38.
1. viel saure (sauere)
2. wenig schwarzes
3. Guten Gute Guten
4. grosse
5. weissen
6. wenig süssen
7. schönes
8. schwarzen
9. dünnes
10. Solch frische
11. solch französichen
12. grosse
13. viel amerikanisches
14. viel heisses

39.
1. Was hast du gegen klassische Musik?
2. Leg es in kaltes Wasser!
3. Ich esse frisches Brot.
4. Wir brauchen deutsches Geld.
5. Er hat solch grossen Hunger.
6. Warum trinkst du kalten Kaffee?
7. Sie nimmt braunen Zucker.
8. Sie hat viel teuren Schmuck.

40.
1. solch grosser
2. langer
3. guter
4. viel warmer
5. grossem
6. solch schönem
7. rostfreiem
8. grosser
9. wenig weissem
10. viel heissem
11. solch bittrer (bitterer)
12. hartem

41.
1. Bei solch schlechtem Wetter fliege ich nicht.
2. Wer schreibt mit grüner Kreide?
3. Nach kurzer Zeit wurde es still.
4. Das Messer ist aus rostfreiem Stahl.
5. Warum schwimmst du in solch tiefem Wasser?
6. Sie wohnt bei solch netter Familie.

7. Ich kenne ihn seit langer Zeit.
8. Er trank nichts ausser viel starkem Kaffee.

42.
1. solch alter
2. dichten
3. freundlicher
4. Traurigen
5. alten
6. wahrer
7. langer
8. neuen
9. solch grosser
10. kurzer

43.
1. Trotz bittrer Kälte spielten die Kinder im Schnee.
2. Er ist Liebhaber moderner Musik.
3. Der Preis manch alten Weines ist hoch.
4. Wegen schlechten Wetters hat er Verspätung.
5. Trotz solch guter Schulung fand er keine Position.
6. Trotz netter Hilfe kam sie nicht vorwärts.

44.
1. es, es
2. em
3. er
4. er
5. e
6. e, er
7. em
8. es
9. es
10. er
11. e
12. en
13. e, en, en
14. em
15. es

45.
1. einige
2. Andere
3. Mehrere
4. viele
5. Wenige
6. Viele

46.
1. gelbe
2. viele gute
3. einige bekannte
4. braune
5. einige graue
6. Mehrere grosse frische
7. andere neue
8. Alte
9. wenige teure (teuere)
10. Manche kleine automatische

47.
1. alten
2. einigen deutschen
3. netten
4. einigen amerikanischen
5. mehreren kleinen
6. schmutzigen
7. dicken
8. vielen intelligenten
9. anderen alten
10. wenigen fremden

48.
1. einiger hoher
2. mehrerer wilder
3. alter
4. vieler alter
5. einiger reicher
6. mancher primitiver
7. hoher
8. fauler
9. herbstlicher
10. einiger moderner

49.
1. er
2. e, e
3. em
4. er, es, e
5. e, e
6. en, en, e
7. er
8. er
9. er, e
10. es
11. en
12. en, en
13. em
14. en
15. e, e
16. e, e
17. em
18. er, er
19. en
20. e

50.
1. Kleinen
2. Blonde
3. Schnelle
4. Alten
5. Fremden
6. Reichen
7. Arme (Armen)
8. Kranken
9. Hübsche
10. Glücklichen

51.
1. e
2. en
3. e
4. e
5. er
6. e
7. en
8. e
9. e
10. en
11. en
12. e
13. e
14. e
15. en
16. en

52.
1. kochende
2. bellenden
3. kommenden
4. weinende
5. Fliegende
6. fliessendem
7. sterbenden
8. brennenden
9. leidende
10. schreiende

53.
1. gekochte
2. geöffneten
3. geschriebene
4. gefrorenen
5. reparierte
6. geschnittenen
7. Vereinigten
8. angebrannte
9. bezahlte
10. zerbrochene

54.
1. Billiges
2. Neues
3. Nürnberger
4. Frankfurter
5. Gutes
6. Dortmunder
7. Altes
8. Modernes
9. Berliner
10. Strassburger

55.
1. Seine
2. Unsre
3. Ihr
4. mein
5. dein
6. Ihr
7. Ihre
8. eure
9. Unser
10. Ihre

56.
1. unsren
2. meine
3. dein
4. eure
5. Ihre
6. ihren
7. sein
8. meine
9. unser
10. eure

57.
1. er
2. er
3. em
4. en
5. em
6. em
7. er
8. en
9. em
10. em

58.
1. seines
2. ihrer
3. unsres
4. meiner
5. ihres
6. deines
7. eures
8. Ihrer
9. unsres
10. ihrer

59.
1. seine
2. mein
3. deine
4. Ihre
5. unsre
6. ihrer
7. seinem
8. eure
9. Ihrem
10. eure
11. Meine
12. seiner

60.
1. länger am längsten
2. teurer am teuersten
3. grösser am grössten
4. schneller am schnellsten
5. mehr am meisten
6. härter am härtesten
7. öfter am öftesten
8. schärfer am schärfsten
9. lieber am liebsten
10. höher am höchsten

61.
1. mehr als
2. dicker als
3. grösser als
4. teurer als
5. lieber als
6. höher als
7. netter als
8. jünger als
9. dunkler als
10. härter als

62.
1. Der Februar ist kürzer als der Januar.
2. Das Kleid ist teurer als die Bluse.
3. Der Vater isst mehr als das Baby.
4. Ute kann besser Spanisch als Marianne.
5. Im Haus ist es wärmer als im Garten.
6. Das Auto fährt schneller als das Motorrad.
7. Robert ist ärmer als Manfred.
8. Mein Vater ist stärker als mein Bruder.
9. Die Lilie ist schöner als die Geranie.
10. Die Limonade ist kälter als das Wasser.
11. Der Kaffee ist bittrer als der Tee.
12. Die Schule ist näher als die Kirche.

63.
1. Es wird immer dunkler.
2. Sie wird immer älter.
3. Er fährt immer schneller.
4. Die Tage werden immer länger.
5. Es kommt immer näher.

64.
1. Ich springe am höchsten.
2. Karl ist am grössten.
3. Wir singen am besten.
4. Meine Mutter spricht am schnellsten.
5. Sabine ist am kränksten.
6. Mein Bruder spart am meisten.
7. Die Kirche ist am nächsten.
8. Klaus und ich gehen am langsamsten.
9. Unsre Nachbarn sind am reichsten.
10. Der Rock ist am kürzesten.

65.
1. Der Brocken ist hoch. Das Matterhorn ist höher. Die Zugspitze ist am höchsten.
2. Ich trinke Wasser gern. Ich trinke lieber Limonade. Ich trinke Bier am liebsten.
3. Das Gedicht ist lang. Die Geschichte ist länger. Der Roman ist am längsten.
4. Der Vogel fliegt schnell. Der Hubschrauber fliegt schneller. Das Düsenflugzeug fliegt am schnellsten.
5. Der Apfel ist sauer. Die Orange ist saurer. Die Zitrone ist am sauersten.
6. Das Brot schmeckt gut. Der Kuchen schmeckt besser. Die Torte schmeckt am besten.
7. Hans arbeitet viel. Josef arbeitet mehr. Franz arbeitet am meisten
8. Das Wollkleid ist warm. Die Jacke ist wärmer. Der Wintermantel ist am wärmsten.

66.
1. Deine Nägel sind so lang wie Katzenkrallen.
2. Pia ist so gross wie Inge.
3. Die Jacke ist nicht so warm wie der Mantel.
4. Deine Augen sind so blau wie der Himmel.
5. Heute ist es so kalt wie im Winter.
6. Peter ist so stark wie Max.
7. Die Hose ist so teuer wie der Pullover.
8. Grossmutter ist so alt wie Grossvater.
9. Renate schreit so laut wie ich.
10. Mein Bruder schreibt so viel wie sein Freund.

67.
1. schönere
2. teurere
3. schärfere
4. ärmere
5. jüngerer
6. kleineres
7. besserer
8. kälteres

68.
1. wärmeren
2. stärkeren
3. schärferes
4. grössere
5. bessere
6. mehr
7. kleinere
8. ältere

69.
1. Wir sind in einer kleineren Wohnung.
2. Er kommt aus einem bekannteren Museum.
3. Er fährt mit einem schnelleren Wagen.
4. Wir helfen einem kränkeren Patienten.
5. Sie erzählt von einer besseren Zeit.
6. Er spricht mit einer kleineren Frau.

70.
1. höheren
2. jüngeren
3. älteren
4. stärkeren
5. kleineren
6. kälteren

71. 1. nächste 2. höchste 3. wärmste 4. teuerstes 5. dünnste 6. härteste 7. bester 8. älteste

72. 1. jüngsten 2. modernste 3. stärksten 4. teuerste 5. beste 6. meisten 7. intelligentesten 8. kleinste

73. 1. teuersten 2. kürzesten 3. ärmsten 4. wärmsten 5. jüngsten 6. neusten 7. teuersten 8. stärkstem

74. 1. besten 2. teuersten 3. ältesten 4. jüngsten 5. längsten 6. hübschesten

75. 1. e 2. e 3. en 4. ____ 5. en 6. e 7. ____ 8. e 9. en 10. en 11. e 12. en 13. en 14. en 15. e 16. en 17. en 18. e 19. en 20. e

76.
1. Er ist sehr alt.
2. Sie haben sehr gute Lehrer.
3. Er ist ein sehr intelligenter Mann.
4. Es ist sehr kalt.
5. Sie singt sehr schön.

77. 1. nun, jetzt 2. heute 3. selten 4. gestern 5. nie 6. abends 7. damals 8. täglich 9. bald 10. immer 11. manchmal 12. morgens

78. 1. natürlich 2. gern 3. leider 4. nicht 5. so 6. wirklich 7. zu 8. ziemlich 9. schon 10. Vielleicht

79. 1. da, dort 2. oben 3. drinnen 4. draussen 5. hier 6. weg 7. links 8. hinten 9. rechts 10. überall

80.
1. Er bleibt natürlich hier.
2. Maria wohnt nicht unten.
3. Karl sieht uns täglich.
4. Wir waren gestern wirklich drinnen.
5. Ich arbeite abends nicht draussen.
6. Vater suchte dich damals überall.
7. Wir sitzen manchmal gern dort.
8. Ich habe morgens wirklich grossen Hunger.
9. Sie ist jetzt ziemlich dick.
10. Sie sind heute leider weg.

81.
1. Wir trinken nie Wein.
2. Sie war heute schon hier.
3. Ich bin abends nicht dort (da).
4. Sie sind jetzt leider oben.
5. Sie ist morgens immer drinnen.
6. Er war damals hier.
7. Ich sitze immer draussen.
8. Er ist vielleicht hinten.
9. Ich bin selten weg.
10. Sie ist sicherlich überall.

82. 1. noch 2. denn 3. doch 4. doch 5. Doch 6. noch einen 7. ja 8. doch

Chapter 4

1.
1. acht
2. sechzehn
3. einundzwanzig
4. vierunddreissig
5. einundfünfzig
6. sechsundfünfzig
7. siebzig
8. neunundachtzig
9. einundneunzig
10. hundert
11. hunderteins
12. neunhundertsechsunddreissig
13. tausendzweihundertvierundsiebzig
14. neunzehnhundertachtzig
15. zweitausendeinunddreissig
16. zehn Millionen
17. acht komma neun
18. siebzehn komma einundsechzig
19. zwanzig Mark dreissig
20. hunderteinundneunzig Mark siebenundsechzig

2. 1. achten 2. zweites 3. vierte 4. erste 5. dritten 6. der Achte 7. fünfte 8. der Erste 9. des Fünfzehnten 10. dem Zweiten

3.
1. Wer hat meine Hälfte?
2. dreiviertel Pfund
3. ein halbes Glas
4. ein Drittel der Arbeit
5. zwei einviertel Stunden
6. fünf Achtel der Bevölkerung
7. eineinhalb Pfund (anderthalb) (ein und ein halbes)
8. ein Zwanzigstel
9. ein Viertel des Brotes
10. ein halbes Pfund

4.
1. am Mittwoch
2. im Herbst
3. im August
4. am Dienstag
5. im Winter
6. im Mai
7. an dem Donnerstag
8. am Freitag
9. im Frühling
10. am Montag
11. am Samstag
12. im Sommer
13. im Juli
14. in dem September
15. an dem Montag
16. am Sonntag

5.
1. Er hat am 20. (zwanzigsten) Januar Geburtstag.
2. Heute ist der 13. (dreizehnte) Oktober 1977.
3. Ich komme am Freitag, den 9. (neunten) März an.
4. Er ist 1970 gestorben.
5. Ich habe am 10. (zehnten) Dezember Geburtstag.
6. Im Jahre 1980.
7. 30. 5. 1978
8. Sie ist am 4. (vierten) April 1966 geboren.
9. Er wurde 1822 geboren.
10. Sie hat am 10. (zehnten) August Geburtstag.
11. Ich komme am 2. (zweiten) Februar an.
12. Er ist 1974 geboren.
13. Heute ist der 3. (dritte) März 1984.
14. Er ist 1975 gestorben.

6.
1. Es ist acht Uhr abends.
2. Es ist halb elf Uhr vormittags.
3. Es ist (ein) Viertel nach fünf.
4. Es ist fünf nach halb acht.
5. Es ist fünfundzwanzig nach sechs. (Es ist fünf vor halb sieben)
6. Es ist (ein) Viertel vor fünf. (Es ist drei Viertel fünf.)
7. Es ist zwanzig nach elf. (Es ist zehn vor halb zwölf.)
8. Es ist zehn nach drei.
9. Es ist ein Uhr nachmittags.
10. Es ist zwölf Uhr mittags.

7.
1. Es ist zwanzig Uhr dreissig.
2. Es ist dreizehn Uhr.
3. Es ist ein Uhr.
4. Es ist vierundzwanzig Uhr.
5. Es ist null Uhr fünfunddreissig.
6. Es ist einundzwanzig Uhr fünfundzwanzig.
7. Es ist zwölf Uhr vierzig.
8. Es ist zehn Uhr fünfundvierzig.
9. Es ist vierzehn Uhr.
10. Es ist dreiundzwanzig Uhr.

8.
1. Um fünf Uhr.
2. Um zwei Uhr.
3. Um halb vier Uhr.
4. Um sieben Uhr.
5. Um elf Uhr.

9.
1. am Morgen
2. Am Nachmittag
3. In der Nacht
4. am Mittag
5. am Abend

10.
1. Ja, ich bin immer abends hier.
2. Ja, ich habe immer sonntags Zeit.
3. Ja, ich gehe immer mittwochs mit.
4. Ja, ich schreibe immer nachmittags.
5. Ja, ich fahre immer morgens zur Schule.

11.
1. Er kommt morgen abend.
2. Er war gestern nachmittag zu Hause.
3. Otto, hast du gestern abend geschlafen?
4. Sie kommen übermorgen.
5. Sie ist heute morgen abgefahren.
6. Er kommt morgen nachmittag.

12.
1. en
2. en
3. e
4. en, en
5. e
6. e, e

13.
1. er
2. em
3. em
4. en
5. em
6. er
7. en
8. em
9. em
10. em

14.
1. eines Tages
2. eines Nachts
3. eines Abends
4. eines Nachmittags
5. eines Morgens

15.
1. en
2. es, s
3. um
4. heute abend
5. im

6. ie, e
7. am
8. es
9. In der Nacht
10. Morgen nachmittag
11. in einem Monat.
12. Um
13. Am Morgen
14. vor einer Woche (vor acht Tagen)
15. sonntags
16. am Mittag
17. In vierzehn Tagen (In zwei Wochen)
18. eines Tages
19. e, e
20. heute morgen

Chapter 5

1.
1. Hörst
2. trinken
3. kommt
4. schicke
5. singt
6. brennt
7. fliege
8. bellt
9. bleibt
10. Denkst
11. weint
12. stehen
13. beginnt
14. bringt
15. renne
16. parkt
17. schreit
18. Rauchen
19. Kennt
20. Liebst
21. studiert
22. besuchen
23. holt
24. springt
25. ruft
26. riecht
27. schreiben
28. Steigt
29. glaubt
30. probiere
31. telefoniert
32. höre
33. brauchen
34. wohnt
35. holen
36. gehen

2.
1. wartet
2. Schneidest
3. arbeitet
4. bittest
5. Begegnest
6. reitet
7. Findet
8. Rechnet
9. redest
10. rettet
11. öffnet
12. Beobachtet
13. atmest
14. ordnet
15. blutet
16. Sendest
17. antwortest
18. wendet
19. Arbeitest
20. Badest

3.
1. Wie heisst du?
2. Was mixt du?
3. Du tanzt gut.
4. Warum grüsst du mich nicht?
5. Wohin reist du?
6. Was hasst du?
7. Wo sitzt du?
8. Beisst du in den Apfel?

4.
1. klettert
2. wandern
3. bewundere
4. behandelt
5. fütterst
6. ändern
7. lächle
8. behandeln
9. klingelt
10. sammeln
11. behandle
12. füttern
13. sammle
14. klettern

5.
1. Schläfst du die ganze Nacht?
2. Er wächst schnell.
3. Wäschst du die Wäsche?
4. Ich halte die Ballons.
5. Was trägt er zum Ball?
6. Lässt du mich gehen?
7. Ich backe Brot.
8. Warum gräbt er ein Loch?
9. Er schlägt das Kind.
10. Das Tier säuft Wasser.
11. Er bläst ins Feuer.
12. Wohin läufst du?
13. Er fällt.
14. Fängst du den Ball?
15. Ich schlafe schon.
16. Was trägst du?

6.
1. Hilfst du mir?
2. Er stirbt bald.
3. Siehst du uns?
4. Ich esse Suppe.
5. Der Hund frisst.
6. Was gibst du ihm?
7. Ich spreche gern.
8. Er sieht uns.
9. Er steht beim Haus.
10. Gehst du auch?
11. Was nimmst du?
12. Wann triffst du uns?
13. Was liest er?
14. Warum erschrickst du?
15. Was bricht er?
16. Was stiehlst du?
17. Was sticht er?
18. Warum hilft er nicht?
19. Was vergisst er?
20. Empfiehlst du dieses Hotel?

7.
1. bin
2. ist
3. sind
4. sind
5. seid
6. Sind
7. ist
8. Bist

8.
1. haben
2. habe
3. Hast
4. haben
5. Habt
6. hat
7. haben
8. hast

9.
1. werde schon wieder gesund.
2. werdet schon wieder gesund.

3. wirst schon wieder gesund.
4. wird schon wieder gesund.
5. werden schon wieder gesund.
6. werden schon wieder gesund.
7. wird schon wieder gesund.
8. werden schon wieder gesund.

10.
1. wissen
2. wissen
3. wisst
4. weiss
5. weiss
6. Weisst
7. weiss
8. wissen

11.
1. tust
2. tue
3. tun
4. tut
5. Tut
6. Tun
7. tun
8. tut

12.
1. Ja, ich komme morgen.
2. Ja, er hat übermorgen Geburtstag.
3. Ja, wir gehen morgen abend ins Theater.
4. Ja, ich fliege im Juli nach Frankfurt.
5. Ja, ich fahre nächstes Jahr nach Regensburg.
6. Ja, ich besuche dich heute in acht Tagen.
7. Ja, ich bin nächsten Monat in Deutschland.
8. Ja, ich bin morgen abend zu Hause.
9. Ja, wir haben nächste Woche Zeit.
10. Ja, sie spielt nächsten Samstag Golf.

13.
1. warte
2. wohnt
3. ist
4. arbeiten
5. Singst
6. kenne
7. sind
8. fliegt
9. regnet
10. Schreibt

14.
1. Ich lese schon seit einer Stunde.
2. Er studiert schon zehn Tage.
3. Ich bin seit fünf Minuten hier.
4. Ich kenne ihn schon sechs Jahre.
5. Ich telefoniere schon zwanzig Minuten.

15.
1. gräbst
2. komme
3. läuft
4. änderst
5. füttern
6. Seid
7. wird
8. reist
9. arbeitet
10. Liest
11. atmen
12. frisst
13. fahrt
14. fängt
15. wasche
16. grüssen
17. Sind
18. wissen
19. schläfst
20. wird
21. steht
22. studieren
23. blutest
24. klingle
25. heisst
26. isst
27. gibst
28. sieht
29. behandeln
30. sitzt

16.
1. haben . . . gefragt
2. haben . . . gewohnt
3. haben . . . geglaubt
4. Hast . . . gekauft
5. hat . . . geliebt
6. haben . . . gehört
7. habe . . . gesucht
8. haben . . . geraucht
9. habt . . . geparkt
10. hast . . . geweint
11. Hast . . . gelegt
12. hat . . . geschenkt
13. habe . . . gekämmt
14. habt . . . gelernt
15. haben . . . gesagt

17.
1. habt . . . bezahlt
2. Hast . . . verkauft
3. haben . . . repariert
4. hat . . . erzählt
5. habe . . . studiert
6. haben . . . probiert
7. hat . . . zerstört
8. Hat . . . gehört
9. Hast . . . telefoniert
10. haben . . . bestellt
11. hat . . . besucht
12. hat . . . entdeckt
13. hat . . . erklärt
14. hast . . . zerstört
15. hat . . . entschuldigt

18.
1. Wir haben viel studiert.
2. Hast du Geld gebraucht?
3. Warum hat der Hund gebellt?
4. Er hat viel gearbeitet.
5. Man hat das Haus zerstört.
6. Haben Sie den Jungen gesucht?
7. Habt ihr oft geträumt?
8. Sie hat sehr laut geatmet.
9. Ich habe stark geblutet.
10. Die Kinder haben gerne gebadet.
11. Wo habt ihr gewohnt?
12. Ich habe Papier geholt.
13. Wir haben die Bücher auf den Tisch gelegt.
14. Sie hat oft telefoniert.
15. Die Katze hat dem Mädchen gehört.
16. Wer hat dafür bezahlt?

19.
1. Er hat meine Schwester gekannt.
2. Die Kinder haben die Antwort gewusst.
3. Ich habe Blumen gebracht.
4. Hast du daran gedacht?
5. Die Häuser haben gebrannt.
6. Wir haben das Paket gesandt.
7. Habt ihr den höchsten Berg genannt?
8. Ich habe das Blatt gewandt.

20. 1. sind . . . gerannt
2. seid . . . gereist
3. bin . . . geklettert
4. Ist . . . gereist
5. Seid . . . gewandert
6. bin . . . gerannt
7. sind . . . begegnet
8. ist . . . gereist
9. Bist . . . geklettert
10. bin . . . begegnet

21. 1. Hast . . . gelesen
2. hat . . . geschlagen
3. habe . . . gegeben
4. habt . . . gesehen
5. haben . . . gebacken
6. habe . . . gemessen
7. hat . . . gefressen
8. haben . . . gegraben
9. hat . . . getragen
10. habe . . . gewaschen
11. Habt . . . gefangen
12. hat . . . gegessen
13. Hast . . . gelassen
14. habt . . . geschlafen

22. 1. Mein Bruder ist schnell gefahren.
2. Bist du ins Haus getreten?
3. Wir sind schon wieder gewachsen.
4. Seid ihr nach Bremen gefahren?
5. Die Kinder sind immer gewachsen.
6. Ich bin gestern gefahren.
7. Seid ihr ins Haus gelaufen?
8. Wann bist du gekommen?
9. Die Leute sind schnell gelaufen.
10. Ich bin ins Wasser gefallen.

23. 1. Bist du oft geritten?
2. Wir haben laut geschrien.
3. Warum habt ihr nicht geschrieben?
4. Die Sonne hat geschienen.
5. Warum hat er gebissen?
6. Seid ihr lange geblieben?
7. Die Kranken haben gelitten.
8. Warum habt ihr geschwiegen?
9. Bist du auf die Leiter gestiegen?
10. Ich habe dir Geld geliehen.
11. Er hat dem Kind das Haar geschnitten.
12. Habt ihr nicht gelitten?
13. Ich habe nicht geschrien.
14. Hast du den Breif geschrieben?

24. 1. Hast . . . verloren
2. hat . . . gerochen
3. Seid . . . geflogen
4. hat . . . gewogen
5. hast . . . geschossen
6. hat . . . gezogen
7. ist . . . geflohen
8. ist . . . geflossen
9. hast . . . geschlossen
10. haben . . . gefroren
11. hat . . . gebogen
12. hat . . . gelegen
13. hat . . . gesoffen
14. habe . . . verloren

25. 1. Die Sonne ist ins Meer gesunken.
2. Die Vorlesung hat begonnen.
3. Seid ihr von der Brücke gesprungen?
4. Ich habe das Lied gesungen.
5. Bist du über die Nordsee geschwommen?
6. Er hat den Preis gewonnen.
7. Das Gas hat gestunken.
8. Hast du den Hund an den Baum gebunden?
9. Die Männer sind über die Hürde gesprungen.
10. Habt ihr oft gesungen?
11. Ich habe Wasser getrunken.
12. Wir haben gestern begonnen.
13. Er hat auf dem Sofa gesessen.
14. Habt ihr die Frau gebeten?
15. Wer hat den Schmuck gefunden?
16. Er hat kaltes Bier getrunken.

26. 1. Habt ihr sie getroffen?
2. Sie haben den Ball geworfen.
3. Warum hast du es in Stücke gebrochen?
4. Ich habe ihr geholfen.
5. Das Kind hat nichts genommen.
6. Der Verletzte ist gestorben.
7. Warum hast du gestohlen?
8. Fräulein Knauer, Sie haben zu schnell gesprochen.
9. Wir haben dem Kranken geholfen.
10. Hast du viel gesprochen?
11. Bist du ins Kino gegangen?
12. Ich habe hier gestanden.
13. Wir haben die Suppe empfohlen.
14. Der Kran hat das Auto gehoben.
15. Was hast du getan?

27. 1. Hast du Hunger gehabt?
2. Ich bin krank gewesen.
3. Wir haben Hunger gehabt.
4. Sie sind immer dicker geworden.
5. Er ist wieder gesund geworden.
6. Wann sind Sie dort gewesen?
7. Ich habe Kopfweh gehabt.
8. Wir sind nass geworden.
9. Bist du auch müde gewesen?
10. Ich bin böse geworden.
11. Habt ihr Geld gehabt?
12. Ich habe Sorgen gehabt.
13. Sie ist unglücklich gewesen.

14. Die Pferde sind unruhig gewesen.
15. Bist du nervös geworden?
16. Seid ihr krank gewesen?

28.
1. Haben . . . besichtigt
2. hat . . . gegeben
3. hast . . . gewohnt
4. hat . . . gekauft
5. haben . . . gekannt
6. hast . . . gebacken
7. Habt . . . gesehen
8. haben . . . geschrien
9. hat . . . telefoniert
10. habe . . . gearbeitet
11. Habt . . . bestellt
12. bist . . . begegnet
13. hat . . . geschwiegen
14. haben . . . verloren
15. hat . . . gefressen
16. bist . . . gewachsen
17. Seid . . . gesprungen
18. habe . . . geträumt
19. hat . . . zerstört
20. Hast . . . studiert
21. bist . . . gekommen
22. habe . . . erzählt
23. Habt . . . gegessen
24. Haben . . . gewartet
25. haben . . . getrunken
26. haben . . . verkauft
27. Hast . . . geblutet
28. bin . . . gestiegen
29. hat . . . gesagt
30. hat . . . repariert
31. Hast . . . empfohlen
32. ist . . . gesunken
33. habt . . . getroffen
34. hast . . . geschlafen
35. haben . . . geschlossen

29.
1. Sie spielten.
2. Er wohnte in Köln.
3. Wir glaubten daran.
4. Ich studierte gern.
5. Der Hund bellte.
6. Ich bezahlte die Rechnung.
7. Man gratulierte ihm.
8. Wir brauchten Milch.
9. Meine Eltern bauten es.
10. Das Telefon klingelte.

30.

1. maltest	6. reparierte
2. besichtigten	7. zeigten
3. fragten	8. besuchtet
4. schenkte	9. kauften
5. lernten	10. störte

31.
1. Ich atmete ganz regelmässig.
2. Man tötete ihn.
3. Wir retteten den Verunglückten.
4. Du öffnetest die Tür.
5. Sie begegneten ihren Eltern.
6. Paul beobachtete den Vogel.
7. Ich arbeitete gern.
8. Er ordnete die Bücher.
9. Sie antwortete nicht.
10. Sie bluteten stark.

32.
1. Er wusste das nicht.
2. Ich sandte ihm einen Brief.
3. Es brannte dort.
4. Wir brachten Geschenke.
5. Sie dachten daran.
6. Die Kinder rannten.
7. Man nannte es.
8. Ich kannte ihn auch.
9. Er wandte das Heu.
10. Du kanntest uns.

33.
1. Sie litt.
2. Er schlief schon.
3. Sie schrieben Briefe.
4. Wir ritten gerne.
5. Ich schrie laut.
6. Das Buch fiel auf den Boden.
7. Der Zug hielt dort.
8. Ludwig blieb dort.
9. Sie schwiegen immer.
10. Wir litten sehr.
11. Er schrieb die Aufgabe.
12. Sie schwieg nicht.
13. Ihr schnittet ins Papier.
14. Die Sonne schien.
15. Man lieh dem Kind das Buch.
16. Der Hund biss das Mädchen.

34.
1. Ich liess Gudrun gehen.
2. Das Pferd lief am schnellsten.
3. Hubert ritt den ganzen Tag.
4. Wir liehen Gisela das Buch.
5. Der Rattenfänger fing Ratten.
6. Ich schnitt ins Fleisch.
7. Meine Eltern schrieben den Brief.
8. Wir schrien nicht.

35.

1. flog	8. zogen
2. verlor	9. floss
3. roch	10. floht
4. schlossen	11. soffen
5. schoss	12. flog
6. frorst	13. hob
7. wog	14. bogen

36.

1. assen	16. begann
2. gewann	17. schwammen
3. sprang	18. stank
4. sahen	19. traft
5. kam	20. bat
6. las	21. warf
7. nahm	22. sprachst
8. sprangen	23. sahen
9. tat	24. stahl
10. sank	25. traf
11. band	26. halfen
12. starb	27. standen
13. gaben	28. vergass
14. sassen	29. mass
15. sah	30. traten

37.
1. Der Hund frass das Futter.
2. Die Bücher lagen auf dem Tisch.
3. Wir sprangen aus dem Fenster.
4. Ich sass auf einem Stuhl.
5. Die Sängerin sang die Arie.
6. Die Kinder tranken keinen Wein.
7. Er fand die Diamantbrosche.
8. Wir kamen um acht Uhr.
9. Ich sah Monika im Kino.
10. Er tat alles.

38.
1. Die Lehrerinnen fuhren in die Stadt.
2. Ich schlug ihn nicht.
3. Die Alte grub ein Loch.
4. Wir trugen Lederhosen.
5. Das Baby wuchs schnell.
6. Tante Ida wusch die Bettwäsche.
7. Er trug etwas.
8. Ich fuhr mit dem Zug.

39.

1. war	6. Wart
2. warst	7. waren
3. war	8. waren
4. Warst	9. Wart
5. waren	10. war

40.

1. Hattest	6. Hattet
2. hatten	7. Hattest
3. hatten	8. hatte
4. hatte	9. Hattet
5. Hattest	10. Hatten

41.

1. wurden	6. wurde
2. wurden	7. wurdest
3. wurde	8. Wurdet
4. wurde	9. Wurde
5. wurde	10. wurdet

42. Peter besuchte mich gestern. Wir tranken Limonade. Er ass auch ein Stück Schokoladenkuchen. Wir fuhren ins Zentrum. Wir trafen dort seine Freunde und (wir) gingen ins Kino. Der Film war prima. Er gefiel mir sehr. Wir kamen um acht Uhr nach Hause. Wir spielten eine Stunde Platten und sprachen über Musik. Meine Mutter machte noch Wurstbrote. Peter ging danach nach Hause.

43.
1. schlief, las
2. lächelte, sang
3. assen, tanzten
4. schrieb, klingelte
5. kaufte, traf
6. gingen, wurde
7. lachte, erzählte
8. waren, kamst
9. half, blutete
10. schwammen, schnitt

44.
1. Wir fuhren gewöhnlich in die Schweiz.
2. Ich war immer krank.
3. Die Damen tranken gewöhnlich Tee.
4. Die Schauspielerin wurde immer nervös.
5. Wir gingen sonntags gewöhnlich zur Kirche.
6. Er arbeitete immer.
7. Karin trank gewöhnlich Limonade.
8. Wir gaben den Kindern immer Geld.
9. Ich half Renate immer.
10. Wir spielten gewöhnlich moderne Musik.

45.

1. wurdest	11. waren
2. litt	12. nahm
3. arbeitete	13. trank, war
4. öffnete	14. zeigten
5. reparierte	15. klingelte
6. besichtigten	16. lief
7. Wart	17. wusch
8. sah	18. vergass
9. schlief, kam	19. waren
10. Hattest	20. las, studierte

46.
1. Werdet . . . bleiben
2. Wirst . . . telefonieren
3. werden . . . glauben
4. werde . . . bezahlen
5. wird . . . lesen
6. werden . . . machen
7. Werdet . . . helfen
8. werden . . . schreiben
9. werde . . . öffnen
10. Wirst . . . kaufen
11. werdet . . . bestellen
12. wird . . . kommen
13. werde . . . vergessen
14. werden . . . biegen
15. werden . . . schreien
16. wirst . . . frieren

47.
1. Wir werden das Auto bringen.
2. Ich werde nach Berlin fahren.
3. Wirst du kommen?
4. Er wird das Gedicht schreiben.
5. Werdet ihr euren Eltern das Haus zeigen?
6. Sie werden arbeiten.
7. Ich werde bei Inge essen.
8. Wirst du es kaufen?

48.
1. Sie wird vielleicht krank sein.
2. Wir werden wohl kommen.
3. Sie werden vielleicht weinen.
4. Kinder, ihr werdet wohl Hunger haben.
5. Peter, du wirst es wohl wissen.
6. Ich werde wohl gehen.
7. Er wird wohl arbeiten.
8. Sie werden vielleicht helfen.

49.
1. Wir hatten getanzt.
2. Hattest du gesungen?
3. Sie waren gefahren.
4. Hattet ihr gefragt?
5. Man hatte es genommen.
6. Sie hatten viel getrunken.
7. Hattest du studiert?
8. Ich hatte es repariert.
9. Wann war er gekommen?
10. Er hatte mich besucht.
11. Hattest du den Wagen gewaschen?
12. Konrad war dort geblieben.
13. Ich hatte die Jacke getragen.
14. Sie war in Rom gewesen.
15. Hatte er dem Kranken geholfen?
16. Wir hatten gearbeitet.

50.
1. Wir waren arm, denn wir hatten alles verloren.
2. Sie hatte Angst, denn sie war schon oft im Krankenhaus gewesen.
3. Ich wusste alles, denn ich hatte viel studiert.
4. Sie bestellten viel, denn sie hatten den ganzen Tag nichts gegessen.
5. Laura war traurig, denn ihr Freund hatte sie nicht besucht.
6. Sie waren schwach, denn sie waren krank gewesen.
7. Ich war müde, denn ich hatte schlecht geschlafen.
8. Wir hatten Durst, denn wir hatten nichts getrunken.
9. Es roch nach Gas, denn er hatte die Flasche zerbrochen.
10. Ich hatte kein Geld, denn ich hatte viel gekauft.

51.
1. Ihr werdet wohl getanzt haben.
2. Sie werden wohl gekommen sein.
3. Maria wird wohl geschlafen haben.
4. Wir werden es wohl nicht gesehen haben.
5. Du wirst wohl nicht gefragt haben.
6. Er wird wohl das Gedicht geschrieben haben.
7. Der Hund wird wohl Manfred gebissen haben.
8. Du wirst wohl lange gewartet haben.

52.
1. bekommt
2. zerbreche
3. verkauft
4. verstehen
5. empfange
6. bestellt
7. Gefällt
8. Besucht
9. erkläre
10. Erzählst
11. empfehlen
12. vergisst

53.
1. Wir haben das Wort verstanden.
2. Es hat mir nicht gefallen.
3. Sie haben die Wahrheit gestanden.
4. Warum ist es zerfallen?
5. Ich habe das Examen bestanden.
6. Wer hat dich besucht?
7. Habt ihr das Haus verkauft?
8. Er hat den Brief empfangen.
9. Warum hast du alles erzählt?
10. Was hat er entdeckt?

54.
1. steigt . . . ein
2. kommen . . . zusammen
3. fahre . . . mit
4. ziehst . . . an
5. Legt . . . nieder
6. lernen . . . kennen
7. kommst . . . zurück
8. gehe . . . hin
9. steht . . . auf
10. fahren . . . spazieren

55.
1. Er ass alles auf.
2. Ich schrieb das Lied ab.
3. Wir lernten ihn kennen.
4. Arnim sammelte für die Armen ein.
5. Die Kinder machten alles nach.
6. Wer machte das Fenster zu?
7. Wie nähte er das Leder zusammen?
8. Wann gingen die Studenten heim?

56.
1. Gisela, lauf nicht weg!
2. Frau Bayer, machen Sie schnell zu!
3. Konrad, fahr bitte mit!
4. Ursula und Theo, tretet leise ein!
5. Fräulein Breu, stehen Sie langsam auf!
6. Helga, komm doch her!
7. Mutter, mach die Schachtel zu!
8. Arno, schau es nicht an!

57.
1. Wir werden fortgehen.
2. Ich werde hinausgehen.
3. Er wird es zurückbringen.
4. Sie werden nichts wegnehmen.

5. Wirst du ausgehen?
6. Ich werde das Album anschauen.

58.
1. Sie haben auch mitgelacht.
2. Wir haben bei ihr nachgeschaut.
3. Ich habe ihn kennengelernt.
4. Der Zug ist bald angekommen.
5. Wir sind spazierengegangen.
6. Ich bin mit ihm heimgefahren.
7. Gudrun ist dann aufgestanden.
8. Sie haben bald nachgeschaut.

59.
1. war . . . eingestiegen
2. hatte . . . ausgemacht
3. hatten . . . abgeschrieben
4. hatten . . . niedergelegt
5. Wart . . . zusammengekommen
6. hatte . . . kennengelernt
7. waren . . . fortgeblieben
8. hatte . . . zugehört

60.
1. Ich weiss, dass er fortgegangen ist.
2. Ich weiss, dass sie herkommen wird.
3. Ich weiss, dass wir morgen abfliegen.
4. Ich weiss, dass ihr Peter kennengelernt habt.
5. Ich weiss, dass der Zug angekommen war.
6. Ich weiss, dass ich nachkomme.
7. Ich weiss, dass er ausging.
8. Ich weiss, dass wir heimkommen werden.
9. Ich weiss, dass du mitfährst.
10. Ich weiss, dass er nachgeschaut hatte.

61.
1. Ich zeige dem Kind das Buch.
2. Er schickt deiner Mutter eine Karte.
3. Wir glauben dem Mann.
4. Ich bringe der Studentin den Roman.
5. Dankst du deinem Lehrer?
6. Wir helfen unsrer Grossmutter.
7. Das Haus gehört meinen Eltern.
8. Antwortet ihr der Lehrerin?
9. Maria kauft ihrer Freundin eine Kette.
10. Der Wagen gehört meinem Bruder.
11. Wer holt dem Kranken eine Pille?
12. Die Blumen gefallen unsrer Tante.
13. Warum gratulierst du deiner Schwester?
14. Er schenkt dem Baby eine Puppe.
15. Wir schicken dem Präsidenten einen Protest
16. Die Kinder folgen dem Kindermädchen.

62.

1. er	10. em
2. em	11. er
3. ie	12. en
4. em, e	13. er
5. em	14. er
6. er	15. en
7. er	16. er, e
8. em	17. em
9. er	18. er

63.
1. interessiere mich
2. unterhalten uns
3. regst dich . . . auf
4. setzt . . . euch
5. erkälte mich
6. stellst . . . dich vor
7. ziehen sich um
8. freut sich
9. legt sich
10. freuen uns
11. rasiert sich
12. amüsiere mich
13. bewegt sich
14. Freust . . . dich
15. Wascht . . . euch
16. entscheidet sich
17. verspäte mich
18. Erinnern . . . sich
19. zieht sich . . . an
20. Entschuldigst . . . dich

64.
1. Er hat sich vor Pferden gefürchtet.
2. Wir haben uns für die Sammlung interessiert.
3. Sie haben sich ganz nett benommen.
4. Habt ihr euch über das Geschenk gefreut?
5. Ich habe mich schon umgezogen.
6. Wir haben uns heute vorgestellt.
7. Hast du dich oft erkältet?
8. Sie hat sich schon gewaschen.
9. Die Männer haben sich rasiert.
10. Habt ihr euch verspätet?

65.
1. Ich habe mich auf seine Ankunft gefreut.
2. Wir legen uns aufs Bett.
3. Ich habe mich am Freitag verletzt.
4. Ich interessiere mich für Briefmarken.
5. Ich habe mich schon an die Arbeit gewöhnt.
6. Er hat sich im Winter erkältet.
7. Ich wundere mich über die Explosion.
8. Die Kinder fürchten sich vor dem Gewitter.

66.
1. Unterhalten wir uns!
2. Kinder, verspätet euch nicht!
3. Peter, erkälte dich nicht!
4. Herr Ziegler, stellen Sie sich vor!
5. Setzen wir uns!
6. Gisela, wasch dich!
7. Mädchen, entschuldigt euch!
8. Frau Klein, amüsieren Sie sich!
9. Ute, fürchte dich nicht vor dem Hund!
10. Vater, rasier dich!

67.

1. ___	6. ___
2. ___	7. uns
3. mich	8. ___
4. sich	9. ___
5. sich	10. ___

68. 1. tust dir . . . weh
2. putzen uns
3. kaufe mir
4. wascht . . . euch
5. bildet sich . . . ein
6. setzt sich . . . auf
7. bestellt sich
8. stelle mir . . . vor
9. kaufen uns
10. holt sich
11. tun sich weh
12. bildet euch . . . ein
13. wasche mir
14. Nehmt . . . euch
15. machst . . . dir

69. 1. Ich stelle mir das Haus vor.
2. Ich habe mir das Papier geholt.
3. Wir bestellen uns das Essen bald.
4. Ich habe mir am Fuss weh getan.
5. Die Gäste ziehen sich im Schlafzimmer an.
6. Gisela bildet sich etwas ein.

70. 1. Herr Müller, bestellen Sie sich das Buch!
2. Kinder, putzt euch die Zähne!
3. Peter und Heinz, kauft euch etwas!
4. Marlene, tu dir nicht weh!
5. Kinder, wascht euch die Hände!
6. Frau Wimmer, nehmen Sie sich etwas!

71. 1. dürfen 5. darf
2. dürfen 6. darfst
3. darfst 7. Dürft
4. Darf 8. darfst

72. 1. Er muss schwer arbeiten.
2. Sie müssen Brot holen.
3. Musst du studieren?
4. Müssen Sie heute singen?
5. Wir müssen aufstehen.
6. Wann müsst ihr im Büro sein?
7. Die Kinder müssen zu Hause bleiben.
8. Ich muss das Essen bestellen.

73. 1. Ich kann die Geschichte nicht glauben.
2. Könnt ihr morgen mitkommen?
3. Wir können unsrem Freund nicht helfen.
4. Max kann gut tanzen.
5. Kannst du langsamer sprechen?
6. Ich kann alles hören.

74. 1. mag 5. Mögt
2. mag 6. mag
3. mögen 7. Mögen
4. Magst 8. mögen

75. 1. Wir wollen helfen.
2. Ich will es nicht sehen.
3. Er will kommen.
4. Wollen sie schlafen?
5. Ursel, willst du gehen?
6. Sie will studieren.
7. Erika und Frank, wollt ihr arbeiten?
8. Ich will das Museum besuchen.

76. 1. Ich soll dem Kind etwas kaufen.
2. Er soll schnell kommen.
3. Sollst du die Wahrheit sagen?
4. Die Studenten sollen lernen.
5. Man soll nicht stehlen.
6. Wir sollen nicht kommen.
7. Sollt ihr bleiben?
8. Ich soll das Auto reparieren.

77. 1. Wir können Englisch.
2. Ich mag keine Suppe.
3. Sie müssen nach Hause.
4. Kann er Deutsch?
5. Sie muss in die Stadt.
6. Er mag keine Milch.

78. 1. Wir wollten mitmachen.
2. Ich mochte keinen Reis.
3. Konntest du bleiben?
4. Durftet ihr denn rauchen?
5. Du konntest nicht heimgehen.
6. Luise wollte bezahlen.
7. Warum wollten Sie helfen?
8. Musstest du studieren?
9. Ich wollte es sehen.
10. Konntet ihr das machen?

79. 1. Konntet ihr ihm helfen?
2. Ich wollte etwas kaufen.
3. Sollte er auch mitmachen?
4. Wir mussten ihn anrufen.
5. Die Kinder mochten kein Gemüse.
6. Durftest du nicht gehen?

80. 1. Herr Maier, wollten Sie schlafen?
2. Durftet ihr rauchen?
3. Konntest du ausgehen?
4. Mochtet ihr Bananen?
5. Fräulein Lang, sollten Sie daran glauben?
6. Musstet ihr helfen?
7. Solltest du es kaufen?
8. Wolltet ihr fragen?
9. Durftest du mitmachen?
10. Konntet ihr es sehen?
11. Mussten Sie alles nehmen?
12. Solltet ihr Bier bestellen?
13. Mochtest du keine Milch?
14. Wollten Sie Konrad kennenlernen?

81. 1. Ich habe ihn nicht gemocht.
2. Sie hat nach Köln gewollt.
3. Hast du das gedurft?
4. Wir haben zur Schule gemusst.

5. Hat er das gekonnt?
6. Die Leute haben nicht gemocht.
7. Ihr habt doch Deutsch gekonnt.
8. Sie haben Englisch gekonnt.
9. Ich habe zur Arbeit gemusst.
10. Wir haben es gedurft.
11. Hast du keine Limonade gemocht?
12. Ich habe in die Stadt gesollt.

82. 1. Wir haben nicht mitfahren sollen.
2. Ich habe nicht schreiben können.
3. Habt ihr hier bleiben müssen?
4. Warum hat er anrufen wollen?
5. Ich habe es bringen dürfen.
6. Man hat Musik hören können.
7. Sie haben nicht aufstehen mögen.
8. Warum hast du es zerstören wollen?
9. Er hat es sehen dürfen.
10. Habt ihr dort parken wollen?
11. Ich habe heimgehen wollen.
12. Hast du zu Hause bleiben müssen?
13. Sie haben gut lesen können.
14. Hubert hat studieren müssen.
15. Wir haben Maria helfen wollen.
16. Haben Sie schwimmen können?

83. 1. Wir hatten es gekonnt.
2. Ich hatte abfahren müssen.
3. Er hatte es gewollt.
4. Sie hatten keinen Kuchen gemocht.
5. Sie hatte mich anrufen sollen.
6. Hattest du sie besuchen dürfen?
7. Ich hatte nicht davon sprechen wollen.
8. Ihr hattet es ja wissen dürfen.
9. Sie hatte das Fenster aufmachen können.
10. Ich hatte zur Schule gemusst.
11. Wir hatten Peter nicht gemocht.
12. Hattest du hinausgehen wollen?
13. Ich hatte Russisch gekonnt.
14. Er hatte den Wagen reparieren müssen.

84. 1. Sie werden nicht schlafen können.
2. Wir werden den ganzen Tag studieren müssen.
3. Er wird es sehen wollen.
4. Ich werde klingeln müssen.
5. Ihr werdet nichts kaufen dürfen.
6. Wirst du es schicken können?
7. Gudrun wird nicht mitmachen wollen.
8. Werdet ihr die Suppe probieren wollen?
9. Sie werden nicht schreien dürfen.
10. Wir werden nicht arbeiten können.

85. 1. Wir lassen das Bild in der Schule.
2. Ich helfe Rita den Hund suchen.
3. Siehst du deine Schwester arbeiten?
4. Hören Sie die Sonate?
5. Er hört seine Frau schreien.
6. Lasst ihr Hans gehen?
7. Die Leute hören uns sprechen.
8. Ich sehe die Kirche.
9. Frau Berger hilft heute.
10. Er lässt Gerda mitkommen.

86. 1. Ich habe es liegen lassen.
2. Wir haben sie lachen hören.
3. Er hat seinen Freund gesehen.
4. Sie haben Heinz das Auto reparieren helfen.
5. Er hat nichts gehört.
6. Ich habe Pia reiten sehen.
7. Sie haben Sonja weinen hören.
8. Wir haben die Zeitungen zu Hause gelassen.
9. Wir haben den Kindern geholfen.
10. Vater hat uns gehen lassen.

87. 1. Er wird Peter schreiben sehen.
2. Ich werde Otto kommen hören.
3. Wir werden den Kindern zeichnen helfen.
4. Wirst du Dieter lachen sehen?
5. Sie werden Rainer sprechen hören.
6. Werden Sie Anneliese lesen helfen?
7. Ich werde den Mantel hier liegen lassen.
8. Werdet ihr Grossmutter rufen hören?

88. 1. Er sagt, dass du die Jacke hast liegen lassen.
2. Er sagt, dass wir Josef haben studieren helfen.
3. Er sagt, dass sie Franz haben singen hören.
4. Er sagt, dass ich es habe machen lassen.
5. Er sagt, dass sie das Geschenk hat öffnen dürfen.
6. Er sagt, dass du den Bleistift hast zurückgeben wollen.
7. Er sagt, dass wir Peter haben kommen lassen.
8. Er sagt, dass ihr das Auto habt bringen müssen.

89. 1. ohne Norma zu sehen.
2. anstatt zur Schule zu gehen.
3. um Gertrud zu helfen.
4. ohne anzurufen.
5. um mich umzuziehen.
6. um die Kinder einzuladen.
7. anstatt es Helga zu bringen.
8. ohne den Mantel anzuziehen.
9. um zu fragen.
10. ohne es zu lernen.

90. 1. sich zu entschuldigen.
2. uns zu fragen.
3. den Kindern zu helfen.
4. die Geschichte zu erzählen.
5. sich zu rasieren.
6. mitzukommen.
7. es zu holen.
8. Geld zu nehmen.

9. den Hund zu füttern.
10. den Kuchen zu essen.

91.
1. anzurufen
2. zu schreiben
3. mitzugeben
4. einzuladen
5. zu schneiden
6. zu sein
7. zu lesen
8. zu besuchen
9. zu begleiten
10. mitzunehmen
11. zu sehen
12. zu glauben

92.
1. Er braucht nicht zu studieren.
2. Ich brauche nicht zu lesen.
3. Wir brauchen das Buch nicht zurückzugeben.
4. Sie braucht nicht zu arbeiten.
5. Ihr braucht es nicht zu machen.
6. Du brauchst Herbert nicht zu helfen.
7. Ich brauche Bert nicht zu besuchen.
8. Renate braucht nicht zu lesen.
9. Sie brauchen die Geschichte nicht zu erzählen.
10. Ich brauche es nicht zu bestellen.

93.
1. beim Gehen
2. beim Tanzen
3. beim Singen
4. beim Arbeiten
5. beim Malen
6. beim Reparieren
7. beim Studieren
8. beim Spielen
9. beim Telefonieren
10. beim Schwimmen

94.
1. leidend
2. lesende
3. fliessendem
4. bellenden
5. Blutend
6. singende
7. weinenden
8. schlafende
9. lächelnde
10. Grüssend

95.
1. zerstörte
2. angebrannt
3. gestohlenen
4. geschriebene
5. gebackene
6. begonnene
7. gefangen
8. gefütterte
9. reparierte
10. geöffnete

96.
1. en
2. er
3. e
4. e
5. e
6. en
7. en
8. e
9. e
10. e

97.
1. Ja, schreiben Sie bitte!
2. Ja, schlafen Sie bitte!
3. Ja, gehen Sie bitte!
4. Ja, tanzen Sie bitte!
5. Ja, lächeln Sie bitte!
6. Ja, reden Sie bitte!
7. Ja, arbeiten Sie bitte!
8. Ja, erzählen Sie bitte!
9. Ja, essen Sie bitte!
10. Ja, fahren Sie bitte!

98.
1. Findet
2. Sprecht
3. Trinkt
4. Holt
5. Schlaft
6. Parkt
7. Studiert
8. Geht
9. Bleibt
10. Ruft
11. Esst
12. Nehmt
13. Reitet
14. Bestellt
15. Schreibt

99.
1. Sing lauter!
2. Komm jetzt!
3. Such das Geld!
4. Bleib hier!
5. Mach es!
6. Grüss Tante Ida!
7. Geh ins Haus!
8. Probier die Wurst!
9. Wein nicht!
10. Spring ins Wasser!
11. Schwimm mehr!
12. Sag die Wahrheit!
13. Ruf die Polizei!
14. Frag den Lehrer!
15. Rauch nicht!

100.
1. Ja, warte!
2. Ja, rede!
3. Ja, lächle!
4. Ja, füttere es!
5. Ja, behandle ihn!
6. Ja, öffne es!
7. Ja, antworte!
8. Ja, ändere es!
9. Ja, beobachte es!
10. Ja, rechne!
11. Ja, schneide es!
12. Ja, sammle es!
13. Ja, wandere!
14. Ja, arbeite!

101.
1. Hilf dem Kind!
2. Sprich lauter!
3. Gib es dem Lehrer!
4. Stiehl nicht!
5. Lies die Zeitung!
6. Brich es nicht!
7. Triff die Frau!
8. Stirb nicht!
9. Erschrick nicht!
10. Iss das Fleisch!
11. Nimm den Schmuck!
12. Vergiss nichts!

102.
1. habt
2. sei
3. werden Sie
4. wisst
5. seien Sie
6. werde
7. sei
8. hab
9. haben Sie
10. wissen Sie
11. seid
12. seien Sie

103.
1. Kochen wir das Abendessen!
2. Fragen wir den Lehrer!

3. Trinken wir warme Milch!
4. Kaufen wir Wein!
5. Gehen wir jetzt!
6. Schreiben wir die Aufgaben!
7. Rufen wir den Hund!
8. Holen wir das Buch!
9. Arbeiten wir viel!
10. Ändern wir nichts!

104. 1. Wir würden nichts nehmen.
2. Würdest du bezahlen?
3. Ich würde den ganzen Tag schwimmen.
4. Sie würden viel arbeiten.
5. Er würde nicht studieren.
6. Würdet ihr nach Deutschland fahren?
7. Würden Sie laut singen?
8. Ich würde nicht ins Wasser springen.
9. Würdest du das Buch lesen?
10. Er würde den Wagen reparieren.
11. Würdet ihr kommen?
12. Sie würden das Geschenk bringen.
13. Würdet ihr mir helfen?
14. Ich würde auch gehen.
15. Würden Sie die Jacke tragen?
16. Würden die Kinder laufen?

105. 1. Würden Sie bitte kommen?
2. Würdest du das bitte nehmen?
3. Würdet ihr bitte hier bleiben?
4. Würden Sie bitte schneller fahren?
5. Würdest du mir bitte das Messer geben?
6. Würden Sie bitte langsamer sprechen?
7. Würden Sie bitte gehen?
8. Würdest du bitte das Auto parken?
9. Würdet ihr bitte das Essen bestellen?
10. Würden Sie es bitte den Kindern zeigen?
11. Würden Sie bitte Ihren Vater besuchen?
12. Würdest du bitte hier warten?

106. 1. Sie besuchten uns.
2. Wir machten viel.
3. Kauftet ihr es?
4. Ich erzählte es.
5. Zerstörtest du es?
6. Arbeiteten Sie dort?
7. Ich fragte ihn.
8. Wir zahlten.
9. Er glaubte es.
10. Ich sagte es.
11. Wohntest du dort?
12. Hörtet ihr es?
13. Sie lernten es.
14. Wir weinten nicht.
15. Ich bezahlte.
16. Er studierte.
17. Bautet ihr das Haus?
18. Spielten Sie dort?
19. Sie hörten alles.
20. Maltest du?

107. 1. Ich weinte.
2. Wir spielten.
3. Sie holten es.
4. Er glaubte es nicht.
5. Kinder, studiertet ihr?
6. Gerda, kauftest du Blumen?
7. Frau Treibl, wohnten Sie dort?
8. Sie arbeitete.
9. Wir lernten.
10. Sie probierten die Suppe.

108. 1. Das Haus brennte.
2. Dächtet ihr daran?
3. Ich brächte etwas.
4. Nenntest du es?
5. Sie rennten schnell.
6. Wir wüssten es.
7. Ich sendete den Brief.
8. Ich wendete das Blatt.
9. Ich wüsste das.
10. Brächtest du das Buch?

109. 1. Ich schriebe das Gedicht.
2. Wir tränken nichts.
3. Liessest du ihn gehen?
4. Die Alten gingen zur Kirche.
5. Die Sonne schiene nicht.
6. Die Studenten läsen das Buch.
7. Er flöge auch.
8. Schliefest du lange?
9. Ich gäbe Anna alles.
10. Er liefe schnell.
11. Die Leute führen mit dem Auto.
12. Wir schrien laut.
13. Er schnitte das Haar.
14. Ich bliebe hier.
15. Wir kämen auch.
16. Nähmest du das Papier?
17. Ich ässe Brot.
18. Das Pferd zöge den Schlitten.
19. Er verlöre das Geld.
20. Wir sprängen hoch.

110. 1. Er stürbe.
2. Sie hülfen.
3. Wir würfen den Ball.
4. Sie stünde hier.
5. Ich hülfe.
6. Sie stürben.
7. Wir stünden hier.
8. Helga, hülfest du?

111. 1. Wir hätten kein Auto.
2. Ich wäre reich.
3. Sie hätten keine Ferien.
4. Du wärest nicht glücklich.
5. Ich hätte keinen Hund.
6. Sie wäre böse.
7. Sie wären nicht intelligent.

8. Ihr hättet kein Geld.
9. Er hätte nichts.
10. Hättet ihr Geld?
11. Wir wären krank.
12. Hättest du Angst?
13. Wir hätten alles.
14. Wäret ihr müde?
15. Wärest du froh?
16. Ich wäre arm.

112.
1. Könnten Sie mir helfen?
2. Wolltest du auch zeichnen?
3. Müsstet ihr nicht studieren?
4. Dürfte er mitgehen?
5. Solltest du Marianne besuchen?
6. Könnte ich ein Stück nehmen?
7. Müsstest du nicht lernen?
8. Wolltet ihr den Film sehen?
9. Könnte sie es holen?
10. Dürfte ich bleiben?

113.
1. Möchtest
2. möchte
3. möchten
4. möchten
5. Möchten
6. Möchtest
7. Möchten
8. möchte
9. Möchtet
10. Möchtest

114.
1. Ich wollte, er bliebe nicht dort.
2. Ich wollte, sie könnten nicht abfahren.
3. Ich wollte, wir lebten in keinem Dorf.
4. Ich wollte, ich hätte kein Zahnweh.
5. Ich wollte, ihr arbeitetet nicht so viel.
6. Ich wollte, ich müsste nicht studieren.
7. Ich wollte, wir wären zu Hause.
8. Ich wollte, du kauftest dir etwas.
9. Ich wollte, sie weinte nicht.
10. Ich wollte, ich wäre nicht arm.
11. Ich wollte, wir hätten es nicht.
12. Ich wollte, er nähme es nicht.
13. Ich wollte, er sähe Paula nicht.
14. Ich wollte, sie besuchten Oma nicht.

115.
1. Wenn wir nur in München wären!
2. Wenn er nur das Fenster öffnete!
3. Wenn ihr doch ein Auto kauftet!
4. Wenn die Leute nur nicht so laut schrien!
5. Wenn ich nur alles wüsste!
6. Wenn er nur nicht krank wäre!
7. Wenn die Kinder nur zu Hause blieben!
8. Wenn ich nur Deutsch könnte!
9. Wenn ihr nur mehr hättet!
10. Wenn Georg nur nicht abführe!

116.
1. Sagte sie nur die Wahrheit!
2. Könnte ich doch schlafen!
3. Reparierte er nur das Auto!
4. Tränken sie nur nicht so viel!
5. Schwiege er doch!
6. Hätten wir nur keine Angst!
7. Wärest du nur hier!
8. Bliebe er nur hier!
9. Glaubte sie es nur!
10. Lerntet ihr nur mehr!

117.
1. würde ich arbeiten.
2. würde ich nicht hier wohnen.
3. würde ich dir nichts geben.
4. würde ich nicht nach Hamburg fliegen.
5. würde ich mir nichts bestellen.
6. würden wir Kaffee trinken.
7. würden wir uns unterhalten.
8. würde ich mich freuen.
9. würde ich mich umziehen.
10. würde ich mich nicht fürchten.

118.
1. hätte, hülfe
2. wäre, wäre
3. brauchte, nähme
4. bliebest, besuchten
5. studiertet, wüsstet
6. bestellten, ässen
7. lerntest, könntest

119.
1. Hülfest du mir, dann wäre ich froh.
2. Käme er, dann bliebe ich dort.
3. Fragten wir ihn, dann würde er uns antworten.
4. Wollte sie es, dann gäbe ich es ihr.
5. Hätte ich Angst, dann würde ich schreien.

120.
1. Wäre ich krank, bliebe ich zu Hause.
2. Wüssten wir es, erzählten wir es Alexander.
3. Hätte sie Geld, kaufte sie den Mantel.
4. Arbeiteten sie, wären sie glücklicher.
5. Käme er an, holte ich ihn ab.

121.
1. hätten
2. liebtest
3. ginge
4. wären
5. wollte
6. könnte
7. bliebe
8. arbeiteten
9. sähe
10. nähmen

122.
1. Wenn wir nur in der Schule gewesen wären!
2. Wenn du nur angerufen hättest!
3. Wenn ich mich nur gebadet hätte!
4. Wenn er nur Angst gehabt hätte!
5. Wenn ihr nur gekommen wäret!

123.
1. Hättest du nur geschrien!
2. Wären wir ihr nur begegnet!
3. Wäre ich nur hingegangen!
4. Wäre er nur nicht gestorben!
5. Hätte sie nur geschrieben!

124. 1. gegessen hätte, hätte . . . gehabt
2. zurückgebracht hättest, hätte . . . geholt
3. zugemacht hättet, hättet . . . erkältet
4. angerufen hättest, hätte . . . gesagt
5. geblutet hätte, hätte . . . geschrien

125. 1. Hätte es geklingelt, hätten wir aufgemacht.
2. Hättest du angerufen, wäre ich gekommen.
3. Hätten wir es gefunden, hätten wir es wieder zurückgegeben.
4. Hättet ihr geschrieben, hätten wir euch dort getroffen.

126. 1. Er tut, als ob er es gekauft hätte.
2. Sie tun, als ob sie nicht geschlafen hätten.
3. Sie tut, als ob sie krank gewesen wäre.
4. Er tut, als ob er mitgekommen wäre.

127. 1. Hätte er nur bleiben dürfen!
2. Wenn ich doch nicht hätte gehen müssen!
3. Er tut, als ob er es hätte sehen können.
4. Du tust, als ob ich es hätte schreiben sollen.
5. Wenn ich hätte reiten wollen, hätte ich es dir gesagt.
6. Hätte er nur singen können!
7. Wenn du nur nichts hättest essen wollen!
8. Wenn wir hätten fragen dürfen, hätten wir die Antwort gewusst.
9. Hätte sie nur helfen können!
10. Sie tun, als ob sie auf mich hätten warten müssen.

128.

1. sei	10. schicke
2. bleibe	11. schenke
3. wohne	12. habe
4. studiere	13. wisse
5. arbeite	14. könne
6. gebe	15. wolle
7. kaufe	16. finde
8. bringe	17. trinke
9. hole	18. esse

129. 1. er habe schon geschrieben
2. ich sei ins Kino gegangen
3. sie sei im Krankenhaus gewesen
4. er habe etwas geholt
5. ich habe es repariert
6. er habe nicht kommen dürfen

130. 1. Sie sagte, Mutter wäre krank gewesen.
2. Sie sagte, Grossvater hätte Geld gehabt.
3. Sie sagte, Peter hätte Angst.
4. Sie sagte, sie wäre allein gewesen.
5. Sie sagte, er hätte ihn gesehen.
6. Sie sagte, Christa wäre nach Köln gefahren.
7. Sie sagte, Onkel Werner wäre in Hamburg.
8. Sie sagte, ich hätte dich besucht.

131. 1. Er hat gesagt, Mutter sei krank gewesen.
2. Er hat gesagt, Grossvater habe Geld gehabt.
3. Er hat gesagt, Peter habe Angst.
4. Er hat gesagt, sie sei allein gewesen.
5. Er hat gesagt, er habe ihn gesehen.
6. Er hat gesagt, Christa sei nach Köln gefahren.
7. Er hat gesagt, Onkel Werner sei in Hamburg.
8. Er hat gesagt, ich habe dich besucht.

132. 1. wird vom . . . gebacken
2. wird durch . . . gerettet
3. wird . . . serviert
4. werden von . . . angeschaut
5. wird von . . . genommen
6. wird vom . . . geholfen
7. wird von . . . geschrieben
8. wird von . . . gewaschen
9. wird von . . . gegraben
10. wird durch . . . zerstört
11. werden von . . . gesehen
12. werde von . . . geschlagen
13. wird von . . . gehört
14. wird durch . . . zerstört
15. wird von . . . repariert

133. 1. Das Kind wird von dem (vom) Hund gebissen.
2. Das Haus wird durch das (durchs) Feuer zerstört.
3. Der Kaffee wird von meinen Freunden getrunken.
4. Das Pferd wird von ihm gefüttert.
5. Dem Kranken wird von dem (vom) Vater geholfen.

134. 1. Wir wurden abgeholt.
2. Die Rechnung wurde von Renate bezahlt.
3. Wurdest du beobachtet?
4. Das Auto wurde geparkt.
5. Es wurde schon von den Leuten gemacht.
6. Das Museum wurde von der Klasse besucht.
7. Das Wort wurde von dem Studenten buchstabiert.
8. Ich wurde gesehen.
9. Die Maschine wurde von dem Mechaniker repariert.
10. Das Haus wurde durch die Bombe zerstört.

135. 1. Er wurde gesehen.
2. Das Fenster wurde von Marlene geöffnet.
3. Sie wurden von ihrem Vater gefragt.
4. Sie wurde gehört.
5. Es wurde von meiner Tante gewaschen.
6. Uns wurde von dem Jungen geholfen. (Es wurde uns von dem Jungen geholfen.)
7. Ich wurde beobachtet.

8. Die Stadt wurde durch eine Bombe zerstört.

136.
1. Das Museum ist 1911 erbaut worden.
2. Der Löwe ist vom Wärter gefüttert worden.
3. Es ist ihr darüber erzählt worden.
4. Das Kleid ist rot gefärbt worden.
5. Es ist ihm gegeben worden.
6. Du bist überall gesucht worden.
7. Ich bin von ihm gesehen worden.
8. Das Restaurant ist durch das Feuer zerstört worden.
9. Er ist vom Arzt behandelt worden.
10. Die Kinder sind von den Hunden gebissen worden.

137.
1. Das Haus wird von meinen Freunden gebaut werden.
2. Die Geschichte wird erzählt werden.
3. Die Tiere werden durch Gift getötet werden.
4. Das Geschenk wird von den Kindern bewundert werden.
5. Die Rechnung wird von meinem Vater bezahlt werden.
6. Der Brief wird geholt werden.
7. Das Haus wird beobachtet werden.
8. Der Brief wird vom Lehrer geschrieben werden.
9. Rudi wird gefragt werden.
10. Franz wird abgeholt werden.

138.
1. Man zerstört die Ruine.
2. Man ruft uns an.
3. Man bestellt das Essen.
4. Man erzählte die Geschichte.
5. Man holte den Doktor.
6. Man schickte den Katalog.
7. Man hat das Bild verkauft.
8. Man hat den Mann angerufen.
9. Man hatte den Brief geschrieben.
10. Man hatte die Limonade getrunken.
11. Man wird wohl die Stadt aufbauen.
12. Man wird wohl das Auto parken.

139.
1. Es wird gefunden.
2. Es wurde zerstört.
3. Es wurde gezeigt.
4. Es wurde gerettet.
5. Es wird repariert.
6. Es wird begonnen.
7. Es wird geschnitten werden.
8. Es war gebaut worden.
9. Es wurde bezahlt.
10. Es wird gesagt.

140.
1. Es ist gefunden.
2. Es war zerstört.
3. Es war gezeigt.
4. Es war gerettet.
5. Es ist repariert.
6. Es ist begonnen.
7. Es wird geschnitten.
8. Es war gebaut gewesen.
9. Es war bezahlt.
10. Es ist gesagt.

141.

1. kennst	6. kennt
2. kenne	7. weiss
3. können	8. Kannst
4. Wisst	9. Kennt
5. weiss	10. wissen

142.
1. Wir kennen den Präsidenten.
2. Sie können Französisch.
3. Inge, hast du meine Tante gekannt?
4. Ich weiss die Antwort.
5. Er weiss alles.

143.

1. liegt	5. leg
2. liege	6. liegen
3. Liegt	7. legt
4. legst	8. lege

144.

1. setzt	5. setzt
2. sitzt	6. sitze
3. setze	7. sitzt
4. setzt	8. Sitzt

145.

1. stehen	5. stelle
2. stellt	6. steht
3. stelle	7. stellen
4. Stellst	8. Stehst

146.
1. lassen
2. lässt . . . bleiben
3. lassen . . . gehen
4. lasse . . . singen
5. Lässt
6. lässt . . . rufen (anrufen)
7. lass
8. lasse

147.
1. Wir haben die Kinder spielen lassen.
2. Er hat das Fahrrad dort gelassen.
3. Hast du die Jacke zu Hause gelasssen?
4. Sie haben uns mitmachen lassen.
5. Rudi hat Inge mitmachen lassen.
6. Ich habe die Katze im Garten gelassen.

Chapter 6

1.
1. Kommt er morgen?
2. Bringt Herbert es zurück?
3. Setzte er sich aufs Bett?

4. Weisst du alles?
5. Arbeiteten die Männer viel?
6. Braucht ihr es?
7. Amüsiert ihr euch?
8. Bestellte Petra auch Bier?
9. Besichtigen die Touristen das Schloss?
10. Will er nicht?
11. Hörst du nichts?
12. Muss sie in die Stadt?
13. Bleiben sie dort?
14. Rauchte er viel?
15. Schwimmst du nicht?

2. 1. Hat er schon geschrieben?
2. Haben sie sich gestern kennengelernt?
3. Habt ihr alles verloren?
4. Wird sie es aufmachen?
5. Darfst du es nehmen?
6. Hat er sich verletzt?
7. Werdet ihr euch umziehen?
8. Hättest du es gekauft?
9. Ist er gestorben?
10. Können sie nicht dort bleiben?
11. Lässt du Peter helfen?
12. Sieht sie die Kinder spielen?
13. Hat er die Geschichte erzählt?
14. Habt ihr die Oper gesehen?
15. Haben sie immer studiert?

3. 1. Ist er nicht hier?
2. Fährst du nicht mit?
3. Dürft ihr nicht nach Bonn fahren?
4. Kommst du nicht mit?
5. Hilft sie nicht den Kindern?

4. 1. Wann
2. Wie
3. Wie oft
4. Wie
5. Wie lange
6. Wieviel
7. Wie
8. Wie oft
9. Wie lange
10. Um wieviel Uhr
11. Wann
12. Wann
13. Warum
14. Um wieviel Uhr
15. Wann

5. 1. Wo
2. Woher
3. Wohin
4. Woher
5. Wohin
6. Wohin
7. Wo
8. Woher
9. Wohin
10. Wo

6. 1. Wohin fährt sie?
2. Wann bringen sie es?
3. Wie oft besuchte uns Alexander?
4. Wie ist es heute?
5. Wo ist sie?
6. Wie oft sieht er dich?
7. Woher kommt Ella?
8. Wie lange bleiben sie dort?
9. Wo sind sie?
10. Wieviel kostet es?

7. 1. Was
2. Wem
3. Was
4. wem
5. Wer
6. wem
7. Wen
8. Wessen
9. wen
10. wem
11. Wem
12. Wen
13. Wer
14. Wem
15. Wessen
16. wem
17. wen
18. Wessen
19. Was
20. Was

8. 1. Wovon
2. Was
3. Womit
4. Wen
5. Wonach
6. Wofür
7. Worauf
8. Für wen
9. Über wen
10. Was
11. Mit wem
12. Wofür
13. Worin
14. Wozu
15. Hinter wen

9. 1. Welche
2. welchen
3. welcher
4. Welchen
5. welchem
6. Welches
7. welcher
8. welchen
9. welchem
10. Welche
11. Welcher
12. Welche

10. 1. Welcher
2. welchem
3. welche
4. Welche
5. Welchen

11. 1. Welche nimmst du?
2. Welche hat er gekauft?
3. Von welchen erzählt er?
4. Welche brauchst du?
5. Für welche kauft er es?

12. 1. Was für ein Auto ist das?
2. Was für ein Mädchen ist das?
3. Mit was für Leuten fährt er nach Deutschland?
4. In was für einem Haus wohnen sie?
5. Was für Bücher schreibt er?

Chapter 7

1. 1. Er kennt den Herrn nicht.
2. Wir geben es den Leuten nicht.
3. Ich wasche mich nicht.
4. Heinz weiss es nicht.
5. Sie kamen vorgestern nicht.
6. Ich kaufe den Mantel nicht.
7. Sie nimmt es nicht.
8. Er dankt mir nicht.

9. Ich zeige ihr den Roman nicht.
10. Wir rauchen nicht.

2.
1. Sie haben nicht gespielt.
2. Ich wollte die Rechnung nicht bezahlen.
3. Wir haben sie nicht schreien hören.
4. Maria hat nicht neben dem Hotel gewartet.
5. Ich weiss, dass er nicht fliegen will.
6. Das ist nicht meine Tante.
7. Er sagte, dass er sie nicht gesucht hätte.
8. Das Mädchen fährt nicht heim.
9. Wir sind nicht zur Schule gegangen.
10. Ich bin nicht dort geblieben.
11. Wir sind nicht im Kino.
12. Ich sehe sie nicht kommen.
13. Er kommt nicht mit.
14. Ihr könnt es nicht sehen.
15. Sie sind nicht reich.
16. Er hat nicht hier gewartet.
17. Wir haben es nicht geholt.
18. Das sind nicht meine Bücher.
19. Ich hoffe, Inge nicht zu besuchen.
20. Du hast sie nicht genommen.

3.
1. Sie ist nicht bei ihrer Tante geblieben . . .
2. Er hat nicht das Auto repariert . . .
3. Wir haben nicht das rote Buch gekauft . . .
4. Ich brauche nicht den Löffel . . .
5. Ihr habt das Radio nicht gewonnen . . .
6. Ich lese nicht die Zeitung . . .

4.
1. Habt ihr ihnen nicht geholfen?
2. Sind sie nicht abgefahren?
3. Holt sie es nicht?
4. Macht sie nicht mit?
5. Darfst du nicht bleiben?
6. Hast du ihn nicht gefragt?
7. Ist das nicht dein Freund?
8. Hast du nicht mitgesungen?
9. Rasiert er sich nicht?
10. Hat sie es nicht vergessen?
11. Willst du ihm nicht helfen?
12. War das nicht seine Frau?
13. Ist sie nicht schön?
14. Kaufst du die Blumen nicht?
15. Kann er sich nicht daran erinnern?

5.
1. Ja, er war krank.
2. Doch, er ist gestorben.
3. Ja, ich habe es gekonnt.
4. Doch, wir brauchen es.
5. Doch, er hat es gefressen.
6. Doch, sie ist intelligent.

6.
1. Sie braucht nicht zu kommen.
2. Hans braucht nicht zu schreiben.
3. Ihr braucht nicht abzufahren.
4. Wir brauchen nicht zu gehen.
5. Ich brauche nicht zu studieren.
6. Sie brauchen nicht zu arbeiten.
7. Wir brauchen nicht zu springen.
8. Du brauchst den Roman nicht zu lesen.

7.
1. Er fragt uns nie.
2. Wir sind gar nicht müde.
3. Sie wohnt nicht mehr in Bonn.
4. Ich kann noch nicht fahren.
5. Er hat sie noch nie gesehen.
6. Er hilft nie.
7. Sie geht nicht mehr ins Kino.
8. Er war noch nie in Deutschland.
9. Wir sind noch nicht nach Hause geflogen.
10. Sie sind gar nicht freundlich.
11. Ich habe Schnecken noch nie gegessen.
12. Er kennt mich nicht mehr.
13. Sie lernte den Präsidenten nie kennen.
14. Wir machen gar nicht mit.
15. Er hat die Sammlung noch nicht verkauft.

8.
1. Er erzählte kein Märchen.
2. Wir besuchten keine bekannte Stadt.
3. Er hat unser Kind nicht gesehen.
4. Hat sie keine Blumen gekauft?
5. Trinkt er kein Wasser?
6. Ich habe keinen warmen Mantel.
7. Das sind keine Haselnüsse.
8. Ich habe mich nicht auf die Ferien gefreut.
9. Wir essen keine Bananen.
10. Ich habe keinen Freund.
11. Ich kenne den Herrn nicht.
12. Sie singt das Lied nicht.
13. Er hat keine Kinder.
14. Dieser Ring ist nicht teuer.
15. Hier liegt kein Buch.
16. Wer isst kein Brot?
17. Das ist kein Tachometer.
18. Die Lehrerin schreibt nicht.
19. Ist die Milch nicht sauer?
20. Ich habe keine Zeit.

9.
1. Er kann nichts sehen.
2. Niemand hilft uns.
3. Ich habe nichts Altes.
4. Sie wissen nichts.
5. Er fragt niemand.

Chapter 8

1.
1. er
2. du
3. Sie
4. sie
5. du
6. Ihr
7. Es
8. Sie

9. ihr
10. Sie
11. Sie
12. Sie
13. Sie
14. Sie
15. es
16. ihr
17. Sie
18. du

2.
1. er, ihn
2. sie, sie
3. wir, sie
4. sie, es
5. sie, sie
6. er, sie
7. ich, ihn
8. sie, sie
9. ich, es
10. wir, ihn
11. ich, dich
12. er, sie
13. wir, ihn
14. ich, es

3.
1. Renate braucht es.
2. Wir kaufen ihn.
3. Ich setzte mich neben sie.
4. Wir essen sie.
5. Ich darf ihn lesen.
6. Wer hat ihn gefüttert?

4.
1. Ja, er hat dich erkannt.
2. Ja, er schreibt uns.
3. Ja, ich habe es für dich gekauft.
4. Ja, er geht ohne uns.
5. Ja, wir können euch dort besuchen.

5.
1. Er gab es ihr.
2. Wir helfen ihm.
3. Gibst du ihm das Futter?
4. Wir unterhielten uns mit ihr.
5. Er erzählte von ihm.
6. Wohnst du bei ihnen?
7. Ich schrieb ihnen Ansichtskarten.
8. Sie holte ihm Medizin.
9. Es gehört ihnen.
10. Sie bringen ihr Essen.
11. Es gefällt ihm.
12. Ich kaufe ihr etwas.
13. Er kommt von ihm.
14. Wir stehen hinter ihm.

6.
1. Ja, er hat mir etwas gebracht.
2. Ja, ich zeige euch die Stadt.
3. Ja, wir sagen euch die Wahrheit.
4. Ja, er hat mir geholfen.
5. Ja, ich bringe dir etwas mit.
6. Ja, er hat mir dafür gedankt.
7. Ja, sie hat uns geholfen.
8. Ja, ich kaufe ihm etwas.
9. Ja, das Bild gefällt mir.
10. Ja, wir kaufen dir den Wagen.

7.
1. Er gab es seiner Mutter.
2. Ich habe ihr ein Paket geschickt.
3. Sie zeigte sie ihrem Kind.
4. Sie erzählen ihnen die Neuigkeit.
5. Sie bringen sie den Kranken.
6. Er kauft sie seiner Tante.
7. Ich schreibe ihm eine Karte.
8. Sie glaubt ihm die Geschichte.
9. Ich gebe sie der Dame.
10. Wir kaufen ihnen Geschenke.

8.
1. Wir bringen es ihm.
2. Ich hole ihn ihm.
3. Wir erzählten sie ihnen.
4. Er gibt ihn ihm.
5. Er hat sie ihr geglaubt.
6. Johann zeigte es ihnen.
7. Der Professor erklärte sie ihnen.
8. Ich kaufe sie ihnen.
9. Er schreibt sie ihm.
10. Dieter holt es ihm.

9.
1. Ja, er hat sie mir geschenkt.
2. Ja, ich habe sie ihnen gezeigt.
3. Ja, er hat sie uns gekauft.
4. Ja, ich bringe ihn dir.
5. Ja, sie hat ihn uns gegeben.

10.
1. Hilft ihnen Ellen?
2. Ich glaube, dass es Maria gekauft hat.
3. Wir wissen nicht, ob er sie besichtigt hat.
4. Ich habe Zeit, weil ihn Norma abholt.
5. Morgen kauft ihr Susi den Pullover.

11.
1. Jeden Tag holt Pia ihm die Zeitung.
2. Ich weiss, wann Peter ihr geholfen hat.
3. Bringt Gabriele es?
4. Hat er es genommen?
5. Weisst du, wo Dieter sie getroffen hat?

12.
1. Er lachte über sie.
2. Wir sprechen von ihnen.
3. Er fragt nach ihr.
4. Was weisst du von ihm?
5. Er denkt an sie.
6. Warten Sie auf ihn?
7. Warum hast du Angst vor ihm?
8. Wir sprechen über ihn.
9. Ich habe von ihm gehört.
10. Er lädt sie zu ihnen ein.

13.
1. dir
2. ihm
3. uns
4. sie
5. uns
6. ihm
7. dir
8. dich
9. euch
10. mich
11. uns
12. dir
13. sie
14. Sie

14.
1. Ja, ich denke daran.
2. Ja, ich liege darunter.

3. Ja, ich warte auf sie.
4. Ja, wir sprechen darüber.
5. Ja, ich spreche von ihr.
6. Ja, ich fahre damit.
7. Ja, ich stehe davor.
8. Ja, ich warte darauf.
9. Ja, wir stehen neben ihnen.
10. Ja, er denkt an sie.
11. Ja, sie fragt nach ihr.
12. Ja, ich sitze hinter ihm.
13. Ja, ich arbeite damit.
14. Ja, wir fahren mit ihnen.
15. Ja, ich weiss etwas davon.
16. Ja, ich habe Angst vor ihm.

15. 1. mich 2. sich 3. uns 4. euch 5. sich 6. sich 7. dich 8. dich 9. mich 10. sich

16. 1. euch 2. mir 3. sich 4. dir 5. mir 6. dir 7. sich 8. mir 9. dir 10. uns

17.
1. Heute morgen haben sich die Kinder weh getan.
2. Auf die Ferien freut sich Max.
3. Wegen des Unfalls hat sich der Beamte verspätet.
4. Vor einer Stunde hat Vater sich das Auto gekauft.
5. An seine Ferien erinnert sich mein Freund.
6. Am Abend putzt Barbara sich die Zähne.
7. Ein Motorrad kauft sich Herr Obermeyer.
8. Am Morgen rasiert sich Vater.

18. 1. deine 2. eurer 3. unsre 4. meines 5. deinen 6. seine 7. ihren 8. unsrem 9. meinen 10. ihrem

19. 1. der dort (da) 2. dem hier 3. die dort (da) 4. dem hier 5. die hier 6. denen dort (da)

20. 1. diese dort (da) 2. diesem hier 3. diese dort (da) 4. dieser hier 5. dieses hier

21. 1. niemand 2. etwas 3. Wenige 4. einigen 5. Jeder 6. nichts 7. Man 8. Viele 9. alle 10. einem nichts 11. viel 12. wenig 13. Jemand 14. andere 15. einige 16. Manche 17. alles 18. Man

22. 1. das 2. der 3. die 4. die 5. der 6. das 7. die 8. der

23. 1. den 2. die 3. den 4. das 5. die 6. die 7. das 8. den

24.
1. Liest du das Buch, das er gebracht hat?
2. Brauchst du die Zeitung, die auf dem Tisch liegt?
3. Kennst du den Herrn, den wir getroffen haben?
4. Heute kam der Junge, der uns damals geholfen hatte.
5. Kennst du die Leute, die dort spazierengehen?
6. Wo sind die Blumen, die ich gekauft habe?

25. 1. dem 2. dem 3. denen 4. dem 5. der 6. der 7. denen 8. dem

26.
1. Dort sitzt der Tourist, welchem du das Essen bringen sollst.
2. Kennst du meine Geschwister, bei welchen ich wohne?
3. Die Leiter, auf welcher er steht, ist kaputt.
4. Hier ist das Auto, mit welchem wir spazieren fahren.
5. Der Stuhl, auf welchem du sitzt, ist alt.

27. 1. deren 2. dessen 3. dessen 4. deren 5. deren 6. deren 7. dessen 8. dessen

28. 1. Wer 2. Was 3. Wer 4. Was 5. Wer

29. 1. was 2. wo 3. wo 4. was 5. was 6. was 7. wo 8. was

30.
1. Der Stuhl, worauf du sitzt, ist eine Rarität.
2. Wir besuchen das Haus, worin Goethe geboren wurde.
3. Ist das das Spielzeug, womit sie sich so amüsiert?
4. Dort ist die Kirche, wonach er fragte.
5. Sind das die Bücher, wofür du dich interessierst?
6. Wo ist der Brief, worauf er wartet?
7. Das Problem, worüber ihr sprecht, ist schwer.
8. Wo ist die Ruine, wovon er erzählt?

31.

1.	was	14.	Wer
2.	den	15.	das
3.	Wer	16.	die
4.	dem	17.	wo
5.	deren	18.	denen
6.	das	19.	deren
7.	dem	20.	was
8.	den	21.	die
9.	wo	22.	die
10.	der	23.	dem
11.	das	24.	was
12.	was	25.	dem
13.	dessen		

Chapter 9

1.
1. Der Schnellzug ist vor einer Stunde angekommen.
2. Norma bleibt bei uns.
3. Der kleine Junge will mitmachen.
4. Die Goldkette wurde von ihm zurückgebracht.
5. Wir haben ihn sehen können.
6. Gerda geht mit Klaus spazieren.
7. Der Hund beisst den Jungen.
8. Ich habe es kaufen dürfen.
9. Er wird die Geschichte erzählen.
10. Er sieht mich kommen.

2.
1. Sie haben schneller laufen müssen.
2. Wir haben die Schachtel aufgemacht.
3. Er hat nicht heimgehen wollen.
4. Ich habe es ihm zeigen wollen.
5. Seine Grosseltern haben es mitgebracht.
6. Mein Vater hat mich gehen lassen.
7. Er hat gut singen können.
8. Der Alte hat sich auf die Bank gesetzt.
9. Ich habe die Kinder schreien hören.
10. Der Zug ist vor einer Stunde abgefahren.

3.
1. Das Auto wollten wir in Deutschland kaufen.
2. Heute kommen sie zurück.
3. Im Kino hat er es vergessen.
4. Meistens ist er am Abend müde.
5. Leider waren meine Eltern zu Hause.
6. Wegen meiner Erkältung konnte ich nicht kommen.
7. Gestern abend haben wir es gemacht.
8. Mit dem Zug fahren sie in die Schweiz.
9. Im Zentrum ist das Museum.
10. Oft habe ich es hören müssen.

4.
1. Wann machst du das Fenster zu?
2. Was darf das Kind wissen?
3. Wieviel kostet die Kamera?
4. Wo wollen die Leute wohnen?
5. Warum setzt du dich nicht nieder?
6. Wohin fährst du mit dem Auto?
7. Worauf sollen die Bücher liegen?
8. Woher kommen die Kinder?

5.
1. ______
2. Vor einer Woche hat uns Axel besucht.
3. Im Theater hat sich Konrad amüsiert.
4. Jeden Tag schickt ihr Mutter etwas.
5. Wo hat dich Ursel getroffen?
6. ______
7. ______
8. Gestern hat uns Vater etwas mitgebracht.
9. Um neun Uhr trifft sie ihr Freund.
10. ______

6.
1. Hast du ihm den Brief geschrieben?
2. Kennt mich Peter?
3. Wollte Gerda das Museum besuchen?
4. Helft ihr ihm den Baum pflanzen?
5. Macht Herr Klein die Tür auf?
6. Kann er Deutsch?
7. Hat sich Erika bei ihr entschuldigt?
8. Hast du dir das schnelle Auto gekauft?
9. Habt ihr es ihm genommen?
10. Hat man dich gefragt?

7.
1. Zeig (Zeigt)
2. Öffne (Öffnet)
3. Frag (Fragt)
4. Komm . . . heim (Kommt . . . heim)
5. Mach . . . nach (Macht . . . nach)

8.
1. Ja, trinken Sie das Bier!
2. Ja, singen Sie das Lied!
3. Ja, lachen Sie darüber!
4. Ja, schicken Sie es mir!
5. Ja, ziehen Sie den warmen Mantel an!

9.
1. Denke ich daran, bestelle ich es.
2. Hätte er es gewollt, hätte ich es ihm gekauft.
3. Wird es kalt, heizen wir das Haus.

4. Willst du mitmachen, musst du dich umziehen.
5. Nehme ich es ihr weg, weint sie.

10.
1. Da ich keine Zeit hatte, konnte ich es nicht machen.
2. Als er ins Zimmer kam, spielte sie Klavier.
3. Wenn ich das Auto habe, werde ich euch besuchen.
4. Während ich krank war, musste ich viel schlafen.
5. Bevor du gehst, musst du mir helfen.

11.
1. Ich weiss nicht, wo er gewohnt hat.
2. Ich weiss nicht, wieviel sie noch machen muss.
3. Ich weiss nicht, wovon er lebt.
4. Ich weiss nicht, warum er es mitbringt.
5. Ich weiss nicht, worüber er erzählen wird.

12.
1. Wo ist der Mantel, den ich gekauft habe?
2. Die Kinder spielen mit der Puppe, die er mitgebracht hat.
3. Dort steht das Flugzeug, mit dem ich abfliege.
4. Hilfst du dem Mädchen, dessen Vater gestorben ist?
5. Wo sind die Karten, die er mir geschenkt hat?

13.
1. Er ist glücklich, weil er hat gehen dürfen.
2. Ich glaube, dass er hat fragen wollen.
3. Kennst du den Mann, den ich habe schreien hören?
4. Weisst du, ob er hat arbeiten müssen?
5. Ich weiss, was er hat machen sollen.

14.
1. Wir zeigten ihr die Lampe.
2. Wann hat er ihm die Karotte gegeben?
3. Ich habe ihr eine Vase geschenkt.
4. Hat er ihm das Motorrad gekauft?
5. Wer hat ihnen das Geld genommen?
6. Weisst du, ob er ihnen Schokolade gegeben hat?

15.
1. Wir zeigten sie der Dame.
2. Wann hat er sie dem Hasen gegeben?
3. Ich habe sie meiner Tante geschenkt.
4. Hat er es seinem Sohn gekauft?
5. Wer hat es den Leuten genommen?
6. Weisst du, ob er sie den Kindern gegeben hat?

16.
1. Willst du es ihr vorlesen?
2. Wann hat er ihn ihnen gebracht?
3. Weisst du, ob er sie ihm erzählt hat?
4. Wann hat er es ihnen gezeigt?
5. Ich habe sie ihr gegeben.

17.
1. Gibt dir Peter den Ring?
2. Warum kann uns Ursula nicht besuchen?
3. Kennt ihn der Professor?
4. Hat sich Frau Schafft schon umgezogen?
5. Sie weint, weil sie die Leute auslachten.

18.
1. Er sieht sie täglich.
2. Wir geben ihnen natürlich alles zurück.
3. Sie besucht sie abends.
4. Ich habe ihn wirklich getroffen.
5. Er kann sie leider nicht abholen.

19.
1. Ich bin am Nachmittag nach Hause gekommen.
2. Wir treffen sie um zehn Uhr im Hotel.
3. Ich war jeden Tag dort.
4. Ich gehe heute abend mit Ursel spazieren.
5. Ich bin sehr schnell in die Stadt gefahren.
6. Wir sind gestern mit dem alten Wagen ins Kino gefahren.

20.
1. Ja, wir besuchen dich morgen um drei Uhr.
2. Ja, wir fahren diesen Sommer im Juli in die Berge.
3. Ja, ich gehe nächste Woche am Mittwoch ins Theater.
4. Ja, wir fliegen heute abend um sechs Uhr ab.
5. Ja, ich bin morgen zwischen sieben und acht Uhr zu Hause.

21.
1. Er ist arm, aber seine Eltern sind reich.
2. Ich freute mich, denn er wollte sofort mit der Arbeit anfangen.
3. Wir sind nicht dort geblieben, sondern wir sind ausgegangen.
4. Sei vorsichtig, oder es wird kaputt!
5. Ich spiele Golf, und er spielt Tennis.
6. Er ist glücklich, denn er hat Geld gewonnen.
7. Wir sind nicht in Deutschland, sondern wir sind in Spanien.
8. Du kannst zu Hause bleiben, aber ich muss zur Schule.
9. Er trinkt Milch, und ich trinke Limonade.
10. Er kommt zu uns, oder wir gehen zu ihm.

22.
1. Wann liest du das Buch?
2. Wenn sie krank ist, bleibt sie zu Hause.
3. Wenn er mich besuchte, brachte er mir etwas.
4. Weisst du, wann er ankommt?
5. Als es kalt wurde, ging ich ins Haus.

23.

1. Sie hat Kopfweh, weil die Kinder viel Lärm gemacht haben.
2. Er ist in Berlin, während seine Frau noch hier ist.
3. Ich fragte ihn, ob sie wieder gesund sind.
4. Es war sehr kalt, als wir in Alaska waren.
5. Sie konnte gut Deutsch, nachdem sie in Deutschland studiert hatte.
6. Wir kauften alles, da wir viel Geld gewonnen hatten.
7. Wir blieben im Wald, bis es dunkel wurde.
8. Konrad musste mithelfen, bevor er ausgehen konnte.
9. Er trägt einen Pullover, damit er sich nicht erkältet.
10. Sie ist immer müde, seitdem sie nicht gut schlafen kann.

24.

1. dass
2. obwohl
3. bis
4. als ob
5. ob
6. Seit (dem)
7. Je
8. damit
9. da
10. während

VERB CHART

PRINCIPAL PARTS OF VERBS

Below is a list of the most commonly used strong and irregular verbs.

Infinitive	*Imperfect*	*Past Participle*	*Present Stem Vowel*	*English*
backen	buk	gebacken	bäckt	to bake
beginnen	begann	begonnen		to begin
beissen	biss	gebissen		to bite
biegen	bog	gebogen		to bend
binden	band	gebunden		to bind
bitten	bat	gebeten		to ask
bleiben	blieb	(ist) geblieben		to stay
brechen	brach	gebrochen	bricht	to break
brennen	brannte	gebrannt		to burn
bringen	brachte	gebracht		to bring
denken	dachte	gedacht		to think
dürfen	durfte	gedurft	darf	to be allowed
essen	ass	gegessen	isst	to eat
fahren	fuhr	(ist) gefahren	fährt	to go, drive
fallen	fiel	(ist) gefallen	fällt	to fall
fangen	fing	gefangen	fängt	to catch
finden	fand	gefunden		to find
fliegen	flog	(ist) geflogen		to fly
fliehen	floh	(ist) geflohen		to flee
fliessen	floss	(ist) geflossen		to flow
fressen	frass	gefressen	frisst	to eat (animals)
frieren	fror	gefroren		to freeze
geben	gab	gegeben	gibt	to give
gehen	ging	(ist) gegangen		to go
gewinnen	gewann	gewonnen		to win
graben	grub	gegraben	gräbt	to dig
haben	hatte	gehabt	hat	to have
halten	hielt	gehalten	hält	to hold, stop
helfen	half	geholfen	hilft	to help
kennen	kannte	gekannt		to know
kommen	kam	(ist) gekommen		to come
können	konnte	gekonnt	kann	can, to be able
lassen	liess	gelassen	lässt	to let, leave
laufen	lief	(ist) gelaufen	läuft	to run
leiden	litt	gelitten		to suffer
leihen	lieh	geliehen		to loan
lesen	las	gelesen	liest	to read
liegen	lag	gelegen		to lie

messen	mass	gemessen	misst	to measure
mögen	mochte	gemocht	mag	to like
müssen	musste	gemusst	muss	must, to have to
nehmen	nahm	genommen	nimmt	to take
nennen	nannte	genannt		to name, call
reiten	ritt	(ist) geritten		to ride
rennen	rannte	(ist) gerannt		to run
riechen	roch	gerochen		to smell
saufen	soff	gesoffen	säuft	to drink (animals)
scheinen	schien	geschienen		to shine, seem
schiessen	schoss	geschossen		to shoot
schlafen	schlief	geschlafen	schläft	to sleep
schlagen	schlug	geschlagen	schlägt	to hit
schliessen	schloss	geschlossen		to close
schneiden	schnitt	geschnitten		to cut
schreiben	schrieb	geschrieben		to write
schreien	schrie	geschrien		to scream
schweigen	schwieg	geschwiegen		to be silent
schwimmen	schwamm	(ist) geschwommen		to swim
sehen	sah	gesehen	sieht	to see
sein	war	(ist) gewesen	ist	to be
senden	sandte	gesandt		to send
singen	sang	gesungen		to sing
sinken	sank	(ist) gesunken		to sink
sitzen	sass	gesessen		to sit
sollen	sollte	gesollt	soll	ought, to be supposed to
sprechen	sprach	gesprochen	spricht	to talk, speak
springen	sprang	(ist) gesprungen		to jump
stehen	stand	gestanden		to stand
stehlen	stahl	gestohlen	stiehlt	to steal
steigen	stieg	(ist) gestiegen		to climb
sterben	starb	(ist) gestorben	stirbt	to die
stinken	stank	gestunken		to stink
tragen	trug	getragen	trägt	to wear, carry
treffen	traf	getroffen	trifft	to meet
treten	trat	(ist) getreten	tritt	to step
trinken	trank	getrunken		to drink
tun	tat	getan		to do
verlieren	verlor	verloren		to loose
wachsen	wuchs	(ist) gewachsen	wächst	to grow
waschen	wusch	gewaschen	wäscht	to wash
wenden	wandte	gewandt		to turn
werden	wurde	(ist) geworden	wird	to become
werfen	warf	geworfen	wirft	to throw
wiegen	wog	gewogen		to weigh
wissen	wusste	gewusst	weiss	to know
wollen	wollte	gewollt	will	to want to
ziehen	zog	gezogen		to pull